# DIRTY HANDS AND VICIOUS DEEDS

# DIRTY HANDS AND VICIOUS DEEDS

## The US Government's Complicity in Crimes Against Humanity and Genocide

*Edited by*
Samuel Totten

UNIVERSITY OF TORONTO PRESS

**Library and Archives Canada Cataloguing in Publication**

Dirty hands and vicious deeds : the US government's complicity in
   crimes against humanity and genocide / edited by Samuel Totten.

Includes bibliographical references and index.
Issued in print and electronic formats.
ISBN 978-1-4426-3526-5 (hardcover).—ISBN 978-1-4426-3525-8 (softcover).
—ISBN 978-1-4426-3528-9 (PDF).—ISBN 978-1-4426-3527-2 (EPUB)

   1. Genocide—Case studies. 2. Crimes against humanity—Case studies.
3. United States—Foreign relations—20th century—Decision making—Case
studies. I. Totten, Samuel, editor

E741.D57 2017        327.73009'04        C2017-903414-6
                                             C2017-903415-4

We welcome comments and suggestions regarding any aspect of our publications—please feel free to contact us at news@utphighereducation.com or visit our Internet site at www.utorontopress.com.

*North America*
5201 Dufferin Street
North York, Ontario, Canada, M3H 5T8

2250 Military Road
Tonawanda, New York, USA, 14150
ORDERS PHONE: 1-800-565-9523
ORDERS FAX: 1-800-221-9985
ORDERS E-MAIL: utpbooks@utpress.utoronto.ca

*UK, Ireland, and continental Europe*
NBN International
Estover Road, Plymouth, PL6 7PY, UK
ORDERS PHONE: 44 (0) 1752 202301
ORDERS FAX: 44 (0) 1752 202333
ORDERS E-MAIL: enquiries@nbninternational.com

Every effort has been made to contact copyright holders; in the event of an error or omission, please notify the publisher.

The University of Toronto Press acknowledges the financial support for its publishing activities of the Government of Canada through the Canada Book Fund.

Printed in Canada.

# CONTENTS

# INTRODUCTION

Samuel Totten

## INTRODUCTION

In her Pulitzer Prize–winning book, *"A Problem from Hell": America and the Age of Genocide*, Samantha Power (2002) essentially indicts the United States for its repeated failure to halt genocide throughout the twentieth century and the early part of the twenty-first century. For many, her book was a revelation. Not a few were stunned by the facts she presented in her documentation of the United States' reaction, or lack thereof, to the Ottoman Turk genocide of Armenians, the Nazi-perpetrated Holocaust, the 1971 Bangladesh genocide, the Khmer Rouge genocide of fellow Cambodians, and the 1994 Hutu-perpetrated genocide of Tutsi and moderate Hutu in Rwanda, among others.

What Power merely touched on, though, is how the United States government repeatedly aided and abetted certain regimes as they planned and then carried out atrocity crimes that amounted to either crimes against humanity or genocide over the last half of the twentieth century. This book, *Dirty Hands and Vicious Deeds: The US Government's Complicity in Crimes Against Humanity and Genocide*, explores the issue of such complicity. In doing so, noted scholars variously examine seven cases—Indonesia (1965–66), Bangladesh (1971), Chile (1973–77), East Timor (1975–99), Argentina (1976–83), Guatemala (1981–83), and Rwanda (1994)—in which the United States government was complicit, in one way or another, in the mass atrocities committed by the governments of other nations. The seven cases were

■ 1

selected based on the fact that they are illustrative of such complicit actions by the US government.

Let it be duly noted that none of the contributors to this book accuse the United States of carrying out crimes against humanity or genocide in any of the aforementioned cases. What the contributors do show, though, via concrete evidence—including the very words of US officials in what are now declassified government documents—is that the US was complicit in aiding and abetting such perpetrator governments in a host of ways, including but not limited to the following: providing its imprimatur to carry out attacks against particular groups of people; engaging in dirty tricks that induced fear and the belief by certain government and military officials that major eruptions, if not a coup d'état, were in the making, thus pushing officials in the perpetrator governments to take aggressive and deadly actions against the purported instigators; providing training for top military officials and/or troops that were either on the cusp of or already in the process of perpetrating crimes against humanity, if not genocide; providing weapons to the perpetrator governments; providing funds and other types of aid to the perpetrator governments; consulting with and providing advice to the perpetrator governments; helping to obfuscate the truth about the perpetration of such atrocities; etc. And once the atrocities were under way, and many within the US government simply looked the other way, feigned unawareness of the horrors being perpetrated.

Each chapter in this book comprises two parts: first, each author presents a detailed discussion and analysis of a particular case of crimes against humanity or genocide by a foreign government against its own citizens, and in doing so, discusses why and how the United States government was complicit *in aiding, abetting, and/or remaining silent in the face of such.* Second, each chapter also contains copies of a series of declassified US documents germane to the particular case under discussion. Such documents variously include, for example, memoranda, telegrams, letters, talking points, cables, reports, discussion papers, and situation reports (sitreps), each of which was originally classified along one of the following lines: Confidential, Limited Official Use, Secret, and Top Secret. Those who crafted and disseminated such documents were a rather eclectic group, including but not limited to personnel with the following entities: the Central Intelligence Agency (CIA), the White House, the US Department of State, the US Department of Defense, various US embassies around the world, the Defense Intelligence Agency (DIA), the US Agency for International Development (USAID), the US Senate, the US Mission to the UN (USUN), and the National Security Council (NSC). In certain instances, the authors of such documents were high-level officials, including the US Secretary of State, the US Under-Secretary of Defense, and various US ambassadors.

The inclusion of such documents presents readers with the unique opportunity to glean insights into a host of issues, decisions, and actions by the US government that, until relatively recently, were not within the purview of the general public due to the fact the aforementioned documents were classified. Now that they are declassified, readers are able to learn first-hand about how officials in various presidential administrations reacted to the planning and perpetration of crimes against humanity and/or genocide by other nations' governments. More specifically, readers are able to learn about the knowledge and perceptions of various US officials vis-à-vis foreign governments' planning of and/or engaging in atrocities; the US government's support of foreign governments' plans of action; the perceptions of US officials toward the targeted groups; and what the US government conveyed to American citizens about these matters, and how that compared and contrasted with the complete stories of what had taken place.

Ultimately, due to different ways of looking at, interpreting, and/or understanding the world and geopolitics, some readers may draw conclusions that differ from those of the authors of the various cases as they relate to the culpability of the United States. Readers whose world view is more akin to that of realpolitik may, in fact, conclude that the United States was justified in its decisions and actions in regard to a particular case. On the other hand, those whose view is more akin to pursuing a progressive view of international human rights (those who adhere to realpolitik would deem this group "idealists") may conclude that the US government's decisions and actions regarding that same case were questionable, if not immoral or criminal. Still other readers may come out somewhere in the middle or even be undecided. This, of course, is where discussion and debate come into play in the classroom. Such discussions should not simply be predicated on one's beliefs, but must take into consideration international law and such conventions as the Geneva Conventions and the UN Convention on the Prevention and Punishment of the Crime of Genocide.

While some readers may have a basic knowledge of one or more of the cases of crimes against humanity and genocide highlighted herein, as well as how the United States acted or reacted to such, it is likely that many will be astonished by what they didn't know, particularly in regard to the words, actions, and reactions of US government officials—from the President of the United States to the Secretary of State and right down the line—in support of other governments' perpetration of gross violations of human rights against their own people. Many are also likely to wonder, and possibly fret over, why they have never heard about such US government positions and actions.

*Dirty Hands and Vicious Deeds* was produced for three key reasons: First, it was primarily produced to inform US citizens, university students, human rights activists, and anti-genocide activists why and how various United States presidential administrations responded to the perpetration of crimes against humanity and genocide by foreign nations with which it had close relations. Second, it was produced to raise people's awareness—and particularly that of students at the university level—of how certain decisions with monumental consequences made by various US government officials compare and contrast with the purported ethos of the United States and the promises and/or declarations such individuals have made to their fellow citizens upon entering office. (In a number of ways this plays into why documents circulated within the US government are variously classified/stamped: "Limited Official Use"; "Confidential"; "Secret"; and "Top Secret.") Third, it was produced to motivate readers to ponder whether certain actions by US government officials were reasonable or unreasonable; moral, amoral, or immoral; right or wrong; and/or legal or criminal.

To be absolutely clear, then, this book *was not produced* in an attempt to embarrass or shame the United States, past presidential administrations, or certain government officials. Perhaps some should be ashamed of what they did and did not do in the face of the perpetration of crimes against humanity and/or genocide by foreign partners, but that is another issue altogether. Then again, those who adhere to realpolitik are likely to brush aside any criticism as casually as government officials brush dander off the shoulders of their striped suits. At the same time, they may well consider individuals highly critical of their government's dealings with foreign nations that have perpetrated crimes against humanity and/or genocide to be sorely naive (or idealistic) in the ways of global politics.

Be that as it may, various presidential administrations of the United States have had less than sterling records when it comes to honoring international declarations and conventions to which the United States is a party, including the Universal Declaration of Human Rights and the UN Convention on Genocide. The US has not only engaged in the torture of individuals (Human Rights Watch, 2014) but also condoned the use of torture by other nations against their own citizens, political opponents, and perceived enemies. Likewise, at various times the US has cavalierly targeted innocent civilians and more or less perceived their deaths as "collateral damage" (Griffiths, 2015; Graham-Harrison & Ackerman, 2016; Wood & Hall, 2016). Concomitantly, time and again the US government has overthrown governments not to its liking—*and that includes democratically elected governments.* Even a relatively short list of *those democratically elected governments* that were either directly overthrown by the CIA (i.e., the United States) or whose overthrow was influenced and supported by the US since 1945 is eye-opening: Iran (1953); Guatemala (1954); Ecuador (1963); Brazil (1964); Indonesia (1965); Chile (1973); and Australia (1975). Yes, Australia!

What one has to ask is this: What if the government of one of those nations—or any other nation, for that matter—attempted to overthrow the government of the United States? How would this be perceived by the US government and its citizens? What would the likely reaction be? What should the reaction be?

And finally, to ask what will surely seem to be a bizarre question to many, if not most: Has there ever been a time in US history when a government of the United States should have been overthrown? Or, to put it another way: Was there ever a time in US history when another nation's government would have been justified in overthrowing a particular presidential administration (government) of the United States? It is a fair question, since surely there have been plenty of nations that have looked askance at our own government's positions, decisions, and actions.

## CRIMES AGAINST HUMANITY OR GENOCIDE?

Crimes against humanity and genocide are two distinct entities. Furthermore, they constitute two distinct legal categories.

For any incident of mass killing to be deemed genocide it must meet the criteria set out in the United Nations Convention on the Prevention and Punishment of the Crime of Genocide (UNCG). More specifically, in Article 2 of the UNCG, genocide is defined as "any of the following acts committed with intent to destroy, in whole or in part, a national, ethnical, racial or religious group, as such: (a) Killing members of the group; (b) Causing serious bodily or mental harm to members of the group; (c) Deliberately inflicting on the group conditions of life calculated to bring about its physical destruction in whole or in part; (d) Imposing measures intended to prevent births within the group; (e) Forcibly transferring children of the group to another group" (UN General Assembly, 1948).

The legal definition of genocide is the one spelled out in the UNCG. It is the one used by the United Nations, international criminal tribunals, the International Criminal Court, most genocide early warning systems, and the governments of individual nations, to assess whether a particular crime amounts to genocide or not. Scholars who have found the wording of the definition in the UNCG ambiguous and/or the type and number of groups protected under it too constrictive have crafted new definitions, but none of them have been used in courts of law.

Crimes against humanity refer to any of the following acts when committed as part of a widespread or systematic attack directed against any civilian population, with knowledge of the attack:

(a) Murder;
(b) Extermination;

(c) Enslavement;

(d) Deportation or forcible transfer of population;

(e) Imprisonment or other severe deprivation of physical liberty in violation of fundamental rules of international law;

(f) Torture;

(g) Rape, sexual slavery, enforced prostitution, forced pregnancy, enforced sterilization, or any other form of sexual violence of comparable gravity;

(h) Persecution against any identifiable group or collectivity on political, racial, national, ethnic, cultural, religious, gender as defined in paragraph 3, or other grounds that are universally recognized as impermissible under international law, in connection with any act referred to in this paragraph or any crime within the jurisdiction of the Court;

(i) Enforced disappearance of persons;

(j) The crime of apartheid;

(k) Other inhumane acts of a similar character intentionally causing great suffering, or serious injury to body or to mental or physical health. (UN General Assembly, 1998)

Crimes against humanity "are particularly odious offenses in that they constitute a serious attack on human dignity or grave humiliation or a degradation of one or more human beings. They are not isolated or sporadic events, but are part of either a government policy... or of a wide practice of atrocities tolerated or condoned by a government or a de facto authority. However, murder, extermination, torture, rape, political, racial, or religious persecution and other inhumane acts reach the threshold of crimes against humanity only if they are part of a widespread or systematic practice" (UN General Assembly, 1998).

This means that an individual crime on its own, or even several such crimes, would not fall under the Rome Statute[1] unless they were the result of a state or organizational policy. Isolated inhumane acts of this nature may constitute grave infringements of human rights or, depending on the

---

1   The Rome Statute is the treaty that in 2002 established the International Criminal Court.

circumstances, war crimes, but they may fall short of meriting the stigma attaching to the category of crimes under discussion. On the other hand, an individual may be guilty of crimes against humanity even if he perpetrates one or two of the offenses mentioned above, or engages in one such offense against only a few civilians, provided those offenses are part of a consistent pattern of misbehavior by several persons linked to that offender (e.g., engaged in armed action on the same side or because they are parties to a common plan or for any similar reason.)

While the definition of crimes against humanity is rather straightforward, the same cannot be said about the definition of genocide. That is due to the wording used to define genocide in the UNCG and the seemingly limited number of groups protected by the UNCG.[2] The two main points of contention vis-à-vis wording are "intent" and "with the intent to destroy."[3] The legal definition of genocide used today is exactly the same as definition found in the UNCG when it was adopted by the UN General Assembly in 1948.[4] Scholars have written lengthy book chapters and refereed journal articles on the issue of "intent" as it relates to the definition of genocide,

2   The four types of groups protected under the UNCG are national, ethnical, religious, and racial. Over the years, various international law specialists and other scholars have suggested the need to expand the list of protected groups to include, among others, the following: political, gender, economic or class, mentally impaired, and physically impaired.

3   The other phrase that scholars have discussed and debated at length is "in whole or in part." The main concern is what exactly constitutes "in part." The UNCG does not explain the meaning of "in part"—not even a hint. Perhaps the soundest answer to date is "a substantive part." That, of course, still leaves the issue open to ample debate.

4   Be that as it may, in a few rare instances certain acts not specifically mentioned in the UNCG definition have been deemed examples of genocide as a result of cases in which prosecutors and judges agreed that they were perpetrated with the intent to destroy in whole or in part a particular group as such. The classic case is that of the Akayesu case tried at the International Criminal Tribunal Rwanda (ICTR), where the defendant (Jean-Paul Akayesu) was found guilty of nine counts of genocide, incitement to genocide, and crimes against humanity, including rape as genocide and as a crime against humanity, for directing and encouraging widespread acts of sexual violence in the Taba district of the Gitarama province during the 1994 genocide in Rwanda. As Human Rights Watch (1998) pointed out, "The verdict is the first handed down by the Rwanda Tribunal, the first conviction for genocide by an international court, the first time an international court has punished sexual violence in a civil war, and the first time that rape was found to be an act of genocide to destroy a group" (n.p.).

but we shall be more succinct here. According to international law experts and scholars of genocide studies, establishing the intent to perpetrate genocide requires that the perpetrator *consciously desired* and *sought to achieve the destruction of the group*. Likewise, intent to commit genocide means that the perpetrator *knew the likely consequences that the acts he or she committed would destroy a group in whole or in part*. Put another way, if an alleged perpetrator kills 10,000 people from the same group, but did not have the *intent to destroy the group*, in whole or in part, then, as horrific as that crime is, it does not constitute genocide. It sounds crazy, but that is the way the law works.

As one can see, the focus of genocide is the destruction of groups, not individuals. In that respect, "the aim of the Genocide Convention is to prevent the intentional destruction of entire human groups, and the part targeted must be significant enough (substantial) to have an impact on the group as a whole. The substantiality requirement both captures genocide's defining character as a crime of massive proportions (numbers) and reflects the Convention's concern with the impact the destruction of the targeted part will have on the overall survival of the group (emblematic)" (UN Special Adviser on the Prevention of Genocide, 2016, p. 1).[5]

The legal definitions of genocide and crimes against humanity are used by numerous agencies and organizations for various and significant purposes. For example, genocide early warning agencies, the United Nations, individual nations, and major human rights organizations all use the definitions to assess whether contemporary atrocities being perpetrated somewhere in the world constitute crimes against humanity or genocide. Second, prosecutors at the International Criminal Court (ICC) use the definitions to assess whether atrocities that have been perpetrated in a conflict constitute genocide or crimes against humanity, and then issue warrants on

---

5 A valuable classroom assignment is to have individuals or pairs create a chart in which they delineate the similarities and key differences between crimes against humanity and genocide. To ensure that the assignment engages the students in high-level thinking, they should be required to provide a short rationale (one to five sentences) for each point they make in regard to the similarities and the differences.

charges of crimes against humanity and/or genocide. Third, prosecutors, defense attorneys, and judges at, for example, the ICTR and the International Criminal Tribunal for the former Yugoslavia and the ICC have all used the definitions of the terms during the course of a trial to find the alleged perpetrator guilty or innocent.

It is counterproductive to deem something genocide when it is not, because such claims more often than not result in time-consuming debate in the corridors of the United Nations and the governments of individual nations, among others, while the killing continues unabated. As absurd as it sounds, not infrequently do such debates degenerate into cases where the powers that be refuse to act until they are presented with definitive proof that a particular situation constitutes genocide or not. The absurdity of such a position is at least twofold: First, no one can definitively state a situation constitutes genocide until the genocide has already been played out, and by that time tens, if not hundreds of thousands and possibly millions will have been killed. Second, the time to head off a potential genocide is as soon as there are signs that suggest a conflict is moving toward mass killing. To wait until the conflict is definitively called this or that is simply providing the perpetrators with a window of opportunity to carry out their odious "work."

In light of the above discussion, it only makes sense to assist readers of this book to gain an understanding as to how and why the cases examined herein have been deemed genocide, crimes against humanity, or something else altogether. Only in that way will the reader come to understand the real-world use of such terms and to appreciate the fact that determining what a particular act constitutes requires careful attention to a host of issues. As one reads about the various cases, he or she will begin to see that very good minds often come to quite different conclusions. Furthermore, rarely are cases of mass killing as clearly understood to constitute genocide as those perpetrated by the Nazis against the Jews or the Hutu extremists against the Tutsis.

To assist the reader, each author was asked to clearly state and discuss whether the case he or she was writing about constituted genocide or crimes against humanity, and why that was so. The authors were asked to use the definition of genocide in the UNCG as a guidepost and to make their arguments by comparing and contrasting the definition against the facts of the case under study.

## CONTENTS OF THE BOOK

In chapter 1, "US Action and Inaction in the Massacre of Communists and Alleged Communists in Indonesia (1965–1966)," Kai M. Thaler, a PhD candidate in government at Harvard University, examines the United States' part "in laying the groundwork for the Killings and aiding and abetting the perpetrators." In doing so, he argues that "while the Killings were fundamentally a product of internal Indonesian political tensions, the US, motivated by Cold War fears and economic interests, worked to bolster anti-communist military and civilian leaders in Indonesia and to prepare the military for a takeover of the government and a long-term hold on power. US officials celebrated the military takeover and anti-communist repression as an important Cold War victory and the elimination of a potential threat to US strategic and economic interests, glossing over the fact that it was achieved through the mass killing of hundreds of thousands of civilians."

Among the host of topics and issues Thaler addresses are the overthrow of Sukarno and the rise of Suharto, the events leading up to and eventuating in the Killings of 1965–66, who the victims were and why they were targeted, how the Killings were carried out, the issue as to whether they constituted crimes against humanity or genocide, US complicity vis-à-vis the Killings, and the international response.

In chapter 2, "The Bangladesh Genocide and the Nixon–Kissinger 'Tilt' (1971)," Salim Mansur, associate professor of political science at Western University in London, Ontario, Canada, examines the stance of the Nixon administration—in particular, the US ambassador to Bangladesh; President Nixon; and his National Security Adviser Henry Kissinger—in relation to West Pakistan's position and actions against East Pakistan (which later became Bangladesh). In doing so, Mansur discusses the antecedents to the genocide; the immediate events leading up the 1971 crisis, including the mindset of the Pakistani military, which triggered the massacre; the advice and support that the Nixon administration provided to West Pakistan's President Yahya Khan as he prepared to attack Bangladesh; the unfolding of the massacre; the response of the international media to the genocide; and the ensuing and ongoing controversy over the number of dead.

In chapter 3, "'Our Hand Doesn't Show': The United States and the Consolidation of the Pinochet Regime in Chile (1973–1977)," Christopher Dietrich, assistant professor of history at Fordham University in New York City, examines "the evolving relationship between the US government and the Pinochet regime in Chile between 1973 and 1977, the period in which the military dictatorship implemented its reign of terror and carried out a rash of extrajudicial killings and 'disappearances.'" He also discusses the perspectives of two White Houses (particularly President Richard Nixon, President Gerald Ford, and Secretary of State Henry Kissinger) concerning the mass killing there. Dietrich argues that

> the Nixon and Ford administrations, whose foreign policy was by this time dominated by Secretary of State Henry Kissinger, largely disregarded gruesome reports of state-sponsored torture, executions, and the systematic repression of the regime's political enemies in its first four years. [Essentially], the United States provided extensive political, economic, military, and organizational support for the Chilean dictatorship despite its detailed knowledge of Pinochet's campaign of terror and mass murder. The US government did so, in large part, in the name of fighting communism in Latin America. Simply put, the Cold War was more important for US officials than protecting human rights.

Dietrich addresses a host of key issues in his chapter: the United States' reaction to the coup carried out by the military junta; the atrocities perpetrated in Chile between 1973 and 1977 by the junta; the US government's reaction to the atrocities; US aid to the Pinochet regime; and whether this case constitutes genocide or crimes against humanity.

In chapter 4, "Mass Killing at a Distance: US Complicity in the East Timor Genocide and International Structural Violence (1975–1999)," Joseph Nevins, professor of geography at Vassar College (whose major research areas include imperialism, various forms of political violence, matters of human rights, international law, and social justice in the aftermath of mass atrocities), provides a solid overview as to how and why East Timor became the site of cataclysmic violence perpetrated by Indonesia. Part and parcel of the chapter is a discussion of the United States' support of Indonesia's deadly and massively destructive treatment of East Timor. In his introduction, Nevins asserts that

> myriad Western capitalist countries, particularly the United States, whose support was decisive, strongly backed the invasion and occupation [of East Timor by Indonesia]. Washington, DC, provided Indonesia's Suharto regime the green light for the invasion and supplied it significant military, economic, and diplomatic assistance over the 1975–99 period. Without these various forms of assistance, it is highly doubtful that the invasion would have taken place or that the occupation would have endured to the depth, extent, and duration that it did.

In chapter 5, "The US Role in Argentina's 'Dirty War' (1976–1983)," Natasha Zaretsky, an Argentinian who is currently a visiting scholar at the Center for the Study of Genocide and Human Rights at Rutgers University, examines the overthrow of the presidency of Isabel Perón and how the military officials who assumed power carried an out all-out assault against those they suspected of engaging in alleged terrorism and subversion of "Western and Christian order." Tellingly, the military dictatorship "targeted anyone it considered *potentially* subversive—a large cross-section of society that included priests working with the poor, trade unionists, university students, and activists, among others. To accomplish its goal of maintaining both order and strict control of the society, the junta employed clandestine, extralegal tactics of disappearance, torture, and killing, which resulted in the murder of an estimated 30,000 people." Zaretsky discusses the complex role the United States government (particularly Secretary of State Henry Kissinger) played in Argentina's so-called Dirty War, and how it was driven to a large extent "by a powerful US ideological doctrine of eradicating communism in the Western hemisphere."

In chapter 6, "The United States Government's Relationship with the Guatemalan Government During the Latter's Genocide of the Maya of the Highlands (1981–1983)," Samuel Totten, professor emeritus at the University of Arkansas, Fayetteville, and now an independent researcher on the violent crises that have plagued Sudan under the regime of Omar al-Bashir, presents a detailed overview of the Guatemalan government's genocide of the Maya, and how and why the United States aided and abetted the Guatemalan government in its brutal treatment of the Maya. He delineates how the US government was closely involved with Guatemalan President Efraín Ríos Montt, who oversaw the terror and genocide that engulfed the Maya in Guatemala.

In chapter 7, "Calculated Avoidance: The Clinton Administration and the 100-Day Genocide in Rwanda (1994)," Gerry Caplan, an independent scholar based in Canada and author of *Rwanda: The Preventable Genocide* for the Organization of African Unity's International Panel of Eminent Personalities to Investigate the 1994 Genocide in Rwanda, and Samuel Totten take a new look at the Clinton administration's anemic and disingenuous response to the genocide of the Tutsi by radical Hutus and do so by examining and analyzing recent declassified US government documents obtained by the National Security Archive at George Washington University via the Freedom of Information Act (FOIA).

## ADDITIONAL FOOD FOR THOUGHT

As previously mentioned, when one takes a close look at US history, it is nothing short of astonishing how many governments around the world the United States has overthrown. (The number burgeons exponentially when one also considers unsuccessful US attempts to overthrow governments.) And yet, ironically, for all if its might, the US government's record at attempting to prevent major cases of crimes against humanity and/or genocide is relatively scant.

Interestingly (or, perhaps, *disturbingly* is the mot juste here), Henry Kissinger had his hand in three of the cases examined in this book: East Timor, Chile, and Argentina. In his book *Sideshow: Kissinger, Nixon and the Destruction of Cambodia*, William Shawcross (1987) comments about Kissinger and his involvement in many questionable actions across the globe:

> His critics argued that he took the practice of *real politik* to an unacceptable extreme, and that in his schemes the concept of individual rights had no place....He extended approval to regimes like the Portuguese, Spanish, Greek and post-Allende Chilean, which were most obviously intent on denying the ideals on which European civilization and American government are based. Such support had obvious strategic purpose, but it meant that the United States appeared to care little about human suffering and democratic rights. This policy comforted dictators and discouraged democrats everywhere....
>
> Equally disturbing could be the lengths to which he was prepared to go to effect his plans. He never really concealed his irritation with conventional procedures and restraints of the law. "The illegal we do immediately, the unconstitutional takes a little longer," he once said. It was a joke but Kissinger often attempted to mask his real attitudes in humor. (p. 307)

Kissinger was not alone in his propensity for carrying out nefarious affairs in such an arrogant fashion. Earlier in the century, there were the Dulles brothers (Secretary of State John Foster Dulles and Central Intelligence Agency (CIA) Director Allen Dulles), both of whom were instrumental in overthrowing regimes in Iran (1953) and Guatemala (1954). Both of those situations dramatically impacted the future of each of those nations. In the case of Guatemala, it led to decades of rule by authoritarian governments that did their all to keep the poor and downtrodden subservient and the wealthy, rich. Indirectly, the overthrow of the democratically elected government by the CIA in 1954 led to the genocide of the Maya people in the early 1980s. Stephen Kinzer (2013), author of *The Brothers: John Foster Dulles, Allen Dulles, and Their Secret World War*, notes the following:

> A similar confluence of economic and political factors drove the decisions to overthrow [Mossadegh in Iran and] Arbenz in Guatemala. Arbenz was a figure much like Mossadegh. Both were nationalists who wished to improve daily life for their countries' suffering masses. Neither saw why his government's dispute with a foreign corporation should throw him into the vortex of the great East-West confrontation. The Dulles brothers, however, saw every local conflict through the lens of that confrontation. In their eyes, every leader not explicitly tied to the United States was a potential enemy. Arbenz's sin, like Mossadegh's, was his insistence on embracing the domestic challenge of alleviating poverty rather than the global one of supporting Washington's anti-communist crusade. Neither Mossadegh nor Arbenz was a communist, but that didn't matter. In fact, it helped. Not even the Dulles brothers would have risked nuclear conflagration by attacking China, the Soviet Union or one of their satellites. Yet their desire to strike back against communism was so intense that almost any target would do. Iran and Guatemala were ideal because, by subduing them, the United States would not only remove a perceived enemy but also acquire a strategic platform from which it could project its power across an entire region of the world.... Neither Iran in 1953 nor Guatemala in 1954 posed an imminent danger to the United States. Those early coups were operations of choice, warnings to the world that no regime is safe if it defies the United States. (n.p.)

Tellingly, not a few US officials have done their all to attempt to hide certain decisions and actions from just about anyone and everyone. And here, I am not simply speaking about classifying a document "Secret" or "Top Secret," for that is par for the course of virtually any government. Rather, I am speaking about how certain officials not only hid their decisions and actions from the general public but from those *in the very same administration*. Perhaps the classic case involves, once again, Henry Kissinger. In this regard William Shawcross (1987) reported the following:

> Two new series of memoranda were created: National Security Study Memoranda and National Security Decision Memoranda. The Study Memoranda, to be signed usually by Kissinger, sometimes by Nixon, would direct agencies to review particular problems or situations for the President by a certain date.... When confronted with a policy problem the system enabled Kissinger to send a two- or three-page study memorandum, the NSSM (pronounced Nisim), to the appropriate interagency group requesting all views by a certain date. Each member of the group would have officials in his agency submit papers, and these would be collated to be passed on to the Review Group.... On paper, the system gave the President real choice of genuine alternatives for policy making. But even on paper it conferred exceptional powers on the National Security Adviser [Kissinger]. Access to the President was through him; it was he who, in the President's name, informed the bureaucracies what they were to examine; his staff sat through the entire development of the studies, and when these reached the Review Group he could either accept them, reject them or demand changes in whatever had so far been accomplished. Final papers for the President had his covering memorandum on top of them. Subsequently, many more NSC committees were created to coordinate different aspects of foreign policy. Kissinger was made their chairman.... *But it soon became evident... that one purpose of the many NSSM's was to keep the departments occupied and under the illusion that they were participating in the policy-making process while decisions were actually made in the White House. Kissinger's intentions were, in fact, fairly clear. Nothing in his academic writing had suggested that he was concerned to involve the bureaucracies in policy making. In 1968 he had said, "The only way secrecy can be kept is to exclude from the making the decisions all those who are theoretically charged with carrying them out."* (pp. 81, 82, 84; italics added)

What, one has to wonder, is our government doing in our name today that we have absolutely no idea about and/or would look askance at, if not condemn, if we knew?

## CONCLUSION

Certainly one of the many lessons inherent in this book is the fact that *no one, but no one*, other than those at the very highest levels of government (and even some of them, particularly when a "Kissinger-type" is in charge) truly knows what our "leaders" are doing in our name. Indeed, no one knows whether they are overstepping their authority or sidestepping their responsibility. And unfortunately, it is often extremely difficult, if not impossible, to truly know until much later—either when research is conducted and/or classified documents are declassified—whether what they shared with the public was the truth or something more along the lines of disinformation, distortion, misrepresentation, evasion, obfuscation, if not outright prevarication. And the same is true, of course, in regard to whether such leaders have acted in good faith or harbored dubious motives that were closer to immoral, amoral, or outright criminal.

The upshot is that we must all strive to be vigilant in regard to what our respective governments are doing at home and abroad. We must strive to remain as well informed as possible. We must ask questions. We must not be satisfied with the position of simply "going along to get along." We must not assume that someone with more power or more prestige will take care of "it" for us. And, when we or others perceive and/or discover that there is a problem, we must be proactive and face it head on. Short of that, there is little to no hope that "leaders" are going to be totally honest, forthright, moral, or transparent. A case in point is the Obama administration. On the very first day of his presidency, President Barack Obama famously promised that his administration would be the most transparent in the history of the presidency. Promises, of course, are easy to make; keeping them is another thing altogether. As Margaret Sullivan (2016) of *The Washington Post* notes,

After early promises to be the most transparent administration in history, this has been one of the most secretive. And in certain ways, one of the most elusive. It's also been one of the most punitive toward whistleblowers and leakers who want to bring light to wrongdoing they have observed from inside powerful institutions. . . . The Obama administration hasn't walked its talk. It has set new records for stonewalling or rejecting Freedom of Information requests. And it has used an obscure federal act to prosecute leakers. . . . It has kept the news media—and therefore the public—in the dark far too much over the past 7 ½ years. (n.d.)

As it now stands in the United States, presidents, vice presidents, members of presidential cabinets (especially secretaries of state and secretaries of defense), and members of a slew of agencies, bureaus, and services (including, for example, the CIA, the Federal Bureau of Investigation, and the National Clandestine Service) essentially have free reign—within certain bounds, of course, but those bounds, unfortunately, are incredibly broad—to act as they wish; and as a result, a lot of questionable, tawdry, and potentially criminal practices are a regular part of our governmental process. It doesn't help, of course, that government bureaucracy is so huge and so unwieldy. Indeed, that not only complicates matters but makes it all that much easier to hide questionable, if not immoral or illegal, actions. A popular cliché today is "If it ain't broke, don't fix it." Unfortunately, the truth of the matter is that when it comes to the US government, *a lot needs fixing*.

Hyperbole? I fear not. In fact, there are, sadly, hundreds upon hundreds of examples that can be cited. Herein, seven shall suffice. In a book entitled *The Crimes of Patriots*, the author cited a Wall Street report that had the following to say about the CIA's actions between the late 1940s and the late 1980s:

Instead of fulfilling its intended and proper mission, the CIA spent its time organizing and maintaining full-scale armies fighting wars in various parts of Africa, Asia, and Latin America; promoting economic havoc here and there in all three regions; attempting to bring down foreign governments (those of Guatemala, Nicaragua, Chile, Zaire, Zambia, South and North Vietnam, Iran, Afghanistan, Albania, Cambodia, Laos, Brazil, Guyana, the Dominican Republic, Angola, Cuba, Lebanon, Indonesia, and China, to name a few publicly documented cases) and often succeeding; bringing about the death of any number of foreign heads of state and hundreds of thousands of other foreign political figures (the deaths in Indonesia alone might justify that number); reporting on the domestic political activities of us citizens; and carrying out other assorted adventures. (Kwitny, 1987, p. 99)

Continuing several pages later, but moving beyond the CIA, Kwitny (1987) asserts that "it is a sad commentary on what our irrational, undiscerning war against a vague 'Communist' menace has done to American values [i.e., during the period of the Cold War or from 1947 to 1991]. People everywhere accept it as perfectly plausible that the United States Government is routinely engaged in secret, highly illegal, absolutely stomach-turning activities, with profits to be pocketed privately along the way. Unauthorized crimes have become hard to distinguish from the authorized ones. You can no longer tell the crooks from the patriots" (p. 104).

Not a few, of course, have made similar claims about the us government's "war on terror" today, along with the implementation of the Patriot Act. Others, as might be expected, extol the Patriot Act as being essential in the fight against terrorism. Be that as it may, it is absolutely imperative that the so-called average citizen strive to be well informed and not assume that "all's well with the world." As delineated in this book, even relatively recent history proves the nonsense of assuming that it is. And as the reader now knows, not a few officials from various us presidential administrations in the recent past have on their hands the blood of innumerable innocents murdered in Argentina, Bangladesh, Chile, East Timor, Guatemala, Indonesia, and Rwanda due to these officials' imprimatur or feigned ignorance of certain murderous deeds perpetrated by "friends" of this nation.

Thomas Jefferson (1816) wisely asserted that "if a nation expects to be ignorant & free, in a state of civilisation, it expects what never was & never will be. The functionaries of every government have propensities to command at will the liberty & property of their constituents. There is no safe deposit for these but with the people themselves; nor can they be safe with them without information." But that is only true if citizens seek out and demand information that should not be hidden or kept from them, if citizens are not complacent but rather vigilant, and if citizens have the will and drive to act upon the knowledge they have collected. (Here I am not speaking about information that the US must keep secret from potential and actual enemies. That, though, is where matters get sticky, for those who wish to hide their questionable, immoral, if not criminal, activities, often have a proclivity to see to it that such information is "classified" for "purposes of national security.") In regard to the issue of the critical need for citizens *to always be vigilant*, Jefferson (1821) sagaciously said, "Let the eye of vigilance never be closed." As the editor of this book, I firmly believe that the information presented in the various chapters should raise a host of red flags in regard to what one's government purportedly does in one's name—and behind one's back.

Upon reading and pondering each case presented in this book, some may find themselves thinking, cynically, "So what's new?" Put another way, they are likely to say that nothing the US government has done, is doing, or will do surprises them. Others may assume that, for the most part, the US government does its level best in an often nasty and brutish world to uphold the Constitution and beliefs of the people of the United States of America. Still others may firmly believe that the US government would never knowingly act in a way that is counter to the beliefs on which the United States of America was founded. Undoubtedly there will be those who express a wide range of negative emotions, ranging from outright repulsion, fury, and possibly even depression, at the words, decisions, and actions of their nation's leaders, past and present. And, of course, there are bound to be those who "couldn't care less." Again, this is where the value and beauty of discussion, debate, and more research come into play.

# REFERENCES

Graham-Harrison, E., & Ackerman, S. (2016, July 20). "US Airstrikes Allegedly Kill at Least 73 Civilians in Northern Syria." *The Guardian.* Accessed at: www.theguardian.com/ world/2016/jul/20/us-airstrike-allegedly-kills-56-civilians-in-northern-syria

Griffiths, J. (2015, October 7.). "Collateral Damage: A Brief History of U.S. Mistakes at War." *CNN World.* Accessed at: www.cnn.com/2015/10/06/middleeast/us-collateral-damage-history/

Human Rights Watch. (1998, September 2). "Human Rights Watch Applauds Rwanda Rape Verdict." Accessed at: https://www.hrw.org/news/1998/09/02/human-rights-watch -applauds-rwanda-rape-verdict

Human Rights Watch. (2014, December 9). "USA and Torture: A History of Hypocrisy." Accessed at: https://www.hrw.org/news/2014/12/09/usa-and-torture-history-hypocrisy

Jefferson, T. (1816). "Thomas Jefferson to Charles Yancey, 6 January 1816." *Founders Online,* National Archives. Accessed at: https://founders.archives.gov/documents/ Jefferson/03-09-02-0209

Jefferson, T. (1821). "From Thomas Jefferson to Spencer Roane, 9 March 1821." *Founders Online,* National Archives. Accessed at: https://founders.archives.gov/documents/ Jefferson/98-01-02-1900

Kinzer, S. (2013). *The Brothers: John Foster Dulles, Allen Dulles, and Their Secret World War.* New York: Times Books.

Kwitny, J. (1987). *The Crimes of Patriots.* New York: Norton.

Power, S. (2002). *"A Problem from Hell": America and the Age of Genocide.* New York: Basic Books.

Shawcross, W. (1987). *Sideshow: Kissinger, Nixon and the Destruction of Cambodia.* New York: Simon and Schuster.

Sullivan, M. (2016, May 24). "Obama Promised Transparency. But His Administration Is One of the Most Secretive." *The Washington Post.* Accessed at: https://www.washingtonpost.com/ lifestyle/style/obama-promised-transparency-but-his-administration-is-one-of-the-most -secretive/2016/05/24/5a46caba-21c1-11e6-9e7f-57890b612299_story.html?utm_term =.7691b8e51468

UN General Assembly. (1948). *Convention on the Prevention and Punishment of the Crime of Genocide.* Accessed at: https://treaties.un.org/doc/publication/unts/volume%2078/volume-78- i-1021-english.pdf

UN General Assembly. (1998). *Rome Statute of the International Criminal Court* , 17 July 1998. Accessed at: http://www.refworld.org/docid/3ae6b3a84.html

UN Special Adviser on the Prevention of Genocide. (2016). "OSAPG Analysis Framework." New York: United Nations.

Wood, P., & Hall, R. (2016, February 4). "U.S. Killing More Civilians in Iraq, Syria Than It Acknowledges." *USA Today.* Accessed at: https://www.usatoday.com/story/news/world/ 2016/02/02/us-killing-more-civilians-iraq-and-syria-than-acknowledges-globalpost/ 79686772/

# CHAPTER ONE

# US ACTION AND INACTION IN THE MASSACRE OF COMMUNISTS AND ALLEGED COMMUNISTS IN INDONESIA (1965–1966)

Kai M. Thaler

> *In terms of the numbers killed, the anti-PKI massacres in Indonesia rank as one of the worst mass murders of the 20th century, along with the Soviet purges of the 1930s, the Nazi mass murders during the Second World War, and the Maoist bloodbath of the early 1950s. In this regard, the Indonesian coup is certainly one of the most significant events of the 20th century, far more significant than many other events that have received much greater publicity.*

Written in 1968 in a report by the Central Intelligence Agency (1968, p. 71fn), the statement above still holds true today. The massacres of members of the Indonesian Communist Party (PKI) and associated mass organizations, as well as other alleged communists, (henceforth referred to as "the Killings,"[6])

6    Following Cribb (1990b, 2002).

claimed the lives of hundreds of thousands of people, yet they remain little known in the United States.[7] Among the key differences, however, between the Indonesian Killings of 1965–66 and the other mass killings mentioned is that while the other episodes were perpetrated by US enemies, the killings in Indonesia were committed by military and civilian organizations receiving aid, training, and encouragement from the United States government.

This chapter explores the United States' role in laying the groundwork for the Killings and aiding and abetting the perpetrators. While the Killings were fundamentally a product of internal Indonesian political tensions, the United States, motivated by Cold War fears and economic interests, worked to bolster anti-communist military and civilian leaders in Indonesia and to prepare the military for a takeover of the government and a long-term hold on power. US officials celebrated the military take-over and anti-communist repression as an important Cold War victory and the elimination of a potential threat to US strategic and economic interests, glossing over the fact that it was achieved through the mass kill-ing of hundreds of thousands of civilians. The CIA report quoted at the beginning of this chapter proceeded, over the course of 300 pages, to place the blame for the Killings on the PKI and its associates—the victims, rather than the killers. Like the Indonesian perpetrators, the US officials who were accessories to this mass murder were never held to account for their actions or inaction, and they either acclaimed the Killings or ignored them, downplaying US responsibility.

This chapter begins by examining the historical processes of the Killings. It then considers the Killings in light of legal and scholarly definitions of genocide, after which it discusses the particular role played by the United States government in creating the conditions for the Killings and supporting, rather than restraining or condemning, the perpetrators. The primary-source evidence from the US government about its role in Indonesia before and during the Killings is described, with six key documents included in full.

---

7   Though there has been increased interest sparked by Joshua Oppenheimer and Christine Cynn's 2012 film, *The Act of Killing*, and Oppenheimer's 2014 follow-up, *The Look of Silence*.

The chapter concludes with a brief exploration of the broader historical and political implications of the Killings and the us–Indonesia relationship that they forged, which paved the way in Indonesia for a military dictatorship and future genocidal policies.

## THE KILLINGS OF 1965-1966

Indonesia gained independence from the Netherlands in 1948 and was subsequently led by President Sukarno, a charismatic leader who knit together a nation from diverse ethnic and religious groups across a far-flung archipelago. From the late 1950s through the early 1960s, Sukarno developed closer ties with the previously marginalized PKI, the Indonesian Communist Party. The PKI steadily gained political influence in the government and military, especially in the air force, with whom it shared a distrust of the army (Cribb, 2001, p. 229; Crouch, 1978). The PKI grew to become the third-largest communist party in the world (behind only those in the Soviet Union and China), claiming 2.5 to 3.5 million members and candidate members, as well as up to 20 million members of associated "fronts" for labor, women, youths, and other groups (Boden, 2007, p. 510; van der Kroef, 1965). Total affiliates therefore represented about one-fifth of the Indonesian population. The PKI pushed forward plans for land redistribution, which frequently resulted in conflict between dispossessed landowners, and party activists and land occupiers. The party also advocated for the arming of workers and peasants to form a "fifth force" to counterbalance the power of the security apparatus (Mortimer, 1972; Young, 1990; Robinson, 1992). An economic crisis, military conflict with Malaysia and the United Kingdom over Borneo (1963–66), and the uncertain health of Sukarno (who suffered from kidney problems) led to a tense atmosphere in the early 1960s, with many Indonesian and foreign observers unsure what the near future would bring in terms of economic development, political leadership, and international affairs (Sutter, 1966, pp. 523–33; Mackie, 1974; May, 1978; Cribb, 2002).

Tensions came to a head on the night of September 30, 1965, when a group of mid-level army officers, claiming they were acting to counter a plot against Sukarno, kidnapped and executed six generals from the military high command, also fatally wounding the young daughter of General Abdul Haris Nasution, the minister of defense. Major General Suharto of the Army Strategic Reserve (KOSTRAD) quickly organized troops to crush the officers, who were dubbed the 30th of September Movement (G-30-S) or *Gestapu*. By the night of October 1, Suharto and the remaining army command were in control of Jakarta.

In the subsequent weeks and months, the army, under Suharto's leadership and working with Nasution, whom the G-30-S plotters had not killed, moved to consolidate their power and to sideline President Sukarno. Key to Suharto's strategy was stirring up public anger against the PKI, accusing them of murdering the generals as part of a coup plot. To this day, uncertainty lingers about the exact nature of the events of September 30–October 1,[8] but while PKI leader D.N. Aidit was involved in the plot (Roosa, 2006, ch.1), he was not its leader or chief architect; there is no evidence that it was aimed at a larger communist takeover; the list of members of the G-30-S's proposed "Indonesian Revolutionary Council" included known anti-communists; and allegations of Sukarno's involvement in the plot have been unsubstantiated (Crouch, 1978; May, 1978; Roosa, 2006). Meanwhile, Suharto and Nasution had been staunchly anti-PKI and had been advocating to the murdered generals that a stronger stance against the party was needed (Crouch, 1978, p. 136; Roosa, 2006, p. 188).

In the wake of G-30-S, Suharto "took steps to consolidate the already widespread public presumption that the PKI had masterminded the coup (and was probably planning further actions) and encouraged rumors that the communists had been planning to torture and murder their enemies" (Cribb, 2002, pp. 551–52). The army seized control of the public sphere, using newspapers to disseminate false propaganda about the viciousness of the PKI and claim that the generals had been tortured and mutilated, with their genitals cut off by members of Gerwani, the women's organiza-

---

8   See Roosa (2006, ch. 2) for a review of different interpretations of the events and the evidence for them.

tion associated with the PKI. The latter, allegedly, was followed by Gerwani members engaging in a sexual orgy (Anderson, 1987; Wieringa, 2003; Drakeley, 2007).[9] As discussed below, the United States endorsed these propaganda efforts, and the CIA helped spread stories of the PKI's guilt. Press reports and editorial cartoons systematically dehumanized the PKI and Gerwani, portraying them as bloodthirsty monsters threatening common Indonesians (van Langenberg, 1990, p. 50; Drakeley, 2007, p. 21). Communism was equated with atheism and as anathema to the Indonesian nation; one military newspaper argued that a campaign of vengeance against the PKI would be a holy war (Robinson, 1995, p. 281; Drakeley, 2007, p. 21). Rumors were spread that the PKI was compiling lists of non-communists to execute, creating a perception that the country had descended into life-or-death polarization (Young, 1990, p. 80; Cribb, 2002, p. 552; Farid, 2005).

Having whipped the population into an anti-PKI rage, the military coordinated with student and Muslim organizations to initiate attacks on PKI targets and alleged communists, forming the "Action Front to Crush Gestapu" (*Kap-Gestapu*). On October 8, Muslim student groups attacked and destroyed PKI headquarters in Jakarta with military complicity (Crouch, 1978, p. 141; May, 1978, p. 121), and shortly thereafter, massacres began. In devoutly Muslim Aceh, youth groups joined with the regional military command to capture and kill thousands of PKI members, alleged supporters, and in some cases their families and household employees (Crouch, 1978). The military commander for the region, Brigadier General Ishak Djuarsa, boasted to the press in December 1965 that "the PKI is no longer a problem for Aceh because the region has been entirely purged in a physical sense of PKI elements" (Crouch, 1978, p. 143). Late October brought massacres to East and Central Java, where the Army Paracommando Regiment (RPKAD) armed and trained local Muslim and Christian youth groups with whom they traveled from village to village,

---

9   Autopsies on the generals found no evidence of mutilations to support these sensational claims (Anderson, 1987, pp. 111–13).

killing suspected PKI members and sympathizers and at times slaughtering entire villages alleged to support the PKI, and eventually bringing its reign of terror to Bali as well (Crouch, 1978; May, 1978; Scott, 1985; van Langenberg, 1990, p. 49; Cribb, 2001, p. 233). Other than in Aceh, massacres did not begin without instigation from the military (Young, 1990).

PKI members and other victims offered little organized resistance in the face of the overwhelming tide of organized and popular violence (Cribb, 2001; Farid, 2005). The Killings claimed victims throughout Indonesia, with the most violent areas being Aceh, Bali, Central Java, East Java, and Northern Sumatra. Victims were subjected to torture, mutilation, and extreme brutality. While the target of the violence was ostensibly "communists," and many PKI members and supporters were among the victims, the chaos of the Killings provided an opportunity for settling local and personal scores related to land, religion, sexual jealousy, or ethnicity, with victims labeled as communists after the fact (Kalyvas, 2003, p. 478; Dwyer & Santikarma, 2003).[10] These local motivations, however, should not distract from the military's role in promoting and supporting the "popular" side of the Killings (Roosa, 2006, pp. 24–25).

By the end of 1965, the Killings slowed, in part due to the desire of the Indonesian military to rein in civilian groups to avoid anarchy (Crouch, 1978, p. 154; Robinson, 1995, p. 296). Massacres carried over into 1966, though, as the military engaged in "mopping up" operations against remaining actual and alleged PKI cells, and abuses continued over the next several years. In the worst of the known later episodes, over 800 alleged communist prisoners were massacred at Purwodadi in late 1968 (May, 1978, pp. 203–6). Throughout the late 1960s, hundreds of thousands of PKI members and alleged communists were also kept in detention camps in harsh conditions and at times used as slave labor (see Kammen & McGregor, 2012). Despite the mass scale of the Killings and the elimination

---

10 While there was some targeting of ethnic Chinese during the Killings, following allegations that communist China was behind G-30-S, there were not large-scale massacres of Chinese, and violence against them was similar to prior outbursts of anti-Chinese violence in Indonesia (Cribb & Coppel, 2009, pp. 447–65).

of the PKI as a political force, the military government, which came to be known as the "New Order," frequently invoked the threat of communism to justify its authoritarian policies and discrimination against the descendants of victims, whom it labeled "children of the PKI...'infected' by 'political uncleanliness'" (Dwyer & Santikarma, 2003, pp. 297–99).

The ultimate number of victims murdered during the Killings remains uncertain, with estimates ranging from a clearly biased Indonesian government figure of 78,000 up to a high estimate of 2 million (Cribb, 1990a, p. 12). US foreign correspondents who were able to travel within Indonesia after March 1966 estimated that at least 300,000, and most likely 500,000 people had been killed (Roosa, 2006, p. 25), while an Indonesian army officer estimated the death toll at about 500,000 in January 1966 (Easter, 2005, p. 61). The best recent estimate suggests that the mid-range figures were correct and approximately half a million deaths occurred due to the Killings (Cribb, 2004, p. 233), though some argue this figure is still an underestimation (Dwyer & Santikarma, 2003, pp. 290–91).

Despite the high death toll, according to the Articles of the United Nations Convention on the Prevention and Punishment of the Crime of Genocide (UNCG), the Killings do not constitute a genocide, since victims were killed on the basis of their membership or alleged affiliation with the PKI, a political organization, rather than a national, ethnic, religious, or racial group. Political groups were excluded from the Convention on the basis of objections from Eastern Bloc countries, and recent judicial precedent in trials on Rwanda and the former Yugoslavia have reinforced the idea that victims of genocide must be members of "stable" rather than "mobile" groups, with political group membership considered more mutable (Ratner & Abrams, 2001, pp. 36–38). Scholarly definitions of genocide, however, that include the collective mass victimization of members of political or social groups targeted as such and that are aimed at group destruction (Charny, 1988; Chalk & Jonassohn, 1990; Fein, 1993) clearly do apply to the Killings. Furthermore, some scholars have argued that the Killings should be recognized and accepted as genocide under an alternative term and somewhat broader definition of genocide, that is, "politicide" (Cribb, 2001).

Perhaps most significantly, the Killings would also appear to meet the legal standards of intent for group destruction that are necessary for a crime to be considered genocide, with many previous cases setting the precedent that knowledge of the destructive consequences for a group of individual actions may create culpability, even if an individual him- or herself did not specifically possess genocidal intent (e.g., Ratner & Abrams, 2001, pp. 35–37). In this regard, then, the Killings definitely constitute genocide, for group destruction did in fact exist among the Indonesian military high command. The military did not merely target the actual plotters behind G-30-S but everyone considered communist—meaning millions of PKI members and members of associated organizations (Roosa, 2006). The military also called for and aimed to carry out the elimination of communists and viewed communism as a biological phenomenon, able to be inherited and thus necessitating extermination (Thaler, 2012, p. 215), suggesting that in this case, as in civil war-era and Francoist Spain (Balcells, 2012), political identity came to be viewed not as ascriptive but as an integral, unchangeable part of a person. Under these conditions, the legal rhetoric of the UNCG, which excludes the targeting of political groups, is incommensurate with the Convention's mission to condemn and eliminate targeted violence against essentialized collectivities. A strong argument can therefore be made that those who aided and abetted the Killings were complicit in genocide.

The political identity of the victims contributed to a lack of international outcry or action over the Killings. US officials were pleased with the anti-communist nature of the Killings, and no members of the Johnson administration spoke out against them, despite US Senator Robert Kennedy's (D-NY) plea during a January 1966 speech: "We have spoken out against inhuman slaughters perpetrated by the Nazis and the communists. But will we speak out also against the inhuman slaughter in Indonesia, where over 100,000 alleged communists have been not perpetrators, but victims?" (Roosa, 2006, p. 26).

In Australia and the United Kingdom, government policy was to avoid doing anything to impede the Killings and to aid in the propaganda campaign against the PKI. Australian Ambassador to Indonesia Keith Shann was strongly anti-communist and embraced the military takeover. Radio Australia, the most popular foreign station in Indonesia, was instructed not to broadcast anything that could contradict the official Indonesian army line and to "highlight reports discrediting the PKI and showing its involvement" in G-30-S (Easter, 2005, pp. 62–63, 68), while Shann also acted to reassure Indonesian military commanders that they "would be completely safe in using their forces for whatever purpose they saw fit" (Easter, 2005, p. 65).

The British were of a similar mindset, spreading anti-PKI propaganda through radio and print outlets and passing messages via US officials that they would not escalate the fight in Malaysia while the anti-communist purge was ongoing (Easter, 2005, pp. 63–64). The British ambassador in Jakarta, Andrew Gilchrist, wrote to the British Foreign Office on October 5, 1965, that he had "never concealed from you my belief that a little shooting in Indonesia would be an essential preliminary to effective [political] change…" and worrying that the Indonesian army was not acting with enough urgency to target PKI leaders (Curtis, 2003, p. 387), while the Foreign Office wanted to "encourage anti-Communist Indonesians to more vigorous action in the hope of crushing Communism in Indonesia altogether" (Easter, 2005, p. 63).

Gilchrist later came to have doubts about what the Indonesian military had done (in part with his assistance), writing to propaganda chief Norman Reddaway, "What have we to hope from the [Indonesian] generals? 400,000 people murdered, far more than total casualties in Vietnam—nobody cares. 'They were communists.' Were they? And are communists not human beings?" (Easter, 2005, p. 65). Neither the British nor the Australians, however, ever publicly condemned either the military takeover or the Killings.

The Soviet Union, which had been supplying the Indonesian military with arms in the early 1960s, kept its distance, distrusting the PKI, which was more closely aligned with China. Soviet officials and official news sources, however, did condemn the Killings, decrying them as the result of actions by right-wing counterrevolutionaries seeking the elimination of communism, and asking in *Pravda* in February 1966, "What for and according to what right are tens of thousands of people being killed?" (Boden, 2007, pp. 514–16).

Soviet anger over the Killings was expressed to Indonesia's Foreign Minister Adam Malik, who had himself been heavily involved in the Killings (see below), during a visit to Moscow in October 1966, and the Soviets continued to show concern over the treatment of Indonesian communists (Boden, 2007, pp. 521–22). China, which had enjoyed close relations with Sukarno and the PKI, condemned the military and popular organizations' conduct during the Killings, but was concerned primarily with attacks on Chinese citizens and ethnic Chinese, as well as diplomatic facilities. The Chinese government had no leverage to press for an end to the violence. Chinese Ambassador Yao Zhongming left Jakarta for China in April 1966 and was neither sent back nor replaced (Corcoran, 2005).

The Cold War mentality of Western powers prevented any questioning of the New Order government established under Suharto, and the Killings were interpreted as part of a victory against communism. Within Indonesia itself, there was no effort for accountability and the Killings have either been ignored or celebrated. Communists continued to be demonized up until the fall of Suharto in 1998, and the killings of the generals by G-30-S were the only deaths deemed worthy of commemoration (Heryanto, 1999; Farid, 2005; Roosa, 2006). Furthermore, the lack of condemnation and general impunity for the perpetrators of the Killings may have encouraged Suharto and the New Order to engage in genocidal mass killing a second time in their invasion of East Timor (Thaler, 2012), when the United States and other Western powers were once again complicit (Simpson, 2005).[11]

## THE US ROLE IN THE KILLINGS

While some scholars may overplay the US role in the reaction to G-30-S, the rise of Suharto, and the sidelining of Sukarno (Scott, 1985), the United States clearly sought to undermine Sukarno and the PKI and to bolster the

---

11  See also Nevins, this volume.

military through covert action, propaganda, aid programs, and diplomatic activities. US relations with Indonesia under Sukarno were conflictual due to Sukarno's close relations with the PKI and communist countries, his policy of confrontation with Malaysia, the threat his alliance with the PKI posed to US business interests (see Kim, 2002), and his strong anti-imperialist rhetoric. Though it restricted aid to Indonesia significantly in response to Sukarno's policies, the United States left open military assistance and "civic action" programs to maintain ties with the military (Brands, 1989; Evans, 1989),[12] part of close relations with the military developed at the beginning of the 1960s. According to a memo from Secretary of State Dean Rusk to President Lyndon Johnson, these assistance programs were aimed primarily at *"permitting us to maintain some contact with key elements in Indonesia... interested in and capable of resisting Communist takeover"* (Scott, 1985, p. 248; italics in original), and civic action programs also likely provided cover for covert anti-communist activities (Roosa, 2006, p. 184).

The United States government had a history of meddling in Indonesian affairs, supporting failed armed insurgencies aimed at deposing Sukarno in the 1950s, including large-scale covert paramilitary actions and even a bombing campaign (Kahin & Kahin, 1995; Conboy & Morrison, 1999). After that debacle, however, the United States turned to a policy of heavily aiding the Indonesian military. The National Security Council described the Indonesian army as the "principle obstacle to the continued growth of Communist strength," arguing that the army, in concert with civilian anti-communist politicians, could turn the tide against the PKI (Roosa, 2006, pp. 181–82). These military aid policies carried over through the Kennedy administration.

Members of President Lyndon Johnson's administration and US diplomats in Indonesia sought to constrain Sukarno's leftist tendencies and to undermine the PKI while ensuring that the Indonesian military, and

---

12 "Civic action" was the term used to denote the training and use of military personnel in general economic development and infrastructural projects (see Simpson, 2008).

especially the army, remained in a position of strength as a US ally and a "bulwark against the PKI" (Roosa, 2006, p. 182). US officials in Indonesia in 1964 thus had close ties to the military and General Nasution, whom they knew was a staunch anti-communist and who was considered "America's 'golden boy'" (Roosa, 2006, pp. 182–83). In January 1964, as deteriorating relations with Sukarno led some in the US government to call for a cutoff of military assistance to Indonesia, National Security Council staff member Michael Forrestal argued that the United States needed to be careful not to give "Nasution an unintended indication that the U.S. is abandoning its political support of the Indonesian armed forces."[13] In March 1964, US Ambassador to Indonesia Howard Jones asked Nasution how the military would respond if the PKI "attempted [to] exploit current economic difficulties through strikes, riots, etc.," to which "Nasution replied that Madiun (1948 crushing of PKI attempted coup) would be mild compared with army crackdown today."[14] In response to later calls to end nearly all aid ties with Indonesia, Special Assistant for National Security Affairs McGeorge Bundy wrote to President Lyndon Johnson in August 1964, stating that the United States "ought to keep a few links, however tenuous, to the Indo military, still the chief hope of blocking a Communist takeover." Meanwhile, Secretary of State Dean Rusk argued that military assistance "was an important link to the Indonesian military, and this long-term asset value is still considerable," while also suggesting the "continuation of technical assistance, non-military training, and supply of non-sensitive equipment for the National Police

---

13 US Department of State (1992). "Memorandum from Michael V. Forrestal of the National Security Council Staff to the President's Special Assistant for National Security Affairs (Bundy)." (1964, January 6). In E.C. Keefer (Ed.), *Foreign Relations of the United States, 1964–1968 [FRUS]* (vol. XXVI, doc. 5, pp. 10–12). Washington, DC: Author. Accessed at: http://history.state.gov/historicaldocuments/frus1964-68v26/d5

14 "Telegram from the Embassy in Indonesia to the Department of State." (1964, March 19). In E.C. Keefer (Ed.), *FRUS* (vol. XXVI, doc. 40, pp. 80–82). Washington, DC: US Department of State. Accessed at: http://history.state.gov/historicaldocuments/frus1964-68v26/d40 The Madiun uprising was a communist revolt during Indonesia's independence war against the Dutch and was seen by many Indonesians as a treasonous stab in the back (see Swift, 1989).

including the Mobile Brigade, to preserve US influence in this important power center."[15] In February 1965, Forrestal wrote to Jones to suggest that the United States, despite rough relations with Sukarno, "should let the Army have the Java portion of the telecommunications equipment we promised them" to maintain good relations with the army, because "it would probably also help them in the event there were trouble with the P.K.I. on Java."[16]

Throughout 1964 and 1965, the United States was aware that tensions were rising within Indonesia and sought to ensure that events played to its advantage. The US did not want to lose "100 million people, vast potential resources, and a strategically important chain of islands" to the communist camp.[17] Beyond Nasution and the military, US officials in Indonesia developed close ties to Minister of Trade Adam Malik, one of the leading civilian anti-communists, who met with Ambassador Jones in November 1964 to discuss the formation of an anti-communist coalition among Muslim and right-wing political parties, labor federations, and youth groups,[18] the civilian demographics later heavily involved in the Killings with Malik's organizational support and fundraising. At a particularly low point in US–Indonesian relations in March 1965, Special Representative for Indonesia Ellsworth Bunker wrote a lengthy report, after consultations with Nasution and Malik among others, in which he recommended that the United States meet its commitments to provide communications equipment to the

---

15 "Memorandum from President's Special Assistant for National Security Affairs (Bundy) to President Johnson." (1964, August 31). In E.C. Keefer (Ed.), *FRUS* (vol. XXVI, doc. 67, pp. 144–48). Washington, DC: US Department of State. Accessed at: http://history.state.gov/historicaldocuments/frus1964-68v26/d67

16 "Letter from Michael V. Forrestal of the National Security Council Staff to the Ambassador to Indonesia (Jones)." (1965, February 19). In E.C. Keefer (Ed.), *FRUS* (vol. XXVI, doc. 107, pp. 226–28). Washington, DC: US Department of State. Accessed at: http://history.state.gov/historicaldocuments/frus1964-68v26/d107

17 "Memorandum from the President's Special Assistant for National Security Affairs (Bundy) and James C. Thompson, Jr., of the National Security Council Staff to President Johnson." (1965, March 24). In E.C. Keefer (Ed.), *FRUS* (vol. XXVI, doc. 107, p. 253). Washington, DC: US Department of State. Accessed at: http://history.state.gov/historicaldocuments/frus1964-68v26/d119

18 "Intelligence Memorandum." (1964, December 2). In E.C. Keefer (Ed.), *FRUS* (vol. XXVI, doc. 89, pp. 89–91). Washington, DC: US Department of State. Accessed at: http://history.state.gov/historicaldocuments/frus1964-68v26/d89

Indonesian military and that even if other programs were cut, the United States should retain military assistance, training officers at the embassy to "keep maximum contact with the Indonesian military."[19] The sale of the communications equipment, to be stationed in Java, was approved and moving forward by July 1965.[20]

US officials at this time were worried that an anti-communist movement would have a hard time gaining traction while Indonesia's confrontation with Malaysia was still ongoing, concerned that efforts to undermine the PKI, given its close ties to Sukarno, would be seen as an effort to divide the nation in a time of war and would in fact strengthen the PKI, and so they tried to determine ways to resolve the conflict.[21] The CIA was also concerned that in the event of Sukarno's death, considered a strong possibility due to uncertainty over his health, "the initial struggle to replace him would be won by Army and non-Communist elements," but that "unless the non-Communist leaders displayed more backbone, effectiveness, and unity than they have to date, the chances of eventual PKI dominance of Indonesia would quickly mount."[22] By February 1965, the US government was determined to more actively influence the internal situation in Indonesia, developing a covert action plan for the State Department and CIA to support Indonesian anti-communist groups and

---

19 "Report from Ambassador Ellsworth Bunker to President Johnson." (n.d.). In E.C. Keefer (Ed.), *FRUS* (vol. XXVI, doc. 121, pp. 255–63). Washington, DC: US Department of State. Accessed at: http://history.state.gov/historicaldocuments/frus1964-68v26/d121

20 "Memorandum of Conversation." (1965, July 20). In E.C. Keefer (Ed.), *FRUS* (vol. XXVI, doc. 127, p. 272). Washington, DC: US Department of State. Accessed at: http://history.state.gov/historicaldocuments/frus1964-68v26/d127

21 "Telegram from the Embassy in Indonesia to the Department of State." (1964, December 15). In E.C. Keefer (Ed.), *FRUS* (vol. XXVI, doc. 93, pp. 198–200). Washington, DC: US Department of State. Accessed at: http://history.state.gov/historicaldocuments/frus1964-68v26/d93; "Telegram from the Embassy in Malaysia to the Department of State." (1964, December 17). In E.C. Keefer (Ed.), *FRUS* (vol. XXVI, doc. 95, pp. 203–4). Washington, DC: US Department of State. Accessed at: http://history.state.gov/historicaldocuments/frus1964-68v26/d95

22 "Special Memorandum Prepared by the Director of the Office of National Estimates of the Central Intelligence Agency (Kent)." (1965, January 26). In E.C. Keefer (Ed.), *FRUS* (vol. XXVI, doc. 103, pp. 219–20). Washington, DC: US Department of State. Accessed at: http://history.state.gov/historicaldocuments/frus1964-68v26/d103

to "chip away at the PKI." According to the planning document, "Specific types of activity envisaged include covert liaison with and support to existing anti-Communist groups, particularly among the [*less than 1 line of source text not declassified*], black letter operations, media operations, including possibly black radio, and political action within existing Indonesian organizations and institutions" [bracketed material included in the declassified document].[23]

Though the United States did not take any direct actions aimed at toppling Sukarno, they certainly were not opposed to his removal from power if it involved the military or other anti-communist forces taking power. In March 1964, Ambassador Jones met with Nasution and hinted that the United States would support the military in the event of a coup (Evans, 1989, p. 28). In April 1965, Jones wrote to Assistant Secretary of State for Far Eastern Affairs William Bundy that he was "privy to plans for a coup here" and that while "to play safe, I informed my contact that the U.S. Government can in no way participate in any effort of this kind. I nevertheless conveyed clearly my own sympathy with his objectives," though this particular coup plot did not come to fruition.[24] While Jones was considered a moderate by the US standards of the time, in early June 1965 he was replaced as ambassador by Marshall Green, who took a harder anti-communist line and sought to ensure that the United States "maintain whatever contact possible with military and other elements in power structure, looking toward post-Sukarno period."[25]

The United States likely expected neither the G-30-S plot nor the swift and successful reaction by Suharto and the army. It was also unlikely to have expected the scale and ferocity of the Killings; intelligence estimates in July

---

23 "Memorandum Prepared for the 303 Committee." (1965, February 23). In E.C. Keefer (Ed.), *FRUS* (vol. XXVI, doc. 110, pp. 234–37). Washington, DC: US Department of State. Accessed at: http://history.state.gov/historicaldocuments/frus1964-68v26/d110

24 "Editorial Note." (n.d.). In E.C. Keefer (Ed.), *FRUS* (vol. XXVI, doc. 120, pp. 254). Washington, DC: US Department of State. Accessed at: http://history.state.gov/historicaldocuments/frus1964-68v26/d120

25 "Telegram from the Embassy in Indonesia to the Department of State." (1965, August 23). In E.C. Keefer (Ed.), *FRUS* (vol. XXVI, doc. 135, pp. 285–87). Washington, DC: US Department of State. Accessed at: http://history.state.gov/historicaldocuments/frus1964-68v26/d135

1965 suggested that in the event of Sukarno's death or marginalization, the "military would almost certainly exercise greater authority than at present, but would be unlikely to risk civil war to initiate a roll back of the Communists."[26] As Frederick Bunnell (1990) put it, the US plan was to lie low, and "there was always the cautious confidence that the army could and would prevail in a post-Sukarno showdown with the PKI, but the form and timing of such a showdown could not be predicted" (p. 59). Jones had been told in January 1965 by a reliable source that the military might undertake a "coup that would be handled in such a way as to preserve Sukarno's leadership intact," and Jones and other Western diplomats thought that "an unsuccessful coup attempt by the PKI" could provide the spark for a military reaction (Roosa, 2006, pp. 181–91). Yet when their hopes came true and G-30-S happened, the United States was caught off guard. The State Department was unsure of the extent of PKI involvement in G-30-S, and this was one case in which the CIA stated that it "had had absolutely nothing to do with it."[27]

With the news that the army was establishing control, however, US officials began to be cautiously optimistic that their dreams for an anti-PKI military reaction might come to fruition. Acting Secretary of State George Ball thought that if the army could take power, Nasution and his ilk might purge the PKI to consolidate control.[28] Already on October 5, Ambassador Green sought to ensure that the United States maintain its contacts with the military and distribute anti-PKI propaganda, suggesting that the failure of G-30-S and the army's reaction "may embolden [the] army at long last to

26 "National Intelligence Memorandum." (1965, July 1). In E.C. Keefer (Ed.), *FRUS* (vol. XXVI, doc. 126, pp. 270–71). Washington, DC: US Department of State. Accessed at: http://history.state.gov/historicaldocuments/frus1964-68v26/d126

27 "Memorandum of Telephone Conversation between Acting Secretary of State Ball and Secretary of Defense McNamara." (1965, October 1). In E.C. Keefer (Ed.), *FRUS* (vol. XXVI, doc. 143, pp. 301–2). Washington, DC: US Department of State. Accessed at: http://history.state.gov/historicaldocuments/frus1964-68v26/d143

28 Memorandum of Telephone Conversation between Acting Secretary of State Ball and Senator William Fullbright." (1965, October 1). In E.C. Keefer (Ed.), *FRUS* (vol. XXVI, doc. 144, pp. 302–3). Washington, DC: US Department of State. Accessed at: http://history.state.gov/historicaldocuments/frus1964-68v26/d144

act effectively against Communists." The memo recommended that the United States "spread the story of PKI's guilt, treachery and brutality (this priority effort is perhaps most needed immediate assistance we can give army if we can find way to do it without identifying it as solely or largely US effort)."[29] Ball replied that the United States should try to avoid publicly being tied to the army and that previous military assistance programs and contacts should have provided the military with sufficient capabilities and assurances as to US support, while Voice of America radio programs should spread the anti-PKI propaganda being produced in Indonesia, "without at this stage injecting U.S. editorializing," though Ball expressed concern to Rusk later that night that the army was not moving fast enough against the PKI.[30] Rusk also worried that the army would not seize the opportunity to go after the PKI and stated, "if [the] army's willingness to follow through against PKI is in any way contingent on or subject to influence by US, we do not wish [to] miss [the] opportunity [to] consider US action."[31]

As of October 12, the United States was already aware that attacks on PKI members were being organized by the army. In a conversation between Ball and US Senator William Fulbright, Ball stated that "although [the army] were afraid to move directly against Sukarno and the PKI, they were encouraging the Muslims and other groups to do so."[32] On October 14, US Army attaché Colonel William Ethel delivered assurances to Nasution's aide that the British would stand down and let the Indonesian army deal

29 "Telegram from the Embassy in Indonesia to the Department of State." (1965, October 5). In E.C. Keefer (Ed.), FRUS (vol. XXVI, doc. 147, pp. 307–8). Washington, DC: US Department of State. Accessed at: http://history.state.gov/historicaldocuments/frus1964-68v26/d147

30 "Telegram from the Department of State to the Embassy in Indonesia." (1965, October 6). In E.C. Keefer (Ed.), FRUS (vol. XXVI, doc. 148, pp. 308–10). Washington, DC: US Department of State. Accessed at: http://history.state.gov/historicaldocuments/frus1964-68v26/d148

31 "Telegram from the Department of State to the Embassy in Indonesia." (1965, October 13). In E.C. Keefer (Ed.), FRUS (vol. XXVI, doc. 153, pp. 320–21). Washington, DC: US Department of State. Accessed at: http://history.state.gov/historicaldocuments/frus1964-68v26/d153

32 "Memorandum of Telephone Conversation between the Under Secretary of State (Ball) and Secretary of State Rusk." (1965, October 12). In E.C. Keefer (Ed.), FRUS (vol. XXVI, doc. 152, p. 319). Washington, DC: US Department of State. Accessed at: http://history.state.gov/historicaldocuments/frus1964-68v26/d152

with the PKI, which the aide commented was "just what was needed by way of assurances that we (the army) weren't going to be hit from all angles as we moved to straighten things out here," before proceeding to tell Ethel that communist cadres and Chinese were being rounded up.[33] Ethel then organized the delivery of portable radio equipment to the Indonesian army's leadership.[34] On October 17, the American Embassy noted that attacks on the PKI were spreading outside Jakarta, with Central Java, East Java, and Northern Sumatra seen as potential tinderboxes for anti-communist violence.[35] Ethel was continuing to work closely with Nasution's aide, and on October 18, Ambassador Green wrote, "I gain [the] distinct impression that [the] army is proceeding methodically against Communists."[36] Only two days later, Green reported on hundreds of executions around Jakarta, expressing pleasure at the army's activities.[37] On October 22, Rusk, in his summation of the situation, showed he was aware that the army was "cleaning up" and aiming for the "elimination of the PKI," as well as that "non-communist civilians... [were] becoming actively anti-PKI," before reaffirming US support for the military in case a PKI insurgency broke out.[38] At the same time, the American Embassy sought to figure out "how to help the Army to win, but without revealing that assistance," in its

33  "Telegram from the Embassy in Indonesia to the Department of State." (1965, October 14). In E.C. Keefer (Ed.), *FRUS* (vol. XXVI, doc. 154, pp. 321–22). Washington, DC: US Department of State. Accessed at: http://history.state.gov/historicaldocuments/frus1964-68v26/d154

34  "Telegram from the Embassy in Indonesia to the Department of State." (1965, October 14). In E. C. Keefer (Ed.), *FRUS* (vol. XXVI, doc. 155, pp. 322–23). Washington, DC: US Department of State. Accessed at: http://history.state.gov/historicaldocuments/frus1964-68v26/d155

35  "Telegram from the Embassy in Indonesia to the Department of State." (1965, October 17). In E.C. Keefer (Ed.), *FRUS* (vol. XXVI, doc. 156, pp. 323–26). Washington, DC: US Department of State. Accessed at: http://history.state.gov/historicaldocuments/frus1964-68v26/d156

36  "Telegram from the Embassy in Indonesia to the Department of State." (1965, October 18). In E.C. Keefer (Ed.), *FRUS* (vol. XXVI, doc. 157, pp. 327–28). Washington, DC: US Department of State. Accessed at: http://history.state.gov/historicaldocuments/frus1964-68v26/d157

37  "Telegram from the Embassy in Indonesia to the Department of State." (1965, October 20). In E.C. Keefer (Ed.), *FRUS* (vol. XXVI, doc. 158, pp. 329–30). Washington, DC: US Department of State. Accessed at: http://history.state.gov/historicaldocuments/frus1964-68v26/d158

38  "Telegram from the Embassy in Indonesia to the Department of State." (1965, October 22). In E.C. Keefer (Ed.), *FRUS* (vol. XXVI, doc. 159, pp. 330–33). Washington, DC: US Department of State. Accessed at: http://history.state.gov/historicaldocuments/frus1964-68v26/d159

power struggle with Sukarno.[39] By late October, the embassy in Jakarta was receiving frequent reports about the massacre of PKI members and alleged communists throughout the country, with army encouragement and often with great brutality.[40] With all of this knowledge, Rusk on October 29 still thought small pockets of PKI resistance constituted a significant threat and laid out plans to aid the army in eliminating this resistance and further sidelining Sukarno. In doing so, he addressed different ways to supply "small arms and equipment" to the army.[41] An interagency task force also began planning to deliver communications equipment and other covert aid to the army.[42] The Department of Defense and the White House Staff agreed that such aid should be unconditional, "because they feel it is important to assure the Army of our full support of its efforts to crush the PKI."[43]

Green soon had knowledge in early November of army forces committing massacres in the outer islands and the RPKAD paratroopers training and arming Muslim youth organizations in Central Java,[44] while extremist youth group leaders bragged to the consulate in Medan in Northern

39 "Telegram from the Embassy in Indonesia to the Department of State." (1965, October 26). In E.C. Keefer (Ed.), FRUS (vol. XXVI, doc. 161, pp. 335–37). Washington, DC: US Department of State. Accessed at: http://history.state.gov/historicaldocuments/frus1964-68v26/d161

40 "Editorial Note." (n.d.). In E.C. Keefer (Ed.), FRUS (vol. XXVI, doc. 162, pp. 338–40). Washington, DC: US Department of State. Accessed at: http://history.state.gov/historicaldocuments/frus1964-68v26/d162

41 "Telegram from the Department of State to the Embassy in Indonesia." (1965, October 29). In E.C. Keefer (Ed.), FRUS (vol. XXVI, doc. 163, pp. 340–43). Washington, DC: US Department of State. Accessed at: http://history.state.gov/historicaldocuments/frus1964-68v26/d163

42 "Memorandum from the Assistant for Indonesia (Nuechterlein) to the Deputy Assistant Secretary of Defense for International Security Affairs (Friedman)." (1965, October 30). In E.C. Keefer (Ed.), FRUS (vol. XXVI, doc. 164, pp. 343–45). Washington, DC: US Department of State. Accessed at: http://history.state.gov/historicaldocuments/frus1964-68v26/d164

43 "Memorandum from the Assistant for Indonesia (Nuechterlein) to the Deputy Assistant Secretary of Defense for International Security Affairs (Friedman)." (1965, November 4). In E.C. Keefer (Ed.), FRUS (vol. XXVI, doc. 168, pp. 351–53). Washington, DC: US Department of State. Accessed at: http://history.state.gov/historicaldocuments/frus1964-68v26/d168

44 "Telegram from the Embassy in Indonesia to the Department of State." (1965, Noember 4). In E.C. Keefer (Ed.), FRUS (vol. XXVI, doc. 169, pp. 353–56). Washington, DC: US Department of State. Accessed at: http://history.state.gov/historicaldocuments/frus1964-68v26/d169

Sumatra about organizing large-scale killings.[45] A US intelligence memorandum in late November stated, "[PKI] members and sympathizers are
being rounded up and interned by the military; others are being purged
from local government positions; and in Central Java PKI adherents are
reported to be shot on sight by the army,"[46] yet no change in US policy took
place. Green stated in a memo at the beginning of November, "Nasution
seems at long last to have been spurred to act on and, in tandem with
Suharto and other [tough?] deeply motivated military leaders, [move]
relentlessly to exterminate PKI as far as that is possible to do."[47] With this
knowledge, in early December, Green even requested 50 million rupiah
(over US$200,000) to channel through Adam Malik to the Kap-Gestapu
civilian anti-communist coalition.[48] The United States also decided in
December to provide requested medicines and medical equipment to the
army, as officials from the CIA, State Department, and National Security
Council agreed on the need for the army to "know who their friends were,"
giving the United States the chance of "getting in on the ground floor" with
the likely new government.[49] The Indonesian army, though, did not necessarily need further assurances of US support, for, as one State Department
official said, "The Army knows that [the Pentagon, the CIA, and the State

---

45  "Telegram from the Consulate in Medan to the Department of State." (1965, November 16).
    In E.C. Keefer (Ed.), *FRUS* (vol. XXVI, doc. 174, pp. 366–68). Washington, DC: US Department
    of State. Accessed at: http://history.state.gov/historicaldocuments/frus1964-68v26/d174

46  "Intelligence Memorandum." (1965, November 22). In E.C. Keefer (Ed.),, *FRUS* (vol. XXVI,
    doc. 178, pp. 375–79). Washington, DC: US Department of State. Accessed at: http://history.
    state.gov/historicaldocuments/frus1964-68v26/d178. This document also highlights that the
    Soviets had continued arms shipments to the Indonesian military, even as it was engaged in
    its "anti-PKI" campaign.

47  "Telegram from the Embassy in Indonesia to the Department of State." (1965, November 1).
    In E.C. Keefer (Ed.), *FRUS* (vol. XXVI, doc. 165, pp. 345–47). Washington, DC: US Department
    of State. Accessed at: http://history.state.gov/historicaldocuments/frus1964-68v26/d165

48  "Telegram from the Embassy in Indonesia to the Department of State." (1965, December 2).
    In E.C. Keefer (Ed.), *FRUS* (vol. XXVI, doc. 179, pp. 379–80). Washington, DC: US Department
    of State. Accessed at: http://history.state.gov/historicaldocuments/frus1964-68v26/d179

49  "Memorandum from the Deputy Director for Coordination, Bureau of Intelligence and
    Research (Koren) to the Director (Hughes)." (1965, December 4). In E.C. Keefer (Ed.), *FRUS*
    (vol. XXVI, doc. 181, pp. 381–82). Washington, DC: US Department of State. Accessed at: http://
    history.state.gov/historicaldocuments/frus1964-68v26/d181

Department] approve of its actions against the PKI, and that all three are disposed to help the Army in this effort."[50] At the end of 1965, the Department of Defense was making plans to supply the army with food and medicine in case they undertook a coup against Sukarno in 1966, along with contingency plans for the resumption of overt military and economic aid if conditions were favorable;[51] and with power shifting ever further toward the military, President Johnson was reportedly intent not to "miss the boat in Indonesia."[52] By February 1966, Green gave an assessment stating that since October 1, 1965, "the PKI [had] been destroyed as an effective political force for some time to come," and that "the Communists... [had] been decimated by wholesale massacre."[53]

The United States had not only been providing material and moral support to the Indonesian army and Kap-Gestapu, they had also been providing information. In a report in 1990, journalist Kathy Kadane unveiled evidence, gathered from former US officials in the Johnson administration, that staff at the US embassy in Jakarta had actually provided lists of PKI members to the Indonesian army for targeting. According to Kadane's report, US officials "systematically compiled comprehensive lists of Communist operatives, from top echelons down to village cadres. As many as 5,000 names were furnished to Adam Malik, who passed them on to Kap-Gestapu and the army, and the Americans later checked off the names of those who had been killed or captured, according to the U.S. officials"

---

50 "Memorandum from the Director of the Office of Southwest Pacific Affairs (Cuthell) to the Assistant Secretary of State for Far Eastern Affairs (Bundy)." (1965, November 3). In E.C. Keefer (Ed.), *FRUS* (vol. XXVI, doc. 167, pp. 348–51). Washington, DC: US Department of State. Accessed at: http://history.state.gov/historicaldocuments/frus1964-68v26/d167

51 "Memorandum from the Joint Chiefs of Staff to Secretary of Defense McNamara." (1965, December 30). In E.C. Keefer (Ed.), *FRUS* (vol. XXVI, doc. 187, pp. 390–92). Washington, DC: US Department of State. Accessed at: http://history.state.gov/historicaldocuments/frus1964-68v26/d187

52 "Memorandum of Conversation." (1966, February 14). In E.C. Keefer (Ed.), *FRUS* (vol. XXVI, doc. 190, pp. 399–401). Washington, DC: US Department of State. Accessed at: http://history.state.gov/historicaldocuments/frus1964-68v26/d190

53 "Memorandum from the President's Deputy Special Assistant for National Security Affairs (Komer) to President Johnson." (1966, February 15). In E.C. Keefer (Ed.), *FRUS* (vol. XXVI, doc. 191, pp. 401–2). Washington, DC: US Department of State. Accessed at: http://history.state.gov/historicaldocuments/frus1964-68v26/d191

(Kadane, 1990, n.p.). Embassy official Robert Martens, who had been interviewed for the article, responded to Kadane's piece in a letter arguing that he had only passed on the names of "a few thousand" senior cadres and that his information was based on published PKI materials.[54] According to Kadane's report, though, based on Martens's statements, these "included names of provincial, city and other local PKI committee members, and leaders of the 'mass organizations,' such as the PKI national labor federation, women's and youth groups" (Kadane, 1990, n.p.)—clearly a broader swathe of people than Martens was willing to admit and many of whom were unlikely to have been hard-core, militant PKI leaders. This assessment is supported by Roosa (2006), who states that the PKI "Central Committee consisted of about eighty-five people, and each of the roughly twenty provincial committees had about ten people. If one adds the leaders of the various affiliated organizations, such as trade unions, the total is about five hundred. Martens had to be listing district- and subdistrict-level party members" (p. 298). Martens maintained that he acted alone, and subsequent reviews of Kadane's interviews could not conclude that his superiors were definitively aware of his actions (Wines, 1990), though it is clear that his lists were useful to the Indonesian army and to Kap-Gestapu, who had relatively poor information (Kadane, 1990).

In March 1966, the army finally moved decisively to push Sukarno off the scene, and the US embassy was well apprised of the plans. On March 10, a giddy Adam Malik shared with Green the news that a coup by soldiers loyal to Suharto and Nasution was in the offing. Green replied that he hoped for a new, productive intergovernmental relationship and "asked Malik to feel free to share the burden of our conversation with Nasution and Soeharto [Suharto]."[55] Two days later, the coup occurred (though Sukarno nominally remained president), and in the coming weeks, the United States began releasing aid to Indonesia that had been held up while Sukarno was in power. At the same time, Green worked closely with

54 "Editorial Note." (n.d.). In E.C. Keefer (Ed.), FRUS (vol. XXVI, doc. 185, pp. 386–87). Washington, DC: US Department of State. Accessed at: http://history.state.gov/historicaldocuments/frus1964-68v26/d185

Suharto, even as the United States saw that purges of alleged PKI sympa-thizers and attacks on Chinese civilians continued.[56]

US officials were both quick to embrace Suharto, and equally quick to either acclaim or ignore the destruction of the PKI and the violence it entailed. A background paper for a National Security Council meeting in August 1966 described the Killings explicitly, stating that "the Army hunted down and executed the principal Communist leaders. In small cities, towns and villages, groups of youths embarked on a systematic campaign of exter-mination of Communist Party cadres, encouraged by the Army and motivated by religion, historic local grievances, and fear for their own fate had the Communists taken power. While the exact figure will never be known, an estimated 300,000 were killed." The paper went on to recom-mend increasing aid to Indonesia and to further cooperation with the military.[57] As Kolko (1988) mentions, "'The reversal of the Communist tide in the great country of Indonesia' was publicly celebrated, in the words of Deputy Undersecretary of State U. Alexis Johnson in October 1966, as 'an event that will probably rank along with the Vietnamese war as perhaps the most historic turning point of Asia in this decade'" (p. 181). According to Howard Federspiel, who was an Indonesia expert at the State Department in this era, US officials were little bothered by the huge number of victims resulting from the Killings: "No one cared, as long as they were Communists, that they were being butchered" (quoted in Kadane, 1990, n.p.). Finally, in

---

55  "Telegram from the Embassy in Indonesia to the Department of State." (1966, March 10). In E.C. Keefer (Ed.), *FRUS* (vol. XXVI, doc. 199, pp. 414–16). Washington, DC: US Department of State. Accessed at: http://history.state.gov/historicaldocuments/frus1964-68v26/d199

56  "Memorandum from Donald W. Ropa of the National Security Council Staff to the President's Special Assistant (Rostow)." (1966, April 18). In E.C. Keefer (Ed.), *FRUS* (vol. XXVI, doc. 206, pp. 427–28). Washington, DC: US Department of State. Accessed at: http://history.state.gov/historicaldocuments/frus1964-68v26/d206; "Telegram from the Embassy in Indonesia to the Department of State." (1966, May 27). In E.C. Keefer (Ed.), *FRUS* (vol. XXVI, doc. 209, pp. 431–34). Washington, DC: US Department of State. Accessed at: http://history.state.gov/historicaldocuments/frus1964-68v26/d209

57  "Memorandum from Secretary of State Rusk to President Johnson." (1966, August 1). In E.C. Keefer (Ed.), *FRUS* (vol. XXVI, doc. 215, pp. 449–57). Washington, DC: US Department of State. Accessed at: http://history.state.gov/historicaldocuments/frus1964-68v26/d215

his memoirs, Marshall Green (1990), while acknowledging the "deplorable blood-letting" of the Killings, still laid all blame at the feet of the PKI (pp. 58-61).

Suharto and the military meanwhile consolidated their authoritarian rule as the "New Order" regime. Suharto remained in power for the next 32 years until 1998. Green (1990) anticipated this authoritarian outcome already in November 1965, noting that the "Army [was] not thinking purely in military terms or intending [to] turn [the] political future of Indonesia over to civilian elements. Army is moving its people into all aspects of government and organizational framework with view toward keeping control [of] political trends and events" (p. 2).[58]

The United States continued to support Suharto and the New Order regime, and worked with the military despite its record of human rights violations (Simons, 2000). As demonstrated clearly by the publicly available primary documents, in the case of the Killings the US government approved of and was complicit in a mass killing that many consider a genocide and developed close, sustained relations with the perpetrators.

## CONCLUSION

After perpetrating politicide in the Killings with no adverse consequences, the Indonesian military and its New Order regime in subsequent years engaged in genocidal mass killing in East Timor and harsh and possibly genocidal counterinsurgency in West Papua (Roosa, 2006, p. 225; Thaler, 2012), with continued US support, military aid, and investment (see, for example, Simpson, 2005).[59] The fact that impunity and foreign approval for the Killings was followed by further mass killings suggests that perpetrators who face no consequences for engaging in mass killings may decide this is a useful tactic and will employ it repeatedly (Thaler, 2012). US backing of the New Order also set a dangerous precedent of support for

---

58 "Telegram from the Embassy in Indonesia to the Department of State." (1965, November 4). In E.C. Keefer (Ed.), FRUS (vol. XXVI, doc. 169, pp. 353–56). Washington, DC: US Department of State. Accessed at: http://history.state.gov/historicaldocuments/frus1964-68v26/d169

59 See also Nevins, this volume.

right-wing authoritarian regimes engaged in mass killings, prioritizing ideology and realpolitik over human rights, with parallels to the Killings in Bangladesh (Mansur, this volume) and in Latin America (Dietrich and Totten, both this volume). Finally, this study of the Killings suggests that the language of the UNCG may be too narrow, and that in cases where political affiliations are considered by perpetrators as integral, unchangeable components of one's identity and a political group is targeted as such, this should also be considered genocide. This shift might provide opportunities to survivors of repression during the Killings and descendants of victims for international legal redress for their suffering—suffering that has largely been swept under the rug of history.

# REFERENCES

Anderson, B. (1987, April). "How Did the Generals Die?" *Indonesia*, 43, 109–34. https://doi.org/10.2307/3351215

Balcells, L. (2012). "The Consequences of Victimization on Political Identities: Evidence from Spain." *Politics & Society*, 40(3), 311–47. https://doi.org/10.1177/0032329211424721

Boden, R. (2007). "The 'Gestapu' Events of 1965 in Indonesia: New Evidence from Russian and German Archives." *Bijdragen tot de Taal-, Land- en Volkenkunde*, 163(4), 507–28. https://doi.org/10.1163/22134379-90003693

Brands, H. W. (1989). "Limits of Manipulation: How the United States Didn't Topple Sukarno." *Journal of American History*, 76(3), 785–808. https://doi.org/10.2307/2936421

Bunnell, F. (1990). "American 'Low Posture' Policy toward Indonesia in the Months Leading up to the 1965 'Coup.'" *Indonesia*, 50, 29–60. https://doi.org/10.2307/3351229

Central Intelligence Agency. (1968). *Indonesia—1965: The Coup that Backfired*. Langley, VA: Author.

Chalk, F., & Jonassohn, K. (1990). *The History and Sociology of Genocide: Analyses and Case Studies*. New Haven, CT: Yale University Press.

Charny, I.W. (1988). "The Study of Genocide." In I.W. Charny (Ed.), *Genocide: A Critical Bibliographic Review* (pp. 1–19). New York: Facts on File.

Conboy, K., & Morrison, J. (1999). *Feet to the Fire: CIA Covert Operations in Indonesia, 1957–1958*. Annapolis, MD: Naval Institute Press.

Corcoran, J. R. (2005) "The Jingju-Wayang Encounter: China and Indonesia during the Cultural Revolution and the Gestapu Coup and Countercoup." Unpublished doctoral dissertation, University of Hawai'i at Monoa.

Cribb, R. (1990a). "Introduction: Problems in the Historiography of the Killings in Indonesia." In R. Cribb (Ed.), *The Indonesian Killings of 1965–66: Studies from Java and Bali* (pp. 1–44). Clayton, Australia: Centre for Southeast Asian Studies, Monash University.

Cribb, R. (1990b). *The Indonesian Killings of 1965–1966: Studies from Java and Bali*. Clayton, Australia: Center for Southeast Asian Studies, Monash University.

Cribb, R. (2001). "Genocide in Indonesia, 1965–1966." *Journal of Genocide Research*, 3(2), 219–39.

Cribb, R. (2002). "Unresolved Problems in the Indonesian Killings of 1965–1966." *Asian Survey*, 42(4), 550–63. https://doi.org/10.1525/as.2002.42.4.550

Cribb, R. (2004). "The Indonesian Massacres." In S. Totten, W.S. Parsons, & I.W. Charny (Eds.), *Century of Genocide* (pp. 289–326). New York: Routledge. https://doi.org/10.4324/9780203495698.ch7

Cribb, R., & Coppel, C.A. (2009). "A Genocide that Never Was: Explaining the Myth of Anti-Chinese Massacres in Indonesia, 1965–66." *Journal of Genocide Research*, 11(4), 447–65. https://doi.org/10.1080/14623520903309503

Crouch, H. (1978). *The Army and Politics in Indonesia*. Ithaca, NY: Cornell University Press.

Curtis, M. (2003). *Web of Deceit: Britain's Real Role in the World*. New York: Vintage.

Drakeley, S. (2007). "Lubang Buaya: Myth, Misogyny, and Massacre." *Nebula*, 4(4), 11–35.

Dwyer, L., & Santikarma, D. (2003). "'When the World Turned to Chaos': 1965 and Its Aftermath in Bali, Indonesia." In R. Gellately & B. Kiernan, (Eds.), *The Specter of Genocide: Mass Murder in Historical Perspective* (pp. 289–306). New York: Cambridge University Press. https://doi.org/10.1017/CBO9780511819674.013

Easter, D. (2005). "'Keep the Indonesian Pot Boiling': Western Covert Intervention in Indonesia, October 1965–March 1966." *Cold War History*, 5(1), 55–73. https://doi.org/10.1080/1468274042000283144

Evans, B. (1989). "The Influence of the United States Army on the Development of the Indonesian Army (1954–1964)." *Indonesia*, 47, 25–48.

Farid, H. (2005). "Indonesia's Original Sin: Mass Killings and Capitalist Expansion, 1965–66." *Inter-Asia Cultural Studies*, 6(1), 3–16. https://doi.org/10.1080/1462394042000326879

Fein, H. (1993). *Genocide: A Sociological Perspective*. London: Sage Publications.

Green, M. (1990). *Indonesia: Crisis and Transformation, 1965–1968*. Washington, DC: Howells House.

Heryanto, A. (1999). "Where Communism Never Dies: Violence, Trauma and Narration in the Last Cold War Capitalist Authoritarian State." *International Journal of Cultural Studies*, 2(2), 147–77. https://doi.org/10.1177/136787799900200201

Kadane, K. (1990, May 19). "Ex-Agents Say CIA Compiled Death Lists for Indonesians." *Spartanburg Herald-Journal*, n.p.

Kahin, A.R., and Kahin, G.M. (1995). *Subversion as Foreign Policy: The Secret Eisenhower and Dulles Debacle in Indonesia*. New York: New Press.

Kalyvas, S.N. (2003). "The Ontology of 'Political Violence': Action and Identity in Civil Wars." *Perspectives on Politics*, 1(3), 475–94. https://doi.org/10.1017/S1537592703000355

Kammen, D., & McGregor, K. (Eds.). (2012). *The Contours of Mass Violence in Indonesia, 1965–1968*. Honolulu: University of Hawai'i Press.

Keefer, E.C. (Ed.). (1992). *Foreign Relations of the United States, 1964–1968 [FRUS]* (vol. XXVI). Washington, DC: US Department of State.

Kim, J. (2002). "U.S. Covert Action in Indonesia in the 1960s: Assessing the Motives and Consequences." *Journal of International and Area Studies*, 9(2), 63–85.

Kolko, G. (1988). *Confronting the Third World: United States Foreign Policy 1945–1980*. New York: Pantheon Books.

Mackie, J.A.C. (1974). *Konfrontasi: The Indonesia-Malaysia Dispute, 1963–1966*. Oxford: Oxford University Press.

May, B. (1978). *The Indonesian Tragedy*. Boston: Routledge & Kegan Paul.

Mortimer, R. (1972). *The Indonesian Communist Party and Land Reform, 1959–1965*. Clayton, Australia: Centre for Southeast Asian Studies, Monash University.

Ratner, S.R., & Abrams, J.S. (2001). *Accountability for Human Rights Atrocities in International Law: Beyond the Nuremberg Legacy* (2nd ed.). New York: Oxford University Press.

Robinson, G. (1992). "The Economic Foundations of Political Conflict in Bali, 1950–1965." *Indonesia, 54,* 59–93. https://doi.org/10.2307/3351165

Robinson, G. (1995). *Dark Side of Paradise: Political Violence in Bali*. Ithaca, NY: Cornell University Press.

Roosa, J. (2006). *Pretext for Mass Murder: The September 30th Movement and Suharto's Coup d'État in Indonesia*. Madison: University of Wisconsin Press.

Scott, P.D. (1985). "The United States and the Overthrow of Sukarno, 1965–1967." *Pacific Affairs, 58*(2), 239–64. https://doi.org/10.2307/2758262

Simons, G. (2000). *Indonesia: The Long Oppression*. New York: Palgrave Macmillan. https://doi.org/10.1057/9780333982846

Simpson, B. (2005). "'Illegally and Beautifully': The United States, the Indonesian Invasion of East Timor and the International Community, 1974–76." *Cold War History, 5*(3), 281–315. https://doi.org/10.1080/14682740500222028

Simpson, B.R. (2008). *Economists with Guns: Authoritarian Development and U.S.-Indonesian Relations, 1960–1968*. Stanford, CA: Stanford University Press.

Sutter, J.O. (1966). "Two Faces of *Konfrontasi*: 'Crush Malaysia' and the *Gestapu*." *Asian Survey, 6*(10), 523–46. https://doi.org/10.2307/2642110

Swift, A. (1989). *The Road to Madiun: The Indonesian Communist Uprising of 1948*. Ithaca. NY: Cornell University Press.

Thaler, K. (2012). "Foreshadowing Future Slaughter: From the Indonesian Killings of 1965–1966 to the 1974–1999 Genocide in East Timor." *Genocide Studies and Prevention, 7*(2), 204–22.

van der Kroef, J.M. (1965). *The Communist Party of Indonesia: Its History, Program and Tactics*. Vancouver: University of British Columbia Publications Centre.

van Langenberg, M. (1990). "Gestapu and State Power in Indonesia." In R. Cribb (Ed.), *The Indonesian Killings of 1965–66: Studies from Java and Bali* (pp. 45–61). Clayton, Australia: Centre for Southeast Asian Studies, Monash University.

Wieringa, S.E. (2003). "The Birth of the New Order State in Indonesia: Sexual Politics and Nationalism." *Journal of Women's History, 15*(1), 70–91. https://doi.org/10.1353/jowh.2003.0039

Wines, M. (1990, July 11). "C.I.A. Tie Asserted in Indonesia Purge." *The New York Times Magazine*, n.p.

Young, K.R. (1990). "Local and National Influences in the Violence of 1965." In R. Cribb (Ed.), *The Indonesian Killings of 1965–66: Studies from Java and Bali* (pp. 63–99). Clayton, Australia: Centre for Southeast Asian Studies, Monash University.

# DOCUMENTS

While the United States was not directly involved in the perpetration of the Killings, significant evidence exists regarding US material, diplomatic, intelligence, and rhetorical support for the Indonesian military; US efforts to undermine the PKI and incite the population against it; and US awareness of the Killings and endorsement of them. Documents referenced here are drawn from the *Foreign Relations of the United States, 1964–1968, [FRUS], volume XXVI: Indonesia; Malaysia-Singapore; Philippines* part of the series of books produced by the US State Department compiling declassified primary documents from the State Department, intelligence agencies, and the White House. Many documents related to CIA activities in Indonesia during this period still have not been released, though historian Brad Simpson is heading a project at the National Security Archive at George Washington University to try to get further documents declassified using Freedom of Information Act requests.[60] Due to space restrictions, the texts of only six key documents are reproduced in full below, but see the citations in the previous section for further documents, which are available online or in print. The documents include an "Editorial Note" describing extracts of US documents that were not reproduced in the volume, but which contain key information related to the US role in the Killings. Footnotes from the *FRUS* documents are not included.

## DOCUMENT 1

As the Killings began in October 1965 in the aftermath of G-30-S, US officials in Indonesia were in contact with army officers and were aware of the

---

60 National Security Archive, (n.d.). "The Indonesia/East Timor Documentation Project." Washington, DC: George Washington University. Accessed at: http://nsarchive.gwu.edu/ indonesia/index.html. On its website, the National Security Archive reports the following: "Since its inception in 1985, the goal of the National Security Archive has been to document recent U.S. policy and enrich research and public debate on the often hidden process of national security decision making. . . . Through its collection, analysis and publication of previously classified government documents, the Archive is able to reconstruct U.S. policy making on a variety of foreign, defense and intelligence issues and capture how government decisions are made—with important implications for ongoing policy. "To carry out its mission, the Archive combines a unique range of functions in one institution. It is simultaneously a research institute on international affairs, a library and archive of declassified U.S. documents obtained through the Freedom of Information Act, a public interest law firm defending and expanding public access to government information through the FOIA, and an indexer and publisher of the documents."

ongoing purge of the PKI and mass executions. Yet there was no condemnation of these killings, and the United States was primarily concerned
with ensuring that the Indonesian army stand up to the nonexistent threat
of a PKI insurgency. In a telegram to Washington, Green described anti-PKI
efforts around Jakarta and stated his strong approval for the army's "determination and organization in carrying out this crucial assignment."

## 158. Telegram From the [US] Embassy in Indonesia to the Department of State

Djakarta, October 20, 1965, 0330Z.

1090. 1. Army and other actions against PKI have been covered in
detail in our sitreps and regular reporting. Question now is extent
to which party's effectiveness and potential have actually been
impaired.

2. While situation still fluid, evidence to date indicates party
has received major, though not necessarily mortal, blow to its
image, considerable damage to its communications and command
structures, and some damage to its organizational strength through
arrest, harassment and, in some cases, execution of PKI cadres.

3. Extent of this damage cannot be definitely fixed but is
certainly significant. In area of communications and command, we
have direct evidence ███████████████████████████
████████████ that PKI itself already regarded its communications
to be virtually shattered a week or so ago, even before army
repression had reached its peak. Some thousand[s] of PKI cadres
have reportedly been arrested in Djakarta area alone and several
hundred of them have been executed. We know that Njono, head of
Djakarta PKI and Politburo member, was arrested and may have been
executed and there are unconfirmed reports of other arrests of top
leaders including Anwar Snauee. Army sweeps of Kampung areas have
also disrupted channels of communication, and loss of buildings,
effects of curfew in Djakarta shut-down of telephone and telegraph

system, etc., are forcing PKI to employ inefficient and cumbersome devices no matter how well prepared their underground network may have been.

4. Thus far, however, basic PKI organizational potential would appear to be largely intact and capable of recovering quickly in a purely organizational sense if its status were recognized by the government and army attacks were stopped. However, there would still be severe damage to its image that, taken by itself, would tend to impair recruitment and decrease possibilities for successful prosecution of United Front tactics. Also, even now party will face uphill fight in regaining degree of popular acceptance and ostensible prestige it enjoyed before Sept 30. At same time, if return of PKI did take place and could be shown as sign of anti-PKI weakness and indication that opposition to PKI was useless, loss [of] popular image could be at least partially offset by psychology of intimation [sic] and by terror.

5. If army repression of PKI continues and army refuses to give up its position of power to Sukarno, PKI strength can be cut back. In long run, however, army repression of PKI will not be successful unless it is willing to attack communism as such, including associations with China and other bloc countries and Communist ideology, including many of [the] key pillars of Sukarno doctrine. Army has nevertheless been working hard at destroying PKI and I, for one, have increasing respect for its determination and organization in carrying out this crucial assignment.

6. PKI capability for insurgency reported septel [in a separate telegram].

Green

**Source:** "Telegram from the Embassy in Indonesia to the Department of State." In E.C. Keefer (Ed.), *FRUS* (vol. XXVI, doc. 158, pp. 329-30). Accessed at: http://history.state.gov/historicaldocuments/frus1964-68v26/d158

## DOCUMENT 2

Throughout late October and November, the US embassy in Jakarta was receiving reports of large-scale violence against communists and alleged communists throughout Indonesia, though US priorities were still to ensure that the army was unencumbered and that there was no resistance or resurgence from the PKI. The *FRUS* editors in this editorial note are overly generous to the US officials at the time in stating that "the fact that many of the killings took place in outlying areas tended to obscure their magnitude"—even as reports of hundreds and thousands of people killed by the army and civilians should have warranted further investigation. Rather, ideological blinkers led US officials to see these deaths as unimportant or in fact good, part of an effort to defeat communism.

### 162. Editorial Note

The Embassy in Djakarta was hampered in its reporting on events in the areas outside the capital by the general confusion and chaos of the initial conflict between the Partai Komunis Indonesia (PKI) on one hand and the Indonesian Army and anti-Communist forces on the other. At first the [U.S.] Embassy viewed the fighting and violence as a potential military/guerrilla conflict and concentrated on the PKI's armed activity and its potential for terrorism. In telegram 1215 from Djakarta, October 27, 1965, the Embassy recounted multiple reports of increasing insecurity and mounting bloodshed in Central Java, but could not determine whether it was caused by the PKI moving towards terrorism and sabotage, "local PKI cadres reacting uncoordinatedly to pressures upon them," or the Army "purposely moving to wipe out questionable elements and gain control." (National Archives and Records Administration, RG 84, Djakarta Embassy Files: Lot 69 F 42, POL 23) On October 28 the Embassy reported that a PKI source alleged that the PKI was about to engage in a "war of liberation" and cited incidents of PKI terrorism to support this conclusion. The telegram stated, "There [is] no question, even allowing for exaggeration, that PKI acts of terrorism have increased." (Telegram 1248 from Djakarta, October 28; ibid., RG 59, Central Files 1964-66, POL 23-9 INDON) On October 28 the Embassy Country Team reviewed the situation and sent its appraisal. Although the report emphasized the deteriorating security situation in Central Java, East Java, Bandung, and Djakarta, the team could not say "whether these incidents were isolated acts of local communists or beginning of a coordinated act of terror and sabotage." The report concluded that Indonesia was heading for a "period of chaos, since PKI has residual strength and arms, but balance seems on Army side." (Telegram 1255 from Djakarta; October 28; ibid.)

At the end of October 1965, the Embassy began to receive reports of killings and atrocities against PKI members, which were generally reported upon in the context of continued armed PKI resistance. On October 29 the Embassy reported that "Moslem fervor in Atjeh apparently put all but few PKI out of action. Atjehnese have decapitated PKI and placed their heads on stakes along the road. Bodies of PKI victims reportedly thrown into rivers or sea as Atjehnese refuse 'contaminate Atjeh soil.' " (Telegram 1269 from Djakarta; October 29; ibid., RG 84, Djakarta Embassy Files: Lot 69 F 42, Pol 23-9) By November 8 the Embassy reported that in North Sumatra and Atjeh "the Army with the help of IP-KI Youth organizations and other anti-Communist elements has continued systematic drive to destroy PKI in northern Sumatra with wholesale killings reported." On November 13 the Embassy had a report from the local police chief that "from 50 to 100 PKI members were being killed every night in East and Central Java by civilian anti-Communist troops with blessing of the Army." A missionary in Surabaya reported that 3,500 PKI were killed between November 4 and 9 in Kediri and 300 at Paree, 30 kilometers northwest of Kediri. (Telegrams 1374 and 1438 from Djakarta, November 8 and 13, and telegram 171 from Surabaya, November 13; ibid.) These types of anecdotal reports continued well into the first months of 1966.

In airgram A-527 from Djakarta, February 25, 1966, the Embassy reported estimates of the PKI death toll in Bali at 80,000 with "no end in sight." The Embassy attributed the murders to sharp conflict there between PKI and the Indonesian National Party (PNI), but also to the "tradition of family blood feuds" and suggested that "many of the killings that are taking place under a political cover are actually motivated by personal and clan vendettas." (Ibid., RG 59, Central Files 1964-66, POL 23-9 INDON)

Gradually the Embassy came to realize that Indonesia was undergoing a full scale purge of PKI influence and that these killings were overlaid with long standing and deep ethnic and religious conflicts. The fact that many of the killings took place in outlying areas tended to obscure their magnitude. The Embassy still had no good estimates of the number of Indonesians who perished. In airgram A-641 to the Department, April 15, 1966, the Embassy stated that the problem was the impossibility of weighing "the countervailing effects of exaggeration (which is especially common in Indonesia) and the interests of persons involved to cover up some of the crimes. The truth can never be known. Even the Indonesian Government has only a vague idea of the truth." The Embassy admitted, "We frankly do not know whether the real figure is closer to 100,000 or 1,000,000 but believe it wiser to err on the side of the lower estimates, especially when questioned by the press." (Ibid., POL 2 INDON)

**Source:** "Editorial Note." (n.d.). In E.C. Keefer (Ed.), *FRUS* (vol. XXVI, doc. 162, pp. 338-40). Accessed at: http://history.state.gov/historicaldocuments/frus1964-68v26/d162

# DOCUMENT 3

With the Indonesian army consolidating its hold on power and continuing to pursue the PKI and its supporters, the CIA sought to determine the best ways in which to covertly aid the army. In a memo written in November

1965, the CIA acknowledged the uncertainty around the army's political control and the risks of assisting a military outside of established government channels, but recommended that aid was worth the risks, given the army's strong anti-communist actions. The CIA argued that now that the army was acting against the PKI, "we should avoid being too cynical about its motives and its self-interest, or too hesitant about the propriety of extending such assistance provided we can do so covertly," counseling the provision of small arms, medicine, and other materials should the army request them.

## 172. Memorandum Prepared in the Central Intelligence Agency

Washington, November 9, 1965.

SUBJECT

Covert Assistance to the Indonesian Armed Forces Leaders

1. The requests of the Indonesian military leaders for covert assistance in their struggle against the Partai Kommunis Indonesia (PKI), create a definite risk for us of deliberate assistance to a group which cannot be considered a legal government nor yet a regime of proven reliability or longevity. Early assessment of the political direction and longevity of this military leadership must be accomplished and, before any overt or readily visible assistance could be offered, its legal authority as well as its de facto control must be confirmed explicitly. As long as Sukarno fights a clever rear-guard delaying action politically, this is not likely soon to occur.

2. On the other hand, the Army leaders appear determined to seize the opportunity of the current confused circumstances to break the organizational back of the PKI, to eliminate it as an effective political force, and to prevent emergence of any crypto-Communist successor party. Recent intelligence from

within the PKI party ranks clearly indicates that the PKI has
begun to abandon hope of salvation through Sukarno's political
legerdemain and has therefore decided it must, however ill-
prepared and disorganized, fight back against the Army. Despite
the overwhelming military superiority of the Armed Forces, the
roots of Communism, of PKI membership, and of mass support
nurtured for years by the constant flood of pro-Communist media,
are so deep in many areas that the Army is very likely to be faced
with a lingering insurgency situation. Specifically, much of
Central Java is in very poor shape. Hard intelligence on the area
shows a sizeable potential for resistance, and PKI sources
indicate plans for a redoubt area there. Considering the economic
problems Army leaders will face as they gradually assume more and
more authority under their own program for a non-Communist
future, the law of rising expectations is against them; they
cannot divert popular attention from economic ills as Sukarno has
for many years, and the weight of several years neglect of
economic problems and realities may fall upon them. Therefore if
the PKI can build even small areas of resistance in Central Java
and West Sumatra, they will have the ideal bases from which to
mount campaigns of harassment, subversion and sabotage as the
emergent non-Communist government attempts to grapple with
responsibilities already close to overpowering.

3. In addition, the Army must find some formula for continuing
its relationship with Sukarno in a way that will retain real control
for themselves without necessitating a preemptive hostile move
against Sukarno which might cause him to defy or deny them, and
thus provoke divisions in their own ranks. In this insurgency
situation therefore, the Army has no real guarantee of ultimate
success; hazards to its survival are many and varied.

4. One of the Army's major needs will be civilian support. They
have instituted psychological warfare mechanisms, control of media
prerequisite to influencing public opinion and have harassed or

halted Communist output. They have also mobilized certain bases of mass support, especially among Moslems. Unfortunately in these areas where the PKI has been able to initiate an insurgent campaign or local resistance, as in Central Java, the Army has not been able to protect those anti-Communist civilians who have fought the PKI and pro-Communist rebel troops. If this situation continues, the populace in some of these areas may be intimidated from affording aid to the government forces regardless of their convictions, or they will be decimated.

5. True, the future policy of the Indonesian Army if it should succeed in controlling or eliminating Sukarno as an effective factor is not entirely clear. Two probabilities do however seem fairly significant about its future stance:

a. It will certainly be less oriented towards Asian Communist Bloc and will be decidedly Nationalist (though not without some Marxist and anti-Western concepts), perhaps with a strong neutralist flavor and hopefully with a concentration upon Indonesia's internal welfare.

b. Its future attitude regarding the West and the U.S. in particular will certainly be affected favorably by the degree to which the U.S. can now provide what limited aid the military leaders feel they require in their struggle to survive.

6. In short, we must be mindful that in the past years we have often wondered when and if the Indonesian Army would ever move to halt the erosion of non-Communist political strength in Indonesia. Now that it has seized upon the fortuitous opportunity afforded by the PKI's error in the 30 September affair and is asking for covert help as well as understanding to accomplish that very task, we should avoid being too cynical about its motives and its self-interest, or too hesitant about the propriety of extending such

assistance *provided* we can do so covertly, in a manner which will
not embarrass them or embarrass our government.

7. In reviewing the types of assistance which can be provided
covertly, we believe that mechanisms exist or can be diverted or
created to extend either covert credits for purchases or to
deliver any of the types of the matériel requested to date in
reasonable quantities. ███████████████████████████
███████████████████████ The same can be said of purchasers
and transfer agents for such items as small arms, medicine and
other items requested. ████████████████████████
████████████████wherein we can permit the Indonesians with whom
we are dealing to make desired purchases and even indicate to them
where items may be purchased without our being in on the direct
transaction. Some degree of control can be exercised through
these accounts to insure that the letters of credit cannot be
misused for other than specified purposes. ████████████████
████████████████████████████████████████
████████████████████████ which can be made available on very
short notice. ████████████████████████████████
equipment would be more expensive and would require a little more
time to deliver. It would however probably be more appropriate if
equipment is to be handed by Indonesian Army officers to selected
civilian auxiliaries.

8. We do not propose that the Indonesian Army be furnished such
equipment at this time. This should be determined only after
exhaustive conversations with Sukendro and his associates and, to
the extent securely feasible, with Nasution's subordinates at
Djakarta. In these we would probe for necessary details, e.g.,
precisely why they need additional arms, how they intend to use
them, to whom they intend to give them, how they intend to control
the release and registration of weapons and to control the groups
who receive them, and many other questions.

9. If the Indonesian Army leadership continues to insist to us that they need this type of assistance to crush the PKI, and even if they furnish the above details, we would still be incurring political risk and the possible risk of loose handling of the arms in satisfying the request. These risks, however, must be weighed against the greater risks that failure to provide such aid which the Army claims it needs to win over the PKI might result in reduction of the Army's future political position and concomitant erosion of what may be a unique opportunity to ensure a better future for U.S. interests in Indonesia. It is difficult to predict definitively that aid of this type is absolutely vital to that future. If the Army leaders justify their needs in detail, however, it is likely that at least will help ensure their success and provide the basis for future collaboration with the U.S. The means for covert implementation, either of transmittal of funds for necessary purchases or delivery of the requested items themselves in discreet fashion, are within our capabilities.

**Source:** "Memorandum Prepared in the Central Intelligence Agency." (1965, November 9). In E.C. Keefer (Ed.), *FRUS* (vol. XXVI, doc. 172, pp. 361-63). Accessed at: http://history.state.gov/historicaldocuments/frus1964-68v26/d172

## DOCUMENT 4

As the United States was preparing to aid the Indonesian army if asked, US officials in Indonesia were receiving more information about the scale and nature of the Killings. In mid-November, the US consul in Medan, Theodore Heavner, reported staff conversations with civilian youth movement leaders, whom he described as "bloodthirsty" and engaged in a "reign of terror" against anyone associated with the PKI. This report, though, sparked no change in US policy or criticism against the army or civilian anti-communist groups.

## 174. Telegram From the [US] Consulate in Medan to the Department of State

Medan, Indonesia, November 16, 1965, 0115Z.

65. 1. Two officers of Pemuda Pantjasila separately told Consulate officers that their organization intends [to] kill every PKI member they can catch. November 14 Secretary [of] Medan City Pemuda Pantjasila said [the] policy [of] his organization is to ignore public calls for calm and order by Sukarno and other leaders. He stated Pemuda Pantjasila will not hand over captured PKI to authorities until they are dead or near death. He estimated it will take five years to eradicate all PKI. Similar statements were made [a] few days earlier by leader North Sumatra cultural arm of Pemuda Pantjasila.

2. ███████████████████████████ sources indicate that much indiscriminate killing is taking place (FNM-1516). ███████████████████████████ Consulate sources have connected some of this violence with declaration [of] "holy war" against PKI by local Moslem leaders. While press has carried relatively little on such violence, November 10 newspapers carried account of "revolutionary youth" cornering and beating to death PKI member North Sumatra legislature.

3. Press has also in recent days carried reports of five mutilated bodies discovered in Medan streets. PKI terrorists blamed. Commenting on these reports, above sources stated it is press policy to play up deaths of anti-Communists in order [to] justify attacks on PKI members.

4. Same sources indicate strong hostility toward PNI [Indonesian National Party] and expressed determination [to] "clean up" that organization.

5. Secretary Medan Pemuda Pantjasila at one point said bitterly that only way [to] solve Indonesia's problems is to shoot dead both Subandrio and Sukarno. His companion agreed. Other Pemuda Pantjasila

leader said on separate occasion that if Sukarno refuses ban [on] PKI he [will] likely be overthrown. Comments by other Consulate sources suggest growing hostility toward Sukarno generated by his evident reluctance [to] ban PKI. Worth noting that Medan press to date has carried no word of Sukarno's recent [verbal] attacks on U.S.

6. *Comment*:

(A.) Attitude [of] Pemuda Pantjasila leaders can only be described as bloodthirsty. While reports of wholesale killings may be greatly exaggerated, number and frequency such reports plus attitude of youth leaders suggests that something like real reign of terror against PKI is taking place. This terror is not discriminating very carefully between PKI leaders and ordinary PKI members with no ideological bond to the party. FNM-1515 suggests that army itself is officially adopting extreme measures against PKI with plans to put many thousands in concentration camps.

(B.) PNI was out in force on both November 9, when they presented statement to General Mokoginta, and on November 10 heroes day celebration. PNI avoided endorsement of demand for ban on PKI on both occasions. PNI remains large and apparently strong here and there is real possibility of violence between PNI and militant anti-Communist groups. (Pemuda Pantjasila and PNI youth clashed briefly on November 2, and Pemuda Pantjasila members reportedly carried knives and clubs to November 10 mass meeting in anticipation of clash with PNI.)

Heavner

**Source:** "Telegram from the Consulate in Medan to the Department of State." (1965, November 16). In E.C. Keefer (Ed.), *FRUS* (vol. XXVI, doc. 174, pp. 366–68). Accessed at: http://history.state.gov/historicaldocuments/frus1964-68v26/d174

# DOCUMENT 5

With military leaders setting their plans in motion for the destruction of the PKI, officials on the US National Security Council recommended the provision of communications equipment to Indonesian army officers. Though initially framed as necessary for the personal security of military commanders, the document goes on to describe the need for anti-communist generals "to coordinate planning with trusted subordinates" in order to follow through with Nasution and Suharto's "desires... to crush the PKI," arguing that poor communications had imperiled the fight against the communists. The document concludes by recommending that communications equipment be provided, despite the risks of such assistance.

## 175. Memorandum Prepared for the 303 Committee

Washington, November 17, 1965.

SUBJECT
    Supply of Communications
    Equipment to Key Anti-Communist
    Indonesian Army Leaders

*1. Summary*
    The purpose of this operational proposal is to assure that certain key anti-Communist Indonesian Army leaders will have adequate communications equipment for use in their fight against the Communist insurgents. Such equipment is in insufficient supply in Indonesia. This lack has, in consequence, imperiled the personal security of important anti-Communist Army leaders and has jeopardized their effectiveness in combating the Communists' efforts to eliminate non-Communist influence favorable to us in their Government.
    This request for equipment by several leading Indonesian officials has the support of the U.S. Ambassador to Indonesia and is concurred in by the State Department's Bureau of Far Eastern Affairs.
    There are some risks in the delivery of this equipment, but ■

with proper precautions in making deliveries to the ultimate
recipients will minimize such risks. The Indonesians cannot now
ostensibly nor actually purchase this equipment in the U.S. without
exception being made to U.S. export license controls, thereby
implying U.S. Government collusion. Any exposure of this activity
would embarrass not only the U.S. Government, but certain high Army
officials in the Indonesian Government. Much care will be taken in
this regard.

The cost of the requested equipment is approximately ██████████
████████████████████████████████████. The supplies themselves
come to ████████████████████████████████████████████ will be
required to package and ship.

On 5 November 1965 the 303 Committee approved a similar request to
send medical supplies to Indonesia.[2] This operation is proceeding on an
urgent basis. It is hoped that the 303 Committee will approve the above
program, which it is expected will proceed with the same urgency.

## 2. Problem

The immediate need is to provide on an urgent basis the present
Indonesian Army leadership with secure voice and CW communications.
Such equipment will provide a continuity of communications among
the various Army units and their anti-Communist leaders and between
certain of these leaders and U.S. elements. Given the uncertain
loyalties within various Army commands and within Army communications
proponents, existing communications equipment cannot be relied on
to satisfy this need.

## 3. Factors Bearing on the Problem

On 13 October 1965, ████████████████████████████████████████
were furnished from ████████████████████████████████████
stocks for use of the guards protecting Nasution and other key Army
officers. The continuing insufficiency of this equipment in the hands
of leading anti-Communist Army leaders has imperiled their own

personal security and could make it difficult for them in a crisis to
communicate securely with each other and/or with the U.S. A ████████
█████████████████████████████████ communications expert surveyed
the needs in late October in conjunction with the Djakarta country team.
The Indonesian Army does not have funds to purchase the equipment but
asks that it be given to them covertly and as rapidly as possible.

### a. Origin of the Requirement

The various requirements for communications equipment came
█████████████████████████████████████ from the U.S.
Ambassador to Indonesia, from the Minister of Defense Nasution's
aide, and from General Sukendro.

### b. Pertinent U.S. Policy Considerations

On 5 November 1965 the 303 Committee approved an operational
proposal for Indonesia responding to a request for medical supplies.

### c. Operational Objectives

A covert contact ████████████████████████████
████████████ must be maintained with certain Indonesian Army
leaders who also require additional means of communicating
securely among their own components in their struggle with the
Communists. In the confused situation of conflicting loyalties in
the Indonesian scene today, the security and personal safety of the
leading anti-Communist leaders and safety of their families from
intimidation and kidnapping, is of vital importance to their
continuance of the struggle to prevent any return to the status quo
before the 30 September coup. The possible assassination of
Nasution, Suharto, Umar or a number of other generals would
constitute serious setbacks for the U.S. Furthermore, in order to
coordinate planning with trusted subordinates, they must have
private communication facilities, frequently out of direct
channels, in order to be really secure. There is equipment

available within the Indonesian Army units for routine
communications but recent events have shown clearly that not
everyone, even in high ranks of the Indonesian Armed Forces, can be
relied on to be loyal to, or even sympathetic with, the desires of
Nasution and Suharto to crush the PKI, especially if in virtual
defiance of Sukarno.

### d. Equipment

### e. Risks Involved

Any publicity on this operational program would be highly
embarrassing both to the U.S. Government and to the Indonesian
Army leadership. Extreme care will be taken in all aspects of this
operation, especially that pertaining to shipment of the requested
equipment. A covert delivery procedure has been devised to the
ultimate Indonesian recipient.

### f. Training

A qualified and senior Army communications officer, designated by Sukendro, would be provided ████████████ ███████████████████████████████ with special covert training at a safe site in use of the equipment. He would be required to bring with him the following necessary data: details of the several proposed net patterns, including locations of components and general concept of operations for the net; the frequencies between 45 and 52 megacycles which could be used in Indonesia (to afford maximum security from local monitoring) so that, based upon these specifications, our communicator would be able to tune the equipment to the desired frequencies and provide advice concerning a secure signal plan and communications procedures.

### g. Funding

The overall cost is estimated at ████████████████████ ███████████████████. The equipment itself will be approximately ████████████████████████████████████ for shipping and packaging.

### 4. Coordination

This operational proposal has been recommended by the U.S. Ambassador to Indonesia and has been concurred in by the State Department's Bureau of Far Eastern Affairs.

### 5. Recommendation

That the 303 Committee approve this program.

**Source:** "Memorandum Prepared for the 303 Committee." (1965, November 17). In E.C. Keefer (Ed.), *FRUS* (vol. XXVI, doc. 175, pp. 368-71). Accessed at: http://history.state.gov/historicaldocuments/frus1964-68v26/d175

## DOCUMENT 6

Despite their knowledge of the atrocities being planned and perpetrated by civilian anti-communist groups, US officials decided to aid these groups. US Ambassador to Indonesia Marshall Green in early December 1965 recommended financial assistance to Adam Malik to help the civilian Kap-Gestapu movement, whose "activities to date have been important factor in the army's program, and judging from results, I would say highly successful," with the group "still carrying burden of current repressive efforts targeted against PKI, particularly in Central Java."

### 179. Telegram From the [US] Embassy in Indonesia to the Department of State

Djakarta, December 2, 1965.

1628. For Assist. Sec. Bundy from Amb Green. Ref: Deptel 708, Dec 1, 1965.

1. This is to confirm my earlier concurrence that we provide Malik with fifty million rupiahs requested by him for the activities of the Kap-Gestapu movement. ██████████████████
████████████████████████████████████████████
████████

2. The Kap-Gestapu activities to date have been [an] important factor in the army's program, and judging from results, I would say highly successful. This army-inspired but civilian-staffed action group is still carrying burden of current repressive efforts targeted against PKI, particularly in Central Java.

A. Malik is not in charge of the Kap-Gestapu movement. He is, however, one of the key civilian advisers and promoters of the movement. There is no doubt whatsoever that Kap-Gestapu's activity is fully consonant with and coordinated by the army. We have had substantial intelligence reporting to support this.

B. I view this contribution as a means of enhancing Malik's position within the movement. As one of the key civilians, he is responsible for finding funds to finance its activities. Without our contribution Kap-Gestapu will of course continue. On the other hand, there is no doubt that they need money. The latter, despite inflation, is in tight supply, and the comparatively small sum proposed will help considerably.

C. ████████████████████████████████████████
████████████████████████████████████ Our willingness to assist him in this manner will, I think, represent in Malik's mind our endorsement of his present role in the army's anti-PKI efforts, and will promote good cooperating relations between him and [the] army.

D. The chances of detection or subsequent revelation of our support in this instance are as minimal as any black bag operation can be. ███████████████████████████████████████
████████████████████████████████████████████
██████████

Green

**Source:**"Telegram from the Embassy in Indonesia to the Department of State." (1965, December 2). In E.C. Keefer (Ed.), *FRUS* (vol. XXVI, doc. 179, pp. 379-80). Accessed at: http://history.state.gov/historicaldocuments/frus1964-68v26/d179

# CHAPTER TWO

# THE BANGLADESH GENOCIDE AND THE NIXON–KISSINGER "TILT" (1971)

Salim Mansur

## INTRODUCTION

The South Asian crisis of 1971—the genocide in East Pakistan/Bangladesh—is now mostly forgotten outside the region. More than four decades later, the events that resulted in Pakistan's military crackdown in East Pakistan and the birth of Bangladesh have faded away and are of little interest to people other than those whose lives were seared by them. The publication in 2013 of Gary Bass's book *The Blood Telegram: Nixon, Kissinger, and a Forgotten Genocide*, however, has in some small way reopened the debate over the extent to which the United States bears responsibility vis-à-vis the mass killings in Bangladesh, as a result of either the failure or the refusal on the part of the Nixon administration to push sufficiently hard on the military government of President Yahya Khan of Pakistan to not act as it did.

The Bangladesh tragedy was overtaken by other events of seemingly greater consequences in world politics and hence was more or less forgotten. As Milan Kundera (1981), the Czech novelist, famously wrote, "The bloody massacre in Bangladesh quickly covered over the memory of the Russian invasion of Czechoslovakia, the assassination of Allende drowned out the groans of Bangladesh, the war in the Sinai Desert made people forget Allende, the Cambodian massacre made people forget Sinai, and so on and so forth until ultimately everyone lets everything be forgotten" (p. 7). Bass (2013) placed Kundera's words in the frontispiece of his book, presumably as a reminder for his readers that recalling the past is, in Kundera's words, "the struggle of memory against forgetting" (n.p.). To recall the Bangladesh tragedy all these years later is to be sadly reminded of how, in our world, despite the regularly displayed good intentions of world leaders, the reality turns out to be much different; leaders are often driven to act on the basis of realpolitik, and the resulting amorality, if not immorality, of their decisions leaves the weak and the vulnerable exposed to violence and wars in which the innocents perish and are forgotten.

Herein, I shall succinctly discuss the events of 1971, within the context of Pakistan's domestic politics, that led to the eventual breakdown of the country as a result of a civil war spread over nine months and the war between India and Pakistan. Among the many issues to be considered are the larger history of the 1947 partitioning of British-ruled India, since this history is pertinent to understanding why eventually Pakistan self-destructed; the role of the United States or, more precisely, the Nixon administration, and its moral failure to use its influence and resources to urge the Pakistani government to cease and desist in carrying out the vicious massacres that it did; and the controversy over the numbers of people killed in Bangladesh during the period of military operations by the Pakistan Army in what was then East Pakistan. Here, I might note in passing that I lived through the events of 1971 and, as a first-year college student, witnessed firsthand the ensuing conflict and massacre. Despite the passage of time and every effort since to be objective in discussing the events of that fateful year, I cannot completely erase from my memory the trauma of those months in the lives of the people in East Pakistan nor forget how I was personally fortunate to survive the killings and the war when many known or related to me perished.

## ANTECEDENTS
### The Partitioning of British India in 1947

At the end of World War II, a victorious Great Britain was an exhausted great power, and her resources spent in defeating Hitler's Germany left her hugely weakened in terms of holding on to and continuing to administer her vast overseas empire. In the general election of July 1945, following the end of the war, the people of Great Britain handed the Labour Party, led by Clement Atlee, an overwhelming electoral victory over the Conservative Party led by wartime leader Winston Churchill. The people had spoken, and the vote was for "a sweeping program of nationalization of services and industry" (Keegan, 2002, p. 172), for rebuilding a war-devastated country that required, as most people in Great Britain implicitly understood, a withdrawal from the overseas empire.

India, or the British Raj, was the "crown jewel" of Great Britain's vast overseas empire, and how withdrawal from India was to be arranged would be immensely consequential for both Great Britain and the 400 million people of the subcontinent. On February 18, 1947, Prime Minister Clement Atlee rose in the British parliament and announced, "His Majesty's Government wishes to make it clear that it is their definite intention to take the necessary steps to effect the transference of power into responsible Indian hands by a date not later than June 1948" (Collins & Lapierre, 1976, p. 64). But Atlee's government rushed the process of Great Britain's withdrawal by a hasty decision to partition the subcontinent into two independent states, India and Pakistan, in less than six months. The story of Great Britain's decision to hasten her withdrawal from India in the summer of 1947 by conceding to the demands made by Mohammed Ali Jinnah and his party, the Muslim League, for a separate and independent Muslim-majority state, Pakistan, and, as a result, unleashing one of the most hideous cycles of violence in twentieth-century history has been told in numerous accounts, such as *Freedom at Midnight* by Larry Collins and Dominique Lapierre (1976) and most recently in *Midnight's Furies: The Deadly Legacy of India's Partition* by Nisid Hajari (2015).

One American, Margaret Bourke-White, was an eyewitness to the events leading up to the partitioning of India and what followed as some 2 million people (Hindus, Muslims, and Sikhs) died in the violence that erupted, and some 15 million people made homeless headed in opposite directions to Pakistan and India in the weeks and months after August 14–15, 1947, when Great Britain withdrew from the subcontinent that she had ruled for nearly a century. Bourke-White was a photojournalist for *Life* magazine reporting from India at the time, and later she published her account of what she had witnessed in *Halfway to Freedom* (1949). The proximate cause for hastening Great Britain's withdrawal from the subcontinent came about in the summer of 1946, when communal riots between Hindus and Muslims were ignited in the metropolitan port city of Calcutta, which at one time had been the capital of British India. In witnessing the unfolding events during the final months of the British Raj, Bourke-White wrote,

> The overt act that split India began in the streets of Calcutta. But the decision was made in Bombay. It was a one-man decision, and the man who made it was cool, calculating, unreligious. This determination to establish a separate Islamic state came not—as one might have expected—from some Muslim divine in archaic robes and flowing beard, but from a thoroughly Westernized, English-educated attorney-at-law with a clean-shaven face and razor-sharp mind. Mahomed Ali Jinnah, leader of the Muslim League and architect of Pakistan, had for many years worked at the side of Nehru and Gandhi for a free, united India, until in the evening of his life he broke sharply with his past to achieve a separate Pakistan. (1949, p. 13)

Nearly a quarter of India's vast ethnically diverse population in 1947, estimated at 90 million, was Muslim, and Jinnah's demand for a separate Muslim-majority state, presented in 1940 as the Lahore Resolution of the Muslim League, had turned into a lethal weapon contesting the idea of maintaining India as a united and independent country. Great Britain's political leaders and military commanders feared that denying Jinnah and the Muslim League's demand for a separate Muslim homeland would lead to a civil war within India along religious and communal divisions, and the colonial-imperial administrators would be stretched beyond available resources to keep the peace. Jinnah, as Bourke-White reported, had defiantly announced in a press conference in late July 1946, "If you [meaning the Indian National Congress led by Mahatma Gandhi and Jawaharlal Nehru] want peace, we do not want war. If you want war we accept your offer unhesitatingly. We will either have a divided India or a destroyed India" (Bourke-White, 1949, p. 15).

Jinnah's "two-nation theory" for Pakistan had whipped into frenzy a large segment of Muslims in undivided India with the slogan "Islam is in danger within a Hindu majority India." It mattered for neither Jinnah's supporters nor Jinnah and his colleagues in the Muslim League that partitioning India along communal or religious lines would also divide the Muslim population. Britain's "divide and rule" policy had meant leaning toward the minority, the Muslims, as a means to counter the nationalist demands of the Congress Party, supported by the Hindu majority. But a significant segment of Muslim opinion, led by reputable Muslim religious scholars and political leaders such as Maulana Abul Kalam Azad of the Congress Party and Khan Abdul Ghaffar Khan (a Pathan or Pashtun leader from India's northwest frontier), opposed Jinnah's demand to partition India as un-Islamic and contrary to the history of Muslims in the subcontinent, who had for over a millennium considered India their homeland.

The idea that Muslims in undivided India constituted a "nation" based on Islam was emotive and driven by the fear of a people who, defined by their faith, were a minority alongside a predominantly Hindu, majority non-Muslim population. Muslim nationalism of the Muslim League under Jinnah's leadership in undivided, British-ruled India opposed the Indian nationalism of the Congress Party led by Mahatma Gandhi, Maulana Abul Kalam Azad, and Pandit Jawaharlal Nehru. Jinnah insisted, and mobilized the supporters of the Muslim League accordingly, that Muslims of India deserved a Muslim-majority state of their own. The result was the partition of India, preceded by and accompanied by communal violence. Pakistan emerged as an independent Muslim-majority country, but was physically divided into two halves, or wings—East and West—separated by over a thousand miles of independent India in between the two. During the 24 years of united Pakistan's existence, this geographical reality of a country divided into two distant halves, exacerbated the multiple cleavages of ethnicity and language, class and customs, between the peoples of East and West Pakistan, which the commonality of religion (Islam) was ultimately insufficient to help repair or ameliorate.

In a series of interviews that Lord Louis Mountbatten, the last Viceroy and the first Governor-General of India, gave in the early 1970s to Larry Collins and Dominique Lapierre, the authors of *Freedom at Midnight*, he described his role in achieving the independence of India and Pakistan. Mountbatten mentioned the difficulties of negotiating with Jinnah, Jinnah's unreasonableness, and how Jinnah was ultimately responsible for the partition and the human suffering that followed, as Hindus and Muslims migrated in opposite directions. And then Mountbatten said, "Twenty-five years ago Rajagopalachari [who succeeded Mountbatten as India's second Governor-General in June 1948] and I said it [Pakistan] would last 25 years. It had to... it couldn't go on" (quoted in Collins and Lapierre, 1982, p. 44).

In March 1940, upon his election as president of the Congress Party and as war raged in Europe, Azad addressed the people of British India. He spoke about India's freedom as a necessary element in the war against fascism, and why communal problems in India, referring to Jinnah's demand, should not be an obstruction to India's quest for independence. He refuted Jinnah's claim by stating the following: "Muslims in India are a vast concourse spreading out all over the country. They stand erect, and number between eighty and ninety million. It is true they number only one-fourth of the total population, but the question is not one of ratio, but of large numbers and the strength behind them. If they are in a minority in seven provinces, they are in a majority in five" (R. Gandhi, 1986, p. 237).

Jinnah, however, prevailed, and the creation of Pakistan not only was a geographical oddity but, following the partition in August 1947, also left behind a significantly large Muslim population in India, which in numbers was more than half of the Muslim population of the new Muslim-majority state. In his memoir, *India Wins Freedom*, published after his death in 1958, Azad (1988) wrote that

> Mr. Jinnah and his followers did not seem to realize that geography was against them. Indian Muslims were distributed in a way which made it impossible to form a separate State in a consolidated area. The Muslim majority areas were in the north-west and north-east. These two regions have no point of physical contact. People in these two areas are completely different from one another in every respect except religion. It is one of the greatest frauds on the people to suggest that religious affinity can unite areas which are geographically, economically, linguistically and culturally different. It is true that Islam sought to establish a society which transcends racial, linguistic, economic and political frontiers. History has however proved that after the first few decades or at the most after the first century, Islam was not able to unite all the Muslim countries on the basis of Islam alone. (p. 248)

Azad did not live to see his assessment of Jinnah's Pakistan ironically turn true; Lord Mountbatten, on the other hand, witnessed his prediction fulfilled. In destroying united Pakistan, the Punjabi officers and soldiers of the Pakistan Army were driven as much by their own obduracy, ethnic and religious bigotry, and myth-making as Jinnah and his supporters had been in partitioning united India. No outside power could have likely kept India together in 1947; similarly, none could have saved Pakistan in 1971.

## Internal Turmoil in Pakistan

In 1962 Ayub Khan devised a constitution made to order for a strong, centralized government, and quasi-democratic national and provincial assemblies were elected indirectly under his system by "basic democrats," who formed an electoral college for electing politicians and their parties at the national and provincial levels. Under this system of his own making,

Ayub Khan conducted a presidential election in 1965, which he won over Miss Fatima Jinnah (the sister of Pakistan's founder, Mohammed Ali Jinnah), as the candidate for the Combined Opposition Parties and which gave him some degree of democratic legitimacy in a country where democracy, since its creation in August 1947, had been more or less suffocated by the ineptness and corruption of politicians and the authoritarian intervention of the military in October 1958.

In March 1969, President and Field Marshal Ayub Khan resigned and handed power to General Yahya Khan (the two men were not relatives—the Muslim surname "Khan" is a common one on the subcontinent). There was no one single incident that precipitated Ayub Khan's resignation; it came about as a result of growing discontent within a country under what was largely viewed as "one man rule" disguised as "guided democracy." In the months preceding his resignation, there were rumors about his failing health, and though he appeared to have recovered from his illness (kept secret from the public), his support within the army leadership, the key institution that kept him in power, began to waver. According to G.W. Choudhury's account of this period, the three service chiefs (army, air force, and navy) had concluded that using military force to keep Ayub Khan in power in the face of increasing political discontent and civil unrest was not in their interest. Choudhury (1993) wrote that on joining Yahya Khan's cabinet in 1969, he learned that the three service chiefs had agreed among themselves "to use the armed forces only to the minimum extent needed to keep the administration functioning and prevent the situation from being exploited by any foreign country, presumably India" (p. 35). This loss of critical support from men in uniforms left Ayub Khan at the end with no choice but to hand over power to the army chief, General Yahya Khan. Ayub Khan's resignation was a replay of events from a decade earlier, when he had deposed another military ruler, Iskander Mirza, and seized power as president and chief martial law administrator in October 1958. Ayub Khan's power had rested ultimately on his command over the armed forces of the country and the loyalty of senior officers to him personally; and when this almost two-decade-long institutional loyalty to one man—going back to

1950, when Ayub Khan had become the army chief—dissolved as a result of the army leadership "getting tired" (Choudhury, 1993, p. 35), then his fate as leader was sealed. In handing power to Yahya Khan, Ayub Khan abrogated the constitutional system of his own devising and basically turned the country's political clock back a decade to the situation in 1958, when the country had seemed paralyzed by a lack of political consensus at the center on how and on what basis it was to be governed.

The December 1970 election in united Pakistan was the first and also the last such election in its history as an independent country. It was also by all accounts a fair and free election. Yahya Khan and his advisers anticipated that in a multi-party contest—24 political parties, besides independent non-party candidates, took part in the election for the National Assembly's 300 seats—no single party would emerge as the dominant majority party, and that such a result would necessitate bargaining and compromise among politicians under the watchful directives of the military as the final arbiter and defender of the national interest. But Yahya Khan and his team were misinformed—this was largely due to the mindset or mentality of the men in uniforms, which I discuss below—of the country's prevalent mood, of the degree of alienation between the peoples of the two halves of the country and, as a result, of how strained and weakened the bonds that held the country together were. The results of the election were entirely contrary to expectations and pushed united Pakistan over the precipice three months after the polls closed.

Of the 300 seats in the National Assembly, 162 were to be allocated to East Pakistan as one provincial unit with the largest population in the country. The remaining 138 were to be allocated to West Pakistan, divided into 4 provincial units: Baluchistan with 4 seats, Punjab with 82 seats, the North-West Frontier Province (NWFP) with 25 seats, and Sind with 27 seats. The Awami League (AL), led by Sheikh Mujibur Rahman (or Mujib, as he will be referred to in the rest of the chapter) emerged with an absolute majority in the assembly, with 160 elected members, all of them from East Pakistan; the Pakistan's Peoples Party (PPP) led by Zulfikar Ali Bhutto elected 81 members (62 in Punjab, 18 in Sind, and 1 in NWFP) and emerged as the second-largest party in the assembly. In effect, the election produced an assembly that was clearly polarized between the two wings, with both of the two largest parties, the AL and the PPP, lacking any representation beyond their provincial heartlands in the eastern and western halves of the country and at odds with respect to the fundamental issue—the distribution of powers between the center and the provinces—at the heart of the constitutional vision for the country as a federation.

The AL campaign was based on the six-point program that was first presented by Mujib in March 1966 in Lahore, West Pakistan, following the India–Pakistan war of September 1965 (Government of India, 1971, pp. 23–33). Ayub Khan was then president, and Mujib's six points were viewed by the Pakistani elite, which was predominantly based in West Pakistan, as a veiled scheme for secession disguised as a plan for regional autonomy. The Ayub regime dealt with Mujib's advocacy of the six-point program with a heavy hand, and Mujib was sent to prison for agitating against the national unity of Pakistan. Later, Mujib was also indicted by the Ayub regime for involvement in the Agartala Conspiracy Case, allegedly hatched by India to push for the secession of East Pakistan. The fall of the Ayub Khan regime in March 1969 brought Mujib's release from prison, so that he could participate with his party in the election of December 1970.

The massive electoral support for Mujib and the AL in East Pakistan reflected the extent to which Bengali (i.e., the majority people of the province, whose native language is Bengali) opinion had come to espouse the demand for regional autonomy. The main thrust of the six-point program was the devolution of power from the central government to the provinces, which would leave the center, or the federal government, responsible only for "Defence and Foreign Affairs, and all other residuary subjects shall vest in the Federating States" (Government of India, 1971, p. 25). The program also reflected the grievances of East Pakistan regarding the unfair treatment of the central government and the real or perceived socio-economic disparity between the two wings of the country. The "disparity" thesis pushed by the AL had brought the Bengali "agitating" class—composed of students, teachers, journalists, lawyers, and factory workers—to increasingly view their province as a colony of West Pakistan, a situation that outraged them. The origin of such political sentiment could be traced back to the language movement, which sprang up in opposition to the announcement made by Jinnah during his only visit in 1948 to Dacca (now spelled Dhaka) that Urdu, the language of Muslims of northern India and adopted by the urban elite of West Pakistan as its own, would be the only national language of Pakistan. The demand for Bengali to also be recognized as an official language—Bengali was the language of the people of the eastern province (East Pakistan), and they outnumbered the people in the western (West Pakistan) half of the country—was another secular demand that united the Bengalis, irrespective of their religious beliefs, in marked contrast to the ideology of the "two-nation theory," which, by definition, excluded non-Muslims from the religion-based Muslim nationalism in the making of Pakistan.

The December 1970 election, in effect, turned into a referendum of sorts for the Bengalis, in regard to both the politics of Pakistan and the constitutional need to fix the system of rule so that it would no longer unfairly disadvantage East Pakistan. Before the election, on the night of November 12–13—as if nature and its gods were also aligned to drive home the message of how greatly wronged the Bengalis were—a massive cyclone, accompanied by giant tidal waves, devastated the coastal areas of East Pakistan, resulting in an estimated death toll of a half-million people. The inept response to human suffering by the military regime gave further mileage to the "disparity" thesis of the AL.

In contrast to Mujib with the AL's electoral platform, Bhutto and the PPP had a different task in campaigning across the four provinces of West Pakistan. Bhutto had to find the basis to make a common appeal to an electorate that was not as ethnically homogeneous as the Bengalis in East Pakistan. Consequently, Bhutto's campaign was as emotive and populist as Mujib's was, but with a twist. Bhutto raised the slogan of "Islam is our faith; democracy is our policy; socialism is our economy." It was a campaign of slogans directed to buttress a weak Pakistani nationalism, as opposed to Muslim nationalism, which thrived on the sloganeering of "Islam is in danger"—and to mobilize the patriotic feelings of a people who could be relied on view Hindu-majority India as an archenemy. He spoke vaguely about socialism in terms of fairness and justice for the poor without threatening the interests of the large land-owning class to which he belonged; made promises to students and workers; and stirred the patriotic and martial sentiments of the people in Punjab, who constituted in numbers the bulk of the *jawans* (soldiers) and officers in the armed forces of Pakistan.

The campaigns of Mujib and Bhutto and their consequent electoral results were dramatically and tragically different, each of the campaigns invoking grievances and politics of identity that only served to further widen the distance between the two wings of the country, as if Pakistan was no longer one country in terms of ethnicity, language, and culture. Bhutto's patriotic appeal was designed to strengthen Pakistani nationalism based primarily on religion—Islam—in terms of identity politics, but it found little resonance in East Pakistan, where nationalist identity had turned secular and was based on ethnicity and language. For the Bengalis, West Pakistan had become more or less a foreign country, while the Bengalis of West Bengal in India came to be seen as kinfolk sharing a common Bengali language and culture.

The aftermath of the election exposed the fatal weakness of Pakistan's political culture. Years of authoritarian military rule had deprived the people of Pakistan of an understanding of democracy; in order for it to function, they would need to be tutored in the art of politics. In the period after the election, neither Mujib nor Bhutto demonstrated any understanding of (a) how a country, divided physically and culturally, was to be kept united in the face of tensions pulling it apart or (b) how inflexibility and unwillingness to make concessions when they were most needed were counterproductive in bringing about a peaceful transition from a military dictatorship to civilian rule based on electoral politics. Instead, politics for them, at that critical moment in their country's history, became a zero-sum game, since both Mujib and Bhutto were unwilling to offer any formula for compromise, fearing that their own constituents, in particular the "agitating" class, would readily denounce them for betraying their "cause." This was especially Mujib's situation, given the resounding electoral victory he had won on the basis of AL's six-point agenda. The overwhelming majority of the people in East Pakistan, voting as Bengalis in terms of language and culture, supported Mujib and his party in the expectation of attaining autonomy for their province within a very loose federal arrangement with the people of West Pakistan.

The dominant majority position of the AL in the newly elected National Assembly in session meant that Mujib would be able to draft a constitution for the country in keeping with his six-point agenda. It also meant that Bhutto and his party would not be in a position to obstruct or stop the AL from passing a constitution not to their liking. Consequently, Bhutto demanded that a consensus be reached between the PPP and the AL before the first meeting of the National Assembly. Mujib refused Bhutto's demand, insisting that the proper place for all discussions should be the National Assembly. This back and forth between Mujib and Bhutto illustrated the absence of trust between the two politicians. Bhutto raised the stakes by declaring that he and his party would not attend the opening of the National Assembly unless Mujib relented to his demands.

## THE MINDSET OF THE PAKISTANI MILITARY
The Immediate Events Leading up to
the 1971 Crisis

On March 25, 1971, President and Chief Martial Law Administrator General Agha Mohammed Yahya Khan abruptly ended talks with Sheikh Mujibur Rahman, the Bengali leader of the Awami League (AL), in Dhaka, the provincial capital of East Pakistan, and flew back to Islamabad, the country's capital, located in West Pakistan. Yahya Khan had arrived in Dhaka on March 15 to bridge the differences between Mujib and Bhutto before the National Assembly was called to session. Bhutto had threatened to boycott the National Assembly until Mujib agreed with him that the AL majority would not impose a constitution based on the party's six-point program, which was unacceptable to him. But both Mujib and Bhutto remained intransigent and uncompromising. When Yahya Khan departed from

Dhaka, it ended the two-year experiment by the martial law regime that he headed, aimed at arranging a general election for a National Assembly and the transfer of power to a civilian government. Yahya Khan and his coterie of advisers, mostly military men, had visualized a return to civilian rule for the country within a reasonable time frame and an end to the martial law regime that had been put in place following Ayub Khan's handing of power to the military. A free and fair election, it was thought, would provide legitimacy to the working out of the constitutional arrangements for civilian rule and democracy. According to G.W. Choudhury (1993), a civilian member of the Yahya Khan's military regime, "Yahya's pledge of 'free and fair' elections on the basis of direct voting and giving the Bengalis, for the first time, their due share of representation on the basis of 'one man, one vote' was in a sense a revolutionary development in Pakistan's politics" (p. 108). The failure on the part of Yahya Khan to settle the differences between Mujib and Bhutto derailed the experiment to move the country down the path of electoral politics and democratic rule.

When Yahya Khan boarded his plane in Dhaka on March 25, 1971, to return to Islamabad, essentially giving the green light to his army commanders in East Pakistan to pacify Bangladesh and crush what he deemed to be the politics of secession, he ironically also brought down the curtain on the unseemly and illogical creation of a Pakistan based on Jinnah's "two-nation theory." While Yahya Khan's order for the forced pacification of East Pakistan was the trashing of the script for a united Pakistan that he had prepared, the opening act of this script had been the general election of December 1970. After taking power from Ayub Khan on March 25, 1969, Yahya Khan invested nearly all of his time and energy in preparing the country for this election, based on adult franchise and "one man, one vote," as a prelude to the transfer of power to a civilian government. Yahya Khan's plan for the country had three components: (a) the election; (b) the setting up of a representative assembly to draft the constitution; and (c) the institutionalization of democratic rule. As G.W. Choudhury (1993) wrote in regard to Yahya Khan's plan, "There were three clear and unambiguous promises: first, transfer of power to the elected representatives of the people; secondly, the election would be held on the basis of direct adult franchise—Ayub's system of indirect election through Basic Democrats was rejected; and thirdly, the future constitution of the country would be framed by the elected members" (p. 73).

Throughout the month of February 1971, Yahya Khan made efforts to broker a compromise between Mujib and Bhutto. But Yahya Khan was also under pressure from his military commanders, who were divided over how to proceed into the uncharted political currents with politicians proving to be, in their cynical view, once again thirsting for power more than for doing what was good for the country. Since the military had ruled the country for more than a decade since 1958, the men in uniform simply assumed that they knew best what was good for the country and instinctively held the political class in contempt. But the military in united Pakistan was not entirely representative of the country. All the top-ranking field commanders and senior generals were from West Pakistan, as were the bulk of the *jawans* (soldiers) recruited from Punjab and the NWFP, just as they had been in British India. Only after independence in 1947 was effort directed at recruiting soldiers and commissioning officers from East Pakistan and raising Bengali regiments. This effort, however, had not progressed sufficiently to make a significant difference in the ethnic composition of the armed forces in the country. Thus, in February–March 1971, that critical juncture in united Pakistan's history, the Pakistan Army in East Pakistan appeared to the Bengalis to be more or less an army of occupation.

Bhutto's stand against Mujib and the AL's six-point agenda converged with the thinking of that significant element within the senior leadership of the military who saw Mujib's political stand as a preparation for the secession of East Pakistan. For these senior military commanders, Mujib's alleged involvement in the Agartala Conspiracy Case was proof that the AL's proposal for a loose, hence weak, central government and regional autonomy would spell the beginning of the end for united Pakistan. And while Yahya Khan was engaged in efforts to nudge Mujib and Bhutto into finding an agreeable solution to their impasse before the March 3 opening of the National Assembly he had announced, he also ordered a military buildup of men and matériel to be airlifted and shipped from West to East Pakistan. On February 28, Bhutto announced that he and his party would not be attending the National Assembly when it opened. Threatening a general strike, he called upon his supporters to force non-PPP members elected from the provinces in West Pakistan to do the same. Bhutto demanded, as a condition for his attendance, that the time limit of 120 days to draft the constitution be abandoned, or that the opening of the National Assembly be postponed until his demand for consensus over the key principles of the constitution had been met.

On March 1, a message from Yahya Khan was broadcast on radio, announcing that the National Assembly had been postponed *sine die*, or without giving any appointed date for resumption. The people of East Pakistan were already in a tense mood. The annual language day commemoration on February 21 had seen the slogan of *"Joy Bangla"* ("Victory to Bangladesh") resonate across East Pakistan, as students and workers took to the street, flags for Bangladesh were unfurled, and Bengalis began to address Mujib as *"Bangabandhu"* ("Friend of Bengal"). Yahya Khan's announcement was followed by Mujib's call on March 3 for general strikes, which resulted in practically shutting down all activities across the province. Mujib also refused to attend a roundtable conference that the president had proposed, and instead indicated he would speak at a public rally in Dhaka on March 7.

As the Bengalis watched the military buildup in their province, the public mood began to shift, and extremist elements among the "agitating" class resorted to violent demonstrations as a show of support for independence. There was expectation that Mujib might call for independence when he addressed the announced rally. But a day earlier, on March 6, Yahya Khan made a public broadcast over the radio, informing the country that the National Assembly would begin session on March 25. When Mujib addressed the rally in Dhaka on March 7, instead of declaring independence, as many of his supporters had expected, he announced a series of directives on how public and private businesses were to be conducted, so as to demonstrate Bengali solidarity. He also demanded the lifting of martial law ahead of the National Assembly session as a precondition for his attendance. According to G.W. Choudhury (1993), "Between 3 and 25 March the central Government's writ did not run in East Pakistan" (p. 158). And thus when Yahya Khan arrived in Dhaka for the final time on March 15, he was in effect a "foreign guest" among the Bengalis.

The 10 days of negotiations during Yahya Khan's stay in Dhaka, when Bhutto and other elected members from West Pakistan joined him in talking with Mujib and his team, ended in a stalemate. There was no concession on the key constitutional issue from either Mujib or Bhutto. Opinions are divided over whether this last attempt at negotiation was a farce on the part of Yahya Khan and his top generals, a ploy intended to buy time for the military buildup, or whether Mujib's obstinacy and Bhutto's lust for power proved to be fatal for the survival of Pakistan as a united country. Choudhury (1993), for one, wrote, "The Dacca dialogues had failed. For this the Pakistan Government headed by Yahya and Bhutto and his party put the entire blame on Mujib" (p. 180). Witnessing the events unfold, Anthony Mascarenhas (1971) observed, "The fact that the talks had failed was of no consequence. They were not intended to succeed. The purport had been purely military—the purchase of time for preparedness and the big strike" (p. 4).

## Operation Searchlight

The big strike—Operation Searchlight—began in the midnight hours of March 25–26, uncorking a civil war in East Pakistan that raged until the birth of Bangladesh in December 1971 as a new nation-state in South Asia. What had essentially been a case of domestic political unrest mutated into a regional conflict, which subsequently escalated into tensions among the great powers. The orders given to crush the vanguard of the noncooperation movement (which had, increasingly through the month of March, appeared to the military high command as secessionist), *and* to arrest the leading members of the AL, including Mujib, had been implicit in Yahya Khan's message of March 6. In announcing that he was calling the National Assembly session for March 25, Yahya Khan stated, "I will not allow a handful of people to destroy the homeland of millions of innocent Pakistanis. It is the duty of the Pakistan Armed Forces to ensure the integrity, solidarity and security of Pakistan, a duty in which they have never failed" (Government of India, 1971, p. 216). Addressing the country after the military crackdown in East Pakistan had begun, Yahya Khan declared, "Sheikh Mujibur Rahman's action of starting his non-co-operation movement is an act of treason... They have created turmoil, terror and insecurity" (Government of India, 1971, p. 276). Consequently, he announced, "As for the Awami League it is completely banned as a political party. I have also decided to impose complete Press censorship" (Government of India, 1971, p. 277).

The martial law administration in East Pakistan headed by Lieutenant General Tikka Khan was given free hand to impose law and order, with a news blackout of the repressive measures taken by the military in Dhaka and elsewhere in the province. What followed amounted to a massacre of the civilian population in East Pakistan, and it was genocide when it came to the killings of Hindus. Operation Searchlight was a huge miscalculation of the political reality in East Pakistan when Yahya Khan spoke of "a handful of people" in support of Mujib and the AL who could be eliminated without too much of a blowback; and it was a terrible misreading of Bengalis as a people, wrongly considered weaklings and cowards who could be terrified into meekly submitting to the demands of the military dictatorship by a few thousand soldiers brought in from West Pakistan. As a policy, it was also a grand folly in the way that historian Barbara Tuchman (1985) described "folly" to mean "the pursuit of policy contrary to the self-interest of the constituency or state involved" (p. 5). For Yahya Khan and his generals to believe that, once they had unleashed the military against the majority population of the country and carried out killings, rapes, and torture, Bengali opinion would be malleable to their directives was delusional. But delusional they were, and by their decision the Rubicon was crossed and united Pakistan was undone by measures taken to save it.

The mindset of the Pakistan Army's officer corps, which planned and executed Operation Searchlight, also reflected the ideology of Pakistani nationalism that had taken shape in the years following the independence of the country. It could indeed be said that the prevalent thinking within the army was instrumental in shaping Pakistani nationalism, which carried within it the seeds of its own undoing, as the tragedy in East Pakistan/ Bangladesh illustrated. An army, led by its officer corps, that was prepared and willing to massacre its own people was indicative of the place and role in the country that the army had been indoctrinated to imagine for itself: as a privileged group with the responsibility of defending the country's honor, dignity, and self-respect. In studying the Pakistan Army and the mentality of its officer corps, Stephen Cohen (1992) observed that the officers "stressed that the virtues of Pakistan were their virtues, that the Islamic character of Pakistan was reflected in the Islamic character of the military. In numerous popular publications as well as in the military schools, the history of Pakistan was traced to Muslim dominance in South Asia and Pakistanis were portrayed as the natural conquerors of the region by virtue of their purer religion and their martial characteristics" (p. 42).

In Urdu, the name "Pakistan" means "the land of the pure." The word "pure" in this context signified the purity of Muslim belief in Islam, and the slogan "Islam is in danger" suggested the ever-present peril of this purity of belief becoming contaminated and corrupted by the impurities of Hinduism or subverted by heretical thinking among Muslims through association with non-Muslims. The notion of purity was also extended to describing Muslims as ethnically pure or impure in terms of geographical location or origin, and proximity or distance from Arabia as the birthplace of Islam. In this schema of purity and impurity, the faith of Bengali Muslims of East Pakistan was held suspect by the officer corps of the Pakistan Army, given the distance between Arabia and Bengal, and because the Bengali language, derived from Sanskrit, did not belong to the family of languages (Arabic, Persian, Turkish, and Urdu) considered Islamic. The military campaign to crush the Bengali demand for regional autonomy that the AL's six-point agenda represented was also readily justified by the officer corps in religious and ethnic terms, given the prevalent views that (a) the faith of Bengali Muslims was weak, since they were converts from Hinduism; (b) they considered Rabindranath Tagore (Asia's first Nobel Laureate in Literature) an icon of their literary and musical culture; and (c)

Bengalis were racially inferior to Muslims from West Pakistan who, as descendants of Arabs, Afghans, Persians, and Turks, saw themselves as belonging to the martial races.

The Pakistan Army was predominantly made up of officers and soldiers recruited from Punjabi Muslims and Muslims of the NWFP. This pattern of recruitment originated with the British. According to Stephen Cohen (1992), "The idea of the 'martial races' had complex origins (some of them mythical), but it did partially reflect actual regional, religious, and ethnic differences among Indians. It also led to a serious imbalance of recruitment in the old Indian Army and the dominance of Punjabis in the sepoy ranks. This dominance later spread to the officer corps, and by the beginning of World War II the largest single category in the Indian Army was Punjabi Muslims, just as they had been the largest category recruited to the Indian Army during World War I" (p. 41).

The composition of the new (i.e., post-1947) Pakistan Army was similar to that of the old Indian Army. In effect, the Pakistan Army was a Punjabi army, drilled and indoctrinated to view other ethnic groups in the country (except for the Pathans of the NWFP), and especially Bengalis, as Pakistanis of inferior virtues in terms of religion, culture, and martial qualities.

In his political autobiography, *Friends Not Masters*, President and Field Marshal Ayub Khan recalled how one evening in London, in order to clarify for himself his own thinking, he wrote a memo, which he titled "A Short Appreciation of Present and Future Problems of Pakistan." It seems Ayub Khan, who also served as the commander in chief of the army, was so impressed with what he wrote that evening in London that he reprinted the entire memo for posterity in his autobiography. What he wrote about Bengalis in describing the people of Pakistan was very revealing of the mindset of the officer corps of the army. He wrote,

The people of Pakistan consist of a variety of races each with its own historical background and culture. East Bengalis [i.e., Bengalis of East Pakistan], who constitute the bulk of the population, probably belong to the very original Indian races. It would be no exaggeration to say

that up to the creation of Pakistan, they had not known any real freedom or sovereignty. They have been in turn ruled either by the caste
Hindus, Moghuls, Pathans, or the British. In addition, they have been
and still are under considerable Hindu cultural and linguistic influence. As such they have all the inhibitions of down-trodden races and
have not yet found it possible to adjust psychologically to the requirements of the new-born freedom. (Khan, 1967, p. 187)

The military became a new aristocracy and, as Robert Payne (1973)
wrote, it "proclaimed itself the inheritor of the martial tradition of Islam, the
successor of Timurlane and Nadir Shah and all the other Islamic conquerors
of India" (p. 36). It became a common theme within the ranks of the military,
a matter of unquestioning bravado turned into conviction of their own
innate prowess as soldiers of Islam, that one Pakistani soldier was equal, if
not better, in fighting spirit than 10 Hindus. Out of such thinking, infused
with racial bigotry and religious chauvinism, the senior commanders of the
Pakistan Army were blinded by their own limited vision of the complex
reality of politics. Their contempt for politicians and impatience with politics
led them to believe that punishing the people with their fists would make
political difficulties disappear. And thus the Punjabi generals and soldiers of
the Pakistan Army in East Pakistan saw in Bengalis a lesser breed of people,
insufficient in their faith in Islam and loyalty to Pakistan, and given their
own sense of superiority as a martial race, they felt confident that a military
crackdown would put to an end the obstinacy of the Bengalis, with their
unreasonable political demands. Yahya Khan expressed the sheer unreality
of such thinking in February 1971, even as he engaged in negotiations with
Mujib and Bhutto, when he reputedly told the commanding officers in East
Pakistan, "Kill three million of them and the rest will eat out of our hands"
(Payne, 1973, p. 50). When the tanks rolled out into the streets of Dhaka
around the midnight hours of March 25–26, the fate of united Pakistan was
a chronicle foretold by those who had understood the sheer illogic of Jinnah's
"two-nation theory" and what it might mean eventually.

## The Massacre Unfolds

Operation Searchlight, launched on the night of March 25–26 in Dhaka, was aimed to swiftly decapitate the center of the AL-organized and Mujib-led noncooperation movement, and eliminate the supporting cast of the AL among the Bengali literate class. Mujib was arrested in the early hours of Operation Searchlight's launch. While columns of tanks and soldiers moved during those first hours of the military crackdown against the barracks of the local police force and the militia (the East Pakistan Rifles, made up of recruits from the Bengali population), the two main residences of Dhaka University students (Iqbal Hall for Muslims and Jagannath Hall for Hindus), the homes of professors in the vicinity of the university, and the offices of Bengali newspapers were raided. The first priority of Operation Searchlight was to take control of Dhaka and crush any sign of insurgency before the military regiments began moving against the Bengalis outside of Dhaka, in the port cities of Chittagong and Khulna, and in other towns of East Pakistan. And as the sun rose on the morning of March 26 over Dhaka, a city gripped with fear, "the year of the vulture"—in Robert Payne's memorable description of the slaughter of Bengalis in East Pakistan—had begun.

The military governor and chief martial law administrator in East Pakistan, Lieutenant General Tikka Khan, appointed on March 4, had ordered a news blackout following Yahya Khan's announcement of press censorship. Foreign journalists in Dhaka were ordered to leave East Pakistan and were subsequently taken to the airport by military personnel on the first day of the crackdown. In turn, before their departure, journalists had their notebooks and films confiscated and were warned not to report on what they might have seen during the night. By censoring the press, the generals believed they were erecting a *cordon sanitaire* around East Pakistan, and seemed confident that with their control of the flow of news and information, they could "pacify" the Bengali population with brute force.

The massacre Yahya Khan ordered was genocide by the definition of the UN Convention on the Prevention and Punishment of the Crime of Genocide of December 1948. There was the manifest intent, as evidenced in the planning and execution of Operation Searchlight, against Bengalis, who were deemed by the Punjabi-dominated Pakistan Army to be people of an inferior race. Bengalis were slaughtered both at random and with intent; specifically targeted were students residing at Iqbal Hall and Jagannath Hall within the Dhaka university campus and prominent individuals on a list prepared by the military high command. The thinking behind Operation Searchlight was that a ferocious display of military force in killing and brutally repressing the Bengalis would spread fear across East Pakistan, and that such an experience would make a lasting impression among Bengalis, deemed a "non-martial" race. The lesson of the massacre, the top echelon of the Pakistan Army believed, would deter any thoughts of independence among the Bengalis, who would recognize it to be a painfully losing proposition.

The special animus or hatred of Bengalis, which animated the soldiers of the Pakistan Army, was directed toward Hindus, who made up about 15 per cent of the estimated population of 75 million people in East Pakistan. The slaughter of Hindus, or their forced exodus into India as refugees, was meant to "purify" the country by cleansing it of infidels whose presence within Pakistan was tantamount to a contamination of the "land of the pure." The crime of genocide, according to the UNCG, occurs when any party or authority acts with the *intent* to destroy "a national, ethnical, racial or religious" group of people, as had occurred, for example, in Ottoman Turkey with the destruction of the Armenian people in 1915. The brutal attack by the military against the Bengali Hindu population of East Pakistan, and the rape and murder that accompanied it, was genocidal in both intent and execution.

Yahya Khan and his army *knew* they were committing genocide, but they prepared an alibi and sought to shift the responsibility on to the AL and its "militant" supporters, claiming in the *White Paper on the Crisis in East Pakistan*, published in August 1971, that the military action launched on March 25 was ordered to prevent "genocide" from being perpetrated by the Bengalis. The *White Paper* stated the following:

> On the night of 25–26 March, a few hours before the Awami League plan for an armed uprising and launching of the "Independent Republic of Bangla Desh" was to be put into effect, the President called upon the

armed forces of Pakistan to do their duty and "fully restore the authority of the Government."

The Pakistan Army units, largely deployed along the borders with India, set out to suppress the rebellion and drive out the Indian infiltrators over the next few weeks. During this period, in the areas which came temporarily under the control of the rebels and Indian infiltrators, the Awami League reign of terror, unleashed from 1 March 1971, onwards claimed the lives of more than a hundred thousand men, women and children, besides incalculable damage to public and private buildings, transport and communications an [sic] industrial establishments etc.

The mass killings by the Awami League cadres and EBR/EPR [East Bengal Regiment/East Pakistan Rifles] rebels assumed the character of genocide. (Government of Pakistan, 1971, pp. 40–41)

It was true that there were incidents of violence carried out by mobs of Bengalis against non-Bengalis in various parts of East Pakistan during the month of March, between Yahya Khan's announcement on March 1 of the indefinite postponement of the National Assembly session and his departure from Dhaka on the evening of March 25. But it was a spurious claim, in terms of the alleged number of victims and without evidence supported by independent witnesses, *to suggest*, as the government's white paper did, that despite the presence of the Pakistan Army in East Pakistan and in the presence of the international press corps in Dhaka, AL supporters had been responsible for the killings of "a hundred thousand men, women and children" over the course of about three weeks.

Mob-driven violence was mostly the result of the inflammatory situation created by Yahya Khan's announcement and the failure of the AL—which was insufficiently prepared for such an eventuality—to stop such violence; it may also have been instigated by extremist elements posing as AL followers to take advantage of the situation and precipitate anarchy. No matter what, mob violence provided the military with the rationale it needed as cover for its own planned massacre of Bengalis. Bengali mobs attacked the residential settlements of mostly Muslim migrants from India, who had arrived in 1947 and had been designated as "Biharis." These mob-driven assaults on Biharis were deliberately, though improperly, described as "genocide" by the Yahya regime.

The temper of Bengalis was frayed, putting them on edge, as they learned about the airlift of troops from West Pakistan and news of clashes, such as those between West Pakistani soldiers and Bengali dock workers who refused to unload ships bringing weapons into the port city of Chittagong. But in regard to the violence perpetrated by Bengali mobs during the month of March, the white paper's authors had the cause-and-effect relationship completely backward; instead, Yahya Khan's decision to postpone the National Assembly session for March 3 indicated to Bengalis that he was prepared to trash the election results and deny the people their right to elect a government of their choice. This is what provoked mob violence and then, according to the white paper, compelled the military to act as it did. Yahya Khan wanted the world to believe that the actions of his military government were preventative, were taken to stop a Bengali-led genocide of the non-Bengali population in the province, and constituted the preemption of a well-planned secessionist uprising. In other words, he wanted his actions to appear as if they had been carried out for the sole purpose of maintaining the unity of the country.

## THE BANGLADESH TRAGEDY AND THE INTERNATIONAL MEDIA

Throughout the months of April, May, and June, the repression and killings inside East Pakistan went mostly unreported in the international press. Refugees fled scenes of military carnage, and eventually an estimated 10 million sought shelter in refugee camps in India. On June 13, the *Sunday Times* in London finally carried an extended report by Anthony Mascarenhas, a Pakistani journalist based in Karachi, under the heading "Genocide."

Mascarenhas had been sent by the Pakistani military regime as part of a team of selected reporters from West Pakistan on a guided tour to report "the return of normalcy" in East Pakistan. In the limited time he spent being shown around Dhaka and elsewhere in the province by a military escort, he was shocked by what he saw and heard.

Later, in the preface to his book *The Rape of Bangla Desh*, Mascarenhas (1971) wrote, "What I saw in East Bengal was to me more outrageous than anything I had read about the inhuman acts of Hitler and the Nazis. I knew I had to tell the world about the agony of East Bengal or forever carry within myself the agonizing guilt of acquiescence" (p. v). To report on what he had witnessed, Mascarenhas moved to Britain with his family in June 1971 so as to flee the predictable wrath of the generals. And then, on the front page of the *Sunday Times* on June 13, he lifted the curtain on what he had witnessed: "West Pakistan's Army has been systematically massacring thousands of civilians in East Pakistan since the end of March. This is the horrifying reality behind the news blackout imposed by President Yahya Khan's government since the end of March. This is the reason why more than five million refugees have streamed out of East Pakistan into India, risking cholera and famine."

It was sheer folly on the part of the Pakistani military high command to believe that the enormity of the massacre perpetrated by the army could long be kept hidden from the outside world. The world was bound to find out sooner or later, but what it did after obtaining the knowledge was another matter altogether. Still, being provided with such knowledge was essential, and once Mascarenhas's eye-witness account had been published, there could be no denial of the mass murder, mass rape, and massive refugee flow. After visiting Bangladesh in early 1972, Robert Payne (1973) wrote, "For month after month in all the regions of East Pakistan the massacres went on. They were not the small casual killings of young officers who wanted to demonstrate their efficiency, but organized massacres conducted by sophisticated staff officers, who knew exactly what they were doing. Muslim soldiers, sent out to kill Muslim peasants, went about their work mechanically and efficiently, until killing defenseless people became a habit like smoking cigarettes or drinking wine. Before they had finished, they had killed three million people" (p. 29).

## THE ENSUING AND ONGOING CONTROVERSY OVER THE NUMBER OF DEAD

The figure of 3 million Bengalis killed in less than 10 months between March and December by the Pakistan Army was an astounding figure, and yet this figure came to be accepted, more or less through repetition, as the figure officially cited by subsequent governments in Bangladesh. In the trials of the Bengali collaborators with the Pakistan Army (all of whom were indicted for mass murder) held by the International Crimes Tribunal for Bangladesh (ICT-BD) constituted by an act of the Bangladesh parliament, 3 million dead Bengalis was cited as evidence of the scale of massacres in 1971. In one such trial, the court document of the judgment handed down in February 2013 reads, "Some three million people were killed, nearly quarter million women were raped and over 10 million people were forced to take refuge in India to escape brutal persecution at home, during the nine-month battle and struggle of Bangalee [sic] nation" (International Crimes Tribunal-2, 2013, pp. 4–5).

While there is a general consensus in the literature on Bangladesh that the scale of the both the massacres carried out by the Pakistan Army in 1971 and the counterviolence of Bengalis against non-Bengalis during this period was huge and appalling, the figure of 3 million killed that has now become part of the official record, or the myth of Bengali losses in the struggle for liberation is controversial. Any critical examination of this figure raises the question of how such an industrial-level killing was conducted by the Pakistan Army and how the dead bodies were disposed of, even as the army became increasingly tied down in a losing guerilla warfare against the *Mukti Bahini* (Bengali freedom fighters), who had been trained and supported by the Indian Army.

To arrive at the figure of 3 million dead during this period of less than 10 months would have required in excess of 11,000 individuals killed daily, a number that is not credible, irrespective of how bloody-minded and efficient the soldiers of the Pakistan Army were. Even half of 3 million killed under orders from Yahya Khan, as estimated by R.J. Rummel (1995) in *Death By Government*, his study of mass killings in the twentieth century, is seemingly too high for the rate of daily killings that would be required to reach the number of 1.5 million dead (pp. 315–77). Yet Rummel's study, which reduces by half the official Bangladeshi record of the number of people killed, has been cited on the same page as the figure of 3 million without any irony by Bangladeshi justices of the ICT in their judgment of the Bengali collaborators who worked side by side with the Pakistan Army.

In her 2011 study of the East Pakistan/Bangladesh genocide (*Dead Reckoning: Memories of the 1971 Bangladesh War*), Sarmila Bose has severely dented the figure of 3 million dead by examining historical records of the crisis and combing through interviews with survivors of the massacres. The failure of successive Bangladesh governments to present the evidence on which the figure of 3 million dead was based and to be fully transparent has contributed to the ongoing controversy and debate over the numbers of dead. The least the government could do would be to either exhume the mass graves and identify the victims via the latest available forensic method, or admit its inability to conduct a scientifically credible investigation and invite technical assistance from foreign governments to do this work on behalf of the people of Bangladesh. Until then, doubts about the numbers killed cannot be quelled. Bose (2011) concluded her study by noting, "It appears possible to estimate with reasonable confidence that at least 50,000–100,000 people perished in the conflict in East Pakistan/Bangladesh in 1971, including combatants and non-combatants, Bengalis and non-Bengalis, Hindus and Muslims, Indians and Pakistanis. Casualty figures crossing one hundred thousand are within the realm of the possible, but beyond that one enters a world of meaningless speculation" (p. 181).

Bose's estimate is low, even though her numbers are higher than the figure provided by the *Hamoodur Rahman Commission Report* (1974), commissioned by Bhutto in the aftermath of the 1971 debacle for the Pakistan Army. Hamoodur Rahman was the chief justice of the Supreme Court of Pakistan when Bhutto asked him to investigate the circumstances that led to the surrender of the Pakistan Army to the Indian Army in Dhaka on December 16, 1971. In his report, Rahman dismissed the notion that 3 million Bengalis had been killed and 200,000 women raped as "fantastic and fanciful." Rahman concluded, "Different figures were mentioned by different persons in authority but the latest statement supplied to us by the GHQ shows approximately 26,000 persons killed during the action by the Pakistan Army" (p. 33). This number is much too low to be taken as credible and is likely a low-ball estimate, presented in an effort to minimize the charges leveled against the Pakistan Army.

The probable figure regarding the total number of casualties in East Pakistan/Bangladesh during the 1971 unrest and war is likely in the proximity of 300,000. It has been speculated that this was the figure that Mujib initially cited in Bengali and that was then misstated or mistranslated as 3 million. In a study published by the *British Medical Journal* about the comparative numbers of mass deaths over the past half-century, the authors indicate a large variance between two independent surveys of the figures for deaths during the Bangladesh crisis of 1971: one survey estimated 269,000 deaths and another, 58,000 deaths (Obermeyer, Murray, & Gakidou, 2008). The figure 269,000 seems credible and is not implausibly higher than the estimate provided by Bose. In the end, the total number of deaths amounting to genocide in East Pakistan/Bangladesh will remain a contentious figure, though it needs to be reiterated that the figure 3 million is a gross exaggeration.

## THE UNITED STATES AND THE BANGLADESH GENOCIDE

In *The Blood Telegram: Nixon, Kissinger, and a Forgotten Genocide*, Gary Bass (2013) reminds his readers that the massacres in East Pakistan/Bangladesh ranked with "Vietnam and Cambodia among the darkest incidents in Nixon's presidency and the entire Cold War" (p. 340). It is a stain on the presidency (1969–74) of Richard Nixon, just as the Watergate scandal is, and neither of them will ever be washed away. While the buck stopped with Nixon when it came to who was ultimately responsible for US policy during the 1971 crisis, his national security adviser, Henry Kissinger, also bears responsibility for his role in formulating and executing the president's policy. It is therefore quite right to speak of the Nixon–Kissinger policy, which was hollow at its core in terms of moral concern when confronted with a genocide committed by an ally or, more appropriately, a "client" state, ruled by a military dictator.

In a century of wars, the Holocaust, and various other genocides, it might be said that the massacres of Bengalis and non-Bengalis in East Pakistan were just another sorry episode in the ignoble history of mankind committing evil. Such a view might not be inappropriate when considering history philosophically and with detachment, yet it leaves us unconvinced that we are entirely helpless in the face of evil. We want to know what might or could have been done to thwart evil, or why there was such an inadequate response to prevent the commission of evil. The world community, as represented by the United Nations, utterly failed to stop the genocide in Bangladesh or, in the aftermath, to bring those responsible to answer for their crimes against humanity. As Adam LeBor (2006) indicates in *"Complicity with Evil": The United Nations in the Age of Modern Genocide*, a study of the UN and its reaction to genocides, the record of the world community, or of the great powers that sit as permanent members of the Security Council, has been abysmal. The Bangladesh tragedy was followed by numerous other atrocities, such as the massacre of Iraqi Kurds and the use of chemical weapons against them by the Iraqi regime of Saddam Hussein, the genocide of Tutsi and moderate Hutu in Rwanda, the genocidal massacre of Muslim boys and men in Srebrenica in the former Yugoslavia, the killings in Somalia, the genocide in Darfur, and, even as I write this in the winter of 2015–16, the ongoing massacres of minority Christian and Yazidi populations in Iraq and Syria by the so-called "holy warriors" of the Islamic State or ISIS (the Islamic State of Iraq and Syria). The failure of the UN in the face of such organized criminality is astounding, and I mention this in order to place the genocide in Bangladesh within the context of the broader history of such crimes, committed with the full knowledge of the world community, whose response in confronting them has been inadequate.

The role of Nixon and Kissinger in this tragedy was, at a minimum, shameful. In the case of Bangladesh, the United States could have made a difference by leaning heavily on Yahya Khan. Consequently, even if Nixon and Kissinger are not responsible for what occurred, they are responsible for not attempting to halt Yahya Khan's plan once it became known that he had ordered his army to carry out a campaign of terror and mass murder against an unarmed civilian population. According to Bass (2013), "No country, not even the United States, can prevent massacres everywhere in the world. But these atrocities were carried out by a close US ally, which prized its warm relationship with the United States, and used US weapons and military supplies against its own people. Surely there was some US responsibility here" (p. 339).

Bass's book is based in part on the declassified archival records of the US government vis-à-vis its policy decisions during the period of the Bangladesh crisis. Certain of these documents are available electronically as *National Security Archive Electronic Briefing Book No. 79*, edited by Sajit Gandhi (2002); there is nothing in this particular set of documents that shines a kind light on the roles played by Nixon and Kissinger.

In 1978 Nixon published his memoirs covering the record of his presidency from 1969 to 1974, at which time he resigned and left office in disgrace. It is an impressive tome of over 1,100 pages. In the chapter covering the year 1971, Nixon devoted some 43 pages to domestic problems, the war in Vietnam, the release of the Pentagon Papers, and arms negotiations with the former Soviet Union; he devoted 8 pages to the India–Pakistan war. He made one passing mention of "a rebellion in East Pakistan against the government of President Yahya Khan" and another about Indian officials reporting that "nearly 10 million refugees fled from East Pakistan into India" (Nixon, 1978, p. 525). Even in hindsight, Nixon could acknowledge neither what had occurred in East Pakistan nor how his administration had reacted (or actually, not reacted) to the tragedy. Speaking of the Bangladesh genocide, Nixon (1978) wrote, "We knew that Yahya Khan eventually would have to yield to East Pakistan's demands for independence, and we urged him to take a more moderate and conciliatory line. We could not have known the extent to which India would seize this opportunity not just to destroy Pakistan's control of East Pakistan but to weaken West Pakistan as well" (p. 525).

It was no secret that Nixon personally disliked Indira Gandhi, India's prime minister, and the dislike intensified following the agreement reached between New Delhi and Moscow with the signing of "The Indo-Soviet Treaty of Peace, Friendship and Co-operation" of August 9, 1971. In contrast, Nixon displayed genuinely warm feelings for Yahya Khan and prized his relationship with the dictator, particularly for facilitating the secret diplomacy with the Chinese leadership that culminated in Kissinger's journey to Beijing out of Islamabad in July 1971 and Nixon's visit to China in February 1972. Be that as it may, instead of cautioning Yahya Khan over East Pakistan, as Nixon claims in his memoirs, archival evidence presents a radically different version of the events. For example, in his own handwriting, Nixon scribbled the following note at the bottom of a six-page memorandum dated April 28, 1971: "To all hands, Don't squeeze Yahya at this time – RN" (Gandhi, 2002, doc. 9). This April 28 memorandum was prepared for Nixon by Kissinger, the president's national security adviser at the time, and Nixon's handwritten scribbled note was directed at his national security staff in the White House. It went unmentioned in Kissinger's memorandum to Nixon that, a month earlier, the US government had been informed of the military crackdown by Archer Blood, the consul general in Dhaka, in a telegram dated March 28. The opening paragraph of the March 28, 1971, telegram from the consul general stated, "Here in Dacca we are mute and horrified witnesses to a reign of terror by the Pak military. Evidence continues to mount that the MLA [Martial Law Administration] Authorities have a list of Awami League supporters whom they are systematically eliminating by seeking them out in their homes and shooting them down" (Gandhi, 2002, doc. 1).

Nixon was apparently unmoved by the situation in East Pakistan following the "West Pakistani military crackdown," as noted by Kissinger in the aforementioned memorandum of April 28 (Gandhi, 2002, doc. 9), and instead Nixon did not hesitate to indicate his concern for the well-being of the military dictator Yahya Khan.

In *White House Years*, Kissinger described what has come to be known as "The Tilt" in US policy toward Pakistan during the South Asian crisis of 1971. As the shooting war between Pakistan and India began on December 3,

Kissinger informed members of the Washington Special Action Group (wsag), "He [Nixon] wants to tilt in favor of Pakistan" (Kissinger, 1979, p. 897; Jackson, 1975, p. 213). In fact, "the Tilt," had been unmistakably evident since the beginning of the crisis in March. In discussing the rationale behind it, Kissinger devoted 76 pages to a spirited defense of Nixon's policy. In doing so, he clearly stated that it was a policy that he, the president's national security adviser, was in total agreement with and wholly supported. "The Tilt" was meant to indicate that the actions of Yahya Khan and his army in East Pakistan were a sideshow and, therefore, of marginal concern to Nixon and Kissinger when viewed, as they were, within the larger framework of global politics and American interests—at a time when Nixon and Kissinger were engaged in secret diplomacy with the Chinese leadership in Beijing.

Kissinger's *White House Years* was, as all memoirs are, a retrospective effort to present his role as Nixon's top foreign policy aide and adviser in the most favorable light. In that regard, he expended considerable effort on justifying the "tilt" policy, which, in fact, failed to prevent a war, failed to save a "client" state from defeat and dismemberment, and was the one policy that was challenged—on humanitarian grounds—by career officials of the State Department and members of Congress during Nixon's first term, thereby leaving a stain on a record that otherwise could be presented as evidence of the sagacity of the Nixon–Kissinger team in shaping us foreign policy in the first term of the Nixon presidency.

From the perspectives of Nixon and Kissinger, the military crackdown in East Pakistan came at the most inopportune moment. As Kissinger (1979) recalled in his memoir, he and Nixon had "every incentive to maintain Pakistan's goodwill. It was our crucial link to Peking; and Pakistan was one of China's closest allies. We had sent a message in December through Pakistan accepting the principle of an American emissary in Peking. In March and April the signs were multiplying that a Chinese response was imminent. April was the month of Ping-Pong diplomacy" (p. 853). In the midst of such expectations, Archer Blood's dispatch from Dhaka, now famously referred to as the "Blood telegram" of April 6 and signed by 20

American officials in East Pakistan, arrived in Washington with a stinging rebuke of Nixon–Kissinger policy. The "Blood telegram" (readily accessible electronically) read in part,

Aware of the Task Force proposals on "openess" [sic] in the foreign service, and with the conviction that U.S. policy related to recent developments in East Pakistan serves neither our moral interests broadly defined nor our national interests narrowly defined, numerous officers of AMCONGEN Dacca, USAID Dacca, and USIS Dacca consider it their duty to register strong dissent with fundamental aspects of this policy. Our government has failed to denounce the suppression of democracy. Our government has failed to denounce atrocities. Our government has failed to take forceful measures to protect its citizens while at the same time bending over backwards to placate the West Pak [sic] dominated government and to lessen likely and deservedly negative international public relations impact against them. Our government has evidenced what many will consider moral bankruptcy, ironically at a time when the USSR sent President Yahya a message defending democracy, condemning arrest of leader of democratically elected majority party (incidentally pro-West) and calling for end to repressive measures and bloodshed. In our most recent policy paper for Pakistan, our interests in Pakistan were defined as primarily humanitarian, rather than strategic. But we have chosen not to intervene, even morally, on the grounds that the Awami conflict, in which unfortunately the overworked term genocide is applicable, is purely internal matter of a sovereign state. Private Americans have expressed disgust with current policy and fervently hope that our true and lasting interests here can be defined and our policies redirected in order to salvage our nation's position as a moral leader of the free world. (Gandhi, 2002, doc. 8)

Archer Blood was unaware of the secret moves behind the so-called "Ping-Pong diplomacy" that the United States was undertaking in relation to China, as were most people in Washington, since this was a closely guarded and highly confidential presidential initiative. Blood was made to pay a very heavy price for his dissent in terms of his professional career, as Nixon ordered his transfer cum removal from Dhaka, and Kissinger, while in office as secretary of state, remained vindictive over the long haul, denying Blood another diplomatic posting abroad and, in effect, ending a career that had been full of promise.

Essentially, the China policy meant that any other issue or crisis that interfered with it was downgraded in the Nixon White House. This was the justification that Kissinger offered in explaining Nixon's policy toward the South Asian crisis of 1971. But this justification came wrapped in the language of high politics, of a professor turned practitioner of geopolitics, whose thinking on the subject went all the way back to when he was a student and then a teacher of international politics. In this sense, Kissinger was consistent as a realist thinker and scholar devoted to the study of world politics from the traditional perspective of power relations among international actors, and a concern with world order based on equilibrium among great powers, which he explored in his published works, such as *A World Restored: Metternich, Castlereagh and the Problems of Peace 1812–22* (1973), *Diplomacy* (1994), and his most recent book, *World Order* (2014).

As for his critics, in their view Kissinger's thinking and practice as a realist smacked of the amorality that, as many theorists of international relations have contended, was inherent in the realist approach (i.e., realpolitik). But remaining confident in his theoretical framework, Kissinger (1979) explained why he and Nixon were so misunderstood vis-à-vis "the Tilt" and how it impacted their reactions to the crisis in Bangladesh: "There is in America an idealistic tradition that sees foreign policy as a contest between evil and good. There is a pragmatic tradition that seeks to solve 'problems' as they arise. There is a legalistic tradition that treats international issues as juridical cases. There is no geopolitical tradition.... Our geopolitical concerns were given no credence and were attributed to personal pique, anti-Indian bias, callousness toward suffering, or inexplicable immorality" (p. 915).

When reading the above, one cannot fail to notice an exasperated note of self-pity. Kissinger (1979) ended the chapter with the comment, "And then it was all over. The crisis on the subcontinent did not linger and so there was no focal point for festering criticism" (p. 918). There was absolutely no reflection on Kissinger's part of what this crisis on the subcontinent meant to the people of a poor country born in the midst of violence and devastated by genocide: lives ruined by an almost year-long savage war, millions of refugees dislocated and made homeless, poverty and impending famine, and the immense need for assistance in rebuilding a country mostly destroyed. By complaining that the critics were wrong in accusing him and Nixon of callousness and immorality, Kissinger ironically confirmed the allegations that their critics, such as Archer Blood, had leveled at them.

The alternative to Nixon–Kissinger policy of "tilt" was giving stiff warning to the Pakistani generals that they would be held individually accountable for subverting the democratic transition of Bangladesh and terrorizing the civilian population with massacres, rapes, and torture in East Pakistan. Nixon and Kissinger might have posed the question to the generals that G.W. Choudhury (1993) asked: "The most pertinent question is whether the Pakistan Army would have taken such cruel measures *in West Pakistan* if Bhutto had taken the same position as Mujib on March 23, 1971.... Did not the Pakistan Army's action betray a deep-rooted ethnic hatred on the part of the Punjabis against the Bengalis?" (p. 182). Despite their bravado and public posturing, the generals were the oligarchic head of what had become a new aristocracy in Pakistan, squeezing the peasants and crushing any opposition that threatened its privileged status in the country. The military crackdown begun on March 25–26 was designed to crush the most serious challenge posed to this new aristocracy.

Nixon and Kissinger could have called the bluff of the generals on how far they were willing to go not merely against the Bengalis but also against the weight of world public opinion, the principles of the UN Charter, international law, and the understanding that the United States government would not shield them from prosecution—which would undoubtedly be demanded by the victims and a world outraged after having witnessed the carnage. The generals were in greater need of American support for their own survival than were Nixon and Kissinger of them. Nixon had done Yahya Khan an immense favor by choosing him to be his secret channel to Beijing, when an alternative was at hand in the person of the Romanian leader Nicolae Ceauşescu. Nixon and Kissinger could have warned the generals in private and then tested their response. In his memoir, Kissinger (1979) wrote, "There simply was no blinking the fact that Pakistan's military leaders were caught up in a process beyond their comprehension. They could not conceive of the dismemberment of their country; and those who could saw no way of surviving such a catastrophe politically if they cooperated with it. They had no understanding of the psychological and political isolation into which they had maneuvered their country by their brutal suppression" (p. 861).

Of course, Kissinger wrote these views retrospectively. If he had appreciated these facts in *real* time and not in hindsight, the crisis of Bangladesh *may* have been avoided. But Kissinger never broached such issues with the generals and, thus, we cannot know how they would have responded. Instead, Nixon and Kissinger assented to "the night of the generals" in East Pakistan/ Bangladesh and rationalized the slaughter of innocents as the necessary cost of the secret diplomacy with Beijing and the geopolitics of shaping a new equilibrium in world politics by bringing China into the equation.

## CONCLUSION

As I have discussed herein, the tragedy in East Pakistan/Bangladesh arose from the internal contradictions of Pakistan that doomed the country right from the start of its troubled history. Islam proved to be a fragile thread with which to bind into one nation people as ethnically diverse as the Baluchis of Baluchistan, the Bengalis of East Bengal or East Pakistan, the Pathans of the NWFP, the Punjabis of Punjab, the Sindhis of Sind, and the *Muhajirs* (Muslim refugees) from India in the aftermath of the partition in 1947— and that's not to mention the all-but-insurmountable physical divide between the East and the West with India in the middle. Among Bengalis there was a commonly told joke with a bitter edge: that although Pakistan was blessed with two wings, the middle of the bird was missing.

Once East Pakistan effectively challenged the dominance of West Pakistan or, more accurately, of the Punjabi military-civil and landed elite, the idea of the "two-nation theory" that had brought about the partition of India and the making of Pakistan snapped. Jinnah's formula was a brazen attempt to forge a "nation" out of the religious sentiments of a people, the Muslims of India, contrary to the historical record that Islam was insufficient by itself to bring Muslims together as a "nation" into one political entity. The eventual breakdown of Pakistan had been foreseen, but that such a breakdown would come about as a result of genocide was not imagined. The only question that then remains is whether the massacre begun on the night of March 25–26 was avoidable. In my view, it was avoidable and, therefore, the decision taken by Yahya Khan to launch Operation Searchlight to crush the Awami League in East Pakistan was both foolish and criminal. If, instead, Yahya Khan had allowed the political process he initiated to proceed to its logical end, a constitutionally engineered divorce would likely have been the eventual outcome, with East Pakistan and West Pakistan going their separate ways. The politicians could certainly have negotiated this divorce, thus avoiding war and genocide. I do not discount how hard and difficult it would have been to negotiate the dissolution of a country in this manner, but ultimately the undeniable geographical oddity of Pakistan would bear upon all parties, including the military. A country of "two wings" without a body and soul (the bird in the middle) was simply untenable, and, ultimately, despite the bravado of the Pakistan Army, its perpetration of savage killings could not, and did not, bind the two distant units of this physically divided country together once the Bengalis, as a majority population of Pakistan, became disillusioned with their place within it.

In the fifth century BCE, Thucydides reported, in the "Melian Dialogue" in *The Peloponnesian War*, that representatives of Athens counseled the assembled governing body of Melos to choose rightly in the circumstances of an impending war. The Athenians told the Melians that "the standard of justice depends on the equality of power to compel and that in fact the strong do what they have the power to do and the weak accept what they have to accept" (Thucydides, 1954, p. 402). In more ways than we wish to recognize, "the standard of justice," as reported by Thucydides some two and half millennia ago, remains operative to this day: the strong do what they wish to do in compelling the weak to comply, and when the weak refuse, then terror follows. Such was the tragedy that befell the people of Bangladesh in 1971.

The role of the United States in this tragedy was somewhat akin to that of Thucydides's Athens—one of a distant and mighty power, with the sense of purpose and responsibility that belong to great powers in history. Bangladesh was a faraway land, and its place, in terms of the global balance of power that preoccupied the thinking of both Nixon and Kissinger, was negligible. And just as the Athenians at war with Sparta were dismissive of the claims of the people of Melos, Nixon and Kissinger remained unmoved by what befell the people of Bangladesh, given that their priority was the consummation of the China policy pursued through the backdoor channel of the military regime in Pakistan. It is rare in history to find an example when moral considerations have trumped the politics of any great nation, calculated in terms of power and interest, or realpolitik, and the United States' conduct of foreign policy under Nixon and Kissinger during the South Asian Crisis of 1971 was in this sense, not surprisingly, unexceptional.

# REFERENCES

Azad, M.A.K. (1988). *India Wins Freedom*. New Delhi: Orient Longman.

Bass, G.J. (2013). *The Blood Telegram: Nixon, Kissinger, and a Forgotten Genocide*. New York: Alfred A. Knopf.

Bose, S.B. (2011). *Dead Reckoning: Memories of the 1971 Bangladesh War*. New York: Columbia University Press.

Bourke-White, M. (1949). *Halfway to Freedom*. New York: Simon and Schuster.

Choudhury, G.W. (1993). *The Last Days of United Pakistan*. Karachi: Oxford University Press.

Cohen, S.P. (1992). *Pakistan Army*. Karachi: Oxford University Press.

Collins, L., & Lapierre, D. (1976). *Freedom at Midnight*. New York: Avon Books.

Collins, L., & Lapierre, D. (1982). *Mountbatten and the Partition of India (vol. 1)*. New Delhi: Vikas Publishing House.

Gandhi, R. (1986). *Eight Lives: A Study of the Hindu-Muslim Encounter*. Albany: State University of New York Press.

Gandhi, S. (Ed.). (2002). *National Security Archive Electronic Briefing Book No. 79: 'The Tilt': The U.S. and the South Asian Crisis of 1971*. Washington, DC: George Washington University. Accessed at: http://nsarchive.gwu.edu/NSAEBB/

Government of India. (1971). *Bangla Desh Documents (vol. 1)*. New Delhi: Ministry of External Affairs.

Government of Pakistan. (1971). *White Paper on the Crisis in East Pakistan*. Islamabad: Ministry of Information and National Affairs.

Hajari, N. (2015). *Midnight's Furies: The Deadly Legacy of India's Partition*. New York: Houghton Mifflin Harcourt.

*Hamoodur Rahman Commission Report*. (1974). Accessed at: http://img.dunyanews.tv/images/docss/hamoodur_rahman_commission_report.pdf

International Crimes Tribunal-2. (2013). "The Chief Prosecutor vs. Abdul Quader Molla." ICT-BD Case No. 02 of 2012. Accessed at: https://bangladeshtrialobserver.files.wordpress.com/2013/02/qader-full-judgement.pdf

Jackson, R. (1975). *South Asian Crisis: India, Pakistan and Bangla Desh: A Political and Historical Analysis of the 1971 War*. New York: Praeger Publishers.

Keegan, J. (2002). *Winston Churchill: A Life*. New York: Penguin Books.

Khan, A. (1967). *Friends Not Master: A Political Autobiography*. London: Oxford University Press.

Kissinger, H. (1973). *A World Restored: Metternich, Castlereagh and the Problems of Peace 1812–22*. Boston: Houghton Mifflin Company.

Kissinger, H. (1979). *White House Years*. Boston: Little, Brown and Company.

Kissinger, H. (1994). *Diplomacy*. New York: Simon and Schuster.

Kissinger, H. (2014). *World Order*. New York: Penguin Press.

Kundera, M. (1981). *The Book of Laughter and Forgetting*. New York: Penguin Books.

LeBor, A. (2006). *"Complicity with Evil": The United Nations in the Age of Modern Genocide*. New Haven, CT: Yale University Press.

Mascarenhas, A. (1971). *The Rape of Bangla Desh*. New Delhi: Vikas Publications.

Nixon, R. (1978). *Memoirs of Richard Nixon*. New York: Grosset & Dunlap.

Obermeyer, Z., Murray, C.J.L., & Gakidou, E. (2008). "Fifty Years of Violent War Deaths from Vietnam to Bosnia." *BMJ (Clinical Research Ed.)*, *336*, 1482. Accessed at: http://www.bmj.com/content/336/7659/1482

Payne, R. (1973). *Massacre*. New York: The Macmillan Company.

Rummel, R.J. (1995). *Death by Government*. New Brunswick, NJ: Transaction Publishers.

Thucydides. (1954). *The Peloponnesian War* (R. Warner, Trans.). Harmondsworth, UK: Penguin Books.

Tuchman, B.W. (1985). *The March of Folly: From Troy to Vietnam*. New York: Ballantine Books.

# DOCUMENTS

More than four decades after the calamitous events that befell East Pakistan in 1971, we now have available declassified US government documents providing ample evidence that senior officials in the US Department of State had been briefed in regard to the planning and implementation of the aggressive actions by West Pakistan, which ultimately led to genocide in

Bangladesh (former East Pakistan). These documents detail why and how United States policy under the direction of President Nixon and Henry Kissinger came to be known as "the Tilt" toward Pakistan, which was under the military rule of General Yahya Khan. The latter was responsible for the bloody massacre, carried out with us-supplied weapons, against the unarmed civilian population of East Pakistan. Collectively, the documents provide damning evidence of the involvement of the Nixon administration, some of it direct and some of it indirect, in the tragedy that befell the people of Bangladesh in that fateful year of 1971.

## DOCUMENT 1

Document 1 is a two-page telegram dispatched by us Consul General Archer Blood from Dhaka, Bangladesh (former East Pakistan) to us Secretary of State William P. Rogers in Washington, DC, and copied to a number of us embassies and consulates in the region. Essentially, Blood reports on "a reign of terror being carried out by the Pak Military" in East Pakistan, indicating that evidence was surfacing that suggested that Awami League supporters and Hindus were being systematically targeted by the Martial Law Administrators.

Dated March 28, 1971, some 48 hours after the Pakistani military crackdown in Dhaka and other towns of Bangladesh had begun in the midnight hours of March 25–26, Blood's message to his superiors in Washington is stark, graphic, urgent, and deeply disturbing, informing them from "ground zero" of the impending genocide, which he fears awaits the Bengalis, especially the Hindus, of East Pakistan. Blood lists by name some of the Bengalis executed by Pakistani soldiers, and mentions reports of non-Bengali Muslims "systematically attacking" residential areas of Bengali Muslims and Hindus. This telegram removes any doubt as to whether or not Washington was informed of what was unfolding in Bangladesh in almost real time.

*Department of State*

**TELEGRAM**

CONFIDENTIAL 206

PAGE 01 DACCA 00959 280718Z

21
ACTION SS-45

INFO OCT-01 SSO-00 CCO-00 NSCE-00 /046 W
------------------------------------- 021278
O P 280540Z MAR 71
FM AMCONSUL DACCA
TO SECSTATE WASHDC IMMEDIATE 2989
AMEMBASSY ISLAMABAD
INFO AMCONSUL KARACHI PRIORITY
AMCONSUL LAHORE
AMEMBASSY LONDON
AMCONSUL CALCUTTA
AMEMBASSY BANGKOK
AMEMBASSY NEW DELHI
CINCSTRIKE
CINCPAC
MAC

C O N F I D E N T I A L   DACCA 0959
EXDIS
SUBJECT: SELECTIVE GENOCIDE

1. HERE IN DACCA WE ARE MUTE AND HORRIFIED WITNESSES TO A
REIGN OF TERROR BY THE PAK MILITARY. EVIDENCE CONTINUES TO
MOUNT THAT THE MLA AUTHORITIES HAVE A LIST OF AWAMI

LEAGUE SUPPORTERS WHOM THEY ARE SYSTEMATICALLY ELIMINATING
BY SEEKING THEM OUT IN THEIR HOMES AND SHOOTING THEM DOWN.

2. AMONG THOSE MARKED FOR EXTINCTION IN ADDITION TO A. L.
HIERARCHY, ARE STUDENT LEADERS AND UNIVERSITY FACULTY. IN
THIS SECOND CATEGORY WE HAVE REPORTS THAT FAZLUR RAHMAN,
HEAD OF APPLIED PHYSICS DEPARTMENT, PROFESSOR DEV, HEAD
OF PHILOSOPHY DEPARTMENT AND A HINDU, M. ABEDIN, HEAD OF
DEPARTMENT OF HISTORY, HAVE BEEN KILLED. RAZZAK OF POLITICAL
SCIENCE DEPARTMENT IS RUMORED DEAD. ALSO ON LIST ARE BULK
OF MNA'S ELECT AND NUMBER OF MPA'S.

3. MOREOVER, WITH SUPPORT OF PAK MILITARY, NON-BENGALI
MUSLIMS ARE SYSTEMATICALLY ATTACKING POOR PEOPLE'S
QUARTERS AND MURDERING BENGALIS AND HINDUS. STREETS OF
DACCA ARE AFLOOD WITH HINDUS AND OTHERS SEEKING TO GET
OUT OF DACCA. MANY BENGALIS HAVE SOUGHT REFUGE IN HOMES
OF AMERICANS, MOST OF WHOM ARE EXTENDING SHELTER.

4. TIGHTNING [SIC] OF CURFEW TODAY ( IT IS BEING REIMPOSED
AT NOON ) SEEMS DESTINED TO FACILITATE PAK MILITARY SEARCH
AND DESTROY OPERATIONS. THERE IS NO RPT NO RESISTANCE
BEING OFFERED IN DACCA TO MILITARY.

5. FULL HORROR OF PAK MILITARY ATROCITIES WILL COME TO
LIGHT SOONER OR LATER. I, THEREFORE, QUESTION CONTINUED
ADVISABILITY OF PRESENT USG POSTURE OF PRETENDING TO
BELIEVE GOP FALSE ASSERTIONS AND DENYING, FOR UNDERSTOOD
REASONS, THAT THIS OFFICE IS COMMUNICATING DETAILED
ACCOUNT OF EVENTS IN EAST PAKISTAN. WE SHOULD BE
EXPRESSING OUR SHOCK, AT LEAST PRIVATELY TO GOP, AT THIS
WAVE OF TERROR DIRECTED AGAINST THEIR OWN COUNTRYMEN BY

PAK MILITARY. I, OF COURSE, WOULD HAVE TO BE IDENTIFIED AS
SOURCE OF INFORMATION AND PRESUMABLY GOP WOULD ASK ME TO
LEAVE. I DO NOT BELIEVE SAFETY OF AMERICAN COMMUNITY
WOULD BE THREATENED AS A CONSEQUENCE, BUT OUR
COMMUNICATION CAPABILITY WOULD BE COMPROMISED. GP-3.
BLOOD


NOTE: BY OC/T: EXDIS CAPTION ADDED PER S/S-O, MR. NADZO, 3/28/71

CONFIDENTIAL


**Source**: US Consulate (Dacca). (1971, March 28). "Cable: Selective Genocide,
Confidential." In S. Gandhi (Ed.), *National Security Archive Electronic
Briefing Book No. 79: The Tilt: The U.S. and South Asian Crisis of 1971* (doc.
1). Washington, DC: George Washington University. Accessed at: http://
nsarchive2.gwu.edu/NSAEBB/NSAEBB79/BEBB1.pdf


## DOCUMENT 2

Document 2 is a one-page telegram sent from New Delhi by Kenneth
Keating, the US ambassador to India, to Secretary of State William P.
Rogers, in Washington, DC. Dated March 29, 1971, it followed the previous
day's telegram from US Consul General Archer Blood in Dhaka,
Bangladesh, to his superiors in Washington, DC (see above). In his telegram, Ambassador Keating expresses his dismay and concern at the
repression unleashed by the Martial Law Administrators, while informing
Secretary Rogers of the reported atrocities committed by the Pakistani
military against a defenseless population, as well as the likely damage to
the United States' reputation in the region and beyond as news trickles out
of the brutal actions of the Pakistani military and the fact that the atrocities
are being carried out with arms provided by the US government. Keating
recommends immediate suspension of US military assistance to Pakistan,
as he is fearful of how communists might exploit the tragedy in Bangladesh
for their ends.

*Department of State*

**TELEGRAM**

CONFIDENTIAL    884

PAGE 01 NEW DE 04494    291437Z

46
ACTION    SS-45

INFO  OCT-01  CCO-00  SSO-00  NSCE-00  /046 W
----------------------------- 026815
O P  291340Z  MAR 71
FM    AMEMBASSY NEW DELHI
TO    SECSTATE WASHDC IMMEDIATE 7787
INFO AMCONSUL DACCA PRIORITY
AMEMBASSY ISLAMABAD

C O N F I D E N T I A L  NEW DELHI 4494

EXDIS

SUBJECT: SELECTIVE GENOCIDE

REF: DACCA 0959
    AM DEEPLY SHOCKED AT MASSACRE BY PAKISTANI MILITARY IN EAST
PAKISTAN, APPALLED AT POSSIBILITY THESE ATROCITIES ARE BEING
COMMITTED WITH AMERICAN EQUIPMENT, AND GREATLY CONCERNED AT UNITED
STATES VULNERABILITY TO DAMAGING ALLEGATIONS OF ASSOCIATION WITH
REIGN OF MILITARY TERROR. I BELIEVE USG: (A) SHOULD PROMPTLY,
PUBLICLY AND PROMINENTLY DEPLORE THIS BRUTALITY, (B) SHOULD
PRIVATELY LAY IT ON LINE WITH GOP AND SO ADVISE GOI, AND (C) SHOULD
ANNOUNCE UNILATERAL ABROGATION OF ONE-TIME EXCEPTION MILITARY

SUPPLY AGREEMENT, AND SUSPENSION OF ALL MILITARY DELIVERIES UNDER
1967 RESTRICTIVE POLICY (SPARE PARTS, AMMO, NON-LETHAL, ETC). IT
[SIC] MOST IMPORTANT THESE ACTIONS BE TAKEN NOW, PRIOR TO
INEVITABLE AND IMMINENT EMERGENCE OF HORRIBLE TRUTHS AND PRIOR TO
COMMUNIST INITIATIVES TO EXPLOIT SITUATION. THIS IS TIME WHEN
PRINCIPLES MAKE BEST POLITICS. GP-3
KEATING

CONFIDENTIAL

**Source**: US Embassy (New Delhi). (1971, March 29). "Cable: Selective Genocide, Confidential." In S. Gandhi (Ed.), National Security Archive Electronic Briefing Book No. 79: The Tilt: The U.S. and South Asian Crisis of 1971 (doc. 3). Washington, DC: George Washington University. Accessed at: http://nsarchive2.gwu.edu/NSAEBB/NSAEBB79/BEBB3.pdf

## DOCUMENT 3

Document 3 is a three-page situation report dated March 31, 1971, sent by Archer Blood, the US consul general in Dhaka, Bangladesh (former East Pakistan), to US Secretary of State William P. Rogers in Washington, DC. Blood vividly describes the situation in Dhaka and elsewhere in the province less than a week after the Pakistani military crackdown began on the night of March 25.

Blood indicates that Martial Law Administrators were now cracking down on and carrying out atrocities in predominantly Hindu areas. More specifically, in his report, Blood informs the recipients of his cable of the systematic brutalities, tortures, rapes, and murder carried out by soldiers of the Pakistan Army and their non-Bengali Muslim collaborators against Bengali Muslims and Hindus. In doing so, he reports that naked female bodies had been found "with bits of rope hanging from ceiling fans," after apparently being "raped, shot, and hung by heels" from the fans. Officials of the US consulate were monitoring the events as reports of the massacre by the army circulated, and eyewitness accounts were collected.

The Martial Law Administrators and commanders of the Pakistan Army in East Pakistan had ordered all foreign journalists to report to the authorities in Dhaka immediately after the crackdown had begun, after which they were flown out of the province. Consequently, the only reliable reports immediately available were the eyewitness accounts collected by the officials in the US consulate, which were dispatched to Washington, DC, and various US embassies and consulates in the region.

### Department of State

### TELEGRAM

C O N F I D E N T I A L     120

PAGE  01  DACCA  01010  311520Z

51
ACTION NEA - 15

INFO  OCT - 01 EUR - 20  EA - 15  CCO - 00   SSO - 00 NSCE - 00  CIAE - 00
      DODE - 00 PM - 05  H - 02  INR - 08  L - 04  NSAE - 00  NSC - 10  P - 03
      RSC - 01 PRS - 01  SS - 20  USIA - 12  CU - 05  AID - 28  FBO - 01 NIC-01
      O - 03  OC - 08  OPR - 02  PER - 02  SCS - 04  SY - 03  RSR - 01   /175 W
      ---------------------------- 046225
P  R 311147Z  MAR 71
FM  AMCONSUL  DACCA
TO  SECSTATE  WASHDC  PRIORITY  3028
AMEMBASSY  ISLAMABAD
INFO AMEMBASSY BANGKOK
AMCONSUL  CALCUTTA
CINCPAC
AMCONSUL  KARACHI
CINCSTRIKE
AMCONSUL  LAHORE

AMEMBASSY LONDON
MAC
AMEMBASSY NEW DELHI

C O N F I D E N T I A L   DACCA   0101

SUBJECT: SITREP: ARMY TERROR CAMPAIGN CONTINUES IN DACCA:
EVIDENCE MILITARY FACES SOME DIFFICULTIES ELSEWHERE

1. DISTURBING ASPECT OF CURRENT SITUATION IS THAT WANTON
ACTS OF VIOLENCE BY MILITARY ARE CONTINUING IN DACCA. AS
CASE PREVIOUS NIGHTS, SCATTERED FIRING HEARD THROUGHOUT
NIGHT FROM VARIOUS PARTS OF CITY. HINDUS UNDENIABLY SPECIAL
FOCUS OF MILITARY BRUTALITY. SEVERAL LARGE FIRES WITNESSED
NIGHT OF MARCH 30-31. SHOTS HEARD EMANATING FROM ONE BURNING
AREA. CONGEN LOCALS SAY MOST OF THESE AREAS PREDOMINANTLY
HINDU. ONE FSL REPORTED HINDU TEMPLE AREA ON HIS STREET
SET ON FIRE BY ARMY THIS MORNING.

2. TRUCKLOADS OF PRISONERS SEEN GOING INTO EPR CAMP AT
PEELKHANA. STEADY FIRING HEARD IN AREA YESTERDAY AND TODAY.
CONGEN OFFICER HEARD STEADY FIRING OF APROXIMATELY 1 SHOT
PER TEN SECONDS FOR 30 MINUTES. TOLD SHOTS HAD BEEN FIRED FOR
WHILE BEFORE THEN.

3. ROUNDUP CONTINUING. ROOM-BY-ROOM CHECK OF HOTEL INTER-
CONTINENTAL CONDUCTED LAST NIGHT BY ARMY NCO AND TWO
ENLISTED MEN. REPORTS STUDENT ACTIVISTS STILL BEING PICKED UP.
TROOPS IN FIVE ARMY VEHICLES VISITED JAS COMPOUND AT
ISPAHANI FLATS WHERE MOTOR POOL ETC. LOCATED AT ABOUT 2215
MARCH 30. SEVERAL SCALED WALLS AND INSPECTED COMPOUND,
ALTHOUGH NO WINDOWS OR DOORS FORCED AND NOTHING SEEMED
DISTURBED. NIGHT WATCHMEN ON DUTY FLED HOWEVER AT APPROACH OF

MILITARY VEHICLES. TROOPS DEPARTED AFTER ABOUT FIFTEEN
MINUTES. GUARDS RETURNED IN MORNING.

4. ATROCITY TALES RAMPANT, INCLUDING THOSE OF RELIABLE EYE-
WITNESSES. BENGALI BUSINESSMAN NOT AL SUPPORTER SAW SIX NAKED
FEMALE BODIES AT ROKEYA HALL, DACCA U. FEET TIED TOGETHER. BITS
OF ROPE HANGING FROM CEILING FANS. APPARENTLY RAPED, SHOT AND
HUNG BY HEELS FROM FANS. WORKMEN WHO WERE FORCED TO DIG ONE
OF TWO MASS GRAVES AT DACCA U. REPORT 140 BURIED WITHIN.
OTHER GRAVE EQUALLY AS LARGE. JAPANESE REPORT [TOLD OF] 400
KILLED THERE. SERVANTS AND UNIVERSITY MAINTENANCE STAFF SHOT
DOWN. NUMEROUS REPORTS OF UNPROVOKED KILLINGS, INCLUDING BANK
OFFICIAL (NEIGHBOR OF AMERICAN USIS EMPLOYEE) WHO DROVE TO
UNIVERSITY TO INQUIRE INTO WHEREABOUTS OF RELATIVE THERE.

5. CENTRAL SHAHID MINAR (MARTYR'S MONUMENT) COMMEMORATING
PERSONS KILLED IN 1952 LANGUAGE MOVEMENT DEMOLISHED
MARCH 27 BY DEMOLITION CHARGES PLACED THERE BY ARMY.

6. ARMY BROADCASTS MONITORED HERE INDICATED ONE UNIT IN
DESPERATE SITUATION NEAR PABNA ON MARCH 30. LOW ON AMMUNITION.
CALLED FOR HELP, INCLUDING AIR STRIKES. TOLD TO HOLD OUT "AT ALL
COSTS." TOLD HELICOPTER DISPATCHED TO DROP FRESH ARMS AND
AMMO. WELL-CONNECTED SENIOR GOEP OFFICIAL (PROTECT SOURCE)
TOLD US ARMY HAS CONTROL OF RAG TOWN BUT UNABLE MOVE OUT.
BRITISH REPORT

MANY BANGLADESH FLAGS SEEN FLYING IN KUSHTIA. ACCORDING [TO]
OTHER REPORTS INDO-PAK BORDER AREA BETWEEN DINAJPUR AND
RAJSHAHI OPEN FOR MOVEMENTS BACK AND FORTH BY "RESISTANCE
FORCES." (COMMENT: WE HAVE NO WAY OF EVALUATING THIS
INFORMATION. FROM ARMY RADIO BROADCAST IT IS GATHERED
HOWEVER THAT AT LEAST SOME MILITARY UNITS MAY BE FACING

DIFFICULTIES IN PABNA AREA. TWO F-86'S SEEN TAKING OFF IN THAT GENERAL DIRECTION EARLY THIS MORNING). GP-3.
BLOOD

C O N F I D E N T I A L

**Source:** US Consulate (Dacca). (1971, March 31). "Cable: Sitrep: Army Terror Campaign Continues in Dacca; Evidence Military Faces Some Difficulties Elsewhere." In S. Gandhi (Ed.), *National Security Archive Electronic Briefing Book No. 79: The Tilt: The U.S. and the South Asian Crisis of 1971* (doc. 6). Washington, DC: George Washington University. Accessed at: http://nsarchive2 .gwu.edu/NSAEBB/NSAEBB79/BEBB6.pdf

## DOCUMENT 4

Document 4 is a five-page telegram labeled "Confidential" and was sent by Archer Blood, the US consul general in Dhaka, Bangladesh (former East Pakistan) to US Secretary of State William P. Rogers in Washington, DC, and copied to the US embassy in Islamabad and the US consulates in Karachi and Lahore, Pakistan. Dated April 6, 1971, it was sent nearly two weeks after the Pakistani military crackdown began on the night of March 25.

This dispatch by Archer Blood to Secretary Rogers would come to be referred to within the US government as "The Blood Telegram." Essentially, US officials in Dhaka, those attached to the consulate and others working in various US aid missions, expressed their dissent with US policy toward Pakistan and in doing so, expressed their outrage that Washington had not denounced the actions of the Pakistani military despite the mounting evidence of what was taking place in the eastern province of the country. This was one of the first of the "Dissent Cables" sent from the US consulate in Dhaka and signed by Archer Blood, in which he questions US morality at a time when "unfortunately, the overworked term genocide is applicable."

Archer Blood was fully aware that he was placing his own reputation and diplomatic career on the line by indicating to his superiors in Washington that he did not support the Nixon administration's support of the military run Pakistani Government, not to mention his expression of support concerning the right of those US citizens listed in the cable "to voice their dissent" as well. Blood was eventually recalled to Washington, and his diplomatic career was essentially terminated as Henry Kissinger saw to it that Blood was never again named US ambassador to another country.

Blood died in 2004. In gratitude for his courageous stand during their hour of greatest need and his support for their struggle to win independence, Bangladeshis honored him posthumously with an Outstanding Service Award, as well as their naming the American Center Library at the US embassy in Dhaka in his honor.

### Department of State

#### TELEGRAM

CONFIDENTIAL   084

PAGE 01   DACCA   01138   061008Z

21
ACTION   NEA - 08

INFO OCT -01 SS - 20 AID - 12 USIE -00  NSC - 10  NSCE - 00  CIAE - 00
        INR - 07  SSO - 00  RSR - 01  RSC - 01  /060  W
        --------------------------   092431
P  060730Z   APR 71
FM:  AMCONSUL DACCA
TO:   SECSTATE WASHDC PRIORITY 3124
AMEMBASSY ISLAMABAD
INFO AMCONSUL KARACHI
AMCONSUL LAHORE

C O N F I D E N T I A L   DACCA   1138
LIMDIS
SUBJ: DISSENT FROM U.S. POLICY TOWARD EAST PAKISTAN

JOINT STATE/AID/USIS: MESSAGE

1. AWARE OF THE TASK FORCE PROPOSALS ON "OPENESS" [SIC] IN THE FOREIGN SERVICE, AND WITH THE CONVICTION THAT U.S. POLICY RELATED TO RECENT DEVELOPMENTS IN EAST PAKISTAN SERVES NEITHER OUR MORAL INTERESTS BROADLY DEFINED NOR OUR NATIONAL INTERESTS NARROWLY DEFINED, NUMEROUS OFFICERS OF AMCONGEN DACCA, USAID DACCA AND USIS DACCA CONSIDER IT THEIR DUTY TO REGISTER STRONG DISSENT WITH FUNDAMENTAL ASPECTS OF THIS POLICY. OUR GOVERNMENT HAS FAILED TO DENOUNCE THE SUPPRESSION OF DEMOCRACY. OUR GOVERNMENT HAS FAILED TO DENOUNCE ATROCITIES. OUR GOVERNMENT HAS FAILED TO TAKE FORCEFUL MEASURES TO PROTECT ITS CITIZENS WHILE AT THE SAME TIME BENDING OVER BACKWARDS TO PLACATE THE WEST PAK DOMINATED GOVERNMENT AND TO LESSEN LIKELY AND DESERVEDLY NEGATIVE INTERNATIONAL PUBLIC RELATIONS IMPACT AGAINST THEM. OUR GOVERNMENT HAS EVIDENCED WHAT MANY WILL CONSIDER MORAL BANKRUPTCY, IRONICALLY AT A TIME WHEN THE USSR SENT PRESIDENT YAHYA A MESSAGE DEFENDING DEMOCRACY, CONDEMNING ARREST OF LEADER OF DEMOCRATICALLY ELECTED MAJORITY PARTY (INCIDENTALLY PRO-WEST) AND CALLING FOR END TO REPRESSIVE MEASURES AND BLOODSHED. IN OUR MOST RECENT POLICY PAPER FOR PAKISTAN, OUR INTERESTS IN PAKISTAN WERE DEFINED AS PRIMARILY HUMANITARIAN, RATHER THAN STRATEGIC. BUT WE HAVE CHOSEN NOT TO INTERVENE, EVEN MORALLY, ON THE GROUNDS THAT THE AWAMI CONFLICT, IN WHICH UNFORTUNATELY THE OVERWORKED TERM GENOCIDE IS APPLICABLE, IS PURELY INTERNAL MATTER OF A SOVEREIGN STATE. PRIVATE AMERICANS HAVE EXPRESSED DISGUST. WE, AS PROFESSIONAL PUBLIC SERVANTS EXPRESS OUR DISSENT WITH CURRENT POLICY AND FERVENTLY HOPE THAT OUR TRUE AND LASTING INTERESTS HERE CAN BE DEFINED AND OUR POLICIES REDIRECTED IN ORDER TO SALVAGE OUR NATION'S POSITION AS A MORAL LEADER OF THE FREE WORLD.

2. OUR SPECIFIC AREAS OF DISSENT, AS WELL AS OUR POLICY
PROPOSALS, WILL FOLLOW BY SEPTEL.

3. SIGNED:
BRIAN  BELL
ROBERT  L.  BOURQUEIN
W.  SCOTT  BUTCHER
ERIC  GRIFFEL
ZACHARY  M.  HAHN
JAKE  HARSHBARGER
ROBERT  A.  JACKSON
LAWRENCE  KOEGEL
JOSEPH  A.  MALPELI
WILLARD  D.  MCCLEARY
DESAIX  MYERS
JOHN  L.  NESVIG
WILLIAM  GRANT  PARR
ROBERT  CARCE
RICHARD  L.  SIMPSON
ROBERT  C.  SIMPSON
RICHARD  E.  SUTTOR
WAYNE  A.  SWEDENGURG
RICHARD  L.  WILSON
SHANNON L.  WILSON

4. I SUPPORT THE RIGHT OF THE ABOVE NAMED OFFICERS TO VOICE
THEIR DISSENT. BECAUSE THEY ATTACH URGENCY TO THEIR EXPRES-
SION OF DISSENT AND BECAUSE WE ARE WITHOUT ANY MEANS OF
COMMUNICATION OTHER THAN TELEGRAPHIC, I AUTHORIZE THE USE OF
A TELEGRAM FOR THIS PURPOSE.

5. I BELIEVE THE VIEWS OF THESE OFFICERS, WHO ARE AMONG THE
FINEST US OFFICIALS IN EAST PAKISTAN, ARE ECHOED BY THE VAST

MAJORITY OF THE AMERICAN COMMUNITY, BOTH OFFICIAL AND
UNOFFICIAL. I ALSO SUBSCRIBE TO THESE VIEWS BUT I DO NOT THINK
IT APPROPRIATE FOR ME TO SIGN THEIR STATEMENT AS LONG AS I AM
PRINCIPAL OFFICER AT THIS POST.

6. MY SUPPORT OF THEIR STAND TAKES ON ANOTHER DIMENSION. AS I
HOPE TO DEVELOP IN FURTHER REPORTING, I BELIEVE THE MOST LIKELY
EVENTUAL OUTCOME OF THE STRUGGLE UNDERWAY IN EAST PAKISTAN IS A
BENGALI VICTORY AND THE CONSEQUENT ESTABLISHMENT OF AN
INDEPENDENT BANGLADESH. AT THE MOMENT WE POSSESS THE GOOD WILL
OF THE AWAMI LEAGUE. WE WOULD BE FOOLISH TO FORFEIT THIS ASSET BY
PURSUING A RIGID POLICY OF ONE-SIDED SUPPORT TO THE LIKELY LOSER.
GP-3
BLOOD

NOTE BY OC/T: LIMDIS CAPTION ADDED PER S/S-O, MR. PASSAGE, 4/6/71.

## DEPARTMENT OF STATE
### Washington, D.C. 20520

### CONFIDENTIAL

April 6, 1971

The Honorable
William P. Rogers
Secretary of State
Washington, D.C.

Dear Mr. Secretary:

The undersigned officers, all of who have specialized in
South Asian affairs for the major portion of their service,
wish to associate themselves with the views expressed in

Dacca 1138 (copy attached) and to urge that the United
States Government take immediate steps to meet the
objections raised in paragraph one of the telegram.

                              Sincerely yours,


                         Craig Baxter  NEA/PAF
                         A. Peter Burleigh  NEA/INC
                         Townsend S. Swayze  AID/NESA
                         Joel M. Woldman    NEA/PAF
                         Anthony C.E. Quainton  NEA/INC
                         Howard B. Schaffer   NEA/EX
                         Douglas M. Cochran  INR/RNA
                         John Eaves, Jr.   NEA/P
                         Robert A. Flaten  NEA/PAF


                         CONFIDENTIAL

**Source:** US Consulate (Dacca). (1971, April 6). "Cable: Dissent from U.S. Policy Toward East Pakistan." In S. Gandhi (Ed.), *National Security Archive Electronic Briefing Book No. 79: The Tilt: The U.S. and the South Asian Crisis of 1971* (doc. 8). Washington, DC: George Washington University. Accessed at: http://nsarchive2.gwu.edu/NSAEBB/NSAEBB79/BEBB8.pdf

## DOCUMENT 5

Document 5 is a six-page secret "Memorandum for the President" prepared by Henry Kissinger for President Nixon. It is dated April 28, 1971, and in it Kissinger sets forth various policy options toward Pakistan for Nixon to choose from. Nixon had opted for quiet diplomacy in dealing with Pakistan's President and Chief Martial Law Administrator General Yahya Khan during the period leading up to the military crackdown in Bangladesh (former East Pakistan), which began on the night of March 25, 1971. During that period Nixon and Kissinger were preoccupied with the war in Vietnam and their secret effort to open relations with Communist China, and Yahya Khan had become instrumental in providing the backdoor channel for the US–China secret talks. Nixon had expressed his feelings to a Pakistani delegation about their military leader, declaring, "Yahya is a good friend." Kissinger shared Nixon's views.

In his six-page memorandum Kissinger comments that of the three policy options he believed that the third is the best. According to Kissinger, the third option "would have the advantage of making the most of the relationship with Yahya, while engaging in a serious effort to move the situation toward conditions less damaging to US and Pakistani interests." It was obvious Nixon read the memorandum, for he wrote in his own hand at the bottom of the last page for Kissinger and his White House staff, "To all hands: Don't squeeze Yahya at this time."

It might be said now, as we read these documents from 1971, that the Nixon and Kissinger "tilt" toward Pakistan was calculated and deliberate. It is also of interest that this memorandum was prepared a couple of weeks after the US national table tennis team had attended the World Table Tennis Championship in Nagoya, Japan, and from there had proceed onto China on April 10, 1971, for a friendly tournament with the Chinese team. This visit by the American table tennis team would be the first visit by any Americans to mainland China since the Communist takeover in 1949. The visit would be publicized in the US as "Ping-Pong diplomacy" and mark the beginning of the thaw in the US–China relations. In the context of this great geopolitical realignment that was secretly set in motion by Nixon, the quiet diplomacy and support for Pakistan throughout the South Asian Crisis of 1971 meant keeping General Yahya Khan close to Washington and not allowing the human tragedy unfolding in East Pakistan to become an obstacle in the path of Nixon's China initiative.

**MEMORANDUM**

**THE WHITE HOUSE**

**WASHINGTON**

ACTION

27870

APRIL 28, 1971

SECRET

MEMORANDUM FOR THE PRESIDENT

FROM:     Henry A. Kissinger

SUBJECT:    Policy Options Toward Pakistan

I do not normally bother you with tactical judgments. But in the
case of the present situation in Pakistan, policy depends on the
posture adopted toward several major problems. The purpose of
this memo  is to seek your guidance on the general direction we
should be  following.

The Situation

Three weeks after the West Pakistani military crackdown, these
three judgments seem to characterize the situation we must deal
with:

    -- The West Pakistani military seem likely to regain physical
    control of the main towns and connecting arteries. The
    resistance is too poorly organized and equipped to prevent that
    now.

    -- Physical control does not guarantee restoration of essential
    services like food distribution and normal economic life because
    that requires Bengali cooperation which may be withheld.

    -- Suppression of the resistance, even if achieved soon, will
    leave widespread discontent and hatred in East Pakistan, with

all that implies for the possibility of effective cooperation between the populace and the military, for eventual emergence of an organized resistance movement and for the unity of Pakistan.

-- Tension between India and Pakistan is at its highest since 1965, and there is danger of a new conflict if the present situation drags on.

Those judgments suggest that there will probably be an interim period, perhaps of some length, in which (a) the West Pakistanis attempt to re-establish effective administration but (b) even they may recognize the need to move toward greater East Pakistani autonomy in order to draw the necessary Bengali cooperation.

What we seem to face, therefore, is a period of transition to greater East Pakistani autonomy and, perhaps, eventual independence. How prolonged and how violent this period is will depend heavily on the judgments made in East and West Pakistan.

-- In the East, leaders of the resistance will be faced with the problem of weighing the political disadvantages of cooperating with a West Pakistani administration against the need to restore essential services, especially food distribution. Without that restoration, large-scale starvation seems unavoidable.

-- The West Pakistanis, on their part, face serious financial difficulties within the next several months. They have told us that unless they receive emergency foreign exchange help they will have to default on outstanding external loan repayments and restrict imports to the point of stagnating the economy and possibly bringing on a financial crash. It may well be that, as these costs become apparent to a wider group in West Pakistan, the pressure on President Yahya to let East Pakistan go will mount.

Outside actors will also play roles of varying significance:

-- India will be the most important. By training and equipping a relatively small Bengali resistance force, India can help keep active resistance alive and increase the chances of a prolonged guerrilla war. From all indications, the Indians intend to follow such a course. They could also make it difficult for Yahya to negotiate a political transition in East Pakistan by recognizing a Bengali government. They seem more cautious on this.

-- The US will be an important factor from outside the area: (a) We still have influence in West Pakistan and remain important to India. (b) US economic support--multiplied by US leadership in the World Bank consortium of aid donors--remains crucial to West Pakistan. Neither Moscow nor Peking can duplicate this assistance. (c) Our military supply, while relatively small and unlikely to affect the outcome of the fighting, is an important symbolic element in our posture.

-- The USSR is concerned that instability will work to China's advantage and has shown perhaps more inclination in recent years than the US toward trying to settle disputes in the subcontinent. In the short run, Soviet interests seem to parallel our own, although they would certainly like to use this situation to undercut our position in India.

-- Communist China could (a) be West Pakistan's main ally in threatening India with diversionary military moves and (b) eventually enter the contest with India for control of the East Pakistani resistance movement. For the moment, the Chinese seem to have cast their lot with the West Pakistanis.

The Options

The options are most clearly understood in terms of decisions on our ongoing programs. There are three, each described in terms of concrete actions that would be taken:

Option 1 would be essentially a posture of supporting whatever political and military program President Yahya chooses to pursue in the East. Specifically:

-- On economic assistance, we would support debt relief and go on with our full development aid program as soon as the West Pakistanis could assure us that the money would go for development purposes, not to financing the war effort. We would not concern ourselves that most of the aid would go to the West.

-- On food assistance, we would proceed with all shipments at the request of the government and state no conditions about how they distribute or withhold food from specific areas in East Pakistan.

-- On military assistance, we would allow all shipments but ammunition to proceed. We would delay ammunition without taking any formal action.

Option 2 would be to try to maintain a posture of genuine neutrality. Specifically:

-- On economic assistance, we would delay all further aid until the IMF and World Bank were satisfied that Pakistan has a

satisfactory development plan revised to take account of the
recent disruption in economic activity and to assure equitable
allocation of resources between East and West Pakistan.

-- On food assistance, instead of deferring to the West
Pakistani government on distribution, we would insist before
resuming shipments on assurance that food would be distributed
equitably throughout East Pakistan, in the cyclone disaster
area and in the countryside as well as in the army-controlled
towns.

-- On military assistance, we would have to defer all deliveries
of ammunition, death-dealing equipment and spare parts for it.
Non-lethal equipment and spare parts might continue.

Option 3 would be to make a serious effort to help Yahya end the
war and establish an arrangement that could be transitional to
East Pakistani autonomy. Such an effort would have to carry with
it the understood possibility that, if the political effort
broke down, US aid might have to be reduced by virtue of our
being unable to operate in the East. But our approach for the
time being would be to support emergency help for the Pakistani
economy to tide them over while we work with them in
restructuring their development program in both West and East.
We would not withhold aid now for the sake of applying pressure.
We would face that question only after giving the West
Pakistanis every chance to negotiate a settlement in the face of
the costs of not doing so. Specifically:

-- On economic assistance, we would state our willingness to
help in the context of a West Pakistani effort to negotiate a
viable settlement. We would have to point out that it will be

beyond US--or World Bank or IMF--financial capacity to help Pakistan if the situation drags on and Pakistan faces a financial crisis. We would also have to point out that US assistance legislation requires that economic aid be reduced to the extent that there is a possibility of its diversion to military purposes. We would back World Bank and IMF efforts to provide short-term emergency assistance while helping West Pakistan to reshape the rationale for the development lending program--but with the intent of providing a framework to move ahead, not of seeking a facade for cutting aid. To justify this approach, Yahya would have to produce an administration in East Pakistan that would have enough Bengali acceptance to win popular cooperation in restoring essential services and preventing a further constitutional crisis soon. In the meantime, we would continue to process any loans whose development purposes have not been disrupted by the war.

-- On food assistance, we would allow shipments to resume as soon a food could be unloaded and move into the distribution system. We would not stipulate destination, except perhaps for that amount committed to the cyclone disaster area. It would be implicit in our overall approach, however, that our objective would be the broad distribution that would come with restoring essential services.

-- On military assistance, we would take a line similar to that on economic aid. In practical terms, this would amount to allowing enough shipments of non-lethal spares and equipment to continue to avoid giving Yahya the impression we are cutting off military assistance but holding shipment of more controversial items in order not to provoke the Congress to force cutting off all aid.

<u>Comment on the Options</u>. My own recommendation is to try to work within the range described by Option 3 above.

-- <u>Option 1</u> would have the advantage of preserving our relationship with West Pakistan. It would have the disadvantage of encouraging the West Pakistanis in actions that would drag out the present situation and increase the political and economic costs to them and to us.

-- <u>Option 2</u> would have the advantage of creating a posture that would be publicly defensible. The disadvantage would be that the necessary cutback in military and economic assistance would tend to favor East Pakistan. We would be doing enough to disrupt our relationship with West Pakistan but not enough to help the East or promote a political settlement.

-- <u>Option 3</u> would have the advantage of making the most of the relationship with Yahya while engaging in a serious effort to move the situation toward conditions less damaging to US and Pakistani interests. Its disadvantage is that it might lead to a situation in which progress toward a political settlement had broken down, the US had alienated itself from the 600 million people in India and East Pakistan and the US was unable to influence the West Pakistani government to make the concessions necessary for a political settlement.

If I may have your guidance on the general approach you wish taken, I shall calibrate our posture accordingly on other decisions as they come up.

Prefer <u>Option 1</u>-- unqualified backing for West Pakistan_____

Prefer <u>Option 2</u> -- neutrality which in effect leans toward the
East_____

Prefer <u>Option 3</u> -- an effort to help Yahya achieve a negotiated
settlement_____

## SECRET

**Source:** "Memorandum for the President: Policy Options Toward Pakistan." (1971,
April 28). In S. Gandhi (Ed.), *National Security Archive Electronic Briefing
Book No. 79: The Tilt: The U.S. and the South Asian Crisis of 1971* (doc. 9).
Washington, DC: George Washington University. Accessed at: http://nsarchive2.
gwu.edu/NSAEBB/NSAEBB79/BEBB9.pdf

**Note:** In the original document, Kissinger writes his initials to choose
Option 3. His handwritten note also includes, "<u>Don't</u> squeeze Yaya [sic] at
this time."

# CHAPTER THREE

# "OUR HAND DOESN'T SHOW": THE UNITED STATES AND THE CONSOLIDATION OF THE PINOCHET REGIME IN CHILE (1973-1977)

Christopher Dietrich

## INTRODUCTION

On the night of October 16, 1998, London police arrested General Augusto Pinochet Ugarte in a hospital where he was recovering from surgery on a herniated disc. The police were serving an international arrest warrant issued by the Spanish judge Baltasar Garzón under the principle of "universal jurisdiction" vis-à-vis human rights atrocities. The reasons for Pinochet's arrest and trial are well known, and the phrasing of the arrest warrant was straightforward: The general was wanted for questioning for "crimes of genocide and terrorism that include murder" resulting from his government's reign of terror against political opponents in Chile from 1973 to 1990 (Kraus, 1998, p. A1). By the time of Pinochet's arrest, as Garzón noted in his warrant, precise statistics had been compiled by the high-profile Chilean National Commission on Truth and Reconciliation (CNCTR) that built on the early documentation work of human rights activists: 28,000 people tortured, 2,279 executed, and 1,248 disappeared (Chilean National Commission on Truth and Reconciliation, 1993).

But if Pinochet's government had come to symbolize the excesses of military rule in Latin America in the last third of the twentieth century, the question of whether or not the state-sponsored campaign of mass killing and terror constitutes genocide under the UN Convention on the Prevention and Punishment of the Crime of Genocide remains open. The Spanish court's extradition warrant claimed jurisdiction in part on the basis that Pinochet had been complicit in genocide and, under the UNCG, any signatory can undertake action against any individual who has been involved in genocide. Some critics of the Spanish warrant, including many who believed Pinochet should be charged with lesser human rights violations, held that the charge of "genocide" surpassed its definition, debased the term, and vitiated its moral force.[61]

This chapter does not seek to enter the legal or semantical debates about what constitutes genocide, terrorism, or a crime against humanity. Instead, in line with the focus of this book, it discusses the evolving relationship between the US government and the Pinochet regime between 1973 and 1977, the years in which most of the killing in Chile occurred. In that regard, it argues that the Nixon and Ford administrations, whose foreign policy was by this time dominated by Secretary of State Henry Kissinger, largely disregarded gruesome reports of state-sponsored torture, executions, and the systematic repression of the regime's political enemies in its first four years. In other words, the United States provided extensive political, economic, military, and organizational support for the Chilean dictatorship despite its detailed knowledge of Pinochet's campaign of terror and mass murder. The US government did so, in large part, in the name of fighting communism in Latin America.

This chapter first briefly discusses the question of whether or not the Chilean case constituted genocide. It then presents the consensus among historians of US foreign relations regarding US involvement in the September 11, 1973 coup against the government of Chilean President Salvador Allende. The next two sections delineate the human rights violations that occurred in the immediate aftermath of the coup, the Nixon and

---

61  For a review of the literature, see Totten (2008).

Ford administrations' knowledge of state repression in Chile, and US support for the dictatorship of Pinochet. The last section examines dissent within the United States to the policy of consolidating the power of Pinochet and, eventually, the curtailment of official aid in the late 1970s. The conclusion catalogs the efforts of groups in the United States from the 1980s to the present to examine and understand the meaning and context of US support for Pinochet in his first years in power.

## THE QUESTION OF GENOCIDE VERSUS CRIMES AGAINST HUMANITY

Various scholars, human rights organizations, and judicial bodies have cited the 1948 UN Convention on the Prevention and Punishment of Genocide (UNCG) to argue that the Chilean case amounted to genocide. Yet the Chilean Truth and Reconciliation Commission Report, also known as the Rettig Report, which documents the 3,200 victims over the course of the dictatorship, avoids the use of the term. Although it is not the purpose of this essay to make a determination of whether or not the Pinochet government committed genocide, the debate provides important contextual information for understanding the history of US involvement described below.

Political scientists Maureen S. Hiebert and Pablo Policzer provide an admirable discussion of the genocide debate in a recent edited volume on state violence in Latin America during the Cold War era (Hiebert & Policzer, 2009, pp. 64–80). They identify three key aspects of the definition of genocide: the identity of the victim group; the intent of the culprits; and the extent of the crime. In regard to the first issue, the identity of the victims, they note that the prey of the Pinochet regime were political actors—not ethnic, national, or religious minorities. It is common when defining genocide to note the exclusion of political groups from the definition of genocide victims in the 1948 Convention, based on a legal argument that members of political groups choose their identity, as opposed to members of racial, ethnic, or religious groups who "cannot escape their more 'primordial' identity and their resulting genocidal victimization" (Hiebert & Policzer, 2009, p. 65). Be that as it may, Hiebert and

Policzer argue that this definition is too narrow: it arose out of the political expediency of the early Cold War, and several scholars agree that there isn't much of a difference between the mass killing of political opponents and the mass killing of people of a different ethnicity or religion. What is most important, they argue, is the similarity between political genocide and other types: "It is the fact that the perpetrator defines them as members of a threatening group who must be destroyed which constitutes the basis of genocide" (Hiebert & Policzer, 2009, pp. 65, 67).

On the second question, the intention of the perpetrator, Hiebert and Policzer note that the debate over whether genocide should be characterized by outcomes or intention is an open one. Crucial to this question is whether or not there exists "special intent" to destroy a group of people based on their collective identity, which the authors describe as "an intentional and systematic attempt to physically eliminate an innocent, defenseless group of people" (Hiebert & Policzer, 2009, p. 70). In the Chilean case, they believe there is enough evidence of purposeful action and the explicit targeting of victims from left-wing parties to regard the Pinochet government's policies not just as dirty killings, but as genocide (Hiebert & Policzer, 2009, p. 70).

On the third criterion, the method of destruction, the UNCG defines five methods of destruction, of which two clearly occurred in Chile: killing members of the group and causing serious bodily or mental harm to members of the group. A third method defined in the UNCG also took place, according to Hiebert and Policzer, when considered in conjunction with the question of intent. This is the idea that Pinochet's opponents were targeted in the hope that they would not return to their former political activities (Hiebert & Policzer, 2009, p. 74).

This analysis is helpful in the sense that it raises the question of how scholars think about the killing and political violence in Chile. Less important than the question of genocide, what this and other discussions imply is the human cost of the Pinochet regime's gross human rights violations. It is to that cost, and the US' role in it, that this essay now turns.

## THE UNITED STATES AND THE 1973 COUP

There is no doubt that the Nixon administration used several policies to destabilize the democratically elected government of Pinochet's predecessor, Salvador Allende, between November 1970 and September 1973.[62] Allende's election, said Henry Kissinger, who wrote a memorandum to Nixon on November 5, 1970, "poses for us one of the most serious challenges ever faced in this hemisphere" (McElveen & Siekmeier, 2014b, n.p.). Not only was Allende a "tough, dedicated Marxist," but he came to power with "a profound anti-U.S. bias" that would likely lead to the nationalization of close to $1 billion in US investments (see Document 2; McElveen & Siekmeier, 2014b, n.p.).

Nixon and Kissinger called a meeting of the National Security Council to set policy toward Allende's Chile immediately after the election. In the meeting, Secretary of State William P. Rogers argued that the United States should "put an economic squeeze on him" so that his "economic troubles will generate significant public dissatisfaction," and Secretary of Defense Melvin Laird agreed that "we have to do everything we can to hurt him and bring him down" (McElveen & Siekmeier, 2014b, n.p.).

Informed by that and other discussions, Nixon and Kissinger set a public and covert policy toward Chile on November 9, 1970, just days after Allende's inauguration. According to National Security Decision Memorandum 9, the "public posture of the United States would be correct and cool." But the Nixon administration would also "seek to maximize pressures on the Allende government to prevent its consolidation," in particular through punitive economic diplomacy and the promotion of close relations with the "friendly military leaders" in Argentina and Brazil (McElveen & Siekmeier, 2014b, n.p.).

As a result, the Nixon administration conducted economic and psychological warfare against the Allende government until its ouster on September 11, 1973, with the object of making the Chilean economy "scream," as Nixon put it to CIA Director Richard Helms (McElveen &

---

62 The following section is indebted to Rabe (2012, pp. 122–43) and Harmer (2011). For an alternative interpretation, see Brands (2010, pp. 106–19).

Siekmeier, 2014b). Economic aid to Chile, which had reached a high point of $260 million in 1967, was lowered to less than $8 million in 1972. Food aid was cut. The Nixon administration also used its power at the International Monetary Fund, the World Bank, the Export-Import Bank, and the Inter-American Development Bank to limit loans to Chile. At the same time, the CIA helped fund a conservative propaganda campaign against Allende, in which opposition parties, business and trade associations, newspapers, and even a right-wing paramilitary group vocally cast into doubt the democratic credentials of Allende and his ruling coalition (Harmer, 2011, pp. 88–90, 130, 155–57, 183–86).

At the same time, the Nixon administration increased military aid and military equipment sales to Chile, in large part because it believed "the Chilean military were the key to any coup that might develop now or in the future" (Kornbluh, 2013, p. 147).[63] Between 1970 and 1973, the US government trained hundreds of Chilean soldiers on counterinsurgency, counterintelligence, subversion, interrogation, surveillance, and population control at the US Army School of Americas in the Panama Canal Zone (Harmer, 2011, pp. 90–91). The CIA also maintained close contact with top military leaders, including Augusto Pinochet Ugarte. A CIA spy reported in September 1972, for example, that Pinochet, "previously a strict constitutionalist, reluctantly admitted he was now harboring second thoughts: that Allende must be forced down or be eliminated." These options, Pinochet reportedly said, had become "the only alternatives" (Kornbluh, 2013, p. 144).

Hostility toward Allende was so visceral in the Nixon administration that US military officers exceeded their portfolio, and in a September 1972 meeting in the Panama Canal Zone, one even told Pinochet that "the U.S. will support a coup against Allende 'with whatever means necessary' when the time comes" (Kornbluh, 2013, p. 145). But most historians believe US involvement in the actual plotting and implementation of the coup was

---

63 This document, a CIA record of an October 18, 1972 meeting on Chile, is from the essential document collection by Peter Kornbluh of the National Security Archive, *The Pinochet File* (Kornbluh, 2013).

limited,[64] and existing evidence supports this interpretation. For example, CIA Director William Colby sent a memo to Kissinger on September 13, 1973, two days after the coup. In it, he concluded that a combination of US covert activity and Allende's own political-economic bungling had "strained the fabric of Chilean society to the breaking point." But he also noted that, "while the Agency was instrumental in enabling opposition political parties and media to survive and to maintain their dynamic resistance to the Allende regime, the CIA played no direct role" in the events that led to the seizure of the government and the bombing of the presidential palace on September 11, 1973 (Kornbluh, 2013, p. 160).

The imprecise role of the United States in the coup is reflected in the most famous declassified document about it: a telephone conversation between Nixon and Kissinger five days afterwards. After discussing the season opener of the Washington Redskins football team, Kissinger turned to the administration's common critique of the liberal media, this time for what he considered their gnashing of teeth over the overthrow of Allende: "Of course the newspapers are bleeding because a pro-Communist government has been overthrown." In the Eisenhower era, he continued, "we would be heroes." Nixon responded, "Well we didn't—as you know—our hand doesn't show on this one though." Kissinger agreed: "We didn't do it. I mean we helped them—created the conditions as great as possible" (McElveen & Siekmeier, 2014b, n.p.).

## THE ATROCITIES IN CHILE, 1973-1977

At one and the same time, Kissinger and Nixon were being both forthright and disingenuous when they claimed that the United States had nothing to do with the coup. It is clear that the United States contributed to what CIA Director Colby called "the political polarization" of Chile and engaged in policies designed to encourage political violence and stimulate economic ruin. A contingency paper written for the US National Security Council less than two weeks before the coup noted the effect of

---

64  See the discussions about "the blame game" in Harmer (2011, pp. 7–10, 272–73).

US policies in Chile: "The nation's political life is characterized by inflamed rhetoric, ever increasing civil violence and unchecked economic deterioration," the policymakers wrote. More and more, it seemed likely that the military would take action: "The nation's armed forces, traditionally remaining outside the political arena, have been increasingly drawn to the center of the political struggle" (McElveen & Siekmeier, 2014a, n.p.). Colby was even more forthright in a memorandum the next day to Kissinger, in which he noted the approval of continued funding for Chilean opposition parties: "Allende and his forces appear to be on the defensive, fearing a military coup and unsure of their ability to deal effectively with it if it comes," he wrote the secretary of state (McElveen & Siekmeier, 2014b, n.p.).

But if or how the United States aided the coup mattered little in the months that followed. More important was the immediate support the Nixon administration provided to consolidate the power of the military junta. This initial support came despite immediate evidence—known in the US government and, for that matter, across the world—that the arrival of the Pinochet regime was cruel in its violence.

Violence was endemic, despite claims to the contrary. The military junta released a series of radio declarations in its first hours in power that were meant to legitimize its rule. They claimed the military had a "moral duty" to overthrow the "illegitimate" government of Allende. "This is not a coup d'état, but a military movement," Pinochet said on the radio. The junta would not divide the nation into "victors or vanquished," but rather would work for all Chileans (Constable & Valenzuela, 1993, p. 19). These statements meant little in practice. The day after the coup, September 12, the military used constitutional war provisions to limit civilian rights and increase the use of military courts. Within the week, the junta declared all of Chile an official "emergency zone," ending any civilian authority. Several declarations followed that banned political parties, closed Congress, and declared independent newspapers subject to censorship. It was announced that any citizen who took a "belligerent attitude" was to be "executed on the spot" (Constable & Valenzuela, 1993, pp. 19–20).

Such a pitiless policy appears to have been more vindictive than necessary. According to the Rettig Report, resistance actions "can truly be said
to be minimal... they were uncoordinated and had not the slightest chance
of success, even locally" (Chilean National Commission on Truth and
Reconciliation, 1993, pp. 153–54). Within 48 hours, all armed activity had
come to a virtual halt and public order was restored. Deposed government
officials ceded their positions and most of those ordered by decree to hand
themselves in did so voluntarily.[65]

These policies allowed the armed forces and police to achieve their
primary objective, which was to bring the country under control and eliminate any resistance from Allende supporters. Yet they were followed by
wholescale and increasingly deathly repression. Arrest lists were drawn up
and used in a methodical fashion, and initially were aimed at the top leaders of the overthrown government, mid-level leaders that had worked in
agrarian reform or the Ministries of Health and Housing, leaders of labor
unions and local civil society organizations, and members of the media.
Soon, roundups became routine in the countryside, where police arrested
local officials, political party leaders, and anyone else considered an "agi-
tator." Raids were also carried out in large factories in major cities, whereby
thousands more were arrested (Chilean National Commission on Truth
and Reconciliation, 1993, pp. 155–56, 161–62).

By the new year, the military regime had arrested 45,000 Chileans. There
were several detention sites, as police stations, regimental army bases, and
even ships were repurposed to handle the overflow of the nation's jails. These
locations were not prepared to handle prisoners, and the conditions were
degrading: bedding, toilets, food, medicine, and other basic services were
inadequate. The prisoners were also completely cut off from the outside
world. The situation also began to gain permanency. If the prisoners were
not released after the initial interrogations in these locations, they were set
to appear before war tribunals. After interrogation and sentencing by the war

---

65 On the Rettig Report and other truth and reconciliation commissions in general, see
Grandin (2005, pp. 46–67).

tribunals, they were generally sent to jails or prison camps (Chilean National Commission on Truth and Reconciliation, 1993, pp. 156–57).

To understand the situation as it was lived, it is best to turn to the Report of the Chilean National Commission on Truth and Reconciliation: "Their families were waiting outside these places. They knew or had been told that their relatives had been arrested, that they were here—or over there—at some prison site. They even regularly took clothing or food to that site. Then on some fateful day . . . their loved ones were no longer there. Sometimes families were told that they had never been there. Or that they had been transferred somewhere else—where it was then denied. Or that they had been released. Other times the answer was ridicule, a threat, a sinister hint" (Chilean National Commission on Truth and Reconciliation, 1993, p. 157). As political repression became more normal in the following months, information about living conditions and the fortune of political prisoners became "more acceptable" to the regime. War tribunals began to publicly sentence people to prison terms, and inmates were allowed visits and other contact (Chilean National Commission on Truth and Reconciliation, 1993, pp. 157–58).

Many people did not have the benefit of a trial or a sentence, though. For them, arrest was a prelude to execution. Many of the killings immediately following the coup, for example, were executions of individuals who were deemed political threats. The United States again played a central, and enveloping, role. There is substantial evidence that the extent of this sort of killing derived from the more general trend, led by the United States, of the development of counterinsurgency campaigns in Latin America—the effect of a 15-year search by the US military for a tactical response to the guerilla warfare techniques that concerned US officials during and after the 1959 Cuban Revolution.[66] Chileans, of course, were among the generations of Latin American officers that passed through US military training schools,

---

66 On counterinsurgency in general, see Grandin & Joseph (2010). Of particular importance is the chapter by Peter Winn in this collection, "The Furies of the Andes: Violence and Terror in the Chilean Revolution and Counterrevolution" (pp. 239–75).

and the military junta pursued a spontaneous but organized "cleanup" operation aimed at those citizens regarded as dangerous for their political activities or ideas (Chilean National Commission on Truth and Reconciliation, 1993, pp. 162–63).[67]

The killing also stretched to the common citizenry. At the beginning, the two most notorious detention sites were sports facilities: the Chile Stadium and the National Stadium, where torture and executions were commonly carried out. In one famous example, the body of the folk singer and official of the Allende government Victor Jara, who was tortured in the Chile Stadium, was found with 44 bullet holes and his face and hands extremely disfigured. Jara's murder became the most famous case of the new Chilean atrocities, because his British wife, Joan Turner Jara, pursued a relentless campaign against the regime in Europe (Jara, 1983). But Victor Jara was just one of many Chilean citizens, activists, and national, regional, and local officials who supported Allende that were also murdered in the days following the coup. The violence also extended further into society. The bodies of habitual criminals, youth drug addicts, long-standing alcoholics, and petty thieves were found mysteriously in morgues, on the street, or they simply "disappeared." Many other people were killed for breaking curfew. In the six weeks after the coup, it is estimated that at least 1,500 civilians were killed, many tortured to death or executed by firing squads (Chilean National Commission on Truth and Reconciliation, 1993, pp. 164, 167, 181–82).

Thousands were also shipped to prison camps, where torture became common. Methods were extremely varied, but several manners of torture reappeared again and again. The Rettig Report again provides a telling summary:

> An almost universal technique was violent and continual beating until blood flowed and bones were broken. Another form was to make detention conditions so harsh that they themselves constituted torture,

---

67  On the development of counterinsurgency as a widespread policy in Latin America, see Rabe (1999, pp. 127–47).

for example, keeping prisoners lying face down on the ground or keeping them standing rigid for many hours; keeping them many hours or days naked under constant light or the opposite, unable to see because of blindfolds or hoods, or tied up.

It was also common to hang prisoners up by their arms for very long periods or hold them under water to the brink of suffocation. Simulated firing squads were also commonly used, as were sexual degradation and rape. It was less commonplace, but still ordinary, that prisoners would be mistreated in front of loved ones. (Chilean National Commission on Truth and Reconciliation, 1993, pp. 157–58)

The Academy of Military Engineers of the Tejas Verde Military School, located in the town of San Antonio, was an important site in the first six weeks after the coup. Prisoners were transported in refrigerated trucks requisitioned from fishing companies to the school for interrogation. They were kept blindfolded or hooded during their trips and, once at the school, they were taken to one of two interrogation rooms. Once in the interrogation room, the prisoner was stripped naked, tied to a metal bed frame, and beaten. Electric current was often applied, normally in the mouth or on the genitals. Doctors, also hooded, were present to prevent unwanted deaths and give emergency treatment when necessary. Often, following the torture, prisoners were sent to what were called "niches" underneath the guard towers. Constructed out of gates welded together, these cages were used to keep prisoners immobile for days, without food or toilet facilities (Chilean National Commission on Truth and Reconciliation, 1993, pp. 159–60).

The institutional history of the Tejas Verdes Military Engineer School also reveals how the deadly state of suppression and human rights abuses became permanent after the awful first four months of the dictatorship. This is because Tejas Verdes became the main operations center of the Directorate of National Intelligence (DINA), the notoriously violent police agency led by Manuel Contreras Sepulveda from 1974 to 1977. In the words of one historian, Contreras became the man who "worked behind the scenes, controlling life and death in the country through the intimacy of the bond with Pinochet" (Dinges, 2012, p. 65). Between 1974 and 1977, DINA became the dominant national intelligence service engaged in political repression. Tejas Verdes was transformed into a detention center known as Prison Camp No. 2, and it became the prototype of a web of secret detention facilities where Contreras and his growing forces tortured and executed thousands of Chilean citizens. Historians estimate that approximately 1,100 Chileans were "disappeared" during the Pinochet regime, most at the hands of DINA (Kornbluh, 2013, pp. 166–71).

## US AID TO CHILE

The nature of Pinochet's rule was well known in the US government and the international community from its earliest days. The brutality that followed the coup was also immediately plain to the larger American public, through media reports and high-profile congressional investigations. "The death toll is unprecedented in Latin American history," Amnesty International officials wrote in September 1974. In December of that year, the Inter-American Commission on Human Rights charged the Pinochet government with "extremely serious violations" of human rights (Schoultz, 1981, pp. 12–13). "A documented case can be made for the proposition that the current regime in Chile is militaristic, fascistic, tyrannical and murderous," one State Department official wrote in February 1974 (Kornbluh, 2013, p. 209). Critics had "plenty of ammunition based on the excesses accompanying Salvador Allende's overthrow and the alleged abuses that still mark Chile's security and detention practices," CIA analysts reported later. "The Pinochet regime moves across the world scene like a metal duck in a shooting gallery" (Kornbluh, 2013, p. 171).

The top decision-makers in the US government knew of these abuses from the moment the coup began. CIA Director William Colby testified before Congress in October 1973 that between 2,000 and 3,000 people had been killed in Chile, many by summary execution. Colby's declaration about these statistics reveal two important facts: first, that the CIA knew that the death toll was abnormal and, second, that the death toll was so excessive that the CIA could not accurately tally the casualties. The CIA station in Santiago reported on September 20 that more than 4,000 deaths had resulted from the coup and "subsequent clean-up operations" (see Document 3). By the end of that month, reports from the CIA, including a "highly sensitive" report prepared within the Chilean Junta, were used to prepare a secret briefing paper for Kissinger entitled "Chilean Executions" (see Document 4). The report, which lists the number of deaths at around 1,500, confirms knowledge, if imprecise, at the highest levels of US foreign policymaking of the detention and executions of Chilean citizens (see Document 5).

It is clear too, that US intelligence agents knew about specific atrocities. For example, the CIA reported in detail on the massacres of the "Caravan of Death" of October 1973, in which a five-man team of military officers traveled through the countryside, trying and executing the old government's local officials and others identified as "dangerous" to the new regime. The actions of General Sergio Arellano Stark, the leader of the tour, were an example of the fact that the military would "continue to act against any person taking belligerent action against law and order," the CIA reported. Analysts described Stark's operation as part of the larger campaign to "neutralize extremists" (Kornbluh, 2013, pp. 164–65).

Despite these abuses, and his immediate knowledge of the savage nature of the new regime, there was never any doubt for Henry Kissinger that the United States would support Pinochet. After all, it had been the Nixon administration's policy to destabilize the Allende government. President Nixon held off on official recognition of the new government for public relations reasons, but Kissinger directed US officials to reassure their Chilean military counterparts of US support. On September 13, 1973, two days after the coup, Kissinger instructed the US ambassador in Chile to "make clear its [that is, the US government's] desire to cooperate with the military junta" (Rabe, 2012, p. 137). The State Department also urged the ambassador to tell top Chilean officials that it was US policy to make relations "as positive and constructive as friends can make them" (McElveen & Siekmeier, 2014b, n.p.). "We want GOC [Government of Chile] to know of our strongest desire to cooperate closely and establish firm basis for cordial and close constructive relationship," Kissinger and his deputy at the National Security Council, Brent Scowcroft, wrote to the American Embassy again later that month (Kornbluh, 2013, p. 210).

Secretary of State Kissinger discussed his policy and rationale with Assistant Secretary of State for Latin America Jack Kubisch at a staff meeting on October 1. The United States would press the regime to end atrocities, but it would "not support moves against them [the Pinochet government] by seeming to disassociate ourselves from the Chileans," he said. "I think we should understand our policy—that however unpleasant they act, this government is better for us than Allende was" (Digital National Security Archive, n.p.). Kubisch thus told a House Foreign Affairs subcommittee that "if the Chileans want our help and we can give it, it would be my hope and expectation that we would do everything we could to provide it" (Schoultz, 1981, p. 188).

Such help to "maintain and strengthen the present Chilean government," to use the words of a declassified State Department record, was extended at massive levels between 1973 and 1977 (US Department of State, 1999b, n.p.). It took several different forms: direct economic and military aid, the training of military and economic experts, support in multilateral financial institutions, and covert aid in propaganda and to DINA. This assistance was vital for the regime's consolidation of power and ability to continue to suppress political opposition.

American largesse began with the disbursal of food aid on October 6, 1973, when the US Department of Agriculture granted $24 million in commodity credits for wheat to alleviate food shortages. In November, the US government granted another $24 million for feed corn. Kissinger's report of this credit was attached to the same memorandum, "Chilean Executions," described above. This was just the beginning of massive food aid for the regime—aid which had been denied to the Allende government. Under the Public Law (PL) 480 program of food aid, Chile received $132 million in the first three years of the military government. In 1975 and 1976, the Pinochet regime received 80 per cent of all PL 480 Title 1 funds for Latin America (Kornbluh, 2013, p. 212).

The exceptional amount of food aid was complemented by new loans from the World Bank and the International Development Bank, pushed through by the United States. Loans from the two institutions totaled $11.6 million dollars for the Allende government. From 1974 to 1976, that number rose to $237.8 million from International Development and $66.5 million from the World Bank for the Pinochet regime. The US government also helped Chile renegotiate its debt with private lenders and secure private loans from commercial banks (Kornbluh, 2013, pp. 212–13).

Food and economic aid opened up foreign exchange for Chile, much of which was used to buy arms from the United States. Chile was the fifth best customer of US arms manufacturers in the world by 1977, and the only nation in the top five not located in the Middle East (Kornbluh, 2013, pp. 213-14). A significant part of their purchases included equipment that could be used for repression, including "tear gas grenades and riot control items," armored personnel carriers, communications systems, rifles, submachine guns, and ammunition (US Department of State, 1999c; US Department of State, 1999g; see also Kornbluh, 2013, pp. 213–14).

On top of this, the CIA and the US military also continued their clandestine activities in Chile. A week after the coup, US Ambassador Nathaniel Davis approved a local CIA request to finance a "small network" of media outlets that would mount "a propaganda campaign to popularize the Junta's programs." This program would support their ongoing news asset, the *El Mercurio* newspaper empire of Agustín Edwards. CIA officials also helped the Junta write the *White Book of the Change of Government in Chile*, a manual that was widely distributed in Chile, in the United States, and abroad. The *White Book* argued for the societal benefits of the Allende overthrow, based on a critique of the ostensibly authoritarian Allende government and the promise of market-led economic growth. In October 1973, the CIA secretly underwrote an international tour in which a group of prominent Christian Democrats—the main opposition party to Allende—justified the coup to the international community (CIA, 2000).

After a series of internal debates, the CIA's covert propaganda action was closed down in the summer of 1974. But the CIA continued to operate in Chile, shifting the emphasis from propaganda to the creation of a working relationship with DINA. Throughout the period in which Manuel Contreras and his subordinates constructed and used their network of detention and torture centers, the CIA provided organizational training to "combat subversion and terrorism from abroad." This training explicitly prohibited CIA support for "any activities which might be construed as 'internal political repression,'" but CIA officials acknowledged that the support "could be adaptable to the control of internal subversion as well" (CIA, 2000).

Although the CIA has not declassified much information on the details of its support of DINA, US officials at the time clearly understood the nature of DINA. In February 1974, for example, the US air[force] attaché in Santiago reported to the Pentagon on the power of Contreras and DINA to control the country's judicial system: "No judge in any court or any minister in the government is going to question the matter any further if DINA says that they are now handling the matter" (Dinges, 2012, p. 65). His sources said, "there are three sources of power in Chile: Pinochet, God, and DINA." Other US military officers called DINA a "modern day Gestapo" and "a KGB-type organization." There is also conclusive evidence that Contreras was on the CIA payroll, at the very least, in May and June of 1975 (Kornbluh, 2013, p. 244).

## DISSENT AND THE END OF AID

All this support came despite recognition by the Ford administration that the extent of Chilean brutality would eventually force a change in diplomacy. The viability of supporting such a malevolent and bloody regime became clear in September 1974, when an aide in Senator Frank Church's office leaked evidence of covert activities approved by Nixon and Kissinger from 1970 to 1973. In July 1975, CIA Director William Colby testified to a closed Senate hearing on Agency activities designed to unseat the Allende government. These were leaked, adding further fuel to the scandal (Kornbluh, 2013, pp. 226–30).

Media outlets in the United States, most notably Seymour Hersh at *The New York Times*, consistently reported on the abuses of the Pinochet regime in the mid-1970s, including those of Manuel Contreras and DINA.

Meanwhile, the new regime continued to govern under martial law. The military junta censored the media, held book burnings, and continued to imprison, torture, and execute its political opponents. A steady flow of often harrowing information emerged out of the country, often through first-hand reports gathered by Amnesty International, the UN High Commissioner for Refugees, university faculty fact-finding missions, or clergy groups (Keys, 2014, pp. 168–70). One Amnesty International board member, Rose Styron, published an account of Chilean torture in *The New York Review of Books*. It was filled with horrific detail. In one instance, she wrote, before the singer Victor Jara's body was disposed of, his captors in the National Stadium had commanded him to play his guitar while they broke and then cut off his fingers. "As an example," she continued, his body was "strung up in the foyer of the stadium" (Styron, 1974, n.p.).[68]

In that context, Hersh revealed that Kissinger was actively preventing his staff from fulfilling human rights instructions from Congress, especially those regarding military aid. The secretary of state rebuked his ambassador in Chile for bringing up human rights issues during those discussions, Hersh explained in *The New York Times*. This led officials in the State Department and White House to tell Hersh that Kissinger's actions were part of a broader "demonstration of the Administration's unwillingness to press fully the human rights issue with the junta now ruling Chile" (Hersh, 1974, p. 18). As a result of these revelations and others, Chile became the topic of a protracted battle over human rights and US foreign policy between the White House and Congress from 1974 to 1976. Led by Donald Fraser, Tom Harkin, and others in the House, and Edward Kennedy, James Abourezk, and George McGovern in the Senate, Congress passed groundbreaking legislation linking human rights to foreign aid that was designed to block the support the Ford administration had given to Pinochet (Keys, 2014, pp. 75–102).

The Ford administration essentially ignored the limits to economic and military aid set by Congress and continued apace to send food, materials, and

---

68  Keys (2014, pp. 168–70).

credits to Chile in 1975 and 1976. Kissinger was again instrumental in this process, scorning human rights in foreign policy as "easy slogans," "empty posturing," "sentimental nonsense," and "malarkey" (Keys, 2014, p. 166). For Kissinger, this also had to do with the executive branch's control over foreign policy. When an assistant secretary argued that compromising with Congress on aid was necessary, Kissinger responded, "There is a more fundamental problem. It is a problem of the whole foreign policy that is being pulled apart, pulling it apart thread by thread, under one pretext or another." Essentially, Kissinger argued, if the State Department began to give way to Congress on human rights violations in Chile, no non-democratic US ally would be safe from sanctions. "There isn't going to be any end to it," Kissinger said. "We have to make a stand now" (Keys, 2014, p. 171).

Secretary of State Kissinger made it abundantly clear that this general opinion on human rights applied directly to the Pinochet regime: "The Chilean aid cut is disastrous," he told President Ford on December 20, 1974. "I want to do everything possible to get arms to Chile" (see Document 6). In the following year, Kissinger and other officials in the Ford administration disparaged the idea that human rights should affect aid policy. "I hold a strong view that human rights are not appropriate in a foreign policy context," Kissinger told Chilean Foreign Minister Patricio Carvajal in 1975. The Ford administration, he assured Carvajal, "did not intend to harass Chile on this matter" (Kornbluh, 2013, p. 236). In another meeting with Carvajal, Kissinger complained that State Department briefing papers were "nothing but Human Rights. The State Department is made up of people who have a vocation for the ministry. Because there were not enough churches for them, they went into the Department of State." In the same meeting, Kissinger and Carvajal discussed continued arms sales, PL 480 aid, and the attempts of the Pinochet regime to "bring the country back to normalcy" (see Document 7).

But faced with the trenchant critique described above and continued evidence of what the UN Commission on Human Rights called in February 1976 "barbaric sadism," the Ford administration began to distance itself from the Pinochet government (Schoultz, 1981, p. 13). This made sense to several US officials, including Richard Bloomfield in the policy planning section of the State Department's Latin American Bureau. In response to suggestions by the US ambassador in Chile, David Popper, that lower amounts of aid would upset the Pinochet regime, Bloomfield wrote in July 1975 that "actions speak louder than words." He took umbrage with Popper's statement that "preventing the re-emergence of a Chilean Government essentially hostile to us is our chief interest and the human rights problem is secondary." For Bloomfield, human rights was not secondary but a major interest: "In the minds of the world at large, we are closely associated with this junta, ergo with fascists and torturers.... Chile is just the latest example for a lot of people in this country of the United States not being true to its values" (see Document 8).

Such arguments led to a change in the United States' public position. In November 1975, the United States voted to support a US General Assembly resolution conveying the international community's "profound distress at the constant, flagrant violations of human rights, including the institutionalized practice of torture" in Chile (Schoultz, 1981, p. 131). In June 1976, Kissinger told the foreign ministers of the Organization of American States (OAS) that human rights violations had "impaired our relationship with Chile and will continue to do so." He told the delegates there, who had been presented with a very critical report of human rights abuses by the Inter-American Commission on Human Rights, that he had sought to persuade Pinochet to reconsider and accept responsibility for his government's actions. He also said he believed the Pinochet government's human rights violations had "undergone a quantitative reduction."[69]

But this was window dressing for Kissinger, not a shift in policy toward the Chilean regime. In June 1976, he went to Santiago to meet with Pinochet and forewarn him of the OAS speech. The declassified transcript of his conversation with Pinochet reveals that his intent was actually to let Pinochet know that the speech was intended to appease the critics in the US Congress, not to pressure him. "This speech is not aimed at Chile," he assured Pinochet.

---

69  Department of State, 1976, p. 4.

"None of this is said with the hope of undermining your government. I want you to succeed and I want to retain the possibility of aid" (see Document 9).

Such a hands-off policy became far less likely on September 21, 1976, when Chilean agents assassinated Orlando Letelier, the former Chilean ambassador, and his American assistant, Ronni Karpen Moffitt, with a car bomb on embassy row in Washington, DC. Letelier was a vocal critic of the Pinochet regime because of his own and others' torture, as well as the role of the famous "Chicago Boys" free market economists in the new regime. His assassination, not to mention that of his American assistant, strained US–Chilean relations. The US State Department moved to reinforce earlier Congressional sanctions and, after the election of Jimmy Carter as president in 1976, US–Chilean relations reached a nadir (Walker, 2011). By the end of the day, several US senators and representatives had publicly eulogized Letelier and Moffitt (Dinges & Landau, 1980). When it came into office in January 1977, the Carter administration immediately recommended sanctions against Chile because of the Pinochet's pitiful human rights record. The administration is well known for its diplomatic commitment to human rights, and Carter himself had sent a telegram to Letelier's widow. But, despite a nod or two toward change, including the disbandment of DINA, the Pinochet government continued to employ repressive tactics to snuff out pockets of opposition. The CIA reported in May 1977 that the Pinochet government was "reverting to the practices that have jeopardized its international standing since the 1973 coup" (Walker, 2011, pp. 109, 119–20).

In 1978, after a year and a half of investigations, the federal government extradited US citizen and former DINA agent Michael Townley from Chile. His testimony and confession in the Letelier assassination led to the US indictment of three Chilean officials, including former head of DINA Manuel Contreras. The Chilean refusal to extradite the men led to calls by Senators Edward Kennedy and Frank Church for the Carter administration to impose heavy sanctions on the regime. Assistant Secretary Patricia Derian, the director of the Office of Human Rights and Humanitarian Affairs, also argued for sanctions. She was opposed, however, by the Latin American Bureau in the State Department, whose head, Viron Vaky, believed sanctions would upset ongoing bilateral relations between Chile and the United States. Vaky argued, successfully, that the harshest sanctions—the termination of private bank loans or the complete withdrawal of the US ambassador from Chile—"would have no positive effect on the Letelier case and would have a negative effect on our pursuit of our other interests in Chile" (Walker, 2011, pp. 121, 130).

The battle between Vaky and Derian revealed the tension between the Carter administration's affirmation of the principle of human rights and its ability to abandon the regime of Pinochet. This difficulty is revealed in a long memo from Policy Planning Director Tony Lake to Deputy Secretary of State Warren Christopher about human rights sanctions. The shift toward prioritizing human rights policies in the Carter administration now confronted the administration with a "new problem: whether to continue denying economic and security benefits... to a country if arbitrary arrest, torture, and other violations of the person are ended, but there is not meaningful progress on political rights and the legal and institutional instruments of repression remain." In particular, Lake found compelling arguments against "limiting programs which are designed primarily to help American exporters and investors" (see Document 10).

In acknowledging the negative link between rights and profit, the debate between Vaky and Derian thus also summarizes the policy bind in which the Carter administration found itself. The problem was made more difficult because Pinochet had not been responsive to previous policies, including the severe limitation of economic and military aid to Chile in 1976 and after. On October 19, 1979, Secretary of State Cyrus Vance told Carter of the final decision on human rights sanctions. The State Department recommended 6 of Derian's 19 suggested sanctions, but had removed what Vance called the "extreme measures," like the cutoff of private loans or the recall of the ambassador (see Document 11). Still, scholars who have studied the effects of Carter's human rights policies have noted a significant impact. In Chile, in particular, the Pinochet regime murdered or "disappeared" fewer citizens between 1977 and 1980 than in any other four-year period between 1973 and 1990 (Rabe, 2012, p. 147).

## CONCLUSION

In the end, the sanctions imposed by the Carter administration lasted just more than a year. When the Reagan administration arrived at the White House in January 1981, it used its first policy statement on Latin America to announce that it would cancel the sanctions (see Document 12). The contrast between the cold treatment by the Carter administration of the Pinochet regime and the warm embrace from Reagan was stark. In 1981, following the doctrine of new UN Ambassador Jeane Kirkpatrick, the Reagan administration praised the military junta's free-market policies and defended the Chilean government against censure for its human rights record (Kaufman & Valenzuela, 1982).[70] Chile's hard-line on communism and free-market approach outweighed human rights concerns for the Reagan administration. The administration also lifted the bans on exports and moved toward the resumption of arms sales. In 1983, the United States even denied Salvador Allende's widow an entry visa, saying her presence would be "prejudicial to U.S. interests" (Smith, 1994, p. 214).

By 1984, National Security Council Official Oliver North would turn to the Pinochet regime, albeit unsuccessfully, to deliver British-made Blowpipe missile systems to the Contras in Nicaragua (Kornbluh, 2013, pp. 420–22). But then, beginning with a new rise of popular protest in 1984, the Pinochet regime crushed mass demonstrations, declared a state of siege, and closed its public universities. This forced the hand of the Reagan administration, which finally criticized Chile openly in the UN Human Rights Commission in 1986 (Morley & McGillion, 2015). In 1988, the United States publicly supplied funds to support the founding of democratic institutions in Chile, and that October, Pinochet lost a plebiscite that would have indefinitely continued his rule. Free elections in 1990 returned democracy to Chile (Smith, 1994, p. 215).

Pinochet's arrest in London in October 1998 brought public pressure on the administration of Bill Clinton to grant Spanish requests for US-generated records on human rights abuses in Chile and Argentina under the US–Spain

---

70 On the Kirkpatrick Doctrine, see Kirkpatrick, J. (1979). "Dictatorships and Double Standards." *Commentary, 68*: 34-45; Scott, J.M. (1996). "Regan's Doctrine? The Formulation of an American Foreign Policy Strategy." *Presidential Studies Quarterly, 26* (4): 1047-61.

bilateral Mutual Legal Assistance Treaty. In November 1998, Secretary of State Madeleine Albright held a meeting to determine the next step. The consensus was that setting a "Pinochet precedent" in international law would not benefit US interests and that the State Department should respect the Chilean government's calls for Pinochet to be released. At the same, the decision-makers did not believe they could disregard pressure from Congress and the public at large. Morton Halperin, the new policy planning director at the State Department, suggested a major declassification review. The result was the Chile Declassification Project, which released approximately 24,000 records in 1999 and 2000, some of which are cited here. The CIA, however, did not cooperate with the declassification, and several other important records remain classified in the US National Archives and different presidential libraries (Kornbluh, 2013, pp. 477–87).

Pinochet himself would return to Chile in 2000 after 16 months under house arrest in London. He died there in 2006. But his case established a precedent—known in the world of human rights law as the Pinochet Precedent—that has implications for past and future human rights violators, as well as for their accomplices. The Pinochet Precedent is especially important because of the idea of universal jurisdiction over certain crimes, such as genocide, human rights violations, or crimes against humanity, which raises the option of transnational cooperation in the apprehension and prosecution of violators (Roht-Arriaza, 2000, pp. 311–19). This raises one final question: If Pinochet could be indicted in this pioneering case of international human rights law, should an actor like Henry Kissinger, whose policies abetted the state terror of Chile and other US-supported regimes that committed massive rights violations, also be tried? The history of that debate, while interesting, is unfortunately beyond the scope of this chapter.

# REFERENCES

Brands, H. (2010). *Latin America's Cold War*. Cambridge, MA: Harvard University Press.
Chilean National Commission on Truth and Reconciliation. (1993). *Report of the Chilean National Commission on Truth and Reconciliation*. South Bend, IN: University of Notre Dame Press.
CIA. (2000). "CIA Activities in Chile." Langley, VA: Library of the Central Intelligence Agency, General Reports.

Constable, P., & Valenzuela, A. (1993). *A Nation of Enemies: Chile under Pinochet*. New York: Norton.

Digital National Security Archive. (n.d.). "Secretary's Staff Meeting, October 1, 1973." *Chile and the United States: US Policy toward Democracy, Dictatorship, and Human Rights, 1970–1990.* Washington, DC: Author.

Dinges, J. (2012). *The Condor Years: How Pinochet and His Allies Brought Terrorism to Three Continents*. New York: The New Press.

Dinges, J., & Landau, S. (1980). *Assassination on Embassy Row*. New York: Pantheon.

Grandin, G. (2005). "'The Instruction of Great Catastrophe: Truth Commissions, National History, and State Formation in Argentina, Chile, and Guatemala." *The American Historical Review, 110*(1), 46–67. https://doi.org/10.1086/531121

Grandin, G., & Joseph, G.M. (Eds.). (2010). *A Century of Revolution: Insurgent and Counterinsurgent Violence during Latin America's Long Cold War*. Durham, NC: Duke University Press. https://doi.org/10.1215/9780822392859

Harmer, T. (2011). *Allende's Chile and the Inter-American Cold War*. Chapel Hill: University of North Carolina Press.

Hersh, S.M. (1974, September 27). "Kissinger Said to Rebuke U.S. Ambassador to Chile." *The New York Times Magazine*, p. 18.

Hiebert, M.S., & Policzer, P. (2009). "Genocide in Chile? An Assessment." In M. Esparza, H.R. Huttenbach, and D. Feierstein (Eds.), *State Violence and Genocide in Latin America: The Cold War Years* (pp. 64–80). New York: Routledge.

Jara, J. (1983). *Victor Jara: An Unfinished Song*. London: Jonathan Cape.

Kaufman, R., & Valenzuela, A. (1982). "Authoritarian Chile: Implications for American Foreign Policy." In R. Newhouse (Ed.), *Gunboats and Diplomacy*. Washington, DC: Democratic Policy Committee.

Keys, B. (2014). *Reclaiming American Virtue: The Human Rights Revolution of the 1970s*. Cambridge, MA: Harvard University Press. https://doi.org/10.4159/9780674726031

Kornbluh, P. (Ed.). (1998). *Electronic Briefing Book No. 8: Chile and the United States: Declassified Documents Relating to the Military Coup, September 11, 1973*. Washington, DC: George Washington University. Accessed at: http://nsarchive2.gwu.edu//NSAEBB/NSAEBB8/nsaebb8i.htm

Kornbluh, P. (2013). *The Pinochet File: A Declassified Dossier on Atrocity and Accountability*. New York: The New Press.

Kraus, C. (1998, October 18). "Britain Arrests Pinochet to Face Charges by Spain." *The New York Times*, p. A1. Accessed at: http://www.nytimes.com/1998/10/18/world/britain-arrests-pinochet-to-face-charges-by-spain.html?mcubz=0

McElveen, J., & Siekmeier, J. (Eds.). (2014a). *Foreign Relations of the United States, 1969–1976* (vol. E-16). Washington, DC: United States Government Printing Office.

McElveen, J., & Siekmeier, J. (Eds.). (2014b). *Foreign Relations of the United States, 1969–1976* (vol. XXI). Washington, DC: United States Government Printing Office.

Morley, M., & McGillion, C. (2015). *Reagan and Pinochet: The Struggle over US Policy toward Chile*. New York: Cambridge University Press. https://doi.org/10.1017/CBO9781316104217

Rabe, S.G. (1999). *The Most Dangerous Area in the World: John F. Kennedy Confronts Communist Revolution in Latin America*. Chapel Hill: University of North Carolina Press.

Rabe, S. (2012). *The Killing Zone: The United States Wages Cold War in Latin America*. New York: Oxford University Press.

Roht-Arriaza, N. (2000). "The Pinochet Precedent and Universal Jurisdiction." *New England Law Review, 35,* 311–19.

Schoultz, L. (1981). *Human Rights and United States Policy toward Latin America.* Princeton, NJ: Princeton University Press. https://doi.org/10.1515/9781400854295

Smith, G. (1994). *The Last Years of the Monroe Doctrine, 1945–1993.* New York: Hill and Wang.

Styron, R. (1974, May 30). "Terror in Chile II: The Amnesty Report." *The New York Review of Books.*

Totten, S. (2008). *The Prevention and Intervention of Genocide: An Annotated Bibliography.* New York: Routledge.

US Department of State. (1999a). "'CIA Directorate of Operations, Station Report, Death Tolls,' September 20, 1973." *Chile Declassification Project.* Freedom of Information Act, Virtual Reading Room. Accessed at: https://foia.state.gov/searchapp/DOCUMENTS/pcia/9ca8.PDF

US Department of State. (1999b). "Fimbres to Rogers, 'US Policy towards Chile,' September 15, 1975." *Chile Declassification Project.* Freedom of Information Act, Virtual Reading Room. Accessed at: https://foia.state.gov/searchapp/DOCUMENTS/pinochet/8b4b.PDF

US Department of State. (1999c). "Kubisch to the Acting Secretary, 'Supply of Lethal Military Items to Chile,' December 25, 1973." *Chile Declassification Project.* Freedom of Information Act, Virtual Reading Room. Accessed at: https://foia.state.gov/searchapp/DOCUMENTS/pcia/9ca8.PDF

US Department of State. (1999d). "Memorandum, 'Ambassador Popper's Policy Paper,' July 11, 1975." *Chile Declassification Project.* Freedom of Information Act, Virtual Reading Room. Accessed at: https://foia.state.gov/searchapp/DOCUMENTS/pinochet/8b4b.PDF

US Department of State. (1999e). "Memorandum of Conversation between Henry Kissinger and Augusto Pinochet, 'U.S.-Chilean Relations,' June 8, 1976." *Chile Declassification Project.* Freedom of Information Act, Virtual Reading Room. Accessed at: https://foia.state.gov/searchapp/DOCUMENTS/StateChile3/0000579F.pdf

US Department of State. (1999f). "Memorandum of Conversation, 'Secretary's Meeting with Foreign Minister Carvajal,' September 29, 1975." *Chile Declassification Project.* Freedom of Information Act, Virtual Reading Room. Accessed at: https://foia.state.gov/searchapp/DOCUMENTS/pinochet/8dcd.PDF

US Department of State. (1999g). "'Pending Requests for Major Items of Military Assistance to Chile,' March 21, 1974." *Chile Declassification Project.* Freedom of Information Act, Virtual Reading Room.

Walker, V. (2011). "At the End of Influence: The Letelier Assassination, Human Rights, and Rethinking Intervention in US-Latin American Relations." *Journal of Contemporary History, 46*(1), 109–35. https://doi.org/10.1177/0022009410383295

# DOCUMENTS

There is a wealth of information that reveals the US government knew about the atrocities committed by the Pinochet regime in the earliest days after the September 11, 1973 coup. Despite knowledge of these and continuing abuses, the US government continued to support the regime, both militarily and economically, in the 1970s. The following documents were made available to scholars and the public as part of the US government's declassification process. They and other related documents can be found in the flagship publication of the Historian's Office of the State Department, *Foreign Relations of the United States (FRUS)*, and at the National Security Archive, which is an independent, non-governmental research institute founded in 1985 to check a rise in government secrecy. Documents 1 to 5 track the initial reactions of the Nixon administration to the election of Allende in 1970 and the coup conducted by Pinochet in 1973. Documents 6 through 12 examine the shifts in policy within the Ford, Carter, and Reagan administrations in response to the continued violence and repression in Chile and the rising importance of human rights concerns in domestic politics and foreign policy.

## DOCUMENT 1

Document 1 is a 1970 memorandum by the chief of the Western Hemisphere Division of the CIA detailing the creation of a special task force to destabilize the Allende government. The memorandum describes the phrase with which CIA Director Richard Helms began the meeting: "President Nixon had decided that an Allende regime in Chile was not acceptable to the United States." It notes a $10 million dollar budget authorization from President Nixon to destabilize the Allende government, or in Helms' words, "to prevent Allende from coming to power or to unseat him." The memo also reveals that these plans were approved by both the president and by National Security Adviser Henry Kissinger.

SEPTEMBER 16, 1970

MEMORANDUM FOR THE RECORD
SUBJECT: Genesis of Project FUBELT

1. On this date the Director called a meeting in connection with the Chilean situation. Present in addition to the Director were General Cushman, DDCI; Col. White, ExDir-Compt; Thomas Karamessines, DDP; Cord Meyer, ADDP; William V. Broe, Chief WH [Western Hemisphere]

Division; ████████████████ Deputy Chief, WH Division, ████
████████████████████████ Chief, Covert Action, WH
Division; and ████████████████ Chief, WH/4.

2. The Director told the group that President Nixon had decided
that an Allende regime in Chile was not acceptable to the United
States. The President asked the Agency to prevent Allende from
coming to power or to unseat him. The President authorized ten
million dollars for this purpose, if needed. Further, The Agency is
to carry out this mission without coordination with the
Departments of State or Defense.

3. During the meeting it was decided that Mr. Thomas Karamessines,
DDP, would have overall responsibility for this project. He would be
assisted by a special task force set up for this purpose in the
Western Hemisphere Division. ████████████████████
████████████████████████████████████████
████████████████████████████████████████

4. Col. White was asked by the Director to make all necessary
support arrangements in connection with the project.

5. The Director said he had been asked by Dr. Henry Kissinger,
Assistant to the President for National Security Affairs, to meet
with him on Friday, 18 September to give him the Agency's views on
how this mission could be accomplished.

William V. Broe
Chief
Western Hemisphere Division

SECRET/SENSITIVE
EYES ONLY

Source: CIA. (1970, September 16). "Genesis of Project FUBELT." In P. Kornbluh (Ed.), *National Security Archive Electronic Briefing Book No. 8: Chile and the United States: Declassified Documents Relating to the Military Coup, September 11, 1973* (doc. 3). Washington, DC: George Washington University. Accessed at: http://nsarchive2.gwu.edu/NSAEBB/NSAEBB8/docs/doc03.pdf

## DOCUMENT 2

Document 2 is a memorandum prepared by the staff of National Security Adviser Henry Kissinger for a meeting of the National Security Council in November 1970. It discusses the election of Salvador Allende, which Kissinger describes as posing "one of the most serious challenges we have ever faced in this hemisphere." He adds that the "model effect" of the Allende government in Latin America—that is, the ability of Allende to inspire other left-leaning groups—could be "insidious." Kissinger thus advises President Nixon that the United States should act to destabilize the Allende regime despite the risks of such actions, because "there is in fact some virtue in posturing ourselves in a position of opposition as a means of at least containing him and improving our chance of inducing others to help us contain him later if we have to."

MEMORANDUM

The White House

Washington

SECRET/SENSITIVE                                     NOVEMBER 5, 1970.

MEMORANDUM FOR THE PRESIDENT

FROM: Henry A. Kissinger

SUBJECT:    NSC MEETING, NOVEMBER 6—CHILE

This meeting will consider the question of what strategy we should adopt to deal with an Allende Government in Chile.

## A. DIMENSIONS OF THE PROBLEM

The election of Allende as President of Chile poses for us one of the most serious challenges ever faced in this hemisphere. Your decision as to what to do about it may be the most historic and difficult foreign affairs decision you will have to make this year, for what happens in Chile over the next six to twelve months will have ramifications that will go far beyond just US-Chilean relations. They will have an effect on what happens in the rest of Latin America and the developing world; on what our future position will be in the hemisphere; and on the larger world picture, including our relations with the USSR. They will even affect our own conception of what our role in the world is.

Allende is a tough, dedicated Marxist. He comes to power with a profound anti-US bias. The Communist and Socialist parties form the core of the political coalition that is his power base. Everyone agrees that Allende will purposefully seek:

-- to establish a socialist, Marxist state in Chile;

-- to eliminate US influence from Chile and the hemisphere;

-- to establish close relations and linkages with the USSR, Cuba and other Socialist countries.

The consolidation of Allende in power in Chile, therefore, would pose some very serious threats to our interests and position in the hemisphere, and would affect developments and our relations to them elsewhere in the world:

-- US investments (totaling some one billion dollars) may be lost, at least in part; Chile may default on debts (about $1.5 billion) owed the US Government and private US banks.

-- Chile would probably become a leader of opposition to us in the inter-American system, a source of disruption in the hemisphere, and a focal point of support for subversion in the rest of Latin America.

-- It would become part of the Soviet/Socialist world, not only philosophically but in terms of power dynamics; and it might constitute a support base and entry point for expansion of Soviet and Cuban presence and activity in the region.

-- The example of a successful elected Marxist government in Chile would surely have an impact on--and even precedent value for-- other parts of the world, especially in Italy; the imitative spread of similar phenomena elsewhere would in turn significantly affect the world balance and our own position in it.

While events in Chile pose these potentially very adverse consequences for us, they are taking a form which makes them extremely difficult for us to deal with or offset, and which in fact poses some very painful dilemmas for us:

a. Allende was elected legally, the first Marxist government ever to come to power by free elections. He has legitimacy in the eyes of Chileans and most of the world; there is nothing we can do to deny him that legitimacy or claim he does not have it.

b. We are strongly on record in support of self-determination and respect for free elections; you are firmly on record for non-intervention in the internal affairs of this hemisphere and of accepting nations "as they are." It would therefore be very costly for us to act in ways that appear to violate those principles, and Latin Americans and others in the world will view our policy as a test of the credibility of our rhetoric.

On the other hand, our failure to react to this situation risks
being perceived in Latin America and in Europe as indifference
or impotence in the face of clearly adverse developments in a
region long considered our sphere of influence.

c. Allende's government is likely to move along lines that will
   make it very difficult to marshal international or hemisphere
   censure of him--he is most likely to appear as an "independent"
   socialist country rather than a Soviet satellite or "Communist
   government."

   Yet a Titoist government in Latin America would be far more
   dangerous to us than it is in Europe, precisely because it can
   move against our policies and interests more easily and
   ambiguously and because its "model" effect can be insidious.

Allende starts with some significant weaknesses in his position:

-- There are tensions in his supporting coalition.

-- There is strong if diffuse resistance in Chilean society to
   moving to a Marxist or totalitarian state.

-- There is suspicion of Allende in the military.

-- There are serious economic problems and constraints.

To meet this situation, Allende's immediate "game plan" is clearly
to avoid pressure and coalescing of opposition prematurely, and
to keep his opponents within Chile fragmented so that he can
neutralize them one by one as he is able. To this end, he will
seek to:

-- be internationally respectable;

-- move cautiously and pragmatically;

-- avoid immediate confrontations with us; and

-- move slowly in formalizing relations with Cuba and other
   Socialist countries.

There is disagreement among the agencies as to precisely how
successful Allende will be in overcoming his problems and
weaknesses, or how inevitable it really is that he will follow the
course described or that the threats noted will materialize.

But the weight of the assessments is that Allende and the forces
that have come to power with him do have the skill, the means and
the capacity to maintain and consolidate themselves in power,
provided they can play things their way. Logic would certainly argue
that he will have the motivation to pursue purposefully aims he has
after all held for some 25 years. Since he has an admittedly
profound anti-US and anti-capitalist bias, his policies are bound to
constitute serious problems for us if he has any degree of ability
to implement them.

B. THE BASIC ISSUE
What all of this boils down to is a fundamental dilemma and issue:

a. Do we wait and try to protect our interests in the context of
   dealing with Allende because:

   -- we believe we cannot do anything about him anyway;

   -- he may not develop into the threat we fear or may mellow in time;

-- we do not want to risk turning nationalism against us and
    damaging our image, credibility and position in the world;

AND thereby risk letting Allende consolidate himself and his ties
with Cuba and the USSR, so that a year or two from now when he has
established his base he can move more strongly against us, and then
we really will be unable to do anything about it or reverse the
process. Allende would in effect use us to gain legitimacy and then
turn on us on some economic issue and thereby caste [sic] us in
the role of "Yankee imperialist" on an issue of his choice.

OR

b. Do we decide to do something to prevent him from consolidating
himself now when we know he is weaker than he will ever be and when
he obviously fears our pressure and hostility, because:

-- we can be reasonably sure he is dedicated to opposing us;

-- he will be able to consolidate himself and then be able to
    counter us in increasingly intense ways; and

-- to the extent he consolidates himself and links to the USSR
    and Cuba the trend of events and dynamics will be
    irreversible.

AND thereby risk:

-- giving him the nationalistic issue as a weapon to entrench
    himself;

-- damaging our credibility in the eyes of the rest of the world
    as interventionist;

-- turning nationalism and latent fear of US domination in the rest
   of Latin America into violent and intense opposition to us; and

-- perhaps failing to prevent his consolidation anyway.

## C. Our Choices

There are deep and fundamental differences among the agencies on
this basic issue. They manifest themselves in essentially three
possible approaches:

1. The Modus Vivendi Strategy:
   This school of thought, which is essentially State's position,
   argues that we really do not have the capability of preventing
   Allende from consolidating himself or forcing his failure; that the
   main course of events in Chile will be determined primarily by the
   Allende government and its reactions to the internal situation;
   and that the best thing we can do in these circumstances is maintain
   our relationship and our presence in Chile so that over the long
   haul we may be able to foster and influencing [sic] domestic trends
   favorable to our interests. In this view actions to exert pressure
   on Allende or to isolate Chile will not only be ineffective, but
   will only accelerate adverse developments in Chile and limit our
   capacity to have any influence on the long-range trend.

   In this view the risks that Allende will consolidate himself and
   the long-range consequences therefrom are less dangerous to us
   than the immediate probable reaction to attempts to oppose
   Allende. Its perception of Allende's long-term development is
   essentially optimistic and benign. Implicit is the argument that
   it is not certain he can overcome his internal weaknesses, that
   he may pragmatically limit his opposition to us, and that if he
   turns into another Tito that would not be bad since we deal with
   other governments of this kind anyway.

2. The Hostile Approach:
   DOD, CIA and some State people, on the other hand, argue that it
   is patent that Allende is our enemy, that he will move counter
   to us just as soon and as strongly as he feels he can; and that
   when his hostility is manifest to us it will be because he has
   consolidated his power and then it really will be too late to do
   very much--the process is irreversible. In this view, therefore,
   we should try to prevent him from consolidating now when he is
   at his weakest.

   Implicit in this school of thought is the assumption that we can
   affect events, and that the risks of stirring up criticism to
   our position elsewhere are less dangerous to us than the long-
   term consolidation of a Marxist government in Chile.

   Within this approach there are in turn two schools of thought:

a. Overt Hostility.
   This view argues that we should not delay putting pressure on
   Allende and therefore should not wait to react to his moves
   with counter-punches. It considers the dangers of making our
   hostility public or of initiating the fight less important
   than making unambiguously clear what our position is and
   where we stand. It assumes that Allende does not really need
   our hostility to help consolidate himself, because if he did
   he would confront us now. Instead he appears to fear our
   hostility.

   This approach therefore would call for (1) initiating punitive
   measures, such as terminating aid or economic embargo; (2)
   making every effort to rally international support of this
   position; and (3) declaring and publicizing our concern and
   hostility.

b. Non-overt Pressure, Cold, Correct Approach.

This approach concurs in the view that pressure should be placed on Allende now and that we should oppose him. But it argues that how we package that pressure and opposition is crucial and may make the difference between effectiveness and ineffectiveness. It argues that an image of the US initiating punitive measures will permit Allende to marshal domestic support and international sympathy on the one hand, and make it difficult for us to obtain international cooperation on the other. It further argues that it is the effect of pressure not the posture of hostility that hurts Allende; the latter gives him tactical opportunities to blunt the impact of our opposition.

Implicit in this approach is the judgment that how unambiguous our public position is and making a public record are all less important in the long run than maximizing our pressure and minimizing risks to our position in the rest of the world.

This approach therefore calls for essentially the same range of pressures as the previous one, but would use them quietly and covertly; on the surface our posture would be correct, but cold. Any public manifestation or statement of hostility would be geared to his actions to avoid giving him the advantage of arguing he is the aggrieved party.

D. ASSESSMENTS
As noted, the basic issue is whether we are to wait and try to adjust or act now to oppose.

The great weakness in the modus vivendi approach is that:

-- it gives Allende the strategic initiative;

-- it plays into his game plan and almost insures that he will
   consolidate himself;

-- if he does consolidate himself, he will have even more freedom
   to act against us after a period of our acceptance of him than
   if we had opposed him all along;

-- there are no apparent reasons or available intelligence to
   justify a benign or optimistic view of an Allende regime over the
   long term. In fact, as noted, an "independent" rational socialist
   state linked to Cuba and the USSR can be even more dangerous for
   our long-term interests than a very radical regime.

There is nothing in this strategy that promises to deter or
prevent adverse anti-U.S. actions when and if Chile wants to pursue
them -- and there are far more compelling reasons to believe that
he will when he feels he is established than that he will not.

The main question with the hostile approach is whether we can
effectively prevent Allende from consolidating his power. There is
at least some prospect that we can. But the argument can be made
that even if we did not succeed -- provided we did not damage
ourselves too severely in the process -- we could hardly be worse
off than letting him entrench himself; that there is in fact some
virtue in posturing ourselves in a position of opposition as a
means of at least containing him and improving our chance of
inducing others to help us contain him later if we have to.

In my judgment the dangers of doing nothing are greater than the
risks we run in trying to do something, especially since we have
flexibility in tailoring our efforts to minimize those risks.

I recommend, therefore that you make a decision that we will oppose
Allende as strongly as we can and do all we can to keep him from
consolidating power, taking care to package those efforts in a
style that gives us the appearance of reacting to his moves.

## E. THE NSC MEETING

Contrary to your usual practice of not making a decision at NSC
meetings, it is essential that you make it crystal clear where
you stand on this issue at today's meeting. If all concerned do
not understand that you want Allende opposed as strongly as we
can, the result will be a steady drift toward the modus vivendi
approach. This is primarily a question of priorities and nuance.
The emphasis resulting from today's meeting must be on opposing
Allende and preventing his consolidating power and not on
minimizing risks.

I recommend that after your opening remarks you call on Dick
Helms to give you a briefing on the situation and what we might
expect. I would then outline the main issues and options along
the above lines, after which you could call on Secretaries
Rogers and Laird for their views and observations. Your Talking
Points, which are appended, are written along these lines.

Also included in your book are:

-- A State/DOD options paper.

-- An analytical summary of that options paper.

**Source**: "Memorandum: Henry Kissinger to Richard Nixon, NSC Meeting, November 6 - Chile." (1970, November 5). In *Foreign Relations of the United States (FRUS), 1969-1976* (vol. XXI, doc. 172).

## DOCUMENT 3

Document 3 is an excerpt of a September 1973 report from the CIA station in Santiago, Chile. It details the summary executions and political repression conducted by the new Pinochet government in the first week after the coup. It notes not only specific information about high-level political prisoners held at Dawson Island but also estimates that 4,000 people had been killed during the coup and the ensuing "cleanup operations."

**CIA**
**DIRECTORATE OF OPERATIONS**

THIS IS AN INFORMATION REPORT, NOT FINALLY EVALUATED INTELLIGENCE

SECRET                                        DIST 20 September 1973

1. ▉▉▉▉▉▉▉▉▉▉▉▉▉▉▉▉▉▉▉▉▉▉▉▉▉▉▉▉▉▉▉▉▉▉▉▉▉▉▉▉▉▉▉▉▉▉

THAT THUS FAR 4,000 DEATHS HAVE RESULTED FROM THE 11 SEPTEMBER 1973 COUP ACTION AND THE SUBSEQUENT CLEAN-UP OPERATIONS, ▉▉▉▉▉▉▉▉▉▉▉▉▉▉▉▉▉▉▉▉▉ THAT CARLOS MORALES, AN OFFICIAL OF THE RADICAL PARTY, AND ERICH SCHNAKE, FORMER SOCIALIST PARTY SENATOR, WERE BEING DETAINED ON DAWSON ISLAND IN THE STRAITS OF MAGELLAN

▉▉▉▉▉▉▉▉▉▉▉▉▉▉▉▉▉▉▉▉▉▉▉▉▉▉▉▉▉▉▉▉▉▉▉▉, 35 POPULAR UNITY (U.P.)

PRISONERS HAVE BEEN TAKEN TO DAWSON ISLAND. AMONG THEM ARE ANIBAL PALMA, FORMER MINISTER OF HOUSING; DANIEL VERGARA, FORMER UNDER-SECRETARY OF THE INTERIOR; CARLOS MATUS, FORMER PRESIDENT OF THE CENTRAL BANK; AND FERNANDO FLORES, FORMER MINISTER OF FINANCE. █████████████████

SECRET

**Source:** CIA Directorate of Operations. (1973, September 20). "Station Report, Death Tolls." In US Department of State, *Chile Declassification Project.* Freedom of Information Act Virtual Reading Room. Accessed at: https://foia. state.gov/searchapp/DOCUMENTS/pcia/9ca8.PDF

## DOCUMENT 4

Document 4 is another intelligence report from the CIA on the repression of political dissent by the Pinochet regime. Dated October 27, 1973, it passes on the military junta's official figures of civilian deaths, including those "executed by firing squads after summary military trials." In addition, the report reveals that the US government had detailed knowledge of other tactics of repression of the regime, including the widespread use of prison camps. The document also notes that CIA's estimates of state-sanctioned violence puts the number of executions at a much higher level than the official Chilean reports.

PAGE 1 **1.5(c)**

DENIED IN FULL

DOCUMENT DATED 27 Oct 73

APPROVED FOR RELEASE

DATE JUN 11 1999

████████████████████████████

████████████████████████████

████████████████████

1. ACCORDING TO ███████████████████████

████████████████████████ HIGHLY SENSITIVE FIGURES

PREPARED FOR THE JUNTA INDICATE THAT A TOTAL OF 1,020 DEATHS OF
CIVILIANS AND ARMED FORCES PERSONNEL OCCURRED DURING THE
PERIOD 11 THROUGH 30 SEPTEMBER 1973 AS A RESULT OF THE 11
SEPTEMBER COUP. DURING THIS PERIOD IN SANTIAGO, 22 MEMBERS OF
THE ARMED FORCES AND 624 CIVILIANS DIED AS A RESULT OF MILITARY
ACTIONS. IN ADDITION, A TOTAL OF 240 CIVILIANS WERE EITHER
EXECUTED BY FIRING SQUADS [SIC] AFTER SUMMARY MILITARY TRIALS
OR EXECUTED ON THE SPOT FOR ARMED RESISTANCE AGAINST MILITARY
FORCES. DURING THE SAME PERIOD OUTSIDE OF SANTIAGO, A TOTAL OF
EIGHT ARMED FORCES MEN WERE KILLED; 46 CIVILIANS WERE KILLED
DURING MILITARY ACTIONS; AND 80 CIVILIANS WERE EITHER EXECUTED
ON THE SPOT OR KILLED BY FIRING SQUADS AFTER MILITARY TRIALS.
███████████████ COMMENT: THESE FIGURES DO NOT REFLECT THE NUMBER
OF CARABINEROS (UNIFORMED NATIONAL POLICE) KILLED DURING THIS
TIME PERIOD NOR DO THE FIGURES REFLECT THE EXECUTION OF KNOWN
CRIMINALS AND DELINQUENTS BY THE DEPARTMENT OF INVESTIGATIONS
(DI, CHILEAN CIVIL POLICE), BECAUSE FIGURES ARE NOT BEING KEPT
ON THESE LATTER CATEGORIES. ███████████████ COMMENT:
    A. ████████████████████████████████████████
████████████████████████████████████████
███████████████████████████ AN UNOFFICIAL ESTIMATE THAT
ABOUT 1,600 CIVILIAN DEATHS OCCURRED BETWEEN 11 SEPTEMBER AND
10 OCTOBER, WITH NO ESTIMATE OF MILITARY AND POLICE CASUALTIES.
IT IS NOT KNOWN IF THE 1,600 FIGURE INCLUDED COMMON CRIMINALS.
ALSO, IT IS IMPORTANT TO NOTE THE DIFFERENCE IN TIME PERIODS
COVERED IN THESE TWO REPORTS.
    B. ON ███ OCTOBER, ████████████████████████████
████████████████████████████████████████
███████████ THAT AT HIGH LEVELS IN THE JUNTA GOVERNMENT THERE
IS A REALIZATION THAT THE OFFICIAL DEATH FIGURES WILL HAVE TO BE
RAISED, BECAUSE THE PUBLIC DOES NOT BELIEVE THE FIGURE (ABOUT
600) USUALLY QUOTED BY THE GOVERNMENT. IF A DECISION IS MADE TO
RAISE THE NUMBER, IT WILL BE PLACED AT SLIGHTLY OVER 1000. THE

HOST [SIC] ACCURATE NUMBER, HOWEVER, IS APPROXIMATELY 1,500.)

2. ████████████████████████████████████████████
████████████████████████████████████████ BETWEEN 11
SEPTEMBER AND 10 OCTOBER A TOTAL OF 13,500 PRISONERS HAD BEEN
REGISTERED AS DETAINED BY THE ARMED FORCES, CARABINEROS AND THE DI
[DEPARTMENT OF INVESTIGATIONS, CHILEAN CIVIL POLICE] THROUGHOUT THE
COUNTRY. AS OF 10 OCTOBER A TOTAL OF 2,300 PRISONERS BEING HELD IN
ARMED FORCES DETENTION CENTERS THROUGHOUT CHILE, BUT NOT INCLUDING
SANTIAGO. 680 PRISONERS HAD BEEN SENTENCED UNDER THE MILITARY
JUSTICE SYSTEM AND WERE SERVING TERMS IN PRISON CAMPS. IN ADDITION, A
TOTAL OF 2,360 PRISONERS WERE BEING HELD IN CARABINERO AND DI
FACILITIES WHILE THEIR CASES WERE BEING TRIED. A TOTAL OF 360 COMMON
CRIMINALS HAD ALSO BEEN DETAINED, TRIED AND SENTENCED BETWEEN 11
SEPTEMBER AND 10 OCTOBER.

3. ████████████████████ THAT AS OF 20 OCTOBER, A TOTAL OF 7,812
PRISONERS HAD BEEN PROCESSED THROUGH THE DETENTION CENTER AT
THE NATIONAL STADIUM IN SANTIAGO. OF THIS NUMBER, 2,112 HAD BEEN
GIVEN UNCONDITIONAL LIBERTY AND HAD NO FURTHER CHARGES AGAINST
THEM; 2,408 HAD BEEN PLACED IN CONDITIONAL LIBERTY AND CONTINUED
UNDER INVESTIGATION; 1,840 INDIVIDUALS CHARGED WITH MINOR CRIMES HAD
BEEN PLACED IN LIBERTY FOLLOWING PAYMENT OF A BAIL; 522 DETAINEES HAD
BEEN SENT TO PUBLIC JAILS AFTER MILITARY TRIALS; AND 680 HAD BEEN
SENT TO PRISON CAMPS CONTROLLED BY THE ARMED FORCES. AN ADDITIONAL
250 CASES WERE PENDING. ONCE THE NATIONAL STADIUM IS CLOSED AS A
DETENTION CENTER, ALL FUTURE DETANIES ARE TO BE SENT TO CARABINERO
AND DI FACILITIES FOR PROCESSING AND CONTROL. (████████████
COMMENT: THE GOVERNMENT HAS ANNOUNCED THAT THE NATIONAL STADIUM IS
BEING CLEARED OF PRISONERS TO ALLOW TIME FOR PREPARATIONS FOR THE
WORLD CUP SOCCER MATCH BETWEEN CHILE AND THE USSR TO BE HELD THERE IN
LATE NOVEMBER.)

4. THE ARMED FORCES IS ADMINISTERING OVER 20 DETENTION SITES
THROUGHOUT THE COUNTRY. OF THIS NUMBER ONLY A FEW, SUCH AS
DAWSON ISLAND, ARE KNOWN TO THE GENERAL PUBLIC.

5.

Source: CIA. (1973, October 27). "Intelligence Report [Executions in Chile
since the Coup]." In P. Kornbluh & Y. White (Eds.), *National Security Archive
Electronic Briefing Book No. 212: Pinochet: A Declassified Document Obit.*
Washington, DC: George Washington University. Accessed at: http://nsarchive.
gwu.edu/NSAEBB/NSAEBB212/19731127%20Chilean%20Executions.pdf

## DOCUMENT 5

Document 5 is an excerpt of a cable from Jack Kubisch, a State Department
official, to Henry Kissinger, who had recently been promoted from national
security adviser to secretary of state and had requested the information
because he faced increasing domestic pressure from human rights groups
and Congress. The cable notes that, although the early violence that followed
the coup had died down, there were weak indications that the Pinochet
regime would put an end to politically motivated executions, such as the fact
that they had delayed in putting prominent Marxists and Allende officials on
trial. Yet Kubisch also noted their "puritanical, crusading spirit—a determination to cleanse and rejuvenate Chile," which is linked to their military code
of justice and common use of death by firing squad. "The Chilean leaders
justify these executions as entirely legal in the application of martial law
under what they have declared to be a 'state of siege in time of war,'" he wrote.

DEPARTMENT OF STATE

BRIEFING MEMORANDUM

S/S

SECRET - NODIS

TO:    The Secretary
FROM: ARA - Jack B. Kubisch

### Chilean Executions

You requested by cable from Tokyo a report on this subject.

-- On October 24 the Junta announced that summary, on-the-spot executions would no longer be carried out and that persons caught in the act of resisting the government would henceforth be held for military courts. Since that date 17 executions following military trials have been announced. Publicly acknowledged executions, both summary and in compliance with court martial sentences, now total approximately 100, with an additional 40 prisoners shot while "trying to escape." An internal, confidential report prepared for the Junta puts the number of executions for the period September 11-30 at 320. The latter figure is probably a more accurate indication of the extent of this practice.

-- Our best estimate is that the military and police units in the field are generally complying with the order to desist from summary executions. At least the rather frequent use of random violence that marked the operations of these units in early post-coup days has clearly abated for the time being. However, there are no indications as yet of a disposition to forego executions after military trial.

-- The Chilean leaders justify these executions as entirely legal in the application of martial law under what they have declared to be a "state of siege in time of war". Their code of military justice permits death by firing squad for a range of offenses, including treason, armed resistance, illegal possession of arms and auto theft. Sentences handed down by military tribunals during a state of siege are not reviewable by civilian courts.

-- The purpose of the executions is in part to discourage by example those who seek to organize armed opposition to the Junta. The Chilean military, persuaded to some degree by years of Communist Party propaganda, expected to be confronted by heavy resistance when they overthrew Allende. Fear of civil war was an important factor in their decision to employ a heavy hand from the outset. Also present is a puritanical, crusading spirit -- a determination to cleanse and rejuvenate Chile. (A number of those executed seem to have been petty criminals.)

-- The Junta now has more confidence in the security situation and more awareness of the pressure of international opinion. It may be a hopeful sign that the Junta continues to stall on bringing to trial former cabinet ministers and other prominent Marxists -- people the military initially had every intention of standing up before firing squads. How the military leaders proceed in this area from now on will be influenced to some degree by outside opinion, and particularly by ours, but the major consideration will continue to be their assessment of the security situation.

At Tab A is a Chile situation report and at Tab B a fact sheet on human rights in Chile.

Attachments:

Tab A - Situation Report

Tab B - Fact Sheet

SECRET - NODIS

**Source:** Kubisch, J. (1973, November 16). "Department of State, Memorandum
for Henry Kissinger, Chilean Executions." In P. Kornbluh & Y. White (Eds.),
*National Security Archive Electronic Briefing Book No. 212: Pinochet:
A Declassified Document Obit.* Washington, DC: George Washington University.
Accessed at: http://nsarchive2.gwu.edu//NSAEBB/NSAEBB212/19731127%20
Chilean%20Executions.pdf

# DOCUMENT 6

Document 6 is an excerpt of a memorandum of conversation between
Kissinger and President Ford. After discussing the difficulties the United
States faced in the Middle East, Kissinger rails against recent moves in the
Congress to limit US aid to Pinochet's government. For Kissinger, it was
clear that the human rights arguments got in the way of a broader strategy
for a pro-American Western Hemisphere. He tells the president that he
wants the White House "to do everything possible" to fulfill the requests
for arms from the Pinochet government.

## MEMORANDUM

THE WHITE HOUSE
WASHINGTON

SECRET/NODIS/XGDS

MEMORANDUM OF CONVERSATION

PARTICIPANTS:   President Ford
                Dr. Henry A. Kissinger, Secretary of State and
                  Assistant to the President for National Security
                  Affairs

Lt. General Brent Scowcroft, Deputy Assistant to
the President for National Security Affairs

DATE & TIME:    Friday – December 20, 1974

PLACE:          The Oval Office

<u>Kissinger</u>: After our talk I wrote warmly to Sadat on your behalf.
Sadat has replied with a long letter.

[...]

<u>Kissinger</u>: The Chilean aid cut is disastrous.  I want us to do
everything possible to get arms for Chile.  They can buy
commercially but Defense says they won't sell if there is any DOD
component.

[...]

<u>SECRET/NODIS/XGDS</u>

**Source:** "Memorandum of Conversation, Henry Kissinger and Gerald Ford."
(1974, December 20). Memoranda of Conversations. Ann Arbor, MI: Gerald R. Ford
Presidential Library and Museum. Accessed at: https://www.fordlibrarymuseum
.gov/library/document/0314/1552894.pdf

# DOCUMENT 7

Document 7 is a 1975 dissent memorandum from the Department of State
that argues that the association of the US government with the Chilean
regime has hurt the United States' reputation at home and abroad. The
document first notes the support offered by the White House to the
Pinochet government, including political, military, technical, and financial
aid extended to the regime, despite its horrendous human rights record.
The authors decry the fact that "the human rights problem is secondary,"

and argue that, both domestically and internationally, human rights was "a major U.S. interest." In particular, the authors note that the alliance with "fascists and torturers" has further alienated the White House from an "increasingly numerous element in Congress" and "the youth of the country." The document also refers to the US policy of supporting the Chicago School economists that sought to liberalize the Chilean economy.

JULY 11, 1975

TO:   ARA: Mr. William D. Rogers
      ARA: Ambassador Hewson Ryan

FROM: ARA/PLC: Richard J. Bloomfield

SUBJ: Ambassador Popper's Policy Paper

The Ambassador characterizes our present stance as one of "disapproval" (p. 20 and p. 21). But the image is otherwise, at least as far as the Executive Branch is concerned:

-- We are solicitous about Chile's debt problem and deploy our diplomacy to promote a debt rescheduling.

-- We use our influence in the IFIS to assure that Chilean loans are not held up.

-- We vote against or abstain on resolutions in international organizations that condemn the GOC's human rights record.

-- We assure the GOC that we want to sell it arms and that we regret Congressional restrictions.

How would the Junta ever get the impression that the USG "disapproves"? As the old saying goes, actions speak louder than words.

The Ambassador says that any stronger signs of our (read Executive Branch) disapproval would not improve the human rights situation (which I am willing to concede). Conclusion: We must provide economic and military assistance; in fact by page 25, we are worrying about our responsibilities for making the Junta's economic program a success. Why? Because "preventing the re-emergence of a Chilean Government essentially hostile to us (p. 22) is our chief interest and the human rights problem is secondary."

This argument overlooks the possibility that the human rights problem in Chile may not be "secondary" but may be a major U.S. interest in the present domestic and international context. In the minds of the world at large, we are closely associated with this junta, ergo with fascists and torturers. This is the way it is perceived by a vocal and increasingly numerous element in Congress whose support we need for other aspects of our Latin American policy (e.g. Panama) and, indeed, for our foreign policy in general. It is one more reason why the youth of the country is alienated from their government and its foreign policy. Chile is just the latest example for a lot of people in this country of the United States not being true to its values.

This is not the emotionalism of a bleeding heart. The Secretary himself has said that no foreign policy will be successful if it is carried in the minds of a few and the hearts of none. Our current Chile policy comes perilously close to fitting that description.

The need to "live with" the absence of human rights in Chile in order to prevent the re-emergence of a hostile government is, to my

mind, a distinctly secondary consideration. We survived a hostile
government in Chile in the recent past. It is really a bizarre
world when the globe's greatest superpower has to worry about the
hostility of the dagger-pointed-at-the-heart-of-Antarctica.

The specific objectives in human rights that Ambassador Popper
sets out on page 21 are fine. The problem is that we will not
achieve them without turning the screws harder and taking the
risks that entails.

cc:    Ambassador Popper
       c/o Mr. Karkashian:ARA/BC


ARA/PLC:RJBloomfield/ahm
7/11/75:x29492

**Source:** "Memorandum, Ambassador Popper's Policy Paper." (1975, July 11). In US
Department of State, *Chile Declassification Project*. Freedom of Information
Act Virtual Reading Room. Accessed at: https://foia.state.gov/searchapp/
DOCUMENTS/pinochet/8b4b.PDF


# DOCUMENT 8

Document 8 is an excerpt of a memorandum of conversation between
Kissinger and the foreign minister of Chile, Patricio Carvajal, from
September 1975. Rather than pressure Carvajal to improve the "human
rights problem" in Chile, Kissinger takes a hands-off approach and asks
only that Carvajal let him know if the Chilean regime did anything he
could use to allay the critics in Congress. Kissinger complains about the use
of human rights arguments, in particular in the State Department and in
Congress, to limit US aid to Chile. He listens closely to Carvajal explain why
the government refused the visit of a United Nations human rights obser-
vation team, and identify government repression as "measures to control
terrorism." After denying personal knowledge of human rights abuses a
number of times and refusing to offer any advice, Kissinger tells Carvajal

he will "treat these requests sympathetically," referring to Chile's appeal for increased economic and military aid. In particular, he promises to reinstate the aid relationship to Chile to the levels at which it stood before the cuts to Allende's government. Furthermore, the discussions about finance and copper production have the opposite tenor of those held with the nationalist and Third Worldist Allende government.

MEMORANDUM OF CONVERSATION

September 29, 1975

SUBJECT:        Secretary's Meeting with
                Foreign Minister Carvajal

PARTICIPANTS:   Chile
                Foreign Minister Patricio Carvajal
                U.N. Permanent Representative
                    Ismael Huerta
                Ambassador to the U.S. Manuel Trucco
                Foreign Ministry Political Advisor
                    Enrique Bernstein
                Foreign Ministry Economic Advisor
                    Thomas Lackington

                US
                The Secretary
                Assistant Secretary William D. Rogers
                Chief Desk Officer Robert S. Driscoll

Foreign Minister: I want to thank you for giving us this opportunity to talk to you.

The Secretary: Well, I read the Briefing Paper for this meeting and it was nothing but Human Rights. The State Department is made up of people who have a vocation for the ministry.  Because there were not enough churches for them, they went into the Department of State.

Foreign Minister: We would like to leave these documents with you.

The Secretary: My God!  What's that?  One of your speeches?

Foreign Minister: It consists of several documents. One explains the current status of the economy.  Another explains the requirements of the armed forces.  Another is the state of the laws under the new level in the state of siege; one concerns the new Council of State, and the final one explains the legal dispositions the government is thinking of taking.

The Secretary: My view on the question of human rights is that it is on two levels.  One that it is a total injustice.  Nobody goes around making statements regarding what is going on in Kampala or the Central African Republic or hundreds of other countries around the world.  The other is the problem of helping your government under the present conditions, which we did not create, but which make it difficult for us.  It would help enormously if something can be done.  We will study the documents.  We understand the problem. It is not in the interest of the United States to turn Chile into another Portugal.  (I'll be in great trouble when this is leaked to the papers.)  However, this is my personal conviction, and I stand behind it.
What can be done visibly to bring about a change in Congressional attitudes?  We do not need to discuss it now.  However, it is our problem.  Otherwise, Congress will place restriction upon restriction against U.S. interests.  Look at Turkey -- the restrictions there do not serve any U.S. interest.
This is the issue we face. (I have not read fully all the Briefing

Papers.) I do not know what can be done. Anything to alleviate that situation, and in a somewhat visible way, would be enormously helpful. This is the basic orientation, but the solution has to be a Chilean one. We don't know the details of what you can do. We have a problem with the Turks. They so adhered to principal that they withdrew 15,000 troops without telling us. This is something we could have used with our Congress. But they were intent on showing they could not yield to pressures. It would have ended the whole thing if we could have issued a communique stating the reduction. They had 35,000 troops, and they only have 20,000. This is not exactly analagous.

Foreign Minister: Regarding Human Rights, first I am convinced that the alleged violations of Human Rights are absolutely false. I have conducted my own personal investigation in my own country to be absolutely convinced in my own conscience to make sure they are not taking place.

The Seretary: Why did you cancel United Nations group? You shouldn't have invited them in the first place. Why did you invite them?

Foreign Minister: We had to cancel because there was a bad atmosphere to begin with. They started badly. Both here in New York and in Lima they talked to people regarding the situation. Th[ey] were supposed to investigate the present situation. However, [they] were hearing old testimony. And the atmosphere inside and out[side] the country was being artificially made into a commotion (sic). The commotion made impossible a thorough and impartial investigation, and I think the government was right in not authorizing the visit. The Working Group has prepared a report which is not fair. My President left the door open for a later visit of the Working Group, but with the report I feel the door is closed.

It was unfortunate. We have admitted the Inter-American Human Rights Commission, and the International Committee of the Red Cross has been there since 1973.

The Secretary: Why did you invite the group to begin with?

Foreign Minister: They created artificially a very bad atmosphere. The Government of Chile has followed a plan to liberalize emergency measures, but the Government of Chile must take measures to control terrorism. Terrorism is a very serious problem all over the world.

The Secretary: That does not happen in the United States. In this country they only shoot at the President.

Foreign Minister: I have asked David Popper whether he would prefer to live in Buenos Aires or Santiago. He answered "no" because his colleague in Buenos Aires lives like a prisoner in his Embassy.

The Secretary: I have no precise suggestions to make. I don't know the conditions. Our point of view is if you do something, let us know so we can use it with Congress.

I see in this document you paroled 200 people, and they have gone to Panama.

Ambassador Trucco: We have authorized more than 200 people to leave the country, and they have no place to go because no one will allow them in. The President of Colombia said he would have to take measures against the Chileans already there. And Facio says some are creating trouble in Costa Rica. Costa Rica is not willing to accept any more Chileans. They are creating problems.

The Secretary: You will know what to do. We cannot go beyond what we have said. What other problem do we have to discuss?

Ambassador Trucco: One problem we are having is with the Ex-Im Bank limitation of the $500,000 (sic).

The Secretary: Why?

Ambassador Trucco: The previous listing on Chile has not changed wth circumstances. This situation dates from the Popular Unity Government.

The Secretary: It took me two years to get our institutions to reduce credit to your country. (To Rogers) Will you call Casey?

Assistant Secretary Rogers: I'll call today. Everything is fine with the IDB and the World Bank?

Ambassador Trucco: With the World Bank we are experiencing certain delays, but we are not pressing the World Bank.

Assistant Seretary Rogers: We should have no problem. We are leaning hard on the bureaucray.

The Secretary: Bill, talk to the Ex-Im Bank. These are vestiges of the previous government.

Your situation with the private banks?

Assistant Secretary Rogers: Do you need any help?

Ambassador Trucco: No, we don't. Our Finance Minister is coming next month, and presently their offers have doubled.

The Secretary: As I understand it, with commercial sales you're alright [sic] -- the problem's with FMS [Foreign Military Sales].

Ambassador Trucco: The problem with commercial sales is that no export licenses have been approved since 1974.

Assistant Secretary Rogers: It is cleared now for purchases made prior to June 1974.

The Secretary: How about the $10 million of sales you are talking about. We could go forward in Congress with a proposal for $20 million in credit, but Congress would throw it out. Our tentative judgment is not to do it. Do you have any problems with that? On cash sales, could we do more?

Assistant Secretary Rogers: The original figure was $6 million, but we changed it to $10 million.

Foreign Minister: On our list here we have items which are in excess of $10 million.

The Secretary: Why do we have to say no commercial sales? Why don't we go through with it? If $10 million are not enough, we could add a few millions.

Assistant Secretary Rogers: We are prepared to be responsive.

The Secretary: If $10 million is not enough, add more. What next, part of south Peru or part of western Bolivia?

Foreign Minister: The new government in Peru is improved. We have hope for better relations with this President. And with Bolivia we are working earnestly to resolve our problems, but we have made no commitments regarding the form of the solution.

The Secretary: Thank you. That would be very helpful.

Foreign Minister: Regarding Peru, we still have Soviet influence. They are receiving a Soviet training vessel in Callao with over 100 "cadets."

The Secretary: But how many Soviets are there now?

Assistant Seretary Rogers: In southern Peru?

The Secretary: What is our position? Soviets in the north are alright; but in the south, they are bad?

Foreign Minister: We have just heard that the Soviets are on board a ship. But this just proves the continued close relation between the armed forces and the Soviet Union.

The Secretary: The new Government of Peru has not been in office long enough to make any changes yet.

Foreign Minister: On the day of the coup -- August 29 -- at 8:00 a.m., the Peruvian colleague of the Chilean military commander in Arica called him to say that they were going to take over the government, "and we are going to eradicate communism and Marxism from Peru." That morning I sent a cable to my Embassy in Lima. The Embassy said it was 9:30 a.m. and all was normal. We hope to have better relations, but there is still some Soviet influence.

The Secretary: We will treat these requests sympathetically. On PL 480 I understand Chile is getting 2/3 of the total for Latin America.

Ambassador Trucco: Yes, this is going well.

The Secretary: How is the economic situation? Is it improving?

Foreign Minister: Yes, it is improving. I believe the economic measures to be sound. The Finance Minister is very strict. I have never seen a Finance Minister like this one in Chile. Traditionally, after the budget was approved, we used to ask the Foreign Minister for more money. But this is not the case with this government. Now he asks for cuts. He has cut us to 80% of the original budget. The measures are very strict, but they are good for the country. I am convinced that next year it will be better. We have been expanding our nontraditional exports, and next year we may not have to renegotiate the external debt. The measures are very good and the people willing to cooperate.

Ambassador Trucco: The Balance of Payments deficit is wiped out and completely financed.

The Secretary: (To a whispered exchange in Spanish between Trucco and Carvajal about a copper producer-consumer conference.) We have agreed to do it.

Ambassador Trucco: We are attending a copper exporters meeting in Lima.

The Secretary: Stay in touch with us. We can set up some sort of ad hoc group which can set objective criteria to define the interests of the producers and the interests of the consumers. This might be according to a percentage of production and consumption.

Ambassador Trucco: Ambassador Popper has had [sic] recent meeting with three Financial Ministers to discuss the Chilean position.

Foreign Minister: Our impression is very good regarding your speech on the matter.

The Secretary: As I stated in my speech we favor this. Why don't you coordinate among the producers? We will set this up.

One other thing: I have heard that you want to invite the OAS General Assembly to Santiago.

Foreign Minister: Yes, in April of next year.

The Secretary: Do you think that would be alright with the other countries?

Foreign Minister: Nobody had made any statement against it.

The Secretary: How about Mexico?

Ambassador Trucco: I have spoken to Colina (of Mexico). He was skeptical. He said the situation had passed. But I do not know what situation he was referring to.

The Secretary: Maybe Echeverria?

Ambassador Trucco: I also talked with President Lopez of Colombia.

The Secretary: We won't oppose.

Ambassador Trucco: I have talked with BurelliRivas [sic] of Venezuela; and he talked to President Perez; and Perez thought it had some merit.  Panama also is in favor.  I believe a meeting of the OAS General Assembly would do a lot of good.

The Secretary: I would rather like it.

Ambassador Truco: It would show the real situation and how it has been distorted.  They would see the effect of the social programs and the economic programs to bring the country back to normalcy.

The Secretary: Would I have to stay the whole week? I would have to listen to too many speeches.

Assistant Secretary Rogers: Last year the meeting was good.  It only lasted two days.

The Secretary: Last year was outstanding.  It was the best I ever attended.  The Foreign Ministers met for two days, and the other sessions were left to the experts.  I would be in favor of such a meeting.

Ambassador Trucco: The only country with which we might have some problems is Mexico, but they can be assured they would receive all courtesies.

The Secretary: Do you have the facilities?

Assistant Secretary Rogers: They are excellent.

Foreign Minister: I am sure they are better than those (OAS) in Washington.

The Secretary: That is not hard to do.

Ambassador Trucco: They would be the same facilities arranged for the 1972 UNCTAD.

The Secretary: If you can get your Latin American friends to support it, the U.S. will have no difficulties.

Ambassador Trucco: (Handing over another document) This is on the talks in Santiago among the countries of the Andean Pact on the limitation of armaments. Ambassador Bernstein presided over these talks.

Assistant Secretary Rogers: Should we make a public statement on these talks?

Ambassador Trucco: Nothing at this time.

This version was agreed upon by Ambassador Lackington, Desk Officer Driscoll, and interpreter Hervas.

**Source:** "Memorandum of Conversation, Secretary's Meeting with Foreign Minister Carvajal." (1975, September 29). In US Department of State, *Chile Declassification Project*. Freedom of Information Act Virtual Reading Room. Accessed at: https://foia.state.gov/searchapp/DOCUMENTS/pinochet/8dcd.PDF

# DOCUMENT 9

Document 9 is the memorandum of a famous conversation between Kissinger and Pinochet from June 1976, when the secretary of state met Pinochet in his office in Santiago. In this conversation, Pinochet first identifies himself with Franco and his victory over communism in the Spanish Civil War. After a discussion of their shared anti-communism, in which Kissinger agrees that Pinochet's government suffers from a "propaganda campaign by the Communists," Kissinger tells the military leader that the United States does not wish to intervene in Chilean domestic affairs. Pinochet mentions his problems with Chilean dissidents in Washington, DC, including

Orlando Letelier. Kissinger also apologizes to Pinochet in advance of his forthcoming statement on human rights at the United Nations General Assembly. "My evaluation of you is that you are a victim of all left-wing troops around the world, and that your greatest sin was that you overthrew a government which was going Communist," Kissinger tells the dictator in conclusion. Later, he adds, "You did a great service to the West in overthrowing Allende. Otherwise Chile would have followed Cuba. Then there would have been no human rights or a Human Rights Commission."

SECRET/NODIS

DEPARTMENT OF STATE<br>Memorandum of Conversation

DATE: June 8, 1976
TIME: 12:00 noon
PLACE: Santiago, Chile
(President Pinochet's
Office)

SUBJECT:       U.S.-Chilean Relations
PARTICIPANTS:  Chile
               Augusto Pinochet, President
               Patricio Carvajal, Foreign Minister
               Manuel Trucco, Ambassador to the United States
               Ricardo Claro, OAS/CA Conference Coordinator for
                   Chilean Government

               United States
               The Secretary
               William D. Rogers, Assistant Secretary for Inter-
                   American Affairs
               Anthony Hervas (Interpreter)

The Secretary: This is a beautiful building. The conference is well organized. Are you meeting with all the delegations?

Pinochet: Yes. Two or three a day. I want to tell you we are grateful that you have come to the conference.

The Secretary: It is an honor. I was touched by the popular reception when I arrived. I have a strong feeling of friendship in Chile.

Pinochet: This is a country of warm-hearted people, who love liberty. This is the reason they did not accept Communism when the Communists attempted to take over the country. It is a long term struggle we are a part of. It is a further stage of the same conflict which erupted into the Spanish Civil War. And we note the fact that though the Spaniards tried to stop Communism 40 years ago, it is springing up again in Spain.

The Secretary: We had the Spanish King recently, and I discussed that very issue with him.

Pinochet: I have always been against Communism. During the Viet-Nam War, I met with some of your military and made clear to them my anti-Communism, and told them I hoped they could bring about its defeat.

The Secretary: In Viet-Nam, we defeated ourselves through our internal divisions. There is a world-wide propaganda campaign by the Communists.

Pinochet: Chile is suffering from that propaganda effort. Unfortunately, we do not have the millions needed for counter propaganda.

The Secretary: I must say your spokesman (Sergio Diaz) was very
effective in this morning's General Assembly session in explaining
your position. In the United States, as you know, we are sympathetic
with what you are trying to do here. I think that the previous
government was headed toward Communism. We wish your government
well. At the same time, we face massive domestic problems, in all
branches of the government, especially Congress, but also in the
Executive, over the issue of human rights. As you know, Congress is
now debating further restraints on aid to Chile. We are opposed.
But basically we don't want to intervene in your domestic affairs.
We can't be precise in our proposals about what you should do. But
this is a problem which complicates our relationships and the efforts
of those who are friends of Chile. I am going to speak about human
rights this afternoon in the General Assembly. I delayed my
statement until I could talk to you. I wanted you to understand my
position. We want to deal in moral persuasion, not by legal
sanctions. It is for this reason that we oppose the Kennedy
Amendment.

In my statement, I will treat human rights in general terms, and
human rights in a world context. I will refer in two paragraphs to
the report on Chile of the OAS Human Rights Commission. I will say
that the human rights issue has impaired relations between the U.S.
and Chile. This is partly the result of Congressional actions. I
will add that I hope you will shortly remove those obstacles.

I will also call attention to the Cuba report and to the hypocrisy of
some who call attention to human rights as a means of intervening in
governments. I can do no less, without producing a reaction in the
U.S. which would lead to legislative restrictions. The speech is not
aimed at Chile. I wanted to tell you about this. My evaluation of
you is that you are a victim of all left-wing troops around the
world, and that your greatest sin was that you overthrew a

government which was going Communist. But we have a practical problem we have to take into account, without bringing about pressures incompatible with your dignity, and at the same time which does not lead to U.S. laws which will undermine our relationship.

It would really help if you would let us know the measures you are taking in the human rights field. None of this is said with the hope of undermining your government. I want you to succeed and I want to retain the possibility of aid.

If we defeat the Kennedy amendment, -- I don't know if you listen in on my phone, but if you do you have just heard me issue instructions to Washington to make an all-out effort to do just that -- if we defeat it, we will deliver the F-5E's as we agreed to do. We held up for a while in others to avoid providing additional ammunition to our enemies.

Pinochet: We are returning to institutionalization step by step. But we are constantly being attacked by the Christian Democratics. They have a strong voice in Washington. Not the people in the Pentagon, but they do get through to Congress. Gabriel Valdez has access. Also Letelier.

The Secretary: I have not seen a Christian Democrat for years.

Pinochet: Also Tomic, and others I don't recall. Letelier has access to the Congress. We know they are giving false information. You see, we have no experience in government. We are worried about our image. In a few days we will publish the constitutional article on human rights, and also another setting up the Council of State. There are a number of efforts we are making to move to institutionalization. In the economic area, we have paid our debts, after the renegotiation. We are paying $700 million in debts with interest this year. We have made land reforms. And we are taking

other constitutional measures. We have freed most detained
prisoners. There have been 60 more just recently. In September 11,
1974, I challenged the Soviets to set free their prisoners. But they
haven't done so, while we have only 400 people who are now detained.
On international relations, we are doing well. In the case of
Bolivia, we have extended our good will. It all depends now on Peru.

The Secretary: I have the impression that Peru is not very
sympathetic.

Pinochet: You are right. Peru does not wish to see the idea
proposed.

The Secretary: Peru told me they would get no port out of the
arrangement.

Pinochet: Peru is arming. Peru is trying to buy a carrier from the
British for $160 million. It is also building four torpedo boats in
Europe. Peru is breaking the arms balance in the South Pacific. It
has 600 tanks from the Soviet Union. We are doing what we can to
sustain ourselves in case of an emergency.

The Secretary: What are you doing?

Pinochet: We are largely modifying old armaments, fixing junked
units. We are a people with energy. We have no Indians.

The Secretary: I gather Chile generally wins its wars.

Pinochet: We have never lost a war. We are a proud people. On the
human rights front, we are slowly making progress. We are now down
to 400. We have freed more. And we are also changing some
sentences so that the prisoners can be eligible for leaving.

The Secretary: If you could group the releases, instead of 20 a week, have a bigger program of releases, that would be better for the psychological impact of the releases. What I mean is not that you should delay, but that you should group the releases. But, to return to the military aid question, I really don't know how it will go tomorrow in the Senate.

Trucco: The Buchanan amendment is workable.

The Secretary: I repeat that if the House version succeeds, then we will send the planes.

Trucco: (Discusses the technical aspects of the 1975, 1976 and 1977 legislation.)

Trucco: The problem is now in the Senate, for the FY 1977 bill. Fraser has already had his amendment passed by the House.

The Secretary: I understand. We have our position on that. My statement and our position are designed to allow us to say to the Congress that we are talking to the Chilean government and therefore Congress need not act. We had the choice whether I should come or not. We thought it better for Chile if I came. My statement is not offensive to Chile. Ninety-five percent of what I say is applicable to all the governments of the Hemisphere. It includes things your own people have said.

Trucco: That's true. We are strongly in favor of strengthening the OAS Commission.

The Secretary: We are not asking the OAS to endorse anything. I have talked with other delegations. We want an outcome which is not deeply embarrassing to you. But as friends, I must tell you that we face a situation in the United States where we must be able to point to events here in Chile, or we will be defeated. As Angola demonstrates, Congress is in a mood of destructiveness. We were in a good position in Angola. We thought Angola could become the Viet-Nam of Cuba. This would have occurred if Cuba had begun to sustain 20 causalities a week. Cuba could not have stood that for long. We had the forces for that. Congress stopped us. But I am persuaded that the Executive, whoever is elected, will be stronger after the election.

Pinochet: How does the US see the problem between Chile and Peru?

The Secretary: (after a pause) We would not like to see a conflict. Much depends on who begins it.

Pinochet: The question is really how to prevent the beginning.

The Secretary: The American people would ask who is advancing on whom.

Pinochet: But you know what's going on here. You see it with your satellites.

The Secretary: Well, I can assure you that if you take Lima, you will have little U.S. support.

Pinochet: We did it once, a hundred years ago. It would be difficult now, in view of the present balance of forces.

The Secretary: If Peru attacked, this would be a serious matter for a country armed with Soviet equipment. It would be serious. Clearly we would oppose it diplomatically. But it all depends, beyond that. It is not easy to generate support for U.S. military action these days.

Pinochet: We must fight with our own arms?

The Secretary: I distinguish between preferences and probabilities. It depends how it happens. If there is naked aggression, that means greater, more general resistance.

Pinoche: Assume the worst, that is to say, that Chile is the aggressor. Peru defends itself, and then attacks us. What happens?

The Secretary: It's not that easy. We will know who the aggressor is. If you are not the aggressor, then you will have support. But aggression does not resolve international disputes. One side can stage an incident. But generally we will know who the aggressor is.

Carvajal: In the case of Bolivia, if we gave Bolivia some territory, Bolivian territory might be guaranteed by the American states.

The Secretary: I have supported Bolivia in its aspirations to the sea, but de la Flor is not happy about it.

Carvajal: If we gave some territory to Bolivia, and then permitted Peru to the use the port, Peru would get everything it needs.

The Secretary: It is my feeling Peru will not accept.

Pinochet: I am concerned very much by the Peruvian situation. Circumstances might produce aggression by Peru. Why are they buying tanks? They have heavy artillery, 155's. Peru is more inclined to Russia than the U.S. Russia supports their people 100%. We are behind you. You are the leader. But you have a punitive system for your friends.

The Secretary: There is merit in what you say.  It is a curious time in the U.S.

Pinochet: We solved the problem of the large transnational enterprises.  We renegotiated the expropriations, and demonstrated our good faith by making prompt payments on the indebtedness.

The Secretary: It is unfortunate.  We have been through Viet-Nam and Watergate.  We have to wait until the elections.  We welcomed the overthrow of the Communist-inclined government here.  We are not out to weaken your position.  On foreign aggression, it would be a grave situation if one were attacked.  That would constitute a direct threat to the inter-American system.

Carvajal: There is massive Cuban influence in Peru.  Many Cubans are there.  The Peruvians may be pushed.  And what happens to the thousands of Cuban soldiers now in Africa, when they are no longer needed there.

The Secretary: If there are Cuban troops involved in a Peruvian attack, then the problem is easy.  We will not permit a Cuban military force of 5,000 Cubans in Peru.

Carvajal: They now have a system, where the Peruvians enter in groups of 20, but the Peruvian registry registers only 1.

The Secretary: The Cubans are not good soldiers.

Carvajal: But there is the danger of irresponsible attack.

Claro: I have sources in Peru.  There is, I am told, a real chance that Cuba could airlift troops to Peru.

<u>The Secretary</u>: This would change the situation, and the question then is easy. We will not permit Cuba another military adventure. A war between Peru and Chile would be a complex thing, but a war between Cuba and Chile or others, we would not be indifferent.

<u>Claro</u>: Your planners were down here in 1974. They did not believe that there was a Cuba threat. The Soviets use Cuba for aggression, I argued. Angola has since confirmed this.

<u>The Secretary</u>: We will not tolerate another Cuban military move. After the election, we will have massive trouble if they are not out of Angola. Secondly, I also feel stronger that we can't accept coexistence and ideological subversion. We have the conditions now for a more realistic policy. It would help if you had some human rights progress, which could be announced in packages. The most important are the constitutional guarantees. The precise numbers of prisoners is subordinate. Right to habeas corpus is also important. And if you could give us advanced information of your human rights efforts, we could use this. As to the Christian Democrats, we are not using them. I haven't seen one since 1969. We want to remove the weapons in the arms of our enemies. It is a phenomenon that we deal with special severity with our friends. I want to see our relations and friendship improve. I encouraged the OAS to have its General Assembly here. I knew it would add prestige to Chile. I came for that same reason. We have suggestions. We want to help, not undermine you. You did a great service to the West in overthrowing Allende. Otherwise Chile would have followed Cuba. Then there would have been no human rights or a Human Rights Commission.

Trucco: We provided the General Assembly the answers to some of the Secretary's suggestions. What will be missing will be our explanation of the coming constitutional acts.

The Secretary: Can you do those while the OAS is here?

Pinochet: We have wanted to avoid doing anything while the OAS is here, since it then looks as though we did it to dampen OAS pressure. We might be able to in 30 days.

The Secretary: If we can, we are prepared to say we have the impression that the constitutional act is helpful.

Pinochet: I discussed it in my inaugural speech.

SECRET/NODIS

Source: "Memorandum of Conversation between Henry Kissinger and Augusto Pinochet, U.S.-Chilean Relations." (1976, June 8). In US Department of State, *Chile Declassification Project*. Freedom of Information Act Virtual Reading Room. Accessed at: https://foia.state.gov/searchapp/DOCUMENTS/StateChile3/0000579F.pdf

# DOCUMENT 10

Document 10 is a memorandum from the Carter administration's director of policy planning in the State Department, Anthony Lake, to the deputy secretary of state, Warren Christopher, on the debates over human rights sanctions against authoritarian countries by the new Carter administration. Although Lake argues that Chile is "the hardest test" for the proponents of the new policy, the memorandum captures the belief of the Carter administration that continued pressure from the United States would "contribute to further progress toward restoration of political freedoms" in Chile. It also refers to the assassination of Orlando Letelier and his assistant, Ronni Moffitt, by car bomb in Washington, DC.

CONFIDENTIAL

ATTACHMENT

Memorandum From the Director of the Policy Planning Staff (Lake) to the Deputy Secretary of State (Christopher)

Washington, August 10, 1978

SUBJECT: Human Rights "Sanctions"

We continue to believe that case-by-case decision making holds the best hope of making our human rights policy effective in varying situations, and of keeping it in balance with other foreign policy interests. But we also see a need for agreement on some general principles which would help guide individual decisions.

Three issues of special concern to us are whether we ever should deny IFI loans which serve basic human needs to countries under repressive regimes; whether to use economic sanctions to press for political change as well as for respect of rights of the person; and how to coordinate all our levers of influence with a given country.

You have our memorandum of last May on the first issue. The attached paper addresses the second and touches on the third. (Other work on the third is in train: the Interagency Group meeting planned for later this month [is] to look at assistance programs a year ahead, and the papers now being prepared on actions taken or planned to integrate human rights advocacy into all our relations with selected countries).

The attached memorandum argues S/P's case for:

— A strong policy bias against opposing IFI loans except in response to gross violations of rights of the person;
— Limiting restrictions on programs designed to help American exporters and investors to the minimum required by law;

— Distancing ourselves from the security forces of countries which deny freedom of expression;

— Channeling more of our bilateral economic assistance to countries with a good or improving record in political as well as personal human rights.

HA has seen this memorandum in draft and will be sending you a separate paper detailing their agreements and disagreements with it.

ATTACHMENT

Memorandum From the Director of the Policy Planning Staff (Lake) to the Deputy Secretary of State (Christopher)

Washington, August 10, 1978

SUBJECT:

Human Rights "Sanctions"

*The Issue*

Successes of the human rights policy to date may now confront us with a new problem: whether to continue denying economic and security benefits (opposition to IFI [International Financial Institution] loans; restrictions on bilateral economic and security programs) to a country if arbitrary arrest, torture, and other violations of the person are ended but there is no meaningful progress on political rights and the legal and institutional instruments of repression remain.

*Discussion*

We believe there should be a strong policy bias against opposing *IFI* [International Financial Institution] *loans* except in response to gross violations of rights of the person and that in general we should limit programs which are designed primarily to help American exporters and investors (*ExIm, CCC, OPIC*) only to the extent required by law. The latter would mean no limits on CCC credits (since there is no applicable law), and might mean using the language of the ExIm

[Export-Import Bank] legislation (to "take into account" human rights situations "and the effects such exports may have on human rights") to deny credits only if the particular export in question might be used in human rights violations or if chances were high that denial might actually produce improvements in rights of the person.

This would be consistent with laws which specifically cite violations of the person as those which require denial of US assistance. It reflects various policy statements, beginning with the Secretary's April 1977 Law Day Speech in which he said we can justifiably seek a rapid end to violations of the person but that promotion of other human rights may be slower to show results. And it reflects both laws and policy directives (and common sense) which call on us to consider human rights trends rather than demand sudden transformations in authoritarian societies.

We can imagine exceptions which we might advocate to this guideline. We might not, for instance, want to vote in one of the Banks for a major non-bhn [Basic Human Needs] loan to a country when its military had just overturned an elected government, even if that move did not include arrests of opposition leaders. Exceptions, however, should be used to express concern about a human rights deterioration or the reversal of a trend—not to maintain maximum pressure until all serious problems are solved.

Chile could be the hardest test of the policy we are advocating. Violations of the person have virtually ended, in part as a result of our pressure. There is a good chance that continued pressure from us could contribute to further progress toward restoration of political freedoms. The latter would, *inter alia*, be the best long-range guarantee of rights of the person. Chile's democratic traditions, moreover, make it hard for that regime to argue that our pressure for a restoration of democracy reflects cultural arrogance. And our own role in its recent history makes it impossible for us to be neutral: to begin now to support IFI loans to it, or to open up ExIm credits, would be seen (in Chile and abroad) as prematurely rewarding Chile.

Finally, those Congressmen who care about Chile are urging that we intensify pressure until and unless democracy is restored.

Thus the arguments for keeping the heat on are strong. Similar cases can be made elsewhere.

Nonetheless we believe that the human rights policy, and American interests in general, ultimately will benefit if we do not seem to be using economic pressure to bring down a particular government. Repressive governments will be more likely to improve their performance if they believe something short of suicide will bring a lifting of economic sanctions. Other IFI donors will be more likely to join our efforts if we do not seem bent on using those institutions not just to work for an end to torture and arbitrary arrest worldwide, but to topple a particular government of which we most strongly disapprove. And in this country, a sense that the human rights policy was hurting American exports (and jobs) could begin seriously to undercut support for the policy itself.

The strongest argument seems to us to be one of principle. To deny a country access to international financial support in order to try to force political change on it is not qualitatively different from the Nixon Administration's efforts to "destabilize" the Allende government. We have not been as successful in cutting off Pinochet's financial sources as Nixon was in doing the same to Allende, and our efforts have not included jawboning commercial banks. But the difference is of degree rather than of kind.

In practice of course we cannot suddenly resume economic business as usual with Chile. Chile is an emotional issue and our attitude toward it is, rightly or wrongly, a symbol to many of our human rights commitment. Moreover, present sanctions are also aimed at getting Letelier's alleged murderers extradited. But if the Letelier issue is satisfactorily resolved and there is no regression on rights of the person, we should begin phasing in some ExIm and CCC financing and supporting bhn loans to Chile in the IFIs, carefully explain both to the Chileans and to human rights activists in this country what we are doing and why, and test the political waters for the feasibility of beginning to support some non-bhn loans.

*Promoting Political Rights*

Our position is only tenable, however, if we can also demonstrate that we are working to promote political rights by other means.

We should avoid supplying the internal *security* forces of governments which deny freedom of expression to their critics, whether or not those governments find it necessary actually to lock the critics up. Here too there might be occasional exceptions. The recent approval of a sale of handguns to South Korea's Presidential guard, even while denying a similar sale to its regular police, is a case in point. But in general we should reverse the past practice in which economic assistance has borne the brunt of the human rights policy, while sales to police (and military) forces remained relatively unscathed. When there is an improving but still unsatisfactory overall human rights situation, we should lift economic sanctions first while continuing to distance ourselves from the security forces of a repressive regime.

*Bilateral economic assistance* might be adjusted to particular situations. You know S/P's aversion to denying assistance which furthers the economic human rights of poor people who have the misfortune to live under a repressive regime. Nonetheless there are more needy people worldwide than we have resources, and the President has directed us to channel bilateral assistance to countries with a good or improving human rights record. Moreover, there is a significant difference between bilateral programs which we can control and adjust, and IFI loans, on which we usually must vote when and as they are presented to us. Thus, we could reprogram aid levels away from repressive regimes and toward governments showing more support for political freedom, rather than continuing to use the IFIs to pressure countries which have ceased violations of the person.

Finally, we need to do more about the *positive promotion of human rights*. For all our rhetoric (in speeches and in PD-30) about preferring positive approaches to sanctions, our policy in practice still is skewed toward the latter. That is understandable since we have to react to IFI loans and arms sales requests as they come to us, while devising positive approaches appropriate to cultures different from our own requires effort and imagination. Some of our Embassies (e.g., Djakarta, Seoul, Nairobi) have volunteered interesting suggestions, based on extensive personal experience in those societies. But too many in the regional bureaus still see the human rights policy as a "problem" of sanctions; if that threat is removed they seem to think no active human rights policy is required of them. If we are going to lift sanctions on governments which still deny political freedoms it will be essential that we demonstrate (not least to human rights activists on the Hill) what we are doing instead to promote the expansion of those freedoms. The reports now being prepared on steps taken and planned to integrate human rights concerns into our policies toward selected countries could be a useful vehicle for this effort.

CONFIDENTIAL

**Source:** "Memorandum from the Director of the Policy Planning Staff (Lake) to the Deputy Secretary of State (Christopher), Human Rights 'Sanctions.'" (1978, August 10). In K. Ahlberg & A.M. Howard (Eds.), *Foreign Relations of the United States (FRUS), 1977-1980* (vol. II, doc. 157). Washington, DC: United States Government Printing Office, 2013.

# DOCUMENT 11

Document 11 provides a glimpse into the US response to the September 1976 assassinations of Orlando Letelier and Ronni Moffit in Washington, DC. Secretary of State Cyrus Vance gives President Carter a series of options in response to the Pinochet government's 1979 refusal to extradite Chilean intelligence officers to the United States. Despite his personal outrage about the actions of the Chilean government, however, Vance suggests that Carter avoid "extreme measures to demonstrate our displeasure," including the suggestions made in Congress that the United States enact legislation to limit Chilean access to private capital. At the same time he does suggest the "extraordinary remedy" of cutting off Chile's Export-Import Bank financing, as passed in Congress. The paper thus also notes both the ongoing difficulties the Chilean problem caused between the legislative and executive branches and the problems the Carter administration faced in enacting its human rights foreign policy.

CONFIDENTIAL

THE SECRETARY OF STATE
WASHINGTON

October 19, 1979

MEMORANDUM FOR: THE PRESIDENT

FROM: Cyrus Vance

RE: Letelier/Moffitt Case

As you know, the Chilean Supreme Court has denied our request for the extradition of the three Chilean intelligence officers indicted by a United States grand jury for the assassination of Orlando Letelier (a former Chilean Ambassador to the U.S.) and Ronni Moffitt. Because the Court's decision also rules out virtually any possibility that these three men will be tried in Chile, it is likely that this act of terrorism, committed on the streets of our nation's capital, will go unpunished. We therefore now face the issue of how to respond to the Government of Chile.

Background. Letelier and Moffitt were killed in September 1976 by a bomb attached to their car. On August 1, 1978, a federal grand jury handed down indictments charging Michael Townley, a member of the Chilean secret police, and two others with having carried out the crime. The same grand jury charged three high-ranking members

of the Chilean secret police with having planned and directed the
killings. Townley and his two accomplices were subsequently tried
and convicted in a U.S. District Court. The United States sought
the extradition from Chile of the other three men.

Recommendations. The Government of Chile bears two-fold
responsibility for these crimes. First, high-ranking officials of that
government have been charged with having planned and directed the
crimes -- and the overwhelming body of evidence that has been amassed
by the Department of Justice makes it likely that those charges would be
upheld if a fair trial could be held either in Chile or the U.S. Second,
the Government of Chile has made no serious effort to investigate or
prosecute these crimes on its own, and its judicial system has refused
either to make the three Chilean officials available for trial in the
U.S. or to order a thorough and effective local investigation.

By its actions -- and its inactions -- the Government of Chile
has, in effect, condoned this act of international terrorism within
the United States. We believe it is essential that we make clear,
both to Chile and to others throughout the world, that such actions
cannot be tolerated.

As you know, there have been suggestions from the Hill and
elsewhere that we take extreme measures to demonstrate our
displeasure, including enacting legislation to limit private bank
lending to Chile, withdrawing our Ambassador, or even breaking
relations altogether. I have considered these options, and while I
share the outrage of those who have suggested them, I believe steps
like this would not serve our interests in Chile or elsewhere.
Instead, I recommend that the following steps be taken:

(1) Diplomatic Steps. During the course of the Letelier matter,
Ambassador Landau has met regularly with Chilean officials to express

the concern of the United States Government. In addition, we have
recalled Ambassador Landau three times on consultations as a
reflection of our displeasure at developments in the case, and Warren
and I have made numerous demarches to Chilean officials. We will be
meeting further with Chilean officials to reiterate our view that the
Government of Chile's failure to investigate this crime is
unacceptable, and to explain the steps we are taking. I believe we
should also make a reduction in the size of our Mission in Chile as a
concrete indication of our displeasure. I am prepared to make such
reductions in the State Department component of the Mission staff, and
I will shortly be submitting to you a proposal for personnel reductions
by other agencies operating in Chile. No further diplomatic steps are
possible at this time, short of recalling Ambassador Landau
permanently or breaking relations, neither of which I recommend.

Approve_____          Disapprove_____

(2) Terminate the FMS Pipeline. A relatively small amount of
equipment remains in the FMS [Foreign Military Sales] pipeline (we
estimate the value to be approximately $7 million). I propose to
terminate the pipeline in an orderly fashion, and to attempt to
minimize any termination costs that might require a Congressional
appropriation. However, I believe we should complete the
termination of the pipeline by January 1, 1980, even if that does
entail some minimal termination costs.

Approve_____          Disapprove_____

(3) Withdraw the MilGroup. There are currently four U.S.
officials in the MilGroup in our Embassy in Santiago. I propose to
withdraw the MilGroup promptly. With the termination of the FMS
pipeline by the end of the year, the MilGroup will no longer have
any function to perform in Chile. I recommend, however, that our
three Defense Attaches remain in Santiago.

Approve_____          Disapprove_____

(4) <u>Suspend EX-IM Financing in Chile</u>. The Chafee Amendment to the Export-Import Bank Act authorizes the denial of EX-IM financing in cases where the President determines that such action would be "in the national interest" and would "clearly and importantly advance U.S. policy in such areas as international terrorism. . . ." We believe that Chile's actions in the Letelier case justify the invocation of this extraordinary remedy. While the Congress intended that this sanction should be used only sparingly, it would be difficult to conceive of a more appropriate case than the present one -- where high officials of a foreign government have been directly implicated in murders committed on United States territory, and where the government has effectively frustrated all attempts to bring the accused perpetrators of these crimes to justice.

Moreover, if the Chafee Amendment were not invoked in the present case, EX-IM activity in Chile would not simply remain at current levels; it would, instead, increase dramatically. Prior to the enactment of Chafee, EX-IM had for several years restricted financing in Chile to a maximum of $750,000 per project. Following Chafee's enactment, that restriction was informally extended pending the final outcome of the Letelier matter and a determination of whether the Amendment would be applicable. In the absence of the Presidential determination described above, EX-IM believes it would not have a legal basis for maintaining the $750,000 ceiling and would therefore be expected to increase sharply.

I therefore recommend that you sign the proposed Presidential determination attached at Tab 1, both as an appropriate response to Chile's actions in the Letelier matter, and to avoid the anomaly of seeming to reward those actions. Some elements of the business community will undoubtedly criticize us for taking this step, but I strongly believe that we must do so.

Approve_____                Disapprove_____

CONFIDENTIAL

**Source:** Secretary of State. (1979, October 19). "Options Paper for President Carter from Cyrus Vance, 'Letelier/Moffit Case.'" Digital National Security Archive. Washington, DC: George Washington University.

## DOCUMENT 12

Document 12 is a memorandum from Secretary of State Alexander Haig to the newly inaugurated President Reagan. It details a proposed shift in US policy toward the Pinochet regime. In it, Haig tells Reagan that he plans to lift Carter-era limits on Chilean financing and reinstate joint military exercises with the government, including the Export-Import Bank financing discussed above. This decision was part of a broader one by the Reagan administration to reverse the human rights-based foreign policy of the Carter administration, in particular toward Chile.

THE SECRETARY OF STATE
WASHINGTON

February 16, 1981                              SECRET

MEMORANDUM FOR:    THE PRESIDENT
From:              Alexander M. Haig, Jr.
Subject:           Our Policy Toward Chile

You asked about our Chile policy. In the next few days I plan to lift the prohibition on Ex-Im Bank financing and approve DOD's [Department of Defense] invitation list for this year's UNITAS

[Annual U.S.-South America Allied Exercise] naval exercise, to include Chile. These are the two most annoying aspects of current policy under Executive Branch control. We will have a full inter-agency review in about one month to decide on further adjustments. We want to maintain appropriate balance in our politics between Argentina and Chile. Both countries are now prohibited by legislation from military sales or training except under very narrow waiver authority.

Among friendly countries looking to the United States for leadership, our relations with Chile are uniquely encumbered by congressional and executive sanctions. Most were imposed because of the repressive policies of the Pinochet regime after it overthrew Allende in 1973. Although there were significant human rights improvements over the past four years, U.S. policy hardened.

In late 1979, the Chilean Supreme Court denied a request for the extradition of three Chilean Army officers involved in the 1976 assassinations of Orlando Letelier and Ronni Moffit [sic] in Washington, D.C. Because the Chilean government had failed to investigate fully or prosecute the three men, the Carter Administration then imposed a series of additional sanctions, most important of these were the suspension of all Ex-Im financing and denying an invitation to Chile for the 1980 UNITAS exercise. The suspension of Ex-Im financing puts U.S. exporters at a competitive disadvantage with other industrialized countries. Because of Chile's strategic location and naval tradition, it is in our interest to maintain military cooperation for hemispheric defense.

SECRET

**Source:** Secretary of State. (1981, February 16). "Secret Memorandum for President Reagan from Alexander Haig, 'Our Policy Toward Chile.'" Digital National Security Archive. Washington, DC: George Washington University.

# CHAPTER FOUR

# MASS KILLING AT A DISTANCE: US COMPLICITY IN THE EAST TIMOR GENOCIDE AND INTERNATIONAL STRUCTURAL VIOLENCE (1975-1999)

Joseph Nevins

## INTRODUCTION

East Timor is one of the world's newest countries, acceding to independence on May 20, 2002, after almost three years of United Nations administration. From 1975 to 1999, upwards of 200,000 East Timorese, almost one-third of the territory's 1975 population, lost their lives as a result of neighboring Indonesia's invasion and almost 24-year occupation.[71]

Myriad Western capitalist countries (Nevins, 2005; Fernandes, 2015), particularly the United States whose support was decisive, strongly backed the invasion and occupation. Washington, DC, provided Indonesia's Suharto regime the green light for the invasion and supplied it significant military, economic, and diplomatic assistance over the 1975–99 period.

---

71 Significant components of this chapter have appeared in previous publications by the authors Jardine (1999) and Nevins (2005, 2007–08).

Without these various forms of assistance, it is highly doubtful that the invasion would have taken place or that the occupation would have endured to the depth, extent, and duration that it did. In the concluding section of this chapter, I explain US involvement by introducing and developing the concept of international structural violence (a concept inspired by Johan Galtung). In the East Timor case, this violence took the form of "normal" relations between states. It is a violence that gives rise to complicity in mass killing and facilitates impunity for the globally powerful (and those with whom they are allied) for their effective participation in war crimes and crimes against humanity.

## THE MAKING OF EAST TIMOR'S KILLING FIELDS

East Timor, as a nation-state, is in large part an imperial creation, as its very territorial definition and the associated national identity of the people grew out of Portuguese colonialism. Portugal laid claim to the island of Timor in the early 1500s in an effort to exploit its lucrative trade in sandalwood. Inter-imperial competition with the Dutch eventually led to the formal division of the island, with the eastern half becoming Portuguese Timor, and most of the western portion becoming part of the Dutch East Indies (what is today known as Indonesia).

In the context of a process of decolonization of Portugal's overseas empire from 1974 to 1975, the military-dominated Indonesian state set its sights on East Timor with the goal of ensuring that the population would opt for integration with Indonesia. Within a few weeks of the April 1974 coup that overthrew the Portuguese military dictatorship and initiated a process of democratization and decolonization in Portugal's overseas colonies, several political parties sprung up in Portuguese Timor (see Jolliffe, 1978; Ramos-Horta, 1987; Dunn, 1996; Taylor, 1999; Hill, 2002), the two largest and most important being the UDT (the Timorese Democratic Union) and the ASDT (the Association of Timorese Social Democrats, later to become FRETILIN, the Revolutionary Front for an Independent East Timor).

While the relatively conservative UDT began as the largest political grouping, it quickly began to lose ground to the ASDT, which, in September 1974, changed the group's name to FRETILIN and demanded an immediate declaration of de jure independence from the Portuguese. It also demanded the establishment of a transitional government that would carry East Timor through a rapid process of decolonization. By early 1975, FRETILIN was, by most accounts (including that of the Portuguese administrators), the grouping that enjoyed the most popular support (Dunn, 1996; Taylor, 1999).

Prior to the overthrow of the Portuguese military government, Indonesia had shown only occasional interest in East Timor, while often publicly stating that Jakarta had no claim on the then-Portuguese colony. Indonesian intelligence reportedly made an assessment in late 1972 or 1973, however, asserting that it could not allow an independent East Timor to exist were the Portuguese to withdraw. Given developments in Vietnam, so went the thinking in Jakarta, an independent East Timor could create security problems for Indonesia. This view grew in strength in the aftermath of the coup in Lisbon. Leading elements of the Indonesian intelligence and security apparatuses feared that an independent East Timor would compound the problems at the archipelago's periphery by strengthening already present separatist sentiments and by possibly serving as a base for leftist subversion. Months later, a small number of Indonesia's top military officials and elements of military intelligence decided to launch a campaign of subversion—codenamed Operasi Komodo or Operation Komodo Dragon—aimed at convincing the East Timorese of the wisdom of "integrating" with Indonesia or, failing that, forcibly annexing the territory (Dunn, 1996; Taylor, 1999).

Central to these efforts was Indonesia's fomenting of a civil war between the UDT and FRETILIN. On the basis of meetings with Indonesian officials and false Indonesian intelligence reports of an imminent FRETILIN power grab, clandestine Chinese arms deliveries, and "Vietnamese terrorists" entering the territory to aid FRETILIN, the UDT decided to try to seize power in the territory and thus launched a coup on August 12, 1975. UDT leaders were convinced that Indonesia would not allow East Timorese independence under FRETILIN leadership and probably not even under the UDT. Nonetheless, the UDT felt that only by purging the territory of "communist" influence would it have any chance of preventing an Indonesian invasion (Jolliffe, 1978; Ramos-Horta, 1987; Taylor, 1999; see also Australian Senate Foreign Affairs, Defence and Trade References Committee, 2000).

The UDT greatly underestimated the strength of FRETILIN, however. On September 24, 1975, the short-lived civil war ended when FRETILIN drove approximately 500 UDT soldiers, along with 2,500 refugees (most of whom were family members of UDT leaders and soldiers), westward into West (Indonesian) Timor. All Portuguese authorities fled the territory. Well aware of Indonesia's designs on the territory and more concerned about its other colonies in Africa and developments at home, Lisbon acquiesced to Jakarta, effectively doing nothing in the face of growing Indonesian interference in the decolonization process and intensifying acts of military aggression (Taylor, 1999; Dunn,1996; Jolliffe, 1978).

As FRETILIN was overcoming the last of the UDT at the end of the civil war, cross-border (from West Timor) incursions by the Indonesian military (Tentara Nasional Indonesia [TNI]) began (Jolliffe, 1978; Van Atta & Toohey, 1982; Taylor, 1999). To present the appearance of an ongoing civil war and to further Indonesia's claim that it was intervening on behalf of East Timorese suffering from FRETILIN-led brutality, Indonesia undertook frequent incursions into Portuguese Timor with the intent of establishing bases along the boundary with Indonesia. This culminated in mid-November when the Indonesians mounted a land, air, and sea attack for about two weeks against the town of Atabae, which finally fell on November 28, 1975 (Budiardjo & Liem, 1984; Taylor, 1999; see also Turner, 1992). On that same date, FRETILIN declared independence from Portugal and its founding of the Democratic Republic of East Timor. Nine days later, on December 7, Indonesia launched a full-scale invasion into the territory.

In the early morning hours of December 7, Indonesian troops parachuted into Dili, near the waterfront. As described by Bishop Martinho Costa Lopes, a Catholic priest who was in the city at the time, the scene was terrifying: "The soldiers who landed started killing everyone they could find. There were many dead bodies in the streets—all we could see were soldiers killing, killing, killing" (Tapol, 1983, p. 3). In the first two days of the invasion, about 2,000 people lost their lives at the hands of the marauding Indonesian troops in Dili alone, according to one estimate (Taylor, 1999). Thereafter, the Indonesian soldiers began looting homes and churches, loading cars, motorcycles, furniture, and even windows onto ships destined for Indonesia. They also compelled young women, especially those related to FRETILIN activists and members of the FRETILIN-associated women's and students' organizations, to join them in a victory celebration. The soldiers arrested and imprisoned most of the women, many of whom they repeatedly tortured and raped (Dunn, 1996; Aditjondro, 1998; Sissons, 1997; Taylor, 1999; Modvig et al., 2000). Such brutality was hardly exceptional: rape and sexual violence against women and girls was widespread throughout the years of the Indonesian invasion and occupation (CAVR, 2005). Here, "Edinha" relates what happened to a relative: "My nephew's wife was a pretty girl pregnant with their first child, soon to give birth.... The wife was home alone and a Javanese soldier came and raped her. The baby died.... Of course it doesn't just happen to this girl, it happens to many other girls. Sometimes they rape the wife in front of the husband. If he does anything he will be killed" (quoted in Turner, 1992, p. 111).

In the face of such brutality—TNI efforts to advance inland from its bases in the territory's principal towns such as Dili and Baucau in the aftermath of the initial invasion and strong resistance from FRETILIN—large numbers of East Timorese lost their lives. In a statement dated February 13, 1976, Francisco Lopes da Cruz, Jakarta's appointee to the position of vice-chairman of the "Provisional Government of East Timor," stated that 50,000 East Timorese had already died at the hands of the Indonesian military. Nevertheless, in the first few months of the invasion, the TNI's territorial control, in the words of the US Defense Intelligence Agency, progressed at "a snail's pace" (Budiardjo & Liem, 1984, p. 23; see also Dunn, 1996; Taylor, 1999). By August 1976, Indonesia only controlled the major towns, some regional centers and villages in the territory, and several "corridors" that connected some of the areas (Budiardjo & Liem, 1984). As of March 1977, the US State Department estimated that two-thirds of the East

Timorese population was still in FRETILIN-dominated areas (Chomsky & Herman, 1979, p. 176).

This situation began to change dramatically in late 1977. In the face of a military stalemate, mounting international publicity of the brutality of the occupation, and growing criticism of the Indonesian occupation within the United States and Western Europe, Jakarta decided it was time to wipe out the resistance once and for all and put an end to any hopes for an independent East Timor (Dunn, 1996; Taylor, 1999). Emboldened by the acquisition of advanced military technology, especially counter-insurgency aircraft like US "Broncos" (OV-10FS) and Australian "Sabres," the TNI began an 18-month campaign characterized by Catholic sources within East Timor as one of "encirclement" and "annihilation" (Taylor, 1999; see also CAVR, 2005). Using tens of thousands of ground troops and aerial bombardment, TNI forces penetrated toward the center from the border and the coasts. The TNI bombed forested areas, hoping to defoliate ground cover, and used chemical sprays to destroy crops and livestock. The objective was to push the resistance into a small area of the country where they could be killed or captured, and to force the population living in the interior of the country to come to the coastal lowlands where they could be more easily controlled by the Indonesians (Taylor, 1999; Budiardjo & Liem, 1984). The campaign had devastating effects on the resistance and the civilian population, killing many thousands (Taylor, 1999). An Australian Parliament Legislative Research Service report described the situation in the territory in the late 1970s as one of "indiscriminate killing on a scale unprecedented in post-World War II history" (quoted in Chomsky, 1979, p. 3).

The Indonesian authorities herded many of the surrendering civilians into a growing number of large, guarded camps. According to a report by the Australian Council for Overseas Aid from July 1979, there were 15 such centers in which there were 318,921 "displaced persons" (almost half the pre-invasion population). Located in both towns and rural areas, the camps were part of a counterinsurgency strategy composed of techniques similar to those employed against guerilla movements in Rhodesia and

Vietnam. The TNI used the camps to "Indonesianize" the population, which included Indonesian language instruction and political education. Forced labor, including the carrying of ammunition and supplies into combat areas, was common (Kohen & Taylor, 1979).

The combined effects of Jakarta's brutal military campaign, the forced relocation program, and the undermining of local food production resulted in famine. Conditions were so bad in one camp (in which 80 per cent of its 8,000 inhabitants suffered from malnutrition) that a visiting delegate from the International Committee of the Red Cross stated that the situation was "as bad as Biafra and potentially as serious as Kampuchea" (quoted in Taylor, 1999, p. 97). Famine-like conditions were hardly limited to the relocation camps, but existed across a wide swath of the country in the early years of Indonesia's war in East Timor, particularly as people fled the terror of the TNI. Herein, Cosme Freitas describes what he experienced in 1978:

When we evacuated from Uaimori, people began to die. From starvation or from illness. As we walked, death stalked us. Death was behind us as we walked, and people died. Not only old people, but children, through lack of food. The old people walked, their strength all gone, carrying just one *maek* [a species of tuber], or a *kumbili* [sweet yam]. And a little water in a bamboo container on their backs. This is how many of us died. The dead were scattered all along the way [from Uamori to Natarbora]. Others died from the mortars, 80 to 100 a day. We wanted to bury them, but the enemy kept shooting, so how could we bury them? We ran on. An old woman said: "Please my son, dig a hole to bury my child's body." We dug a hole, but less than half a metre deep. Before lowering the little angel into the hole we wrapped it in a mat to the sound of continuing gunfire. How could we bury it? We bent our heads and buried it with our hands.

Those we could, we buried. Otherwise they were left behind. How can we now find their bones? They rotted just as they were. We saw seven or eight people were sitting while leaning against a tree. They leaned against the tree and died like that. Flies and dogs were around them. In our hearts we were terrified. (CAVR, 2005, part 7, ch 7.3, p. 39)

In the face of these daunting conditions, the East Timorese resistance adapted and endured. By 1980, Falintil (the military wing of FRETILIN) units were attacking several Indonesian garrisons and even infrastructure and positions around Dili. In response to the guerrilla army's resurgence, the TNI launched Operation Security (*Operasi Keamanan*) in mid-1981, employing a brutal tactic called the "fence of legs" (*pagar betis*) in which the military forced many thousands of East Timorese males to form human chains that would walk across the countryside in front of Indonesian troops to flush out Falintil guerrillas or to surround them at points where they could be massacred. One of those compelled to participate, Cristiano da Costa, recounts the aftermath of the campaign:

> I was forced to go up with a group of soldiers to do a final clean-up.... We smelt the bodies before we found them. The heads had been cut off the first bodies, one women [sic] and four men.... The heads were on the other bodies I saw. We found three other men tied by the feet hanging upside down in trees.... Another two men were tied with their hands behind the trunks of trees. Their faces looked beaten and it looked like knife wounds to their stomach. On the ground beside them there were six others, two women and two children and an old man and an old woman.... There was dried blood on those bodies.... The smell was very bad and the flies.... It was not possible to identify those people; if they were my own brother or sister I would not know them. (Turner, 1992, pp. 185–86)

While many Falintil groups were slaughtered during the operation, some evaded capture, and still others surrendered. The operation as a whole had very detrimental effects on the population as it greatly disrupted agricultural production, leading to severe food shortages in most regions of the country. Many of those forced to participate in the campaign starved to death given the meager food provisions from the Indonesian military (Taylor, 1999).

As before, the resistance was able to reorganize. From that time forward, the military equation changed little, with the two sides in an effective stalemate. The war would continue, however, but at a much lower level, with anywhere from 15,000 to 30,000 Indonesian troops controlling the major towns and strategic points, while facing several hundred Falintil guerrillas, divided into small bands active across the country—in the forests, jungles, and mountainous areas. The two sides would occasionally attack the other, with the TNI launching offensives aimed at eradicating the guerrillas, while the Falintil would engage in much lower-level actions, attacking Indonesian troops as they moved between towns or through the countryside, as well as rural military posts.

This, more or less, remained the situation until 1998–99 when matters in East Timor changed considerably. Early 1998 was a time of political and economic crisis in Indonesia. In May of that year, a rising tide of anti-status quo sentiment forced Suharto, one of the world's longest-reigning dictators, to step down. With Suharto's ouster, fissures within the Indonesian political establishment became more apparent, allowing for initiatives toward East Timor that would have been difficult to imagine previously. In June 1998, B.J. Habibie, the new president, announced that Jakarta would offer the East Timorese "special status," a form of autonomy within Indonesia.

For the first time since December 7, 1975, pro-independence groups were able to operate openly. Beginning in June 1998, huge pro-independence demonstrations took place. These events quickly made it clear that most East Timorese rejected Jakarta's autonomy offer and instead demanded the holding of a referendum through which they could decide their political fate. Given the intensifying international spotlight on East Timor, the military, which opposed Habibie's initiative, could not be as openly brutal as it had in the past. So, in the last few months of 1998, it organized and armed paramilitary death squads, or "civilian militias"; together, they undertook a campaign of terror against East Timorese with pro-independence sympathies, killing hundreds over the next several months (see Robinson, 2009; Nevins, 2005).

The violence within the occupied territory occurred during unprecedented flexibility on the part of Jakarta. In January 1999, Habibie declared that he would grant independence to East Timor if its people rejected the autonomy offer. Several months later (on May 5, 1999), the governments of Indonesia and Portugal concluded negotiations that resulted in a series of historic accords that led to a United Nations-organized and -run referendum on East Timor's political status.

Held on August 30, 1999, the referendum saw the population vote overwhelmingly for independence. In response, the TNI and its paramilitary allies killed many hundreds of civilians, forced at least 400,000 people to flee their homes—almost half of the illegally occupied territory's population—while burning or destroying about 70 per cent of East Timor's buildings and infrastructure over a period of a few weeks (see Robinson, 2009). This was Indonesia's final act before withdrawing from East Timor and a United Nations-run administration took over the devastated territory.

Under the UN administration, a Commission on Reception, Truth, and Reconciliation (CAVR) was established and charged with developing an authoritative account about the human rights violations that occurred between 1974 and 1999. Published in 2005, the CAVR report, *Chega!* (Portuguese for *Enough!* or *Stop!*), provides chilling details of many of the worst atrocities committed during Jakarta's reign. These include torture, extrajudicial killings, disappearances, indiscriminate bombing, and the use of chemical and biological weapons. The CAVR also estimates that Indonesian forces committed thousands of acts of sexual violence—such as torture and mutilation of women, gang rapes, and sexual enslavement—acts that were "widespread and systematic," "widely accepted" within the military hierarchy, and "covered by almost total impunity" (CAVR, 2005, part 7, ch 7.7, pp. 3, 109). Even children "were systematically killed, detained, tortured, raped, and otherwise violated on a widespread scale" (CAVR, 2005, part 8, annex 1, p. 7).

The CAVR established that there were *at minimum* 102,800 East Timorese civilian deaths—84,200 of whom perished due to conflict-induced "displacement-related hunger and illness" (CAVR, 2005, part 7, ch 7.3, p. 5)—while advancing a figure of 201,900 as the *maximum* number of possible conflict-related civilian deaths. (Its estimates did not include what was undoubtedly the very large number of East Timorese combatant deaths.) Whichever of the two figures is more accurate—and there are serious questions about the robustness of the estimates advanced by the CAVR (see Roosa, 2007–08)—both constitute a significant percentage of the country's population.

The CAVR did not deliver judgment as to whether the death toll in East Timor constituted genocide. Certainly many analysts over the years have characterized Indonesia's crimes as such, but without justifying their use of the term (e.g., Kohen & Taylor, 1979; Jardine, 1999; Kiernan, 2003; Robinson, 2009), implicitly suggesting that the size of the death toll relative to the population as a whole is sufficient justification. Others have explicitly shied away from the term, with one calling it a "near-genocide" (see Klaehn, 2003). Such a stance reflects the considerable debate among scholars regarding whether or not what transpired in East Timor fits the definition of genocide. A key issue is the matter of intent and how one would prove it given that "would-be perpetrators [of the crime of genocide] are encouraged by the existing prohibitions and sanctions to disguise their motives and obfuscate their intentions"—an outcome that Derrick Silove (2000) characterizes as an "unintended consequence of establishing international human rights laws such as the Genocide Convention" (p. 75).

One of the first academics to consider the matter was Roger Clark, a specialist in international law, who makes a distinction between what he calls "criminal genocide" and "everyday genocide." Because of the UN Convention on the Prevention and Prosecution of the Crime of Genocide (UNCG)'s emphasis on intent, Clark (from the vantage point of what was known in 1981) concludes that he is "not at all certain that intent is there (or at least that it can be proved)" (Clark, 1981, p. 327). For Clark, rather than his conclusion being first and foremost a manifestation of the nature of what transpired in East Timor, it speaks to a significant gap in the UNCG. Drawing on basic criminal law in the Anglo-American system, in which culpability is based on various elements (not simply intent), he points out that the very design of the UNCG "does not catch cases where the destruction is done negligently [when a reasonable person should have anticipated the destruction in light of the actions]; nor does it encompass cases where the destruction is done 'only' recklessly [when the responsible party continues to carry out particular actions despite knowing their ill effects] or knowingly" (Clark, 1981, p. 326). Given that East Timor, in Clark's estimation, constitutes an "everyday genocide" ("the mass destruction—deliberate or accidental—of a nation, race, people, or culture" [Clark, 1981, p. 321]), he suggests that the UNCG be revised so that it catches reckless and negligent cases, as well as intentional ones (see also Silove, 2000).

Writing almost 20 years later, James Dunn (1998), a former Australian consul-general to East Timor while it was still a Portuguese colony and an adviser to the United Nations on human rights matters, insists that East Timor does constitute a case of genocide. In supporting his assertion, he points to several factors: (1) Indonesian military commanders did nothing to address crimes against humanity committed by their troops when, for example, cases of indiscriminate killings were brought to their attention; (2) the TNI forced East Timorese civilians to flee their homes into the mountains in the early years of the war and then bombed their settlements; and (3) Indonesian authorities refused for several years to allow international aid agencies, particularly the International Committee of the Red Cross, to enter the territory and provide humanitarian rescue. Such actions, Dunn (1998) argues, are a violation of the UNCG in that they reflect "an *intention* to allow the destruction of a significant part of the population of East Timor, at least those who were opposed to integration" (p. 87).

A shortcoming of Dunn's argument as presented above is that it does not distinguish between those targeted by Indonesian authorities for their effective membership in a particular *political* grouping (a category *not* covered by the UNCG)—those resisting Indonesia's occupation—and those targeted for being part of a particular "national, ethnical, racial or religious group" (the categories protected under the UNCG). Concomitantly, legal scholar Ben Saul (2001) contends that those violently targeted in East Timor by the Indonesian forces and their allies "probably do not constitute a recognized group under the *Genocide Convention*"—the killing of Chinese Timorese in the early period of Indonesia's invasion being perhaps the "major exception" (p. 521).

David Lisson also addresses the matter. Writing after the release of the CAVR report in 2005, he argues that, had East Timor been a sovereign nation-state during the 1975–99 period—a status blocked by the Indonesian state via its invasion and occupation—the crime of genocide would likely apply. The direct killing of a large number of East Timorese, the forced displacement, starvation, and sexual violence, Lisson points out, all constitute acts prohibited under the UNCG (Lisson, 2008, p. 1488). That the crimes were of a systemic nature demonstrates "a purpose beyond the destruction of individual victims," while the rhetoric often employed by Indonesian officials "confirms the existence [of] a systemic intent to destroy a group" (Lisson, 2008, p. 1489)—the group being the supporters of East Timorese independence and their loved ones. For such reasons, Lisson suggests that international tribunals interpret the UNCG in an expansive fashion—in this case in terms of how it thinks of a "national group." The working definition of "national," as interpreted in a variety of international legal cases, privileges already-established "nations" (in other words, those identified with a particular nation-state). Lisson thus asserts that the UNCG "should focus *not* on whether the group comprises a state, but instead on whether the group in question possesses the right to self-determination" (Lisson, 2008, p. 1461).

Regardless of whether or not the mass killings in East Timor meet the strict guidelines of the UNCG, which defines genocide as acts intended to destroy "in whole or in part, a national, ethnical, racial or religious group," the scale and nature of the killings were undoubtedly genocide-like, similar to the bulk of the Khmer Rouge's crimes in Cambodia (Kiernan, 2003). This speaks to how the need to suppress and seek justice for genocide should not prevent us from seeing all mass killings of civilians, no matter who commits them and why, as unacceptable, and from acting accordingly.

In this regard, accountability for the countless atrocities that occurred in East Timor in the period of 1975–99 has proven to be quite limited. As part of its post-occupation administration of the territory, the United Nations established the Special Crimes Unit (SCU), an investigative body that prepared indictments, and the "Special Panel for Serious Crimes," an internationally mandated "hybrid" court made up of East Timorese and international judges. While in existence through mid-2005, they prosecuted and convicted several individuals for gross crimes committed in 1999 (and only that year). All of those prosecuted and convicted were low-level East Timorese, typically members of TNI-organized and TNI-directed militias, as Jakarta refused to extradite other persons indicted by the courts (see below) despite having promised to do so. For such reasons, the CAVR (2005, part 11, p. 26) report recommended that the UN Security Council be prepared to establish an international tribunal to try those parties responsible for the crimes committed against the East Timorese people (see Nevins, 2007–08).

The CAVR also hosted numerous hearings at which victims from different sides of the conflict were able to recount their experiences. This, according to *Chega!*, helped to "restore the dignity denied to individual victims" and to dispel "some of the residual anger that fuels continuing division" (CAVR, 2005, part 9, p. 38). In addition, the CAVR established Community Reconciliation Procedures (CRP) to facilitate reconciliation. At a CRP, a person who had harmed his/her neighbors would admit his/her guilt, explain why and how he/she had committed such crimes, and then ask to be accepted back in the community. While significant, such mechanisms involved low-level perpetrators and only East Timorese, proverbial "small fish." Individuals from Indonesia guilty of war crimes and crimes against humanity, particularly those with command and control responsibility ("big fish"), have faced no accountability. Nor have those parties from abroad that supported Indonesia's crimes—most notably the United States.

## THE UNITED STATES AND THE INVASION
## AND OCCUPATION OF EAST TIMOR

A key goal of Operation Komodo Dragon was to win over ruling elites in Western capitals to Jakarta's position on East Timor (Dunn, 1996; Taylor, 1999). This was especially the case in relation to the United States, Indonesia's most important ally. This goal was undoubtedly on Suharto's mind when he visited with US President Gerald Ford at Camp David, Maryland, on July 5, 1975. While there, Suharto asserted that "the only way" forward for East Timor was "to integrate into Indonesia" (see Document 1). Ford responded by thanking Suharto for sharing his views, but said nothing specific about his framing of the situation in the then-Portuguese Timor (see Document 1). Ford's non-response made the Indonesian leader sufficiently confident that he, Suharto, made his first public statement ruling out the viability of an independent East Timor upon his return to Jakarta on July 8, 1975.

An August 17, 1975, diplomatic cable from Australia's Ambassador to Indonesia Richard Woolcott to Don Willesee, Australia's foreign secretary, made clear just how little Washington cared about Indonesian aggression toward East Timor, as well as the potential for the United States government to affect Jakarta's course of action. As Woolcott stated, "the United States might have some influence on Indonesia at present as Indonesia wants and needs US assistance in its military re-equipment programme," but Washington had decided to "allow events to take their course" (see Document 2)—meaning that it would allow Indonesia to swallow its tiny neighbor. This was communicated to Suharto in person by President Ford when he met with the Indonesian leader in Jakarta on December 6, 1975, and gave the green light for the invasion, which took place the following day (see Document 3).[72]

In previous months, the Ford administration had cautioned Indonesia against using US weaponry in any planned aggression. (According to the State Department, about 90 per cent of Indonesia's military equipment at the

---

72 Quoted in Burr & Evans (2001), Document 4.

time was from the United States [United States Congress, 1977, p. 62].) As laid out in a 1958 agreement with the US government, Indonesia assured that it would use US-origin weaponry "solely for legitimate national self-defense"— self-defense as defined by the UN Charter (see Document 4).

Any reservations that the administration might have had about the use of US weaponry seem to have disappeared by December 1975. The invasion and the illegal use of US weapons required a cutoff of US military assistance. But the administration only imposed an administrative delay of additional military aid to Jakarta while continuing to deliver military equipment "already in the pipeline" (United States Congress, 1977, p. 5). To the great satisfaction of the Suharto regime, the Ford administration resumed normal relations with Indonesia, a violation of the law as US Secretary of State Henry Kissinger even seemed to acknowledge (see Document 5). Soon thereafter, the Ford administration ended the pretense of limiting military sales to Indonesia, using as an excuse Suharto's signing into law East Timor's formal integration into Indonesia on July 17, 1976. From then on, the official US position was to accept Indonesia's annexation of East Timor as a fait accompli and, therefore, as a de facto (but not de jure) part of Indonesia—a situation Washington would not contest. The advantage of this position was that it put an end to any discussion regarding the use of US arms in East Timor as the 1958 "mutual defense agreement" between the United States and Indonesia allowed Jakarta to employ US weaponry "to maintain its internal security" (see Document 4). East Timor was now an internal Indonesian matter—at least from the perspective of the White House. Thus, the Ford administration had few qualms about delivering to Indonesia in September 1976 a squadron of US-made OV-10 Bronco ground-attack planes (United States Congress, 1977, p. 8), Vietnam War-era aircraft that were highly useful for counterinsurgency operations, especially against those without effective anti-aircraft weaponry. Only a few months earlier, a US State Department official had explained why Washington condoned Jakarta's actions: "We regard Indonesia as a friendly, non-aligned nation—a nation we do a lot of business with" (Waby, 1976).

A significant component of that "business" involved oil, as Henry Kissinger made clear in a memorandum (circa November 21, 1975) to President Gerald Ford regarding their then-upcoming trip to Indonesia (see Document 6). Kissinger's thinking embodied a perspective that had long been dominant in Washington, one tied to US imperial ambitions made more feasible by World War II and the disruption of colonial rule in the Pacific. In the war's aftermath, the United States emerged as the dominant power of the region. The US war in Vietnam, as American officials often made clear, was in large part about maintaining and enhancing privileged access to the region's resource wealth (see, e.g., Lodge, 1965). For many, the centerpiece of the region's wealth was Indonesia, what *U.S. News & World Report* in interpreting the thinking of the administration of then-US president Dwight Eisenhower characterized in 1954 as "the richest prize in all Southeast Asia" ("Why the U.S. Risks War for Indo-China," 1954, p. 23). Although there were diverse reasons for the various countries' support for Jakarta, the principal rationale was simple: Indonesia was a populous country with great market potential, a very wealthy resource base, and a strategic location. More than a decade later, US thought remained much the same. Not long before he was elected president of the United States, Richard Nixon (1967) echoed the sentiment in nearly identical terms, calling Indonesia "by far the greatest prize in the Southeast Asian area" (p. 111).

Given such perceived imperatives, it is hardly surprising that the essence of US policy toward Indonesia and East Timor did not change during the administration of Jimmy Carter (1977–80). The administration provided weaponry to Jakarta from the outset, including two additional OV-10 Broncos, six of which were already in use in East Timor according to the Pentagon (United States Congress, 1977, pp. 8, 18). In late 1977, when Indonesia was actually running out of military equipment due to its activities in East Timor (McArthur, 1977), the Carter administration responded by authorizing $112 million worth of arms sales for the 1978 fiscal year to Jakarta, up from $13 million the previous year. In February 1978, the administration announced a decision to sell Jakarta 16 F-5 fighter jets. Later that same year, the administration provided Jakarta a squadron of A-4 ground-attack bombers (Nevins, 2005.) Presumably, at least some of the F-5 planes were among those retrofitted by Indonesia to enable the use of napalm—a development, Australian cables indicate, of which US intelligence sources were aware (see Document 7). According to numerous East Timorese sources, the Indonesian military deployed napalm as part of its counterinsurgency efforts. The CAVR, in fact, has documentary footage from the late 1970s of Indonesian military personnel loading bombs labeled "Opalm" (a Soviet version of napalm) onto OV-10 Bronco aircraft at the Baucau airport (CAVR, 2005, part 3, p. 81).

The blank-check approach to US policy toward Indonesia and East Timor continued in the Ronald Reagan (1981–89) and George H.W. Bush Sr. (1989–92) administrations. US military sales to Indonesia peaked during the presidency of Reagan, exceeding US$500 million from 1981 to 1986. Such sales dropped somewhat during the Bush Sr. administration, but still averaged about $28 million annually (Hartung & Washburn, 1997).

As for the Clinton administration (1993–2000), it made steps to change direction upon Clinton's swearing-in—in large part due to growing grassroots and congressional pressure in the aftermath of a November 12, 1991, massacre at Dili's Santa Cruz Cemetery, where Indonesian troops fired on unarmed protesters, killing hundreds (Jardine, 1999). The resulting outcry led Clinton's State Department to block a proposed sale by the Jordanian government of four US-made F-5E fighter jets to Jakarta. And in early 1994, the US State Department announced a ban on the sale of small arms to Indonesia. But Jakarta's continuing economic and strategic importance quickly exposed the limits of Clinton's concern for human rights and international law. Over its eight years in office, Clinton's administration provided over $500 million in economic assistance and sold and licensed the sales of hundreds of millions of dollars in weaponry to Jakarta (Nevins, 2005). It even side-stepped an understanding with Congress to limit engagement with the TNI by continuing joint US-Indonesia military exercises. At least 28 training exercises in sniper tactics, urban warfare, explosives, psychological operations, and other techniques took place between 1993 and 1998 in Indonesia through a Pentagon program. The primary beneficiary was the *Kopassus*, Indonesia's special forces troops responsible for many of the worst human rights violations in East Timor (Nairn, 1998). Various forms of economic and military assistance continued through much of the post-ballot campaign of terror in 1999. It was only on September 11, 1999, during a visit to New Zealand, that Clinton finally announced a suspension of us military sales to Jakarta (Nevins, 2005).

## CONCLUSION

As renowned peace studies scholar Johan Galtung (1969) asserts, violence takes various forms, the most obvious one being direct or physical violence. Another is what he calls indirect or structural violence, whose harmful effects do not emerge directly out of particular actions but provide the fertile soil for those actions. And because the "soil" is all around, one tends not to notice it; it is thus perceived as normal. If, for Galtung, direct violence is like the waves on otherwise tranquil waters, structural violence is the tranquil waters. Thus the violence as violence remains invisible as long as the waters remain tranquil; in other words, as long as the relevant structures or constellation of relations remain stable (Galtung, 1969, p. 173).

The structural violence of the global political economy, one predicated on massive inequality, one in which peoples and places are unworthy to the extent that they challenge the perceived needs and desires of the privileged and powerful, is what facilitated and, in some ways, necessitated, us support for Indonesia's invasion and occupation. The structural violence took the form of the military, diplomatic, and political economic relations that underlay us–Indonesia relations and helped to produce and secure what Nixon called the "greatest prize in the Southeast Asian area" in ways that served the interests of ruling classes in both Indonesia and the United States. To the extent that an independent East Timor in the context of Southeast Asia in the mid-1970s, 1980s, and 1990s threatened those interests, it was effectively sacrificed for a "greater good," albeit one narrowly defined.

That there has been no significant accountability for the horrors that took place in East Timor speaks to another manifestation of international structural violence. As Anarchasis observed long ago in comparing laws to spider webs, laws catch the weak and poor, while the rich and powerful tear them to pieces (Plutarch, 1914, p. 415). Although not always the case, the ancient philosopher has shown himself to be prophetic in the area of contemporary international affairs, a profoundly undemocratic arena in which the powerful demand accountability of their weaker enemies, while insulating themselves and their allies from prosecution. Thus it is hardly surprising that, in terms of international elite opinion, the CAVR report and its recommendations for an international tribunal and reparations have been effectively buried. Indonesia has dismissed the report; Washington, Canberra, London, and their Western allies have ignored it; and the mainstream Western media, following officialdom's lead, has largely paid it no heed. As a result, the Indonesian elite and its international partners-in-crime have thus far enjoyed the luxury of forgetting their crimes. Meanwhile, the East Timorese population is condemned to remember what transpired in their homeland—not least via the enduring physical, socio-economic, and psychological effects of the war and occupation. In this regard, the violence brought about by Indonesia's invasion and occupation, and the complicity of the United States (among others) in enabling it, very much lives on.

# REFERENCES

Aditjondro, G. (1998). "The Silent Suffering of Our Timorese Sisters." In J. Aubury (Ed.), *Free East Timor: Australia's Culpability in East Timor's Genocide* (pp. 243–65). Sydney: Vintage.

Australian Senate Foreign Affairs, Defence and Trade References Committee. (2000). *East Timor: Final Report of the Senate Foreign Affairs, Defense and Trade References Committee.* Accessed at: http://www.aph.gov.au/Parliamentary_Business/Committees/Senate/Significant_Reports/first20years/fdt

Budiardjo, C., & Liem, S.L. (1984). *The War Against East Timor.* London: Zed Books.

Burr, W., & Evans, M. (Eds.). (2001, December 6). *National Security Archive Electronic Briefing Book No. 62: East Timor Revisited: Ford, Kissinger and the Indonesian Invasion, 1975–76.* Washington, DC: George Washington University. Accessed at: http://www.gwu.edu/~nsarchiv/NSAEBB/NSAEBB62/

CAVR (Commission for Truth, Reception, and Reconciliation). (2005). *Chega! Final Report of the Commission for Truth, Reception and Reconciliation (CAVR) in East Timor.* Accessed at: https://www.etan.org/news/2006/cavr.htm

Chomsky, N. (1979). *East Timor and the Western Democracies.* Nottingham, UK: Russell Peace Foundation.

Chomsky, N., & Herman, E.S. (1979). *The Washington Connection and Third World Fascism – The Political Economy of Human Rights* (Vol. 1). Sydney: Hale & Iremonger.

Clark, R. (1981). "Does the Genocide Convention Go Far Enough? Some Thoughts on the Nature of Criminal Genocide in the Context of Indonesia's Invasion of East Timor." *Ohio Northern University Law Review, 8*(2), 321–28.

Dunn, J. (1996). *Timor: A People Betrayed.* Sydney: ABC Books.

Dunn, J. (1998). "Genocide in East Timor: The Attempt to Destroy a Society and Its Culture." In P. Leite (Ed.), *The East Timor Problem and the Role of Europe* (pp. 83–94). Leiden, Netherlands: The International Platform of Jurists.

Fernandes, C. (2015). "Accomplice to Mass Atrocities: The International Community and Indonesia's Invasion of East Timor." *Politics and Governance, 3*(4), 1–11. https://doi.org/10.17645/pag.v3i4.272

Galtung, J. (1969). "Violence, Peace, and Peace Research." *Journal of Peace Research, 6*(3), 167–91. https://doi.org/10.1177/002234336900600301

Hartung, W., & Washburn, J. (1997). *U.S. Arms Transfers to Indonesia 1975–1997: Who's Influencing Whom?* New York: World Policy Institute.

Hill, H. (2002). *Stirrings of Nationalism in East Timor: FRETILIN 1974–1978: The Origins, Ideologies and Strategies of a Nationalist Movement.* Otford, New South Wales, Australia: Otford Press.

Jardine, M. (1999). *East Timor: Genocide in Paradise.* Monroe, ME: Odonian Press/Common Courage Books.

Jolliffe, J. (1978). *East Timor: Nationalism and Colonialism.* St. Lucia, QLD: University of Queensland Press.

Kiernan, B. (2003). "The Demography of Genocide in Southeast Asia: The Death Tolls in Cambodia, 1975–79, and East Timor, 1975–80." *Critical Asian Studies, 35*(4), 585–97. https://doi.org/10.1080/1467271032000147041

Klaehn, J. (2003). "Canadian Complicity in the East Timor Near-Genocide: A Case Study in the Sociology of Human Rights." *Portuguese Studies Review, 11*(1), 49–65.

Kohen, A., & Taylor, J. (1979). *An Act of Genocide: Indonesia's Invasion of East Timor.* London: TAPOL.

Lisson, D. (2008). "Defining 'National Group' in the Genocide Convention: A Case Study of Timor-Leste." *Stanford Law Review, 60*(5), 1459–96.

Lodge, H.C. (1965, January 17). "We Can Win in Vietnam." *The New York Times Magazine,* pp. 15, 73–74.

McArthur, G. (1977, December 5). "Indonesia Anxious to Replace Decrepit Arms." *International Herald Tribune,* n.p.

Modvig, J., Pagaduan-Lopez, J., Rodenburg, J., Salud, C.M., Cabigon, R.V., & Panelo, C.I. (2000, November 18). "Torture and Trauma in Post-Conflict East Timor." *The Lancet, 356*(9243), 1763. https://doi.org/10.1016/S0140-6736(00)03218-9

Nairn, A. (1998, March 30). "Indonesia's Killers." *The Nation* (New York), pp. 6–7.

Nevins, J. (2005). *A Not-So-Distant Horror: Mass Violence in East Timor*. Ithaca, NY: Cornell University Press.

Nevins, J. (2007–08). "The CAVR: Justice and Reconciliation in a Time of 'Impoverished Political Possibilities.'" *Pacific Affairs, 80*(4), 593–602. https://doi.org/10.5509/2007804593

Nixon, R. (1967, October). "Asia After Viet Nam." *Foreign Affairs, 46*(1), 111–25.

Plutarch. (1914). *Plutarch's Lives* (Vol. 1). London: Macmillan.

Ramos-Horta, J. (1987). *Funu: The Unfinished Saga of East Timor*. Trenton, NJ: The Red Sea Press.

Robinson, G. (2009). *If You Leave Us Here, We Will Die: How Genocide Was Stopped in East Timor*. Princeton, NJ: Princeton University Press.

Roosa, J. (2007–08). "How Does a Truth Commission Find Out What the Truth Is? The Case of East Timor's CAVR." *Pacific Affairs, 80*(4), 569–80. https://doi.org/10.5509/2007804569

Saul, B. (2001). "Was the Conflict in East Timor 'Genocide' and Why Does It Matter?" *Melbourne Journal of International Law, 2*, 477–522.

Silove, D. (2000). "Conflict in East Timor: Genocide or Expansionist Occupation?" *Human Rights Review, 1*(3), 62–79. https://doi.org/10.1007/s12142-000-1022-y

Sissons, M. (1997). *From One Day to Another: Violations of Women's Reproductive and Sexual Rights in East Timor*. Fitzroy, Victoria, Australia: East Timor Human Rights Centre.

TAPOL. (1983, September). "Interview with Former Bishop of East Timor." *Tapol Bulletin, 59*, 3–8.

Taylor, J. (1999). *East Timor: The Price of Freedom*. London: Zed Books.

Turner, M. (1992). *Telling East Timor: Personal Testimonies 1942–1992*. Sydney, Australia: New South Wales University Press.

United States Congress, House of Representatives. (1977). *Human Rights in East Timor and the Question of the Use of U.S. Equipment by the Indonesian Armed Forces. Hearing before the Subcommittees on International Organizations and on Asian and Pacific Affairs of the Committee on International Relations. March 23*. Washington, DC: US Government Printing Office.

Van Atta, D., & Toohey, B. (1982 May 30–June5, June 6–June 12). *The Timor Papers* (Parts 1 & 2). *The National Times* (Australia).

Waby, R. (1976, January 22). "Aid to Indonesia Doubled as U.S. Shrugs Off Timor." *The Australian*, n.p.

Way, W., Browne, D., & Johnson, V. (Eds.). (2000). *Australia and the Indonesian Incorporation of Portuguese Timor, 1974–1976*. Carlton, Australia: Melbourne University Press.

"Why the U.S. Risks War for Indo-China." (1954, April 16). *U.S. News & World Report*, p. 23.

# DOCUMENTS

There is extensive documentation—from both official US and Australian sources—now available to the public that illustrates US support for Indonesia's invasion and occupation of East Timor and illuminates the rationale for such support. This is especially the case for the period leading up to the invasion and the early years of the occupation. Herein, I examine seven of those documents, in whole or in part.

# DOCUMENT 1

This document is a four-page excerpt from a "Memorandum of Conversation between Presidents Ford and Suharto" at a July 5, 1975, meeting at Camp David, Maryland, the official retreat of the US President. Produced by the White House and classified until 2001, the memorandum is a transcript of sorts of a wide-ranging discussion on bilateral and international affairs. While Suharto voices support for self-determination and promises that Indonesia will not commit aggression against East Timor (or any other country), he characterizes it as a "small territory with no resources," one that as "an independent country would hardly be viable." In any case, he avers that "a majority want[s] unity with Indonesia," a majority that he describes as under "heavy pressure by those who are almost Communists"— Suharto's characterization of those in favor of independence. Hence, while Suharto asserts that his government "doesn't want to insert itself into Timor self-determination," it faces the problem of figuring out "how to manage the self-determination process" given the alleged majoritarian desire for "unity" with Indonesia. Suharto thus implies that Indonesia might very well have no choice but to "insert itself" to ensure respect for the supposed will of the majority. Of great significance here is that President Ford says nothing to challenge Suharto's presentation, thus, in effect, endorsing it.

MEMORANDUM

THE WHITE HOUSE

SECRET/NODIS/XGDS          Washington

## MEMORANDUM OF CONVERSATION

PARTICIPANTS:   President Ford
                President Suharto, President of Indonesia
                Dr. Henry A. Kissinger, Secretary of State and
                Assistant to the President for NSA

Lt. General Brent Scowcroft, Deputy Assistant to
the President for NSA

Mr. Widodo (Indonesian Interpreter)

DATE & TIME: July 5, 1975 - Saturday

12:40 p.m. - 2:00 p.m.

(1:44 Secretary Kissinger joined)

PLACE:     Laurel Cabin, Camp David, Maryland

President: Let me reiterate how pleased we are to have you visit. Secretary Kissinger told me you were here in 1970 when President Nixon was in office. We are just as concerned about our good relations with Indonesia as we were earlier.

Let me say now that we are as firmly committed and interested in Southeast Asia. The events in Indochina have in no way diminished our interest or commitment in the area.

We are committed to detente with the Soviet Union, but it has to be a mutual relationship. We will not let them have a bigger piece of the benefits. We will continue it as long as it is mutually beneficial. We recognize that the Soviet Union keeps assisting and strengthening its friends, just as we do. But they cannot take advantage of us.

In my trip to Brussels, I told my NATO allies that we were committed to them completely, and I want you and the countries in your area to feel the same.

We want to continue our assistance programs. As you know, that depends on the Congress, which has been cutting our program in recent years. This Congress is interested, but it is my intention to increase aid. We are able to make available some military equipment items to help you in your situation - four navel vessels, which may not be in tip-top condition, some tanks, aircraft such as C-47, and four C-123 transports.

Suharto: May I first convey my appreciation and gratitude, Mr. President, for your invitation to the United States. And on behalf of the Government and people of Indonesia, may I convey our heartfelt congratulations for the 4th of July. I would take this valuable opportunity and discuss the problems affecting not only Indonesia but also all of Southeast Asia in light of recent changes, which have swept the peninsula. I had already obtained valuable information from Mr. Habib and from you in respect to furthering American responsibility to its allies in the Southeast Asia region. After obtaining that information and valuable assessment, we have no fear that the United States will abandon its responsibility toward peace in the Southeast Asia region. Considering the bitter and sad experience of the American people in Vietnam, the U.S. has given such great help and to have it turn out so it is necessary to assess why it happened to come out so very badly after such American sacrifice.

If you would allow me, I will elaborate on Indonesia's problems in our struggles for independence against Communism; it will help us understand. It is not the military strength of the Communists but their fanaticism and ideology which is the principal element of their strength. To consider this, each country in the area needs an ideology of its own with which to counter the Communists. But a national ideology is not enough by itself. The well-being of the people must be improved so that it strengthens and supports the national ideology. From the experience of Laos and Vietnam in the past, they seem to have forgotten this national ideology to get the support of the people. Despite their superiority of arms in fighting the Communists, the human factor was not there. They lacked this national ideology to rally the people to fight Communism.

It is in this spirit that Indonesia has been unifying and nationalizing the people to prepare to fight the threats which eventually will be made against our independence. So we are busily engaged in encouraging and consolidating in Southeast Asia this national ideology and cooperating with others in the areas of culture, economics, and so on. This is of course to prepare for any eventuality of an Indochina eventually dominated by the Communists.

What will happen after Vietnam? There are two possibilities: Whether they will apply Communism just within their borders in order to improve the conditions of their peoples. If so, we are okay. Ho Chi Minh has always wanted to unify all of Vietnam. We don't know yet what is going on and whether they will unify or whether they will be two separate Vietnams.

President: How long do you think it will take for them to decide this?

Suharto: I have been trying to find out from the Communists and Tito, and the judgment is that the consolidation will take five years, but by then, they will be unified.

President: How about the relations between Vietnam, Cambodia and Laos?

Suharto: Let me explain. As far as Cambodia, they recognize the GRUNK and Sihanouk -- although he is still in exile. I asked Tito why he didn't support Sihanouk's return and he said it would take some time. Tito's reply was that due to prevailing conditions in Phnom Penh, it is not safe for Sihanouk to return. There are still some dangerous elements. But my personal opinion is that they don't want him back yet. My information is that it will take Cambodia about five years to consolidate, so it will be similar to Vietnam. Considering that the time for consolidation is so long -- five years -- they might want two Vietnams and one Cambodia, all three joining a non-aligned world. So they may want to stay separate but with their policies aligned.

Even if it takes some time to consolidate, events will certainly encourage similar elements in Thailand, Malaysia, the Philippines and elsewhere. Of course, this Communist ideological solidarity will take the form of encouraging these elements to step up their activities among labor, farmers and youth. When they have built up the Communist movements, the Vietnamese will be able to supply the military equipment necessary for them to undertake military activities.

President: Are all the Communists working together?

Suharto: The Soviet Union and the Chinese don't work together. They are competing to expand their own individual influence in the region.

The second possibility is they may not stay within their borders but seek to Communize the region and the world. If so, we have to find out whether they will support the Soviet Union and China. Right now, I think Vietnam won't take sides, because then it would become a target between the two. Instead it will work for independent national Communists movements. But in any case, these events will have brief impact on the neighboring countries. The question is how to counter it. Knowing well the Communist tactics -- infiltration, fanaticism, etc., it is essential for each country to have a strong national ideology -- to strengthen itself in the political, economic and military areas.

We are fortunate we already have this national ideology --
Pantchestita (?). The question is, is it strong enough? Here it is
important that we strengthen our economic development so we can
support our Pantchestita (?). Therefore if we fail in economic
developments, it will create a lack of confidence of our national
ideology and create doubts in the people and leave them susceptible
to other ideologies.

President: You have done very well in controlling inflation. We have
had problems in that regard, but we are now making progress. I
understand if you don't make economic progress there will be the
growth of a Communist ideology in Indonesia.

Suharto: The principal factor is creating a national stability
principally in the economic and monetary fields. The role of the US
in her responsibility toward this area -- the U.S. won't abandon her
role, but the American assistance role should be reviewed, both in
relation to Indonesia and all of Southeast Asia. Particularly in
assisting and supporting those countries in establishing national
resilience. That would help in creating a regional resilience and
help keep out Communism. But we are running against time because
the Communists are working very hard in these countries to convert
them to Communism.

The best way of fighting subversion is intelligence and territorial
operations, so we can detect Communist activity when it first
arises. In carrying these out when the people are participating, we
rely heavily on communications. Therefore, communication between
areas is very important to knowing when problems emerge, so we can
deal with them immediately. If the danger becomes greater and the
insurgency becomes greater, we will require mobile units to send
to these areas to squelch subversion. To supply and maintain this

mobility we will need both sea and air transport so we can put down insurgency before it becomes too big to stop. Especially in the navy field, we need to improve the conditions of the navy -- not big ships but to be able to transport men and materials to be able to carry out these operations. Particularly, ships which can fight any attempts to interfere with these operations to cope with insurgency. Indonesia has many islands so we will need many of these ships with great mobility. Especially at this moment, intelligence and territorial operations are very important. We are in a better condition to do this than other Southeast nations. With American assistance, we have built a national resilience and we are working hard at building it further.

President: How big a Navy do you have and how big do you need?

Suharto: We have many capable navy men prepared to man the Soviet ships we have – that were gathered to liberate West Iran [sic. Should be West Irian]. These ships are now mothballed and useless, however.

If you will agree with those principles to strengthen the national resilience -- especially in the military field, we can set up a joint committee to decide what is needed in the Navy, Army and Air Force. We don't need equipment, just to make them serviceable.

President: I think we should set up a joint commission to decide what is needed and what we can do to supply those needs. I will talk to Secretary Kissinger.

Suharto: But the most important need is not in the military field but in the economic area. This is where we must build the nation. Indonesia can be an example to other countries of the importance of strengthening their national resilience.

President: Our Ex-Im Bank has been working with your people. I would expect we would continue to work with you on providing more credits and grants. It is important that we help with everything we can make available in order to contribute to the essential development you have described.

Suharto: In view of our efforts to accelerate developments, we have four sources: The IGGI (Inter-Governmental Group for Indonesia), international organizations like the World Bank, the Ex-Im Bank, and private banks. These four go from soft to hard terms for loans. We are already obtaining joint Ex-Im commercial loans, and terms are still lower through commercial banks. We hope to continue these loans.

President: In Fortune I saw a ten-page story urging private investment. Is the investment picture encouraging?

Suharto: The figure has now reached $5 billion. What remains is for industry which requires having capital input. Examples of these huge projects are liquefied natural gas ($800 million), nickel ($900 million), copper, and others. These will require the assistance of other countries to get the credits. With regard to our efforts to strengthen our national resilience, I want to mention the archipelago principle. This principle has been followed by the Indonesian people for years. The purpose is to force ourselves in as a unified nation without any territorial ambition. From various countries we have gotten favorable response, but I see some hesitancy in the U.S. about this principle. Indonesia doesn't want to create difficulties with other countries establishing this principle in its territory.

President: We were encouraged at the progress of the Law of the Sea Conference and we hope for further progress. We do understand your problem. We do have reservations and we would be happy to meet with

your people to work it out. We must have maneuverability if we are
to carry out our responsibility in the world. I assure you we will
work with your people to try to work out a mutual understanding.

Suharto: Talks have been conducted bilaterally between us already. The
third point I want to raise is Portuguese decolonization. Starting
with our basic principle, the new Constitution of 1945, Indonesia will
not commit aggression against other countries. So Indonesia will not
use force against the territory of other countries. With respect to
Timor, we support carrying out decolonization through the process of
self-determination. In ascertaining the view of the Timor people,
there are three possibilities: independence, staying with Portugal,
or to join Indonesia. With such a small territory and no resources,
an independent country would hardly be viable. With Portugal it
would be a big burden with Portugal so far away. If they want to
integrate into Indonesia as an independent nation, that is not
possible because Indonesia is one unitary state. So the only way is
to integrate into Indonesia.

President: Have the Portuguese set a date yet for allowing the
Timor people to make their choice?

Suharto: There is no set date yet, but it is agreed in principle
that the wishes of the people will be sought. The problem is that
those who want independence are those who are Communist-
influenced. Those wanting Indonesia integration are being
subjected to heavy pressure by those who are almost Communists.
The Communist elements practically sabotaged the recent meeting in
Macao. I want to assert that Indonesia doesn't want to insert
itself into Timor self-determination, but the problem is how to
manage the self-determination process with a majority wanting
unity with Indonesia. These are some of the problems I wanted to
raise on this auspicious meeting with you.

President: I greatly appreciate the chance to learn your views, especially on the events in Vietnam as they consolidate -- and the thought it would take five years to consolidate. I would like to mention OPEC.

[Secretary Kissinger enters.]

We appreciate your not joining the embargo in '73-74. We are concerned about OPEC raising prices in the fall meeting. We are concerned about the effect on the economic recovery of the United States, the world, and the Third World. I know you feel badly about the Trade Bill's penalties against OPEC members. We are trying to get Congress to change that to make the penalties selective, not comprehensive.

Suharto: We share with the other OPEC states the view that we should not confront the consumers in this energy crisis. We are also aware that some producers have taken a tough stand. We are a small producer, but the others still listen to us. The September meeting I don't think will focus on a price increase but how to keep the purchasing power of the producers from falling. Therefore Indonesia, with the others, is studying the problem seriously so that oil revenue will benefit the people despite the inflation and recessions which have beset the world.

President: We have been through difficult times and we are now coming out of it. The oil price increase would have an injurious effect on our recovery and thus our ability to help the world's economic recovery.

In the past you have sent a special emissary to contact Secretary Kissinger on occasion. I would like that arrangement to continue under me if you agree.

Suharto: I fully share the importance of sending an emissary to contact Secretary Kissinger. I haven't done it so much recently because of the problems that both our countries have been facing recently. I would also agree to resuming these contacts so we can maintain a similarity of views on problems, like with Japan and Australia.

President: Lunch is ready.

SECRET/NODIS/XGDS

Source: "Memorandum of Conversation between Presidents Ford and Suharto, 5 July 1975, 12:40 pm - 2:00 pm." (1975, July 5). In W. Burr & M. Evans (Eds.), *National Security Archive Electronic Briefing Book No. 62: East Timor Revisited: Ford, Kissinger and the Indonesian Invasion, 1975-76* (doc. 1). Washington, DC: George Washington University. Accessed at: http://nsarchive2.gwu.edu/NSAEBB/NSAEBB62/doc1.pdf

# DOCUMENT 2

This document is the text of a formerly secret Australian government cablegram from Richard Woolcott, ambassador to Indonesia, to Australia's Foreign Secretary Don Willesee. Sent on August 17, 1975, the cable communicates the fact that Indonesia's foreign minister informed Woolcott—information that would undoubtedly be shared with allied Western governments such as Britain and the United States—that Jakarta has decided "to incorporate Timor," to annex the territory in other words. Of particular significance vis-à-vis the United States is Woolcott's statement that the US ambassador to Indonesia had informed him that US Secretary of State Henry Kissinger has "instructed the Embassy to cut down its reporting on Timor." The attitude of the US Ambassador David Newsom is that "the United States should keep out of the Portuguese Timor situation and allow events to run their course."

## 169 Cablegram to Canberra

Jakarta, 17 August 1975

O.JA1240 SECRET PRIORITY

### Portuguese Timor

*For Secretary from Woolcott*

*[matter omitted]*

2. It is of course a decision for the Minister and the Prime Minister but I am somewhat concerned about the proposal that the Prime Minister [Gough Whitlam] might send a message to the President [Suharto].

3. As I stressed in Canberra last month we are dealing with a settled Indonesian policy to incorporate Timor, as even Malik [Indonesian Foreign Minister] admitted to me on Friday (para 9 of our O.JA1233 refers). I believe the Indonesians are well aware of our attitudes to Timor at all levels.

4. Indonesia is simply not prepared to accept the risks they see to them in an independent Timor and I do not believe that we will be able to change their minds on this. We have in fact tried to do so. What Indonesia now looks to from Australia in the present situation is some understanding of their attitude and possible action to assist public understanding in Australia rather than action on our part which could contribute to criticism of Indonesia. They believe they will get this understanding elsewhere in the region, including from Japan and New Zealand.

5. The Department seems to have attached more weight to my discussion with Malik than to the previous discussion with Yoga. This is probably right but only in relation to Indonesia's immediate intentions. In the longer run, I consider that the comments in paras 22-29 in our O.JA1201 are more relevant to the longer term situation we are likely to face. The 'doves', like Malik, hope that the incorporation of Timor can be effected in a reasonably presentable

manner over a period of time. The 'hawks' do not believe Portugal will be able to control the situation or be willing to maintain a 'measured and deliberate approach to decolonisation' which would 'eventually' enable the people to decide their own future. Events in Angola and Portugal itself of course strengthen their hand. They maintain that the situation both in Lisbon and in Timor will deteriorate and that if it does it is better to move earlier rather than later.

6. In considering whether or not there should be another message from the Prime Minister to the President we should also bear in mind that the President has not formally answered the Prime Minister's March letter although it could be argued that he did so orally in Townsville.

7. I am sure that the President would not welcome another letter on this subject at this stage, especially after what he said publicly in Parliament only yesterday (our 0.JA1237 refers). Soeharto [sic] will be looking to Australia for understanding of what he, after very careful consideration, decides to do rather than what he might regard as a lecture or even a friendly caution.

8. The Minister and Prime Minister may feel that domestic pressure puts Australia under an obligation to act. One answer to this would be that Australia has already made more representations to the Indonesian Government and been more active in making its serious concerns known to the Indonesians, than any other country. The upshot of this is that Australia has been singled out by the Indonesians in their planning discussions as the country (along with China) that will be the most vocal in the event of Indonesian intervention in Portuguese Timor. They know that reaction in Australia—unlike other ASEAN countries and New Zealand—will probably be their main problem. I doubt whether we can expect a better result than that.

9. Other alternatives to a message-although I would also not recommend them—would be an answer to a question in the House or a statement, possibly at a press conference. These could assert that

Australia cannot condone the use of force in Timor, nor could we accept the principle that a country can intervene in a neighbouring territory because of concern, however well based that concern might be, over the situation there. At the same time such an answer to a question in Parliament or from the press could concede that Indonesia has had a prolonged struggle for national unity and could not be expected to take lightly a breakdown in law and order in Portuguese Timor, especially when the colony is surrounded by and geographically very much part of the Indonesian Archipelago.

10. While the situation in Portuguese Timor is not likely to get as bad as that in Angola it is going to be a mess for some time. From here I would suggest that our policies should be based on disengaging ourselves as far as possible from the Timor question; getting Australians presently there out of Timor; leave events to take their course; and if and when Indonesia does intervene act in a way which would be designed to minimise the public impact in Australia and show privately understanding to Indonesia of their problems. Perhaps we should also make an effort to secure through Parliament and the media greater understanding of our policy, and Indonesia's, although we do not want to become apologists for Indonesia.

11. The United States might have some influence on Indonesia at present as Indonesia really wants and needs United States assistance in its military re-equipment programme. But Ambassador Newsom told me last night that he is under instructions from Kissinger personally not to involve himself in discussions on Timor with the Indonesians on the grounds that the United States is involved in enough problems of greater importance overseas at present. The State Department has, we understand, instructed the Embassy to cut down its reporting on Timor.

12. I will be seeing Newsom on Monday but his present attitude is that United States should keep out of the Portuguese Timor situation and allow events to take their course. His somewhat cynical comment to me was that if Indonesia were to intervene the

United States would hope they would do so 'effectively, quickly and not use our equipment'.

13. We are all aware of the Australian defence interest in the Portuguese Timor situation but I wonder whether the Department has ascertained the interest of the Minister or the Department of Minerals and Energy in the Timor situation. It would seem to me that this Department might well have an interest in closing the present gap in the agreed sea border and that this could be much more readily negotiated with Indonesia by closing the present gap than with Portugal or independent Portuguese Timor.

14. I know I am recommending a pragmatic rather than a principled stand but this is what national interest and foreign policy is all about, as even those countries with ideological bases for their foreign policies, like China and the Soviet Union, have acknowledged.

15. I am sorry to raise all these issues again with you personally but I do have serious doubts about the wisdom of another Prime Ministerial message at this stage. You may wish to show this to Minister and Prime Minister and to repeat it to Cooper in Lisbon.

**WOOLCOTT**

[NAA: A10463, 801/13/11/1, xi]

**Source:** Department of Foreign Affairs, Canberra. (1975, August 17). "Cable from Ambassador Richard Woolcott to Secretary, Department of Foreign Affairs, Canberra." In W. Way, D. Browne, & V. Johnson (Eds.), *Australian and the Indonesian Incorporation of Portuguese Timor, 1974-1976* (pp. 313-14). Carlton, Australia: Melbourne University Press, 2000.

## DOCUMENT 3

This document is an excerpt (pages 1 and 8–10) from a 12-page telegram in the form of a transcript of the infamous meeting in Jakarta between President Suharto, us President Gerald Ford, and us Secretary of State Henry Kissinger on December 6, 1975, the eve of invasion of East Timor. During the meeting, Suharto raises the issue of Portuguese Timor and asks for us "understanding" if Indonesia deems "it necessary to take rapid or drastic action"—diplomatic speak for invading the territory. Ford responds by telling his Indonesian counterpart that the United States "will not press you on the issue. We understand the problem you have and the intentions you have," thus giving the green light for the invasion. As to the "problem" of the use of US arms by Indonesia and associated public relations challenges, Kissinger suggests that it would be best to "construe" Indonesian actions as "self defense" rather than a "foreign operation." In addition, he and Ford express concerns of what others in the administration might say in response to Indonesia's invasion. For this reason, Kissinger tells Suharto that "it would be better if [the invasion] were done after we returned" to the United States so that he and Ford can better control the message. The US Embassy in Jakarta produced the secret telegram, addressed to the US State Department. It was declassified in 2001.

## Department of State

TELEGRAM

SECRET      NOD267

```
PAGE 01   JAKART  14940        01 OF 03    061141Z
ACTION NODS_00
INFO    OCT-01   ISO-00   /001  W
                        _ _ _ _ _ _ _ _ _ _ 051972
P 06100Z DEC 75
FM AMEMBASSY JAKARTA
TO SECSTATE WASHDC PRIORITY 1579


S E C R E T SECTION 1 OF 3  JAKARTA 14946

NODIS

DEPARTMENT PASS NSC FOR SCOWCROFT
EO 11652 GDS
TAGS: OYIP (FORD GERALD R PRESIDENT)
SUBJ: FORD-SUHARTO MEETING
```

1. FOLLOWING IS MEMCON OF MEETING BETWEEN PRESIDENT FORD AND
PRESIDENT SUHARTO IN JAKARTA DECEMBER 6. ALSO PRESENT WERE
SECRETARY OF STATE KISSINGER, FOREIGN MINISTER MALIK, MINISTER OF
STATE SUDHARMONO, AMEMBASSADOR [SIC] NEWSOM, AND AN INTERPRETER.

2. SUHARTO - I WISH TO EXPRESS MY THANKS AND VERY GREAT APPRECIATION
FOR YOUR WILLINGNESS, MR PRESIDENT, TO ACCEPT MY INVITATION TO VISIT
INDONESIA, ALTHOUGH THE VISIT IS VERY SHORT, I BELIEVE IT WILL BE
MOST USEFUL. THE PROMOTION OF PERSONAL CONTACTS BETWEEN US IS
IMPORTANT AND SIGNIFICANT FOR BOTH OF OUR COUNTRIES.

3. FORD - MY DELEGATION IS EXTREMELY GRATEFUL, MR PRESIDENT, FOR
THE SPLENDID ARRANGEMENTS FOR THE VISIT. I REGRET THAT THE TIME
IS SHORT BUT AFTER ELECTIONS, I HOPE TO COME BACK AGAIN FOR A
LONGER PERIOD. THE OPPORTUNITY FOR SUCH FACE TO FACE MEETINGS
IS ALSO HIGHLY IMPORTANT FOR ME.

. . .

37. FORD - IS THAILAND THREATENED BY VEITNAM [SIC]?

38. SUHARTO - YES. THERE IS A LONG HATRED BEWEEN THAILAND AND
VIETNAM.

39. I WOULD LIKE TO SPEAK TO YOU, MR PRESIDENT, ABOUT ANOTHER PRBELM
[SIC], TIMOR. WHEN IT LOOKED AS IF THE PORTUGUESE RULE WOULD END IN
TIMOR WE SOUGHT TO ENCOURAGE THE PORTUGUESE TO AN ORDERLY
DECOLONIZATION PROCESS. WE HAD AGREEMENT WITH THEM ON SUCH A
PROCESS AND WE RECOGNIZED THE AUTHORITY OF PORTUGAL IN THE
CARRYING OUT OF DECOLONIZATON AND IN GIVING PEOPLE THE RIGHT TO
EXPRESS THEIR WISHES.  INDONESIA HAS NO TERRITORIAL AMBITIONS. WE
ARE CONCERNED ONLY ABOUT THE SECURITY, TRANQUILTY AND PEACE OF
ASIA AND THE SOUTHERN HEMISPHERE. IN THE LATEST ROME AGREEMENT THE

PORTUGUESE GOVERNMENT WANTED TO INVITE ALL PARTIES TO NEGOTIATE. SIMILAR EFFORTS WERE MADE BEFORE BUT FRETELIN DID NOT ATTEND. AFTER FRETELIN FORCES OCCUPIED CERTAIN POINTS AND OTHER FORCES WERE UNABLE TO CONSOLIDATE, FRETELIN HAS DELARED [SIC] ITS INDEPENDENCE UNILATERALLY. IN CONSEQUENCE OTHER PARTIES DECLARED THEI [SIC] INTENTION OF INTEGRATING WITH INDONESIA, PORTUGAL REPORTED THE SITUATION TO THE UNITED NATIONS BUT DID NOT EXTEND RECOGNITION TO FRETELIN. PORTUGUAL, HOWEVER, IS UNABLE TO CONTROL THE SITUATION. IF THIS CONTINUES IT WILL PROLONG THE SUFFERING OF THE REFUGEES AND INCREASE THE INSTABILITY IN THE AREA.

40. FORD – THE FOUR OTHER PARTIES HAVE ASKED FOR INTEGRATION?

41. SUHARTO – YES, AFTER THE UDT, INDONESIA FOUND ITSELF FACING A FATE [SIC] ACCOMPLI. IT IS NOW IMPORTANT TO DETERMINE WHAT WE CAN DO TO ESTABLISH PEACE AND ORDER FOR THE PRESENT AND THE FUTURE IN THE INTEREST OF THE SECURITY OF THE AREA  ND [SIC] INDONESIA. THESE ARE SOME OF THE CONSIDERATIONS WE ARE NOW CONTEMPLATING. WE WANT YOUR UNDERSTADING [SIC] IF WE DEEM IT NECESSARY TO TAKE RAPID OR DRASTIC ACTION.

42. FORD – WE WILL UNDERSTAND AND WILL NOT PRESS YOU ON THE ISSUE. WE UNDERSTAND THE PROBLEM YOU HAVE AND THE INTENTIONS YOU HAVE.

43. KISSINGER – YOU APPRECIATE THAT THE USE OF US-MADE ARMS COULD CREATE PROBLEMS.

44. FORD – WE COULD HAVE TECHNICAL AND LEGAL PROBLEMS, YOU ARE FAMILIAR, MR PRESIDENT, WITH THE PROBLEMS WE HAD ON CYPRUS ALTHOUGH THIS SITUATON IS DIFFERENT.

45. KISSINGER – IT DEPENDS ON HOW WE CONSTRUE IT, WHETHER IT IS IN SELF DEFENSE OR IS A FOREIGN OPERATION. IT IS IMPORTANT THAT

WHATEVER YOU DO SUCCEEDS QUICKLY. WE WOULD BE ABLE TO INFLUENCE THE REACTION IN AMERICA IF WHATEVER HAPPENS HAPPENS AFTER WE RETURN. THIS WAY THERE WOULD BE LESS CHANCE OF PEOPLE TALKING IN AN UNAUTHORIZED WAY. THE PRESIDENT WILL BE BACK ON MONDAY AT 2:00 PM JAKARTA TIME. WE UNDERSTAND YOUR PROBLEM AND THE NEED TO MOVE QUICKLY BUT I AM ONLY SAYING THAT IT WOULD BE BETTER IF IT WERE DONE AFTER WE RETURNED.

46. FORD – IT WOULD BE MORE AUTHORITATIVE IF WE CAN DO IT IN PERSON.

47. KISSINGER – WHATEVER YOU DO, HOWEVER, WE WIL [SIC] TRY TO HANDLE IN THE BEST WAY POSSIBLE.

48. FORD – WE RECOGNIZE THAT YOU HAVE A TIME FACTOR. WE HAVE MERELY EXPRESSED OUR VIEW FROM OUR PARTICULAR POINT OF VIEW.

49. KISSINGER – IF YOU HAVE MADE PLANS, WE WILL DO OUR BEST TO KEEP EVERYONE QUIET UNTIL THE PRESIDENT RETURNS HOME.

50. DO YOU ANTICIPATE A LONG GUERILLA WAR THERE?

51. SUHARTO – THERE WILL PROBABLY BE A SMALL GUERILLA WAR. THE LOCAL KINGS ARE IMPORTANT, HOWEVER, ADN [SIC] THEY ARE ON OUR SIDE. THE UDT REPRESENT FORMER GOVERNMENT OFFICIALS AND FRETELIN REPRESENTS FORMER SOLDIERS. THEY ARE INFECTED THE SAME AS IS THE PORTUGESE ARMY WITH COMMUNISM....

### SECRET

**Source:** "Telegram from US Embassy in Jakarta, Indonesia to US Department of State in Washington, DC, Containing a Transcript of a Meeting in Jakarta, between President Suharto, President Gerald Ford, and US Secretary of State Henry Kissinger." (1975, December 6). In W. Burr & M. Evans (Eds.), *National Security Archive Electronic Briefing Book No. 62: East Timor Revisited: Ford, Kissinger and the Indonesian Invasion, 1975-76* (doc. 4, pp. 1, 8-10). Washington, DC: George Washington University. Accessed at: http://www.gwu.edu/~nsarchiv/NSAEBB/NSAEBB62/

## DOCUMENT 4

This document is entitled "Mutual Defense Agreement Between the United States of America and Indonesia on Equipment, Materials, and Services," which was signed in Jakarta on August 13, 1958. The document, in the form of a letter from US Ambassador Howard P. Jones to Indonesia's Minister of Foreign Affairs Dr. Subandio, summarizes the agreement. It states that "any weapons or other military services purchased by the Government of Indonesia from the Government of the United States shall be used by the Government of Indonesia solely for legitimate national self-defense." What constitutes legitimate self-defense, the document asserts, is defined by the United Nations and thus excludes "an act of aggression against any other state." This document was not classified and informed discussions between and within the United States and Indonesia regarding how to frame the invasion and annexation of East Timor.

### MUTUAL DEFENSE AGREEMENT BETWEEN THE UNITED STATES OF AMERICA AND INDONESIA ON EQUIPMENT, MATERIALS, AND SERVICES

*(Agreement effected by exchange of notes Signed at Djakarta August 13, 1958; Entered into force August 13, 1958.)*

*The American Ambassador to the Indonesian Minister of Foreign Affairs*

### THE FOREIGN SERVICE OF THE UNITED STATES OF AMERICA

DJAKARTA, *August 13, 1958.*

No. 107

EXCELLENCY:

I have the honor to refer to recent conversations between representatives of our two governments, concerning the sale of military equipment, materials, and services to the Government of

Indonesia, as a result of which the following understandings have been reached:

1. The Government of the United States, subject to applicable United States laws and regulations, shall make available to the Government of Indonesia on terms of payment in rupiahs or dollars such equipment, materials, and services as may be requested by the Government of Indonesia and approved by the Government of the United States. Such equipment, materials, and services as may be made available hereunder shall be designated by the Government of the United States in supplementary memoranda, which shall specify the pertinent terms of sale as they are mutually agreed upon.

2. The following assurances provided by the Government of Indonesia on March 14, 1957, shall be applicable to such equipment, materials, and services as may be made available hereunder:

(A) Any weapons or other military equipment or services purchased by the Government of Indonesia from the Government of the United States shall be used by the Government of Indonesia solely for legitimate national self-defense, and it is self-evident that the Government of Indonesia, as a member of the United Nations Organization, interprets the term "legitimate national self-defense" within the scope of the United Nations Charter as excluding an act of aggression against any other state.

(B) Any weapons or other military equipment or services purchased by the Government of Indonesia from the Government of the United Stated shall not be sold or otherwise disposed of to third parties.

3. In addition to the use provided for in subsection (A) of paragraph 2 of this note, the Government of Indonesia may use such equipment, materials, and services as may be made available hereunder to maintain its internal security.

I have the honor to propose that, if these understandings are acceptable to Your Excellency's Government, this note and Your

Excellency's note in reply concurring therein shall constitute an agreement between our two governments, effective on the date of Your Excellency's note.

Accept, Excellency, the renewed assurances of my highest consideration.

HOWARD P. JONES

His Excellency,

Dr. SUBANDRIO,

*Minister of Foreign Affairs,*

*Djakarta.*

**Source:** "Mutual Defense Agreement Between the United States of America and Indonesia on Equipment, Materials, and Services," signed in Jakarta on August 13, 1958. Letter from US Ambassador Howard P. Jones to Indonesia's Minister of Foreign Affairs Dr. Subandio, summarizing the agreement. In: United States Congress, House of Representatives. (1977, March 23)."Human Right in East Timor and the Question of the Use of U.S. Equipment by the Indonesian Armed Forces," Hearing before the Subcommittees on International Organizations and on Asian and Pacific Affairs of the Committee on International Relations. Washington, DC: United States Government Printing Office.

## DOCUMENT 5

This document is an excerpt from the secret transcript (declassified in 2001) of a meeting of Henry Kissinger and his staff on June 17, 1976. The main topic of conversation is whether the United States should accept an invitation from Jakarta and send a representative to occupied East Timor in conjunction with an Indonesian parliamentary delegation. Robert H. Miller, from the us Department of State's Bureau of East Asian and Pacific Affairs, advises against sending a representative in "trying to keep...Congressional sentiment with regard to Indonesia from being rekindled." Philip Habib, the assistant secretary of state, concurs with the advice, opining that us participation is unnecessary in light of the administration's resumption of "normal relations" with Indonesia, which has made Jakarta "quite happy." In reference to the manipulation of Congress, Indonesia's illegal invasion and occupation, or the resumption of "normal relations" with Jakarta (or all three), Kissinger responded: "Not very willingly. Illegally and beautifully"—a likely reference to the bilateral agreement banning Jakarta's use of us-origin weaponry for purposes of aggression (see Document 4).

SECRET

In Attendance -- Thursday, June 17, 1976
Secretary of State Kissinger - Chairman

|      |                                          |
|------|------------------------------------------|
| D    | Mr. Robinson                             |
| P    | Mr. Habib                                |
| M    | Mr. Eagleburger                          |
| C    | Mr. Sonnenfeldt                          |
| AF   | Mr. Schaufele                            |
| ARA  | Mr. Rogers                               |
|      | Mr. Shlaudeman (Asst. Secy. - designate, ARA) |
| EA   | Mr. Miller                               |
| EUR  | Mr. Hartman                              |
| NEA  | Mr. Atherton                             |
| INR  | Mr. Saunders                             |
| S/P  | Mr. Lord                                 |
| EB   | Mr. Greenwald                            |
| S/PRS| Mr. Funseth                              |
| PM   | Mr. Vest                                 |
| IO   | Mr. Lewis                                |
| H    | Ambassador McCloskey                     |
| L    | Mr. Leigh                                |
| S/S  | Mr. Borg (Acting)                        |
| S    | Mr. Aherne                               |
|      | Ambassador L. Dean Brown                 |

GDS                              GDS

MR. LEIGH: It's out of the question to say we're studying assistance.

MR. SHLAUDEMAN: That too. A loan is a loan in the Central Bank for Industrialization.

MR. ROBINSON: They're small businesses. It creates employment.

MR. ROGERS: This is a loan to the needy and it's no loan to us.

SECRETARY KISSINGER: Well, will it be defeated if we vote against it?

MR. SHLAUDEMAN: Yes, I think it will.

MR. ROGERS: I'd like to call Collins and tell him about this. I think he's been getting the full signals from his Chargé here with respect to Parsky, but I think I'll call Collins and Harry Greenwood.

SECRETARY KISSINGER: O.K. Anything else, Harry?

MR. SHLAUDEMAN: No, sir.

MR. MILLER: Mr. Secretary, we have a troublesome, little problem on which we're seeking your decision on whether to accept an invitation to send a diplomatic representative at a Political Officer level with a diplomatic-observer group to accompany an Indonesian Parliamentary Delegation to East Timor.

SECRETARY KISSINGER: Who's going?

MR. MILLER: We.[...]

SECRETARY KISSINGER: I mean which countries have accepted?

MR. MILLER: Well, as of now, practically no countries have accepted. All the EC 9 have turned it down. The UN Security Council President is going to turn it down; the Secretary General of the UN will turn it down.

There will probably be a couple of ASEAN countries that will accept. Japan will probably accept if we accepted. Australia's position is not yet known. The last time, when it was a Provisional Government of East Timor, the Australians decided at the last minute not to accept.[...]

SECRETARY KISSINGER: You're against it. (Laughter.)

MR. MILLER: I think the common recommendation, sir, is that we -- since we would be isolated and since our participation would be

rather high profile, that we would recommend against accepting --
explaining to the Indonesians that we think we can obtain a broader
base of support here in this country for, let's say, our broader
objectives with respect to Indonesia -- including overall support
to Timor, if we don't have high-profile participation.

SECRETARY KISSINGER: Well, how about low-profile
participation?

MR. MILLER: Well, we would intend, at the most, to send only the
Political Counselor. We would not send an Ambassador. On the other
hand, it now looks like there will be very few countries that do
participate. So I think that regardless of what level of officer we
sent, it will be fairly high.

SECRETARY KISSINGER: Am I wrong in assuming if we don't send
somebody there will be some story out of it showing its
disapproval of the United States action in regard to Timor?

MR. HABIB:    Some of the countries won't be going.

SECRETARY KISSINGER: Like who?

MR. HABIB: Singapore won't attend -- probably Thailand.

SECRETARY KISSINGER: Why is it in our interest to? I'm just
trying to understand the rationale.

MR. MILLER: Well, I don't think, sir, we think in terms of it
weakening the Indonesians in Timor; but it's trying to keep, let's
say, Congressional sentiment with regard to Indonesia from being
rekindled -- which we think now is a fairly satisfactory
condition.

MR. HABIB: There's no need to take this action. The
Indonesians are trying to get an international -- and especially
U.S. and other blessing -- before they've done it. Let them go
ahead and do what they've been doing. We have no objection. We've
not objected in UN Security Council debates. They're quite happy
with the position we've taken. We've resumed, as you know, all of
our normal relations with them; and there isn't any problem
involved.

SECRETARY KISSINGER: Not very willingly –

MR. HABIB: Sir?

SECRETARY KISSINGER: Not very willingly. Illegally and beautifully.

MR. MILLER: There's no question that the Indonesians will participate. This will undoubtedly be mentioned in Malik's conversations with you.

MR. HABIB: If we were to go pell-mell in the absence of really anybody else, I think that that could reopen the question of whether the Indonesians are acceptable.

MR. HABIB: The Japanese didn't go last time and they're hesitant to say who's going. The Australians, I'm fairly sure, are not going to go, on the basis of what we know.

SECRETARY KISSINGER: Why don't we ask the Australians?

MR. HABIB: They'll tell us it's under consideration.

MR. MILLER: The Australians asked either the Security Council or Waldheim to send a representative, and that hasn't succeeded. So I think I would agree with Phil that they're not likely. They dropped out at the last minute the last time, and they're likely to drop out this time.

MR. HABIB: It's a political problem.

MR. MILLER: We can ask them directly.

SECRETARY KISSINGER: Well, why don't you ask them?

MR. HABIB: We will.

SECRET

**Source:** "Memorandum of Meeting between Henry Kissinger and His Staff." (1976, June 17). In W. Burr & M. Evans (Eds.), *National Security Archive Electronic Briefing Book No. 62: East Timor Revisited: Ford, Kissinger and the Indonesian Invasion, 1975-76* (doc. 6, pp. 1, 5). Washington, DC: George Washington University. Accessed at: http://www.gwu.edu/~nsarchiv/NSAEBB/NSAEBB62/

## DOCUMENT 6

Document 6, declassified in 2001, is a 6-page except (pages 1–3 and 11–13) from a secret 17-page memorandum (circa Nov. 21, 1975) to President Gerald Ford from US Secretary of State Henry Kissinger regarding their then-upcoming trip to Jakarta. The document demonstrates that Indonesia's oil wealth, its resource wealth more broadly, and its geopolitical importance were underlying reasons for US support for Jakarta. In it, Kissinger characterizes Indonesia as "potentially one of the richest [countries in Southeast Asia]." He goes on, in the section entitled "Background and Strategy," to tout the country's "geographic location and resources" as being "of major strategic importance in the region." That location allows Indonesia, Kissinger gushes, to control "the sea passages between the Pacific and Indian Oceans, including Japan's life line to Middle East oil; its own oil fields provides a significant portion of Japan's oil consumption, and a small but increasing part of our own oil imports. Its other major resources—rubber, tin and tropical products—are also of some significance to the United States." Later, Kissinger writes (in a subsection called "Energy Issues," under "Issues and Talking Points") that although Indonesia is a member of the Organization of the Petroleum Exporting Countries (OPEC), "the country has played a passive moderate role at OPEC meetings and during the latest round kept their price increases significantly below those of other OPEC countries." This is important for US oil sector corporations which account "for the bulk of Indonesia's oil investment (about 86%) and an increasing amount (about 11%) of our crude oil imports are from Indonesia."

As made clear in another subsection called "US Economic Aid to Indonesia," the document pledges that the administration will "maintain a meaningful aid contribution to Indonesia," aid implicitly tied to Indonesia's continued openness to foreign investment. In this spirit, Kissinger advises Ford to call upon Suharto's government to "actively continue to encourage the foreign investor"—presumably and especially the United States.

# THE SECRETARY OF STATE
## WASHINGTON

MEMORANDUM FOR:    THE PRESIDENT
FROM:                      Henry A. Kissinger
SUBJECT:                Your Visit to Indonesia

## I. PURPOSE

Your Jakarta visit will be a dramatic reaffirmation to the
significance we attach to our relations with Indonesia, the
largest and most important non-Communist Southeast Asian state
and a significant Third World Country. In our relations with
Indonesia we are seeking to move progressively away from a
donor-client relationship and from preoccupation with aid
issues toward ties that stress a broader sharing of interests
and views. Your visit offers an excellent opportunity to
encourage a more mature dialogue with the Indonesian leadership
on issues of importance to us and less focused on our aid
relationship.

A key mechanism for moving this process forward will be the
Joint US-Indonesian Consultative Commission first agreed upon
during your Camp David meeting with Suharto on July 5. We expect
that a formal announcement of the Commission's formation can be
made during your brief visit, which provides an occasion to make
the announcement under the most auspicious circumstances. We
expect the Indonesians to welcome this step.

As a result of the Camp David meeting, Suharto is more confident
of the steadiness of our commitment to our friends in Asia and our
close ties with Indonesia in particular. At the same time, the Camp

David meeting may have given the Indonesian side an overly optimistic impression of our ability to assist Indonesian development and security programs and an inadequate appreciation of the growing constraints that are acting to depress US aid levels everywhere. Your visit can be helpful in alerting Suharto to the likelihood of a declining US aid level and making him understand the reasons.

Our goal now is to encourage Indonesia's sense of self-reliance commensurate with its importance to the region, and to focus our dialogue increasingly on broader issues of continuing major interest of the two governments:

-- The US role and US interests in East Asia, both for their own sake and to balance Soviet and PRC pressures;

-- Indonesia's perceptions of its place in Southeast Asia against this broader backdrop;

-- Indonesia's importance in North-South and other multilateral issues and our growing efforts to make a constructive contribution on such issues;

-- Regional cooperation in Southeast Asia;

-- And our increasingly varied and close bilateral relations.

II. BACKGROUND AND STRATEGY

In the post-Vietnam environment, U.S. interests in Indonesia are based both on its present position in the region and, especially, on its anticipated future role. Indonesia, the fifth most populous nation in the world, is more than three times the size of any other

Southeast Asian country and includes within its border about half the region's total population. It is potentially one of the richest. Its geographic location and resources are of major strategic importance in the region. Flanking the Southeast Asian mainland, Indonesia controls the sea passages between the Pacific and Indian Oceans, including Japan's life line to Middle East oil; its own oil fields provides a significant portion of Japan's oil consumption and a small but increasing part of our own oil imports. Its other major resources -- rubber, tin and tropical products -- are also of some significance to the United States.

On the international scene, Indonesia under Suharto has sought to carve out for itself a somewhat unique diplomatic position as an anti-Communist but non-aligned country capable of carrying on a dialogue with both radical "third world" states and the west while cautiously pursuing policies generally compatible with the latter. The government's desire not to offend politicized Moslem elements in Indonesia, however, influences it to side with the Arab states on certain issues, such as zionism [sic]; moreover, it values highly its membership in OPEC and supports OPEC actions, although it has never played a very active role at OPEC meetings.

Within the region, Indonesia is generally recognized as "first among equals" in the five-nation Association of Southeast Asian Nations (ASEAN) and increasingly regards the organization as the cornerstone of its regional policies.

Realization of Indonesia's potential is hampered by severe domestic problems and by economic backwardness which even its increased oil revenues have scarcely begun to overcome. Because of the Suharto Government's decision in the late 1960s to favor economic development over military preparedness, Indonesia's armed forces are poorly equipped and inadequately supplied. At best, it will be years before Indonesia can play a significant regional security role. The speed with which Indochina fell upset Suharto's calculations that Indonesia would have an extended grace period to develop its internal strength before confronting a communist [sic] threat from the north. To meet the changed situation following the loss of Indochina, President Suharto appears to have become, if anything, even more convinced in the months since your meeting at Camp David that Indonesia's policies must be based on the maintenance of close ties with the United States -- although not to the extent that its non-aligned image is tarnished.

> We believe both producer and consumer interests should be taken into account in discussing commodity policies.

-- If we deal with the specifics of these issues we should be able to narrow our differences and reach practical solutions. We hope to discuss these matters with Indonesian policy makers in all appropriate fora: The Joint Commission, the Conference on International Economic Cooperation and elsewhere.

-- Indonesia should also be aware of our political problems in this area. We need the support of the U.S. public to pursue policies to benefit the developing countries. We would welcome Indonesia's help in discouraging Third World positions which can only erode U.S. public support for a forthcoming U.S. posture.

7. Energy Issues

The Indonesians place considerable emphasis on solidarity with OPEC. Nevertheless they have played a passive moderate role at

OPEC meetings and during the latest round kept their price increases significantly below those of other OPEC countries. They did not participate in the Arab oil embargo. The United States accounts for the bulk of Indonesia's oil investment (about 86%) and an increasing amount (about 11%) of our crude oil imports are from Indonesia.

There are two energy related issues which the Indonesians could raise in discussions: (a) Indonesian mandatory exclusion (as a member of OPEC) from the 1974 Trade Act benefits and (b) their hope for a favorable FPC ruling which would permit the GOI to go ahead with a major project to export liquefied natural gas (LNG) to California.

Your Talking Points (if the subject is raised)

-- We have noted Indonesia's recent decision to hold its oil price increases below that sanctioned by OPEC. We have also appreciated Indonesia's moderate stance in other issues relating to OPEC. But we believe that in the long run Indonesia stands to gain most from increasing production and sales.

-- The Federal Power Commission will be taking up the Indonesian LNG case in the very near future. Meanwhile, the Administration's Energy Resources Council will be working toward decisions on our overall energy policies, including the question of LNG imports. While we cannot foretell what these decisions will be, we are very much aware of Indonesia's interest in LNG.

-- We favor Congressional action to enable Indonesia to become eligible to receive those tariff preferences conferred by

the 1974 Trade Act. However, Congressional concern over OPEC
policies will make this difficult.

## 8. US Economic Aid to Indonesia

At Camp David President Suharto emphasized that "Indonesia's
most important need was economic rather than military",
reflecting the realistic Indonesian view that domestic socio-
economic and political problems are the chief threat to the
country's stability. Particularly on Java, where 80 million
people are already as densely crowded as anywhere on earth,
unemployment and grinding poverty are endemic. Compounding
Suharto's political problems are signs that despite ten years of
development under the "New Order" the gap between the rich and
poor is growing, while corruption and maladministration remain
widespread.

In response to Suharto's comments at Camp David, you expressed
your intention to increase aid to Indonesia. Subsequently you
proposed to the Congress an additional $20 million in loans for
Indonesia, bringing the total proposed U.S. assistance package of
$85 million for FY-1976. (Japan this year is providing almost twice
as much, while the other members of the Indonesia aid consortium
are providing roughly $230 million). Prospects for future U.S.
economic assistance are less clear since there are proposals now
under inter-agency review which would cut our aid significantly as
part of worldwide budgetary reductions.

## Your Talking Points

-- We fully recognize Indonesia's continuing need for
   developmental assistance. We have asked Congress for
   $20 million in additional development loans to Indonesia this

year for a total of more than $80 million in aid, the biggest
single increase we have proposed this year for any Asian
country.

-- We intend, within Congressional limits, to maintain a meaningful
   aid contribution to Indonesia. At the same time, Indonesia
   should not gauge U.S. interest in Indonesia solely by bilateral
   aid levels.

-- Private foreign investment can become an increasingly
   important source of capital and technology for Indonesia's
   economic growth. We hope your Government will actively
   continue to encourage the foreign investor.

-- We also hope that Indonesia will support our proposals at the
   UNGA Special Session to protect developing countries
   against cycles in their export earnings, to provide them
   with better access to western capital and to expand
   international facilities to finance development, to promote
   the transfer of technology, and to achieve an international
   consensus governing relations between trans-national
   enterprises and governments.

9. Indonesia and the UN

Indonesia walks a tightrope in its UNGA voting, maintaining a
show of solidarity with the non-aligned majority while attempting
to avoid too frequent opposition to the U.S. and the West. This is
reflected in abstentions and behind-the-scene efforts at
compromise. In 1974 Indonesia worked hard to defend the seat of
the Lon Nol delegation. The 1975 record has been mixed: On Korea
Indonesia voted for the friendly resolution and abstained on the

hostile one; on Zionism, however, it voted with the majority, to some extent because of internal political considerations arising from the pressure of Moslem political parties in Indonesia.

### SECRET

**Source:** "Memorandum from Secretary of State Henry Kissinger to President Gerald Ford." (1975, November). In W. Burr & M. Evans (Eds.), *National Security Archive Electronic Briefing Book No. 62: East Timor Revisited: Ford, Kissinger and the Indonesia Invasion, 1975-76* (doc. 3, pp. 1-3, 11-13). Washington, DC: George Washington University. Accessed at: http://www.gwu.edu/~nsarchiv/NSAEBB/NSAEBB62/

## DOCUMENT 7

This document is a confidential letter from September 26, 1983, from the Australian consul in Bali, Malcolm Mann, to Dennis Richardson, counselor in Australia's embassy in Jakarta. The letter, discovered in Australia's National Archive in 2015, reports a conversation with the US consul in Surabaya (Indonesia), Jay McNaughton. It reveals that both the United States and Australia were aware that Indonesia was deploying napalm in East Timor. Indeed, Indonesia's military was dropping it via retrofitted, US-supplied 5 aircraft. As Mann reports, McNaughton had informed him that "he had seen intelligence reports [presumably US ones] that the Indonesians were fitting napalm tanks to their F5 aircraft for use in East Timor." The letter reveals a small part of the horrific violence unleashed by Indonesian forces in their quest to subjugate East Timor, as well as the complicity of the United States in facilitating it. Dr. Clinton Fernandes, an associate professor in the International and Political Studies Program of the Australian Defence Force Academy and the University of New South Wales, discovered the document. He kindly provided an electronic copy of it to the author.

AUSTRALIAN CONSULATE
BALI
26 September 1983

**Dear Dennis**

The United States Consul in Surabaya, Jay McNaughton, was in Bali late last week in connection with the death (suicide or murder) of an United States citizen here a fortnight ago. As he usually does, Jay called to see me. During our discussion, Jay told me that he had seen intelligence reports that the Indonesians were fitting napalm tanks to their F5 aircraft for use in East Timor. Apparently, American exterts [sic] had been asked to help with the fitting of the napalm tanks as the Indonesians were having difficulty trimming the aircraft.

Jay also told me that when United States Ambassador Holdridge was in the Puncak recently, some men, thought to be Indonesian, attempted to break into his bungalow. The would-be intruders were so persistent in spite of the Ambassador's calls for help that the U.S. authorities suspect that something more than a simple robbery was their motive. It has been widely concluded that the motive of the attempted break-in was either to kidnap or to harm the Ambassador.

You will have probably heard of the above information from other sources. Could you please protect Jay McNaughton.

**Best Regards**

**Malcolm Mann**
( M.D. Mann )
Consul

P.S. Attached are the latest clippings on East Timor.

Mr D. Richardson,

Counsellor,

Australian Embassy,

Jakarta

**Source:** Confidential letter from September 26, 1983, from Malcolm Mann to
Dennis Richardson. Letter discovered in Australia's National Archive in 2015.
Electronic copy of document supplied to author, from Dr. Clinton Fernandes,
Associate Professor, International and Political Studies Program, Australian
Defence Force Academy and the University of New South Wales.

# CHAPTER FIVE

# THE US ROLE IN ARGENTINA'S "DIRTY WAR" (1976-1983)

Natasha Zaretsky

## INTRODUCTION

From 1976 through 1983, Argentina was ruled by a military dictatorship which engaged in what they called a "dirty war" against alleged terrorism and subversion of "Western and Christian order." This "war" was commonly referred to as the *proceso*, or Process of National Reorganization, by the regime—a junta comprised of the navy, army, and air force. Essentially, the junta set out to preserve its vision of national order by annihilating anyone it considered or deemed "subversive"—a category that would come to define virtually anyone who the leaders perceived to be a threat. This included left-wing guerrilla groups, such as the ERP (People's Revolutionary Army) and the Montoneros, whose members had indeed committed acts of violence as a part of their political struggle, which in no way justified the human rights abuses the military committed. The junta also targeted anyone it considered *potentially* subversive—a large cross-section of society that included priests working with the poor, trade unionists, university students, and activists, among others.

To accomplish its goal of maintaining both order and strict control of the society, the junta employed clandestine, extralegal tactics of disappearance, torture, and killing, which resulted in the murder of an estimated 30,000 people. Such systematic violence and repression, of course, did not occur in a political or historical vacuum.

This chapter will address the complex role of the United States in Argentina's "Dirty War" what they saw as a battle against "subversion," driven in many ways by a powerful American ideological doctrine of eradicating communism in the Western hemisphere. This effort involved the US government providing military training in counterinsurgent practices and aid, as well as diplomatic cover in the early years of the military dictatorship. While it is important to acknowledge that the US did not actively intervene in Argentine affairs as they did in other countries, such as Guatemala,[73] it is equally significant to duly note that the US did provide the ideological foundation of anti-communism, which was integral to carrying out the repression. Ultimately, they would also later give the junta tacit approval (essentially a "green light") to drive out what they viewed as subversion and carry out its actions as they saw fit in their eradication of what they understood to be subversive agents.[74]

## THE "DIRTY WAR" AGAINST SUBVERSION

The years that preceded the 1976 military coup were characterized by extreme political and economic upheaval in Argentina. These problems accelerated following Isabel Perón's assumption of the presidency upon her husband Juan Perón's death in July 1974. Under Isabel Perón's ineffective leadership, hyperinflation and political violence by guerrilla groups and right-wing death squads created a sense of heightened instability and insecurity in the nation, setting the conditions for the coup that would become known as the "Dirty War."

Before Isabel Perón became president, Argentina had been experiencing a rise in activist movements. Like other Latin American nations in the

---

73 See, for instance, Rabe (2016).

74 The positive impact of US diplomacy was evident under the Carter administration, when an increased emphasis on human rights did contribute to improving human rights conditions and challenging the military regime.

1950s and 1960s, Argentines sought social change in various sectors, including in the workplace and places of education, which involved labor unions and students seeking reform. It was in 1970, however, that several guerrilla groups that did engage in violence became active, including the Montoneros (left-wing Peronists) and the ERP, or *Ejército Revolucionario del Pueblo* (People's Revolutionary Army—a non-Peronist Marxist-Leninist group). To effect the social change they sought, these left-wing groups resorted to kidnappings, bank robberies, and the assassination of state officials (Rock, 1987, pp. 353–54).[75]

As mentioned, right-wing extremist groups also arose (including those linked to the army and police) that employed extrajudicial violence, targeting students and union members (through kidnapping, "disappearing," and torturing them), in what would become a concerted anti-guerrilla effort. By 1974, the Triple A or Argentine Anticommunist Alliance (*Alianza Argentina Anticomunista*)—a notorious death squad comprised of the police (and later associated with elements of the military)—were responsible for many of the disappearances and killings of those involved in left-wing activities (Rock, 1987, pp. 355–60).[76]

State repression against what became an ever-expanding definition of subversion became the prevailing norm. As historian David Rock (1987) noted, the armed services "imposed repression by the use of unchecked, random, indiscriminate violence that struck without warning or warrant. The definition of *subversion* was broadened and became increasingly capricious, encompassing the mildest protest, whether made by the [various political] parties, the press, the universities, the legal profession, or the

---

75 Although several guerrilla groups engaged in operations involving violence to effect radical forms of social change, it is important not to conflate them. For a discussion of the differences between the Montoneros and the ERP, see Rock (1987, pp. 354–55). For a more detailed analysis of the Montoneros, see Gillespie (1982).

76 Members of the Triple A had received training in counterinsurgency tactics in France and at the School of the Americas. Between 1974 and 1976, the Triple A killed approximately 2,000 people (see McSherry, 2005, p. 74). Although they officially stopped operating after 1976, many of their members would go on to work in other death squads, including Operation Condor, which used the site of Orletti Motors as a clandestine torture and detention center (McSherry, 2005, p. 75).

unions" (p. 363). It is in this context of political violence and severe economic downturn (inflation had reached 700 per cent) that the military
initiated a coup. Comprised of a junta of leading officers from the army,
navy, and air force, they took control to bring "order" back to the country
via what they called the Process of National Reorganization (see National
Commission on the Disappearance of Persons [Comisión Nacional sobre
la Desaparición de Personas or CONADEP], 1986, pp. xii–xiii).

To the outside world, Argentina's military junta framed its actions as a
war against radical left-wing terrorism. In doing so, the junta denied it was
perpetrating any gross human rights violations, while asserting that they had
to do what was necessary to restore order and combat subversion. Ironically,
though, the entire *proceso* was rooted in the idea of subversion (i.e., seeking
or intending to subvert an established system or institution), a concept with
an entrenched history in the US anti-communist National Security Doctrine
for the Western hemisphere. Essentially, anyone and everyone became suspect (or, put another way, a potential suspect). As a result, in addition to
pursuing those actively involved in left-wing guerrilla groups, the military
targeted anyone they wished in Argentine society—anyone they deemed to
be "subversive" or potentially subversive to the national order and to what
they viewed as Argentine civilization. Such "subversives" could then be
detained, jailed, tortured, and "disappeared" or killed.

Both abductions and disappearances had begun before the March 1976
coup; indeed, right-wing death squads had been operating in Argentina
since the early 1970s. But once the military took power in the 1976 coup,
they expanded their repressive tactics in both systematic and clandestine
ways, sowing terror in the population as they sought to eradicate what they
saw as subversion.

To gain a deeper sense of how the military understood the category of
subversion, it is worth turning to witness accounts obtained by the
CONADEP Truth Commission formed in 1984, following the demise of the
dictatorship. An account by a priest found in the Truth Commission report
*Nunca Más* (*Never Again*) asserts that "the person who was interrogating
me lost patience, and became angry, saying, 'You are not a guerrilla, you

don't believe in violence, but you don't realize that when you go to live (in the shanty towns) with your culture, you are joining people, joining poor people, and to unite with poor people is subversion'" (CONADEP, 1986, p. 340). By targeting virtually anyone they thought could potentially undermine their vision of order, the junta recklessly and wantonly violated human rights and ruled through terror.

The Truth Commission was a critical effort in an attempt to establish accountability and transition into democracy. The CONADEP report was based on testimony and evidence that thoroughly documented the systematic nature of torture and repression; indeed, the report clearly indicated that such practices were not isolated incidents or representative of moments of excess, but rather "a concerted plan of repression" that included "murder, rape, torture, extortion, looting and other serious crimes" (CONADEP, 1986, p. 10).

The repression began with abductions: grabbing people from their homes, accosting people on public streets, and taking people from their places of work and study; what is more, at least 8,960 such individuals never reappeared (CONADEP, 1986, p. 11). These sudden abductions generally took place late at night or during early morning hours, often in the presence of adults and other children, and with complete impunity due to the fear and terror that pervaded the society at the time.

Many of the abducted ended up "disappeared" (a term human rights organizations frequently use to refer to those who literally disappear when state officials or their proxies kidnap them from their homes, streets, places of work, school, or other locations, but deny they did so and insist they know nothing about the person). The array of victims was varied, with a wide net cast for those considered to be subversive or potentially subversive, including but not limited to students, nuns and priests, historians, journalists, lawyers, trade unionists, agrarian labor representatives, and those who worked with the poor, among other activists. Even those associated with anyone found to be subversive were potential candidates for disappearance. Not infrequently, the authorities pulled the names of potential victims from the address books of those they already had in custody.

In addition to kidnapping, the authorities also looted and stole from the victims (CONADEP, 1986, pp. 16–18).

Those "disappeared" were often taken to secret detention centers (SDCS) where they were tortured and interrogated for information about their association with organizations and associates considered to be subversive. There were approximately 340 detention centers located throughout the nation, including large cities and regions such as Buenos Aires, Mar del Plata, Córdoba, and Tucumán. According to the CONADEP report *Nunca Más*, the detention centers "worked within the military organizational structure devised for the anti-subversive struggle," with centers linked to different branches of the military. There were also joint action "task forces" comprised of personnel from different branches of the armed forces and security forces (CONADEP, 1986, p. 245).[77]

Officially, the military denied the existence of these centers, but later such centers were confirmed by CONADEP through multiple witness statements and forensic investigations. Some of the spaces had already served as detention centers, while other centers were established in the offices of police and military facilities, such as the Navy Mechanics School (ESMA) in Buenos Aires. According to *Nunca Más*, police stations were most frequently used as concentration camps (CONADEP, 1986, p. 55). The process of dehumanization began for the victims as soon as they were hooded (CONADEP, 1986, p. 56) and unable to see anything as they were transferred to a center—a form of psychological torture (CONADEP, 1986, p. 57). Once incarcerated in a center, their ties with the world outside were severed. Although they were provided food, it was often sporadic (sometimes several days went by without their being provided anything). The same was true in regard to drinking water. Hygiene and health conditions were "deplorable", including situations where prisoners were "left lying on mattresses filthy with blood, urine, vomit and sweat" (CONADEP, 1986, p. 65).

---

77 It is important to note that the repression that took place in Argentina was not just carried out by Argentine forces, but that there were other Latin American nations (via Operation Condor) involved. "The agents of foreign repressive regimes operated in our country and arrested Uruguayans, Paraguayans, Bolivians and other nationals" (CONADEP, 1986, p. 255).

According to the CONADEP report (which documented 8,960 cases of disappearance, although it is suspected that the number was much higher than that), a vast majority of the victims—almost 80 per cent—were between 16 and 35 years of age, with approximately 70 per cent of them being men. Out of those documented, 1 to 2 per cent were children ages 0 to 15, while 3 per cent were pregnant women (CONADEP, 1986, p. 285).

Once in the SDCs or clandestine centers, each person (referred to as a "prisoner") received a number (at times with a letter) to identify them, which would then become their form of identification for the guards and torturers (CONADEP, 1986, pp. 59–60). The detention centers used torture as a primary method for gathering intelligence, with torture engaged at first to "soften up" new prisoners, who, if determined to have any useful information, would then be turned over to special interrogators (CONADEP, 1986, p. 60). Torture methods included the use of the "*picana*" (electric prod), rape, beatings, and psychological torment. Those prisoners who were pregnant had to give birth under deplorable conditions (CONADEP, 1986, pp. 288–94) and were then forced to give up their babies. Ultimately, the newborn babies were placed with military families and raised under new identities.

Because of the arbitrary and widespread nature of the detentions, torture often led to false confessions (CONADEP, 1986, p. 61) since, in many cases, the person being tortured was not engaged in the subversive activity of which they were accused. Torture was also used for arbitrary reasons, including "transgression" of rules (CONADEP, 1986, p. 62).[78]

*Nunca Más* concluded that death was used as a political tool, which included the mass execution of prisoners (in the La Perla detention center, for instance, victims would be taken to the edge of a pit and killed (CONADEP, 1986, p. 210). A great number of victims were also subjected to so-called death flights (*vuelos de la muerte*). Victims were flown out over the Río de la Plata or the Atlantic Ocean in military planes or helicopters and dropped to their deaths, often after they had already been tortured. Generally, the victims were drugged before being loaded onto the aircraft.

---

78 See pp. 76–209 for detailed descriptions of individual detention centers in the *Nunca Más* report.

It is estimated that there were roughly 18 to 200 death flights per year in 1977 and 1978. These flights were documented in the groundbreaking text *El Vuelo* (*The Flight*), written by journalist Horacio Verbitsky (1996) and based on the confession of Adolfo Scilingo, one of the pilots of such death flights. Euphemistically, these murders and executions were referred to as "transfers" (p. 222).[79] Disfigured by the water, corpses would periodically show up on shore. The military would also dispose of bodies in municipal cemeteries or in unmarked graves (CONADEP, 1986, pp. 223–33)—another way the evidence of murder was destroyed.

It is important to understand that the purpose of these executions, and this entire system of repression, was not solely to kill these people but, as previously noted, to "disappear" them. The concealment of documentation of the arrests and deaths of the victims meant uncertainty for the victims' relatives, causing many to forego protests to preserve the possibility of their loved one's return (CONADEP, 1986, p. 234). Some relatives, though, did file writs of habeas corpus in an attempt to locate their relatives. Many also organized to call for what was referred to as "appearance with life," one of the foremost demands of the *Madres de Plaza de Mayo* (the Mothers of the Plaza de Mayo), a powerful force of dissent during the dictatorship and in the years that followed.

Absolute terror pervaded Argentine society, blanketing it in silence during those years—a silence further supported by the impunity enjoyed by the repressors. Only a select number of high profile cases benefited from interventions to some degree, including that of journalist Jacobo Timerman, editor of *La Opinión*, who was kidnapped in 1977 and subjected to torture (including electric shocks) and interrogation before being recognized and subsequently held under house arrest. Eventually, Timerman fled from Argentina to Israel in 1979. He was also one of the first to break the silence, publishing *Prisoner without a Name, Cell without a Number* (1981) after his release in what would become a highly acclaimed and best-selling account, which was extremely important in raising awareness of the repression. (The

---

79 For a more detailed analysis of the significance of language during the repression, see Feitlowitz (1998).

previously mentioned Mothers of the Plaza de Mayo was formed in the late 1970s, as did other organizations advocating for human rights, such as the Center for Legal and Social Studies [*Centro de Estudios Legales y Sociales*, or CELS]). Again, the systematic nature of *all* of these repressive practices was confirmed via the testimony collected in *Nunca Más*. In the years that followed, a robust human rights movement developed, advocating against the impunity that surrounded those responsible for deaths and disappearances due to amnesty laws put into place; only after those laws were overturned in 2005 did trials of those perpetrators begin.

In sum, the years of state repression, understood by the military junta as a war against subversion that they perceived as necessary to preserve their vision of order, would come to leave a profound impact on Argentina as a nation, both in terms of the estimated 30,000 killed, and the way it would shape the development of civil society and democracy in the aftermath.

## CRIMES AGAINST HUMANITY OR GENOCIDE?

Most scholars have deemed the abuses perpetrated by the Argentine military to be crimes against humanity. Remarkably, just two years after amnesty laws were lifted in 2005, more than 300 people had been charged with crimes against humanity in Argentina. As of 2016, over 2,500 people have been charged, with 723 convictions and 76 acquittals (Human Rights Watch, 2017).[80]

According to the Rome Statute of the International Criminal Court (UN General Assembly, 1998), crimes against humanity are understood to mean any of the following acts when committed as part of a widespread or systematic attack directed against any civilian population, with knowledge of the attack:

(a) murder;
(b) extermination;
(c) enslavement;
(d) deportation or forcible transfer of population;

---

80  See ICTJ (2009).

(e) imprisonment or other severe deprivation of physical liberty in violation of fundamental rules of international law;

(f) torture;

(g) rape, sexual slavery, enforced prostitution, forced pregnancy,
enforced sterilization, or any other form of sexual violence of comparable gravity;

(h) persecution against any identifiable group or collectivity on political, racial, national, ethnic, cultural, religious, gender, or other grounds
that are universally recognized as impermissible under international
law, in connection with any act referred to in this paragraph or any
crime within the jurisdiction of the Court;

(i) enforced disappearance of persons;

(j) apartheid;

(k) other inhumane acts of a similar character intentionally causing great
suffering, or serious injury to body or to mental or physical health.[81]

Tellingly, the Argentine military carried out all of the above crimes with
the sole exception of apartheid.

"Genocide," however, has also recently been used as a term to describe
this period of political violence. While what transpired under the military
dictatorship is *clearly* an example of crimes against humanity, state terrorism, and political repression, whether it was truly genocidal in nature has
been met with some disagreement and debate.

The first mention of "genocide" occurred in the *Nunca Más* report
(1986) in relation to the aforementioned disappearances: "at the heart of
this policy of total disappearance lay the prevention by very possible means
of solidarity being shown by the population in general, with all the protests
and demands this would lead to within the country, and the knowledge
abroad that behind the façade of a fight against a terrorist minority lurked
genocide" (CONADEP, 1986, p. 234). However, the report did not explain the

---

81  See Article 7 of the Rome Statute of the International Criminal Court (UN General
Assembly, 1998).

use of the term, and it was only in the early twenty-first century, some 20 years later, that genocide came into more prominence in Argentina regarding the actions of the junta, coinciding with the acceleration of human rights trials that followed the 2005 overturning of the amnesty laws.

In the aforementioned trials of the alleged perpetrators, some courts couched their rulings in terms of crimes against humanity as part of genocide.[82] In 2006, for instance, during the sentencing of Miguel Etchecolatz, former director of intelligence for the Buenos Aires Provincial Police, for a wide array of charges including kidnapping, murder, and torture, the Argentine authorities of the Tribunal lashed out at the former government, accusing it of having perpetrated "crimes against humanity in the context of genocide that took place in Argentina" (see Rozanski, 2016). It was, in fact, the first time that an Argentine court of law used the term "genocide" to describe what had transpired during the "Dirty War" as a result of various actions carried out by the military regime.

In explaining the use of the term genocide, Judge Carlos Rozanski, president of the La Plata Federal Oral Court, asserted that the offenses carried out by Etchecolatz and his associates constituted part of a systematic attack intended to destroy parts of society that the victims represented, and that they rose to the count of genocide. Rozanski (2016) also said, "The reasoning behind the term 'genocide' was to place it in the context of a larger phenomenon instead of the summation of kidnappings, torture, murders and forced disappearances. The idea was to break free from an arithmetic operation and instead use a concept that is in line with the infinite pain of a society in which tens of thousands of people were massacred by a violent and terrorist state and millions were affected by the cultural effects of that terror" (n.p.).

In addition, Rozanski indicated that the Argentine court chose to use the term based on the December 1946 UN General Assembly Resolution, which unanimously adopted the following wording vis-à-vis genocide: "when racial, religious, political and other groups have been destroyed,

---

82  For an overview of the human rights trials, see Argentina Trial Monitor (n.d.).

entirely or in part"—a definition that was not "politically compromised," in Rozanski's words, given the later removal of the category of "political prisoners" from the UNCG due to pressure from the Soviet Union.

The Etchecolatz sentence also affirmed that, "from all that has gone before, it is indisputable that we are not dealing as we previously expected with a mere succession of crimes, but rather with something significantly greater that deserves the name of genocide."[83] Clearly, genocide assumed juridical and social significance in Argentina.

It is useful here to consider the history of genocide as a category for framing specific criminal acts, which can then be applied to Argentina. Raphael Lemkin (1946), a Polish Jewish jurist, created the term "genocide" for the express purpose of providing the international community with a legal and juridical framework for structuring, prosecuting, and, ultimately, preventing the crime of intentionally setting out to destroy a particular group of human beings. He coined the term in 1944, while the horrors of the Holocaust were underway in Europe, to juridically define both what was happening in Europe as well as past genocides, such as the Ottoman Turk genocide of the Armenians between 1915 and 1921.

Lemkin was central to the efforts to create the UN Convention on the Prevention and Punishment of the Crime of Genocide (UNCG) passed by the UN General Assembly in 1948, and ratified by 22 individual nations in 1951. Though Lemkin had originally proposed that genocide be defined as any intent to destroy in part or whole a group, based on ethnic, religious, national, or political reasons, the final version of the UNCG excised the category of "political" from the legal definition. This, in turn, shaped the evolving social understandings of genocide as linked primarily to race or ethnicity (such as that perpetrated by the extremist Hutus against the Tutsi in Rwanda in 1994, or by the Government of Sudan against the black Africans of Darfur in the early- to mid-2000s). However, in critical genocide studies, many contemporary scholars and activists now argue that the definition of genocide

---

83  For the original sentence, see www.ladhlaplata.org.ar/juicios.htm. See also Argentina Trial
    Monitor (n.d.) for additional context.

should be expanded to be more inclusive of various groups, including polit-ical ones.[84] Indeed, if we understand genocide as the intent to destroy, in whole or in part, a group, this is certainly what took place in Argentina.[85]

More recently, this framing of genocide as the intent to destroy, in whole or in part, a national group, shaped the invocation of genocide in Argentina. Debates, however, continue over the accuracy of the term for describing what transpired under the junta during the "Dirty War." In *Genocide as Social Practice: Reorganizing Society under the Nazis and Argentina's Military Juntas*, Argentine sociologist Daniel Feierstein (2014) has argued that what transpired in Argentina should be considered geno-cide, and that it should be understood as "the deliberate annihilation of human groups as a distinctive form of social engineering" (p. 6), with the group in question being those considered "subversive." Essentially, he argues that the junta's hatred of and struggle against "domestic subversion" became an obsession that compelled them to use extreme violence against anyone they perceived to be a threat, prompting them to engage a variety of tactics to destroy said threat: kidnapping, incarceration, terror, wide-spread use of torture, disappearances, and other forms of repression. Feierstein (2014) further describes one of the significant modalities of genocide as "the ways in which annihilation has been used to destroy and reorganize social relations" (p. 1), with a "genocidal social practice as a technology of power—a way of managing people as a group" (p. 14). Feier-stein argues for the expansion of the current understanding of genocide in relation to Argentina, although other scholars, like Martin Shaw (2016), take Feierstein to task for his reconceptualization, especially in relation to the centrality he gives to social reorganization in his definition of genocide.

---

84  See, for instance, Hinton, La Pointe, & Irwin-Erickson (2013).

85  In some ways, the idea of "dirty war" has been found to legitimize the actions of the states in ways that other terms (like repression or genocide) do not, in that it is seen as somehow suggesting that the military's actions were a necessary response to the leftist threat. This also relates to the idea of the "theory of the two demons," used to explain the violence of the right as a logical response to the violence of the left. As noted by historian Stephen Rabe (2016), this "ignores historical chronology and trivializes the methodical abuse of human rights and the campaign of state terror perpetrated by anti-Communists in Latin America" (p. xxxviii).

It appears that there are significant social, political, and juridical impli-cations for the use of the term "genocide" in this case. Be that as it may, debate over whether the military junta's actions constituted crimes against humanity or genocide may not be resolved in the near term. However, what is certain is that the atrocities perpetrated by the military were hor-rific, widespread, and deadly, creating terror throughout the nation in their battle against what they viewed as subversion.

## THE US ROLE IN ARGENTINA'S "DIRTY WAR": ANTI-COMMUNISM AND HUMAN RIGHTS

While Argentina's military forces were clearly responsible for the abuses of the "Dirty War," the conceptual framework that oriented them against the idea of a "subversive" threat was influenced by military aid and training received from the United States, especially during the 1960s and 1970s. In addition, in the first year of the dictatorship, Argentina also received sig-nificant cover from the United States during what proved to be one of the most violent periods of state violence in Argentine history.

Although the political repression of the "Dirty War" took place from 1976 to 1983, the ideological foundation for this period of state-sanctioned violence can be traced earlier to the Cold War, and more specifically, to the anti-communist National Security Doctrine espoused by the United States. Indeed, as human rights scholar Kathryn Sikkink (2004) notes, "although it is difficult to find 'smoking guns' with respect to US human rights pol-icy...US policy makers bear an important responsibility for the peak of repression in Argentina" (pp. 118–19) because of their "tacit support" (p. 120) for what was happening.

This began in the years that followed World War II, when the US felt a pressing hemispheric need to prevent what it saw as the threat of commu-nism spreading in the region, a process that intensified after the successful Cuban revolution in 1959. The US viewed the Western hemisphere and the Americas as a region particularly vulnerable to the spread of communism, thus prioritizing a US National Security Doctrine intent on developing programs to encourage Latin American militaries to focus on what the US referred to as internal security through tactics of counterinsurgency against what it classified as "subversion."[86]

In an attempt to defend against ostensible communist insurgencies in its "backyard," the United States government actively supported its Latin American neighbors in strengthening their internal security efforts. In the case of the Nixon administration, it sought out "friendly dictators to squelch unrest and protect U.S. interests" (Lawrence, 2008, p. 270). Tellingly, the US government viewed authoritarian regimes more favorably, as they were perceived as far more stable than democracies in terms of US interests (Schmidli, 2013, p. 3). In doing so, it more or less created proxies in its Cold War efforts to uphold its anti-communist National Security Doctrine by providing such authoritarian regimes to its south (including Guatemala, Chile, and Argentina, among others) with military aid and counterinsurgency training. To that end, the US provided millions of dollars in military support for internal security efforts in Latin America (Schmidli, 2013, pp. 18–19).

The motivation for supporting authoritarian rule stemmed from the fear of communism spreading not just from the Soviet Union, but from Cuba-inspired Marxist-Leninist movements. The US viewed its role as protecting the hemisphere from communism by directly providing military training and political support for authoritarian regimes to ward off communist subversion, which, according to anthropologist Lesley Gill (2004), "became defined as anything that challenged the status quo" (p. 73). As a result, "broad sectors of the population—students, activists, trade unionists, peasant organizers, and religious catechists—came under suspicion" (Gill, 2004, p. 73). Ultimately, it was expected by the US government that Latin American militaries were to focus on "internal security" against threats of communist subversion.

Ample training was also provided by the School of the Americas (SOA), originally known as the US Caribbean School. First established in 1946 in the Panama Canal Zone, the SOA trained tens of thousands of officers from Latin

---

86 For a detailed analysis of the Cold War in Latin America, see Rabe (2016); Grandin & Joseph (2010); and Grandin (2004). For a comprehensive account of the relationship between the United States and Argentina during the repression, see Sheinin (2006, pp. 150–80).

America, including many who became responsible for committing major human rights violations all across Central and South America. The training at the SOA focused primarily on counterinsurgency, covering subjects ranging from the psychological and the political to paramilitary and military tactics. Untold numbers of Latin American officers traveled to the United States for training, not only at the SOA but such places as the Army Special Warfare Center at Fort Bragg in North Carolina (Schmidli, 2013, p. 20).

The impact of such counterinsurgency training in shaping Argentine military practices is clearly documented in *Nunca Más*. More specifically, it includes information on a 1981 series entitled "The Defeat of Subversion. The Rise and Fall of Guerrilla Groups in Argentina," published in *La Razón*, in which Argentine General Camps was quoted as stating, "In Argentina we were influenced by the French and then by the United States. We used their methods separately at first and then together until the United States' ideas finally predominated. France and the United States were our main sources of counterinsurgency training. They organized centers for teaching counterinsurgency techniques (especially in the US) and sent out instructions, observers, and an enormous amount of literature" (as quoted in CONADEP, 1986, p. 442). This training of military personnel (Sheinin, 2006, p. 15), along with military aid, helped create Argentina's military doctrine, or what Schmidli (2013) called "the blueprint facilitating the systematic use of extralegal tactics against perceived subversives following the military's return to power in March 1976" (pp. 2–3).

The SOA also shaped another aspect of state repression and terror in those years. More specifically, many Latin American officers made connections during their attendance at the SOA, which essentially helped create a hemispheric military network aligned against communism, facilitating regional networks like Operation Condor. Established in 1975 and organized by Chile, Operation Condor involved the cooperation of Chile, Argentina, Paraguay, Bolivia, Uruguay, and later Brazil in a network that coordinated intelligence and repression against those considered subversive in one another's countries.[87]

---

87 For an in-depth analysis of Operation Condor, see Dinges (2004) and McSherry (2005).

The US government supported the efforts of Operation Condor via a telecommunications network located in the Panama Canal Zone, which helped the nations involved coordinate their efforts (Lawrence, 2008, pp. 283–84; McSherry, 2005, p. 95). According to Lawrence (2008), by doing so, the US government essentially "demonstrated that it sympathized with their goals and would not interfere in their repressive activities" (p. 284).

After Richard Nixon resigned, Gerald Ford became president and immediately recognized the junta (Lawrence, 2008). Ultimately, US Secretary of State Henry Kissinger infamously gave what has come to be known as the "green light" for the repressive, criminal, and brutal tactics used by the junta against those it viewed as "subversive." In regard to the latter, Sikkink (2004) reported that "there is evidence that top-level U.S. policymakers gave verbal assurances that were understood as giving a green light to human rights violators.... These verbal green lights were part of a larger normative context in which the struggle against subversion was seen as essential and human rights violations were acceptable, and even necessary, in the struggle against Communist subversion and terrorism" (p. 107). This gave "tacit support" and approval of the tactics used by the military rulers.

Some diplomats, however, saw the situation differently and actually did voice their concerns, such as US Ambassador to Argentina Robert Hill.[88] However, the overall focus of US foreign policy did not begin to emphasize human rights until the Carter administration replaced the Ford administration. Under President Jimmy Carter, there was a marked shift from the "green light" of Secretary Kissinger and other government officials, to a sustained emphasis on human rights as being critical to US–Argentine relations. For example, Carter appointed Patricia Derian, a noted human rights activist, as assistant secretary of state for human rights, who paid several visits to Argentina, during which she forcefully raised human rights concerns and even confronted military rulers like Admiral Massera about the torture and repression underway.[89] The

---

88  This was evident from a September 24, 1976, diplomatic cable from Ambassador Hill (the American Embassy in Buenos Aires) to Washington, DC (see Document 3).

89  For an account of how Derian confronted Massera, see Schmidli (2013, p. 117).

emphasis on human rights by the Carter administration also helped support local human rights organizations on the ground in Argentina.

In addition to diplomacy, the US government during the Carter administration also sought to stop economic and military aid as part of their human rights challenge to Argentina. According to Schmidli (2013), "by mid-1978, the Department of State had blocked an estimated $800 million in U.S. military and commercial transfers to Argentina on human rights grounds" (p. 4). This included stopping arms sales and pushing to withhold a $270 million loan from the Export-Import Bank in 1978 (Sikkink, 2004, pp. 132–33). Ultimately, this economic pressure helped compel Argentina to accept a visit from the Inter-American Commission for Human Rights of the Organization of American States (OAS), a visit that took place in September 1979, which was seen as a key turning point in the history of human rights and repression in Argentina (Schmidli, 2013, pp. 153–54).

All in all, various scholars have found Carter's policies to have, at least, been "partially effective" (Sikkink, 2004, p. 123) in diminishing human rights abuses and supporting democracy. Although it isn't clear that the Argentine military's perception of the threat of subversion shifted radically as a result of Carter's human rights policies (Schmidli, 2013, p. 153), the military did come to understand they needed to portray a different image, and ultimately, human rights advocacy did coincide with a reduction in abuse and a decline in disappearances.

Although the Carter administration's active advocacy for human rights in Argentina would diminish in the final two years of his term (when concerns in Africa and other regions predominated), the work of Carter and his human rights staff, such as Patricia Derian, served an important role in shifting the framework from a "green light" for any and all actions related to suspected subversion (putatively communistic activity) to emphasizing the importance of human rights for all.[90] In

---

90 After the end of the dictatorship in 1983 and the return to democracy, the significance of President Carter and Assistant Secretary Derian's efforts to advocate for human rights were noted by their invitation to the inauguration of Raúl Alfonsín, the first democratically elected ruler after the period of repression.

essence, this reveals a vastly different way US policies affected Argentina's "Dirty War."

This would, though, radically change when Ronald Reagan came into office as president of the United States in 1981, at which time there was a dramatic shift back to an emphasis on anti-communism. Indeed, Reagan sought to end Carter's policies and re-establish ties with a host of authoritarian rulers (see Sikkink, 2004, p. 152). However, by that time, the human rights movement in Argentina had grown much stronger, and the Argentine military government had begun to gradually lose its power because of economic and political problems, including the 1982 military defeat in the Falkland Islands, which would eventually mark the beginning of the end of the dictatorship. Ultimately, Argentina returned to a democracy in 1983.

Overall, the US did not intervene directly in Argentina as it did in other nations, such as Guatemala, and thus cannot be viewed as directly responsible for the "Dirty War." However, US political support, military training, and aid helped shape the course of Argentine repression and the material and ideological framework of the war against what the junta viewed as subversion (just as its advocacy for human rights under Carter helped challenge military abuses). Ultimately, through its ideological, diplomatic, military, and economic support, the US government, under Nixon and then Ford, was complicit in its own way by providing the ideological mission and political cover for many of the horrific human rights violations to which the Argentine people were subjected during the "Dirty War."

## DECLASSIFIED DOCUMENTS

A large collection of US documents related to the "Dirty War" was released in 2002, with a second batch released in August 2016. Many reveal the complex nuances of US diplomacy in relation to the gross human rights violations perpetrated during Argentina's military dictatorship. Although the US did not actively participate in the torture and killing of Argentine citizens, the entire framework of the repression hinged on the idea of subversion that emerged from the US anti-communist National Security Doctrine and its counterinsurgent tactics. Together, the documents provide a unique picture into the constant flow of information between Buenos Aires and Washington, DC, demonstrating the extent of the US government's awareness of human rights violations perpetrated by the junta.

In these documents, we see sober assessments of the initial military coup (1976), evaluated in terms of its impact on and cost to the United States (see Document 1). We also know from other records that President Ford welcomed (as did US Secretary of State Henry Kissinger) the junta and the return to order it represented in Argentina.

As secretary of state—and even as a private citizen—Kissinger would play a particularly important role in the events that unfolded. In a June 1976 meeting with Argentine Foreign Minister Guzzetti, just a few months into the dictatorship, Kissinger essentially gave a "green light" to the junta in Argentina, signaling that the US was aware of the extralegal, extreme measures that it needed to take and understood it as necessary in its war against subversion. More specifically, Kissinger unambiguously said, "if there are things that have to be done, you should do them quickly" (see Document 2).

The aforementioned meeting also included direct evidence of the joint operation of counter-subversive activities that purportedly crossed national boundaries, in that Guzzetti noted the following: "The terrorist problem is general to the entire Southern Cone. To combat it we are encouraging joint efforts to integrate with our neighbors...Chile, Paraguay, Bolivia, Uruguay, Brazil" (see Document 2).

As mentioned earlier, a small number of diplomats did emphasize the significance of honoring human rights, such as Ambassador Robert C. Hill. For instance, in Document 3 we have the record of a September 1976 meeting between Hill and one of the leaders of the junta, Jorge Rafael Videla. In this conversation, Videla suggests that Hill might not fully understand things in the way his superiors would: "Videla said he had [the] impression senior officers of USG [the US government] understood the situation his gov[ern-men]t faces but junior bureaucrats do not." This is indicative of the value Videla placed on Kissinger's support, as well as his perception that human rights were not central to US concerns. Yet Hill stood his ground, telling Videla, "we all hope Argentina can get terrorism under control quickly—but do so in such a way as to do minimum damage to its image and to its relations with other governments. If security forces continue to kill people to [the] tune of [a] brass band, I concluded, this will not be possible" (see Document 3).

In another meeting soon thereafter, on October 6, 1976, Foreign Minister Cesar Augusto Guzzetti complained about how the world perceived the current Argentine government—that is, as "rightist and fascist"—with Acting Secretary of State Charles W. Robinson reaffirming the notion that Argentina was engaged in a legitimate war against subversives. In part, Robinson said, "during this initial period the situation may seem to call for measures not acceptable in the long term. The real question is knowing how long to continue these tough measures" (see Document 4).

During that same period, in a memorandum detailing Secretary of State Kissinger's meeting with Argentine Foreign Minister Guzzetti on October 7, 1976, Kissinger clearly indicates his support for Argentina, essentially justifying the human rights violations: "Look, our basic attitude is that we would like you to succeed. I have an old-fashioned view that friends ought to be supported. What is not understood in the United States is that you have a civil war. We read about human rights problems but not the context. The quicker you succeed the better" (see Document 5).

Foreign Minister Guzzetti returned to Argentina, clearly elated by the reception he had been given in the United States. In a diplomatic cable dated October 19, 1976, Ambassador Hill, for instance, indicates his concern about Guzzetti's perception of his meeting with Kissinger as a "success," further suggesting that his remarks "are not those of a man who has been impressed with the gravity of the human rights problem as seen from the U.S....Guzzetti went to the U.S. fully expecting to hear some strong, firm, direct warning of his gov[ernmen]t's human rights practices. Rather than that, he has returned in a state of jubilation [c]onvinced that there is no real problem with the USG over this issue." Ambassador Hill also indicated in this cable his concern over the ability of the US Embassy to advocate for human rights, given Guzzetti's impressions (see Document 6).

Under Carter's administration, however, a significant shift would emerge in US–Argentine relations, especially evident in the documents chronicling Assistant Secretary Patricia Derian's encounters with the Argentines. The discussion of human rights was much more direct and confrontational, even as the Argentines sought to define this as a fight against terrorism rather than a violation of rights. This was in marked contrast to Kissinger's position. In a March 1977 meeting (see Document 7), Derian confronts her Argentine counterparts with questions about human rights and states unequivocally that the US would not support her counterparts. In that meeting she noted, "although the US government understands the problems faced by the Argentine government, it cannot stand with Argentina due to human rights violations." She would go on to have another important meeting with Admiral Massera in August 1977 (see Document 8), where she actively confronted him about the human rights violations being perpetrated at the notorious torture center ESMA (Navy Mechanics School) and pushed for a return to normalcy and the rule of law. Though Massera denied anything untoward was going on at ESMA, through the CONADEP and other witness testimonies, it was discovered that the ESMA indeed was one of the most notorious torture and detention centers, where an estimated 5,000 people were tortured.

Even under the Carter administration, we still see the powerful influence of Henry Kissinger. In a June 1978 visit, invited by Argentina's leaders to view the World Cup, we see Kissinger confirming that what was done to eradicate terrorism was necessary—essentially legitimizing the use of torture. Even though he traveled as a private citizen, Kissinger's influence was still a concern for the US Embassy, which noted, "despite his disclaimers that the methods used in fighting terrorism must not be perpetuated, there is some danger that Argentines may use Kissinger's laudatory statements as justification for hardening their human rights stance" (see Document 9).

# REFERENCES

Argentina Trial Monitor. (n.d.). "Background 2: The Re-opening of the Trials: 2003–2012." Rutgers University Center for the Study of Genocide and Human Rights and Universidad Nacional Tres de Febrero. Accessed at: http://www.ncas.rutgers.edu/sites/fasn/files/ATM-TrialBackground2_2003-2012.pdf

CONADEP (Comisión Nacional sobre la Desaparición de Personas / National Commission on the Disappearance of Persons). (1986). *Nunca Más (Never Again): The Report of the Argentine National Commission on the Disappeared*. New York: Farrar Straus Giroux.

Dinges, J. (2004). *The Condor Years: How Pinochet and His Allies Brought Terrorism to Three Continents*. New York: The New Press.

Feierstein, D. (2014). *Genocide as Social Practice: Reorganizing Society under the Nazis and Argentina's Military Juntas* (D.A. Town, Trans.). New Brunswick, NJ: Rutgers University Press.

Feitlowitz, M. (1998). *A Lexicon of Terror: Argentina and the Legacies of Torture*. New York: Oxford University Press.

Gill, L. (2004). *The School of the Americas: Military Training and Political Violence in the Americas*. Durham, NC: Duke University Press.

Gillespie, R. (1982). *Soldiers of Perón: Argentina's Montoneros*. Oxford: Clarendon Press.

Grandin, G. (2004). *The Last Colonial Massacre: Latin America and the Cold War*. Chicago: University of Chicago Press.

Grandin, G., & Joseph, G.M. (Eds.). (2010). *A Century of Revolution: Insurgent and Counterinsurgent Violence during Latin America's Long Cold War*. Durham, NC: Duke University Press.

Hinton, A.L., La Pointe, T., & Irwin-Erickson, D. (Eds.). (2013). *Hidden Genocides: Power, Knowledge, Memory*. New Brunswick, NJ: Rutgers University Press.

Human Rights Watch. (2017). "Argentina." *World Report 2017*. New York: Author.

ICTJ (International Committee for Transitional Justice). (2009, November). "Briefing Criminal Prosecutions for Human Rights Violations in Argentina." Accessed at: https://www.ictj.org/sites/default/files/ICTJ-Argentina-Prosecutions-Briefing-2009-English.pdf

Lawrence, M.A. (2008). "History from Below: The United States and Latin America in the Nixon Years." In F. Logevall & A. Preston (Eds.), *Nixon in the World: American Foreign Relations, 1969–1977* (pp. 269–88). New York: Oxford University Press.

Lemkin, R. (1946, April). "Genocide." *American Scholar, 15*(2), 257–80.

McSherry, J.P. (2005). *Predatory States: Operation Condor and Covert War in Latin America*. New York: Rowman & Littlefield.

Rabe, S.G. (2016). *The Killing Zone: The United States Wages Cold War in Latin America* (2nd ed.). New York: Oxford University Press.

Rock, D. (1987). *Argentina 1516–1987: From Spanish Colonization to Alfonsín*. Berkeley: University of California Press.

Rozanski, C. (2016). "Why Using the Figure Genocide to Describe Those Crimes." *Buenos Aires Herald*. Accessed at: http://www.buenosairesherald.com/article/211331/why-using-the-figure-of-genocide-to-describe-those-crimes

Schmidli, W.M. (2013). *The Fate of Freedom Elsewhere: Human Rights and U.S. Cold War Policy toward Argentina*. Ithaca, NY: Cornell University Press.

Shaw, M. (2016). "Book Review: Genocide as Social Practice: Reorganizing Society under the Nazis and Argentina's Military Juntas." *Genocide Studies and Prevention: An International Journal, 9*(3), 183–87.

Sheinin, D.M.K. (2006). *Argentina and the United States: An Alliance Contained*. Athens: University of Georgia Press.

Sikkink, K. (2004). *Mixed Signals: U.S. Human Rights Policy and Latin America*. Ithaca, NY: Cornell University Press.

Timerman, J. (1981). *Prisoner without a Name, Cell without a Number* (T. Talbot, Trans.). New York: Alfred A. Knopf.

UN General Assembly. (1998, July 17). *Rome Statute of the International Criminal Court* . Accessed at: http://www.refworld.org/docid/3ae6b3a84.html

Verbitsky, H. (1996). *The Flight: Confessions of an Argentine Dirty Warrior* (E. Allen, Trans.). New York: The New Press.

# DOCUMENTS

## DOCUMENT 1

This document presents a diplomatic cable ("INR Analysis of Developments in Argentina") from the US Secretary of State's office directed to all American diplomatic posts on the day after the coup that established military rule in Argentina. In Kissinger's assessment, the new military junta did not present a threat to US interests, and indeed, as he noted, "the three service commanders are known for their pro-US, anti-Communist attitudes" that were, moreover, "favorable to foreign capital." Through this cable, Kissinger also indicated that the US was clearly aware of the human rights violations already underway, which he anticipated would intensify.

DEPARTMENT OF STATE

TELEGRAM

PAGE 01 STATE 072468


67

ORIGIN INR-07

INFO OCT-01 ARA-06 CIAE-00 DODE-00 PM-04 H-02 L-03 NSAE-00


NSC-05 PA-01 PRS-01 SP-02 SS-15 USIA-06 ISO-00 /053 R


DRAFTED BY INR/RAR/SA: JEBUCHANAN:BLAP

APPROVED BY: INR: RKIRK

INR/RAR/OD: LEMISBACK
ARA/APU: JSMITH
ARA/LA: HRYAN
------------           056432
R251921Z MAR 76
FM SECSTATE WASHDC
*TO ALL AMERICAN REPUBLIC DIPLOMATIC POSTS*
USCINCSO


C O N F I D E N T I A L   STATE 072468


E.O. 11652; GDS


TAGS: MPOL, PINS, AR


*SUBJECT: INR ANALYSIS OF DEVELOPMENTS IN ARGENTINA*
1. COMMUNIQUES AND STATEMENTS ISSUED BY THE ARGENTINE JUNTA DO
NOT CLARIFY HOW LONG THE MILITARY INTENDS TO REMAIN IN POWER,
NOR WHAT POLICIES WILL BE IMPLEMENTED. SUCH EVIDENCE AS EXISTS,
HOWEVER, INDICATES THAT THE JUNTA HAS PLANNED A MODERATE
CONSERVATIVE APPROACH, FEATURING:

-- A HEAVY LAW-AND-ORDER EMPHASIS WITH TOP PRIORITY ASSIGNED TO
THE COUNTERTERRORIST EFFORT.

-- A HOUSE-CLEANING OPERATION AGAINST ALLEGEDLY CORRUPT
POLITICAL AND LABOR FIGURES, INCLUDING PLANS TO TRY PERON ON
CORRUPTION CHARGES.

-- AVOIDANCE OF A RABIDLY ANTI-PERONIST OR ANTI-LABOR POSTURE,
AND AN ATTEMPT TO WORK WITH AMENABLE SECTORS OF THE POWERFUL
UNION MOVEMENT.

-- IMPLEMENTATION OF A MODERATE AUSTERITY PROGRAM WHICH WILL EMPHASIZE LESS STATE PARTICIPATION IN THE ECONOMY, FISCAL RESPONSIBILITY, EXPORT PROMOTION, FAVORABLE ATTENTION TO THE NEGLECTED AGRICULTURAL SECTOR, AND A POSITIVE ATTITUDE TOWARD FOREIGN INVESTMENT.

2. JUNTA'S CAPABILITY: THERE IS LITTLE REASON TO BE SANGUINE ABOUT THE FUTURE OF THE MILITARY GOVERNMENT AND ITS ABILITY TO PROVIDE SOLUTIONS TO PRESSING PROBLEMS. THE TERRORIST MENACE CAN PROBABLY BE CONTROLLED, IF NOT ERADICATED, BUT DESIGNING AN ECONOMIC STRATEGY WHICH WILL PROMOTE RECOVERY WITHOUT PROVOKING WIDESPREAD OPPOSITION WILL BE DIFFICULT. THE AUSTERITY MEASURES FAVORED BY MANY EXPERTS, AS WELL AS THE JUNTA ITSELF, CANNOT BE ENFORCED WITHOUT CONSIDERABLE SACRIFICE ON THE PART OF A WORKING CLASS NOT INCLINED TO PAY THE PRICE. PERSISTENT EFFORTS TO ENFORCE AUSTERITY WOULD PROBABLY PRODUCE A COMBINATION OF POPULAR RESISTANCE AND POLICY DISAGREEMENTS WITHIN MILITARY CIRCLES THAT WOULD UNDERMINE THE JUNTA'S ABILITY TO RULE. THE PATH WOULD THEN BE OPEN FOR ANOTHER GOVERNMENTAL SHIFT, PROBABLY INVOLVING THE EMERGENCE OF A NEW MILITARY FACTION WITH ITS OWN APPROACH.

3. PERON'S FATE: CONTRARY TO EXPECTATIONS, THE JUNTA HAS DECIDED TO DETAIN PERON WITHIN ARGENTINA AND APPARENTLY INTENDS TO TRY HER ON CORRUPTION CHARGES. THE OBJECTIVE IS PROBABLY TO EXPOSE IN DEFINITIVE FASHION THE ALLEGED IMMORALITY OF PERONIST POLITICS AND POLITICIANS AND, THEREBY, PREVENT PERON'S SUBSEQUENT RESURRECTION AS A MARTYR. HOWEVER, THIS TACTIC COULD EASILY BACKFIRE, AS ARGENTINES WILL NOT BEMOAN THE REMOVAL OF PERON, BUT THEY TEND TO VIEW HER AS A PATHETIC RATHER THAN A SINISTER FIGURE. THE PUBLIC MAY REJECT AN ATTEMPT TO MAKE HER SOLELY RESPONSIBLE FOR THE NATION'S ILLS. THE JUNTA WILL LIKELY MONITOR PUBLIC REACTION TO THEIR PLANS, AND LEAVE OPEN THE POSSIBILITY OF SIMPLY EXILING PERON.

4. US INTERESTS: US INTERESTS ARE NOT THREATENED BY THE PRESENT MILITARY GOVERNMENT. THE THREE SERVICE COMMANDERS ARE KNOWN FOR THEIR PRO-US, ANTI-COMMUNIST ATTITUDES, AND, IN FACT, ONE OF THE JUNTA'S EARLY STATEMENTS REFERENCES ARGENTINA'S NEED "TO ACHIEVE AN INTERNATIONAL STANDING IN THE WESTERN AND CHRISTIAN WORLD." INVESTMENT PROBLEMS WILL BE MINIMIZED BY THE JUNTA'S FAVORABLE ATTITUDE TOWARD FOREIGN CAPITAL, WHILE THE GOVERNMENT'S PROBABLE INTENTION OF SEEKING US AID, TANGIBLE AND/OR MORAL, TO OVERCOME PRESSING ECONOMIC PROBLEMS WILL PROVIDE ADDED INSURANCE AGAINST OPENLY ANTI-US ATTITUDES AND POLICIES.

5. HUMAN RIGHTS IS AN AREA IN WHICH THE NEW GOVERNMENT'S ACTIONS MAY PRESENT PROBLEMS FROM THE US PERSPECTIVE. SEVERAL THOUSAND ALLEGED SUBVERSIVES ARE ALREADY BEING HELD UNDER A STATE OF SIEGE DECLARED IN NOVEMBER 1974, AND THAT FIGURE WILL MOUNT AS THE SECURITY FORCES INTENSIFY THEIR COUNTERTERRORIST EFFORTS. THE MILITARY'S TREATMENT OF THESE INDIVIDUALS HAS BEEN LESS THAN CORRECT IN THE PAST, AND WILL PROBABLY INVOLVE SERIOUS HUMAN RIGHTS VIOLATIONS IN THE FUTURE. A HARBINGER OF THINGS TO COME MAY BE CONTAINED IN THE JUNTA'S DECREE ESTABLISHING THE DEATH PENALTY FOR THOSE ATTACKING SECURITY PERSONNEL. THE SCOPE OF THIS PROBLEM COULD REACH BEYOND THE TREATMENT OF SUBVERSIVES IF, OVER THE COMING MONTHS, THE JUNTA ATTEMPTS TO ENFORCE UNPOPULAR SOCIAL AND ECONOMIC POLICIES.
KISSINGER

**Source:** Secretary of State. (1976, March 25). "INR Analysis of Development in Argentina." In US Department of State, *Argentina Declassification Project (1975-1984)*. Freedom of Information Act Virtual Reading Room. Accessed at: https://foia.state.gov/searchapp/DOCUMENTS/foiadocs/e4f.PDF

## DOCUMENT 2

This document is a Memorandum of Conversation primarily between US Secretary of State Henry Kissinger and Argentine Foreign Minister Cesar Guzzetti during a meeting held several months after the military coup in

Argentina to discuss the current state of affairs in Argentina, filed as SECRET/NODIS. Guzzetti clearly frames the primary issue as that of terrorism, indicating that he wants to re-establish order by focusing on "internal security" and economic stability, both issues that require US support in Guzzetti's view: "Argentina needs United States understanding and support to overcome problems in these two areas."

Immediately, Kissinger notes his support for Argentina's military rulers and his understanding of their need to establish "authority": "We wish the new government well. We wish it will succeed. We will do what we can to help it succeed. We are aware you are in a difficult period....We understand you must establish authority."

Throughout this conversation, we also see a clear tension marked between the issues of human rights and establishing order in Argentine society (both in the need to battle terrorism and re-establish economic order). Kissinger suggests the US cannot directly help in regard to their terrorism problems, but can offer economic support. Guzzetti also reveals to Kissinger the regional cooperation with other Southern Cone nations in combating terrorism.

In what has been interpreted as a "green light," in this memorandum Kissinger clearly signals his awareness of the tactics used by the military, while also suggesting the urgency to return to "normal procedures": "You will have to make an international effort to have your problems understood. Otherwise, you, too, will come under increasing attack. If there are things that have to be done, you should do them quickly. But you must get back quickly to normal procedures."

[Excerpts]

SECRET/NODIS

MEMORANDUM OF CONVERSATION
        Santiago, Chile
        June 6, 1976
        Secretary's Suite
        8:10 a.m. - 9:15 a.m.

PARTICIPANTS:  The United States
                The Secretary
                Under Secretary Rogers
                Under Secretary Maw
                Luigi R. Einaudi, S/P - Notetaker
                Anthony Hervas, Interpreter

              Argentina
                Foreign Minister Guzzetti
                Ambassador Carasales
                Ambassador Pereyra
                Mr. Estrada

DISTRIBUTION: ARA, S/P

. . . .

## Guzzetti

Our main problem in Argentina is terrorism. It is the first priority of the current government that took office on March 24. There are two aspects to the solution. The first is to ensure the internal security of the country; the second is to solve the most urgent economic problems over the coming 6 to 12 months.

Argentina needs United States understanding and support to overcome problems in these two areas.

## The Secretary [Kissinger]

We have followed events in Argentina closely. We wish the new government well. We wish it will succeed. We will do what we can to help it succeed.

We are aware you are in a difficult period. It is a curious time, when political, criminal, and terrorist activities tend to merge

without any clear separation. We understand you must establish
authority.

Guzzetti

   The foreign press creates many problems for us, interpreting
events in a very peculiar manner.  Press criticism creates problems
for confidence.   It weakens international confidence in the
Argentine Government and affects the economic help that we need.
It even seems as though there is an orchestrated international
campaign against us.

The Secretary

   The worst crime as far as the press is concerned is to have
replaced a government of the left.

Guzzetti

   It is even worse than that . . .

The Secretary

   I realize that you have no choice but to restore governmental
authority.  But it is also clear that the absence of normal
procedures will be used against you.

Guzzetti

   We want to restore republican rights.  In the meantime, we must
defeat terrorism and resolve our economic problems. It takes time.

The Secretary

   We can't help you much on the terrorist front.

Guzzetti

   I understand.

The Secretary
  But in the economic field, we may be able to do something....

...We will do what we can on the economic front.  A stable Argentina
is of interest to the hemisphere. That has always been true. It is
basic.

  But this problem of terrorism is strange. There have always been
parts of cities that were not really safe, that had no government.
That in itself was not a political problem. But when it merges with
political terrorism, we have no clear precedents.

  The problem should be studied. Unfortunately, those who have
the time to do so are usually on the side of the guerrillas.

Guzzetti
  The terrorist problem is general to the entire Southern Cone.
To combat it, we are encouraging joint efforts to integrate with
our neighbors.

The Secretary
  Which ones?

Guzzetti
  All of them: Chile, Paraguay, Bolivia, Uruguay, Brazil.

The Secretary [sharply]
  I take it you are talking about joint economic activities?

Guzzetti
  Yes. Activities on both the terrorist and the economic fronts.

The Secretary

Oh. I thought you were referring only to security. You cannot succeed if you focus on terrorism and ignore its causes.

Guzzetti

You are right. People need to develop a broader consciousness that the only way to defeat terrorism in the future in our part of the world is through greater regional integration and economic stability.

The Secretary [mollified]

That sounds like a good idea.

Guzzetti

We must create disincentives to potential terrorist activities. Specifically, terrorism is becoming extraordinarily virulent. People on the outside don't look for details. They don't see the provocations that we face, or our efforts to resolve them.

. . . .

The Secretary

....You will have to make an international effort to have your problems understood. Otherwise, you, too, will come under increasing attack. If there are things that have to be done, you should do them quickly. But you must get back quickly to normal procedures.

Guzzetti

Yes, we must find procedures so as not to alienate people. I will so advise our President.

. . . .

The Secretary

It is certainly true that whatever the origin, terrorism frequently gains outside support. And this outside support also creates pressures against efforts to suppress it.

But you cannot focus on terrorism alone. If you do, you only increase your problems.

. . . .

The Secretary

We want you to succeed. We do not want to harass you. I will do what I can. Of course, you understand, that means I will be harassed. But I have discovered that after the personal abuse reaches a certain level you become invulnerable....

**Source:** "Memorandum of Conversation between US Secretary of State Henry Kissinger and Argentine Foreign Minister Cesar Guzzetti." (1976, June 6). In C. Osorio & K. Costar (Eds.), *National Security Archive Electronic Briefing Book No. 133: Kissinger to the Argentine Generals in 1976: "If There Are Things That Have to Be Done, You Should Do Them Quickly"*. Washington, DC: George Washington University. Accessed at: http://nsarchive2.gwu.edu/NSAEBB/ NSAEBB133/19760610%20Memorandum%20of%20Conversation%20clean.pdf

# DOCUMENT 3

In this document, a diplomatic cable from Ambassador Robert Hill in Buenos Aires addressed to Secretary of State Hill describes a September 21, 1976, meeting with Argentine President Videla. Hill acknowledges the Argentine government's struggle against "left-wing subversion," yet also presses him on human rights issues, indicating that it harms Argentina's international image and could impact Argentina's ability to receive US aid, given the Harkin amendment's prohibition from offering such aid to any nation found to be committing gross human rights violations.

Hill also advocates for the rule of law, both in terms of sanctions for those responsible for violence (such as the murders he mentions), as well as in processing terrorists: "I asked, then, if any sanctions were going to be taken against those responsible, thus showing that his gov[ernmen]t did not condone such acts. Videla avoided reply. I suggested that, in the final analysis, [the] best way to proceed against terrorists was within [the] law."

Videla defended his government's actions based on its battle against terrorism and "international communism." Videla also signaled to Hill that perhaps Hill's assessment (and advocacy for human rights) did not reflect the priorities of higher-level US government officials who understood the situation better than, presumably, Hill. Hill countered that he did in fact understand, and reaffirmed the significance of human rights: "Videla said he had [the] impression senior officers of [the] USG understood [the] situation his gov[ernmen]t faces but junior bureaucrats do not. I assured him this was not the case. We all hope Argentina can get terrorism under control quickly—but do so in such a way as to do minimum damage to its image and to its relations with other governments. If security forces continue to kill people to [the] tune of [a] brass band, I concluded, this will not be possible." Ultimately, Hill left the meeting unsure of Videla's ability or commitment to reign in security forces committing abuses.

[Excerpts]

Current Class: ███████████          Page: 1
Current Handling: ██████████
   Document Number: 1976BUENOS06276          Channel: n/a
                    9/24/76 [hand-written]
                    Case Number: 20 0000044

<<<<.>>>>
PAGE 01      BUENOS 06276  241619Z
43
ACTION SS-25
INFO OCT-01  ISO-00  SSO-00  NSCE-00  /026  W
             ---------------------------------  101650

O 241535Z SEP 76
FM AMEMBASSY BUENOS AIRES
TO SECSTATE WASHDC 7269

 BUENOS AIRES 6276

E.O. 11652: XGDS-2
TAGS: PFOR, SHUM, AR, US
SUBJECT: AMBASSADOR DISCUSSES US-ARGENTINE RELATIONS WITH
PRESIDENT VIDELA

RER: (A) BUENOS AIRES 6177, (B) STATE 227379, (C) STATE 231122

1. AS REPORTED IN REF A, PRESIDENT VIDELA RECEIVED ME AT 11:15
A.M. YESTERDAY, SEPT 21 AND I WAS WITH HIM ABOUT AN HOUR AND A
HALF. I OPENED CONVERSATION BY GOING DIRECTLY INTO HUMAN RIGHTS
ISSUE. I TOLD HIM OF GREAT CONCERN I HAD FOUND IN US. THERE WAS, I
SAID, GREAT SYMPATHY FOR HIS GOVERNMENT, WHICH HAD TAKEN OVER UNDER
DIFFICULT CIRCUMSTANCES AND WHICH ALL UNDERSTOOD TO BE INVOLVED IN
[A] STRUGGLE TO THE DEATH WITH LEFT-WING SUBVERSION. HOWEVER, SUCH
THINGS AS THE MURDER OF THE PRIESTS AND THE MASS MURDER [AT] PILAR
WERE SERIOUSLY DAMAGING ARGENTINA'S IMAGE IN THE US. US WAS
SERIOUSLY CONCERNED WITH HUMAN RIGHTS ISSUE NOT JUST IN ARGENTINA
BUT AROUND THE WORLD, AND WE NOW HAVE LEGISLATION UNDER WHICH NO
COUNTRY DETERMINED TO BE CONSISTENTLY GUILTY OF GROSS VIOLATIONS OF
HUMAN RIGHTS CAN BE ELIGIBLE FOR ANY FORM OF US ASSISTANCE, BE IT
ECONOMIC OR MILITARY. I EXPLAINED TO HIM WHAT WOULD HAPPEN IF
HARKIN AMENDMENT WERE INVOKED AGAINST ARGENTINA (SEE REF B). I
TOLD HIM, HOWEVER, THAT FOR THE MOMENT THIS HAD BEEN AVOIDED.
US WOULD VOTE FOR ARGENTINE LOAN IN IDB (I EXPLAINED THAT
QUESTION OF INTEREST RATES FOR SOME PORTIONS OF LOAN HAD STILL
TO BE RESOLVED BUT THAT THIS [WAS] NOT RELATED TO HARKIN

AMENDMENT). I TOLD PRESIDENT FRANKLY, HOWEVER, THAT I SAW THIS
VOTE AS PROBABLY LAST IME [SIC] US WOULD...BE ABLETO [SIC]
AVOID INVOKING AMENDMENT AGAINST ARGENTINA UNLESS RPT UNLESS
[SIC] GOA [GOVERNMENT OF ARGENTINA] MOVED QUICKLY TO
DEMONSTRATE IT IS TAKING MEASURES TO GET HUMAN RIGHTS SITUATION
IN HAND. I POINTED OUT THAT SO FAR AS I KNEW, NOT ONE SINGLE
PERSON HAS BEEN BROUGHT TO JUSTIC [SIC] OR EVEN DISCIPLINED FOR
EXCESSES OF WHICH ELEMENTS OF SECURITY FORCES HAVE BEEN GUILTY.
I ALSO POINTED OUT TO HIM HUMAN RIGHTS PROVISIONS OF NEW
SECURITY ASSISTANCE LEGISLATION (SEE REFTEL C) AND INDICATED
URUGUAY HAD ALREADY LOST THREE MILLION DOLLARS IN MILITARY AID
BECAUSE OF IT. I PROMISED TO SENT [SIC] TEXTS OF PERTINENT
PROVISIONS OF NEW SECURITY ASSISTANCE LEGISLATION AND HARKIN
AMENDMENT TO FOREIGN MINISTRY.

2. PRESIDENT THANKED ME FOR FRANK EXPOSITION OF PROBLEM AND
EXPRESSED APPRECIATION FOR US AFFIRMATIVE VOTE IN IDB. HE SAID
HE HAD BEEN OUTRAGED BY THE MURDERS AT PILAR, WHICH, INDEED, HAD
BEEN AN AFFRONT TO HIS GOVT.

3. I ASKED, THEN, IF ANY SANCTIONS WERE GOING TO BE TAKEN
AGAINST THOSE RESPONSIBLE, THUS SHOWING THAT HIS GOVT DID NOT
CONDONE SUCH ACTS. VIDELA AVOIDED REPLY. I SUGGESTED THAT, IN
THE FINAL ANALYSIS, [THE] BEST WAY TO PROCEED AGAINST
TERRORISTS WAS WITHIN LAW. AND WHY, I ASKED, DID NOT GOA USE
EXISTING COURT SYSTEM TO BRING MEMBERS OF FORMER GOVT TO TRIAL,
INSTEAD OF LEAVING THEM IN PRISON WITHOUT CHARGES.

4. VIDELA DID NOT ANSWER EITHER QUESTION; RATHER, HE LAUNCHED
INTO LONG EXPOSITION OF DIFFICULT SITUATION HIS GOVT HAD
INHERITED. ECONOMY HAD BEEN ON THE ROCKS AND TERRORISM
RAMPANT. FURTHER, HE SAID, ARGENTINA WAS NOW AT WAR WITH
INTERNATIONAL COMMUNISM, WHICH, THROUGH PENETRATION OF THE

SCHOOLS AND EVEN THE CHURCH, HAD BEEN ON VERGE OF TAKEOVER.
ALTHOUGH HE HAD EARLIER DEPLORED TO ME MASS MURDER AT PILAR,
CERTAIN OF HIS SUBSEQUENT STATEMENTS SUGGESTED THAT HE VIEWS
KILLINGS OF SOME LEFTISTS AS GOOD OBJECT LESSON.

5. HE SAID GOVT WAS TAKING ACTION TO CONTROL PROBLEM OF ANTI-
SEMITISM IN ARGENTINA. HE SAID HE THOUGHT PROBLEM HAD BEEN
EXAGGERATED, BUT THAT GOA WANTS NONE OF THAT SORT OF THING AND
HAS ISSUED DECREE BANNING NAZI-SYMPATHIZING PUBLICATIONS WHICH
WERE PRINCIPALLY RESPONSIBLE FOR STIMULATING ANTI-SEMITISM.

. . . .

6. PRESIDENT SAID HE HAD BEEN GRATIFIED WHEN FONMIN GUZZETTI
REPORTED TO HIM THAT SECRETARY OF STATE KISSINGER UNDERSTOOD THEIR
PROBLEM AND HAD SAID HE HOPED THEY COULD GET TERRORISM UNDER
CONTROL AS QUICKLY AS POSSIBLE. VIDELA SAID HE HAD IMPRESSION
SENIOR OFFICERS OF USG UNDERSTOOD SITUATION HIS GOVT FACES BUT
JUNIOR BUREAUCRATS DO NOT. I ASSURED HIM THIS WAS NOT THE CASE. WE
ALL HOPE ARGENTINA CAN GET TERRORISM UNDER CONTROL QUICKLY--BUT DO
SO IN SUCH A WAY AS TO DO MINIMUM DAMAGE TO ITS IMAGE AND TO ITS
RELATIONS WITH OTHER GOVERNMENTS. IF SECURITY FORCES CONTINUE TO
KILL PEOPLE TO TUNE OF BRASS BAND, I CONCLUDED, THIS WILL NOT BE
POSSIBLE. I TOLD HIM SECRETARY OF STATE HAD TOLD ME WHEN I WAS IN
US THAT HE WANTED TO AVOID HUMAN RIGHTS PROBLEM IN ARGENTINA.

7. VIDELA REPLIED THAT HIS GOVT, TOO, WISHED TO AVOID SUCH A PROBLEM.
NOTHING, HE SAID, MUST BE ALLOWED TO UPSET GOOD RELATIONS WITH US.

. . . .

12: COMMENT: I CAME AWAY FROM MEETING WITH VIDELA SOMEWHAT
DISCOURAGED. HE SAYS HE WANTS TO AVOID PROBLEMS WITH US

....BUT HE GAVE NO INDICATION THAT HE INTENDS TO MOVE AGAINST THOSE ELEMENTS IN SECURITY FORCES WHO ARE RESPONSIBLE FOR OUTRAGES--AND THUS BEGIN TO GET SITUATION IN HAND. INDEED, HE MAY NOT BE IN ANY POSITION TO SO MOVE. I CAME AWAY WITH VERY STRONG IMPRESSION THAT VIDELA IS NOT IN CHARGE, THAT HE IS NOT THE BOSS AND KNOWS HE IS NOT. HE IS PROBABLY NOT GOING TO MOVE AGAINST HARDLINERS. HE IS A DECENT, WELL-INTENTIONED MAN, BUT HIS WHOLE STYLE IS ONE OF DIFFIDENCE AND EXTREME CAUTION. IN THE PRESENT SITUATION, MORE ASSERTIVENESS THAN HE CAN PROVIDE MAY BE NEEDED TO GET HUMAN RIGHTS SITUATION UNDER CONTROL. HILL

**Source:** US Embassy (Buenos Aires). (1976, September 24). "Ambassador Discusses US-Argentine Relations with President Videla." In US Department of State, *Argentina Declassification Project (1975-1984)*. Freedom of Information Act Virtual Reading Room. Accessed at: https://foia.state.gov/Search/results .aspx?searchText=*&beginDate=19760924&endDate=19760924&publishedBeginDate =&publishedEndDate=&caseNumber=

## DOCUMENT 4

This document chronicles an October 6, 1976, Memorandum of Conversation focusing on US–Argentine relations. Argentine Foreign Minister Guzzetti clearly describes their battle against subversion and indicates that he anticipates it being finished in a matter of months. Acting Secretary of State Robinson acknowledges Argentina was grappling with "subversive civil war" (a designation quite different from later understandings which included political repression, crimes against humanity, and possibly genocide). Robinson acknowledges this period as exceptional, perhaps, and urges a longer term view.

The particular urgency to end such violations seemed almost utilitarian in order to avoid disruptions in US aid to Argentina, which would be prompted by continuing human rights abuses. Robinson noted, "The American people, right or wrong, have the perception that today there exists in Argentina a pattern of gross violation of human rights. Under current legislation the administration might be prevented under certain circumstances from voting for loans in the IDB, for example." He further indicated the urgency for Argentina to "soften its countersubversion measures. This will be necessary in order to avoid the concept of a consistent pattern of gross violations, and the changed situation must be perceived by the American public." Robinson also pushed for human rights in more concrete terms, including greater consular access for detained US citizens.

The overall message, however, was one of support: "The United States is anxious to cooperate with Argentina within the limits imposed by our Congress; the United States wishes Argentina success in its endeavors."

[Excerpts]

CONFIDENTIAL

DEPARTMENT OF STATE

*Memorandum of Conversation*

DATE: Oct. 6, 1976

Time: 1:00PM

Place: James Madison Room

SUBJECT: U.S.-Argentine Relations

PARTICIPANTS:  Argentina

His Excellency Rear Admiral Cesar Augusto Guzzetti, Minister of Foreign Affairs and Worship of the Argentine Republic

His Excellency Arnaldo Tomas Musich, Ambassador or [sic] the Argentine Republic

Colonel Repetto Pelaez, Undersecretary General, Ministry of Foreign Affairs

His Excellency Federico Bartfeld, Chief, Latin American Division of Foreign Ministry

United States

The Acting Secretary of State

The Honorable Harry W. Shlaudeman, Assistant
     Secretary for Inter-American Affairs

Mr. Robert W. Zimmermann, Director, Office of East
     Coast Affairs, ARA/ECA

The Honorable Edwin M. Martin, Chairman, Consultative
     Group on Food Production and Investment in
     Developing Countries, IBRD


. . . .


Guzzetti began the substantive conversation by noting that the
military government is now six months old and that its antecedents
and current situation are well known. Nevertheless, he said, he
wished to express his personal views, especially regarding
subversion. In this regard, he noted that the government had
achieved some success and there are hopes that within three to four
months the government will have dealt with the subversive groups.
However, he said, Argentina has other problems as well:
educational, social and economic; the most important of which is
the need to push economic reform. Argentine economic problems are
being effectively attacked by Minister Martinez de Hoz and there
already is clear evidence of substantial recuperation.

One of the most important issues facing the government,
Guzzetti continued, is the capacity of international terrorist
groups to support the Argentine terrorists through propaganda and
funds. The armed forces, when they took over in March, found the
country destroyed economically and psychologically. It was a
country in crisis. But in six months the government is on the road
to recovery. The outside world speaks of the Argentine government
as rightist and fascist. This is far from reality. Argentina had to

face the situation realistically and is trying to find a means to interpret the situation to the outsidw [sic] world. The present regime wishes to establish a democracy; this is the nation's most important task.

. . . .

Acting Secretary Robinson recapitulated the three themes touched upon by Guzzetti: terrorism, progress in the economic area and the problem of the refugees. He said that he was pleased that Guzzetti would be seeing the Secretary [Kissinger] the following day in New York, and that the Foreign Minister would find him sensitive to Argentina's problems. The U.S. is very aware of the progress Argentina has made in restoring its economy in the last six months. He said that he has great respect for the capacity of the Minister of Economics, Martinez de Hoz, to cope with such problems as inflation, severe deficits, foreign debt, and productivity.

Obviously, he continued, Argentina is now facing a kind of subversive civil war. During this initial period, the situation may seem to call for measures that are not acceptable in the long term. The real question, he emphasized, is knowing how long to continue these tough measures and noted that the Foreign Minister had indicated that they might be required for another three or four months.

. . . .

The Acting Secretary said that it is possible to understand the requirement to be tough at first but it is important to move toward a more moderate posture which we would hope would be permanent. It is helpful, he remarked, to hear the Minister's explanation of the

situation. The problem is that the United States is an idealistic
and moral country and its citizens have great difficulty in
comprehending the kinds of problems faced by Argentina today.
There is a tendency to apply our moral standards abroad and
Argentina must understand the reaction of Congress with regards to
loans and military assistance. The American people, right or wrong,
have the perception that today there exists in Argentina a pattern
of gross violation of human rights. Under current legislation the
administration might be prevented under certain circumstances
from voting for loans in the IDB, for example. The government is
placed in a difficult position. In reality there are two elements
that must be considered. First, how long is it necessary to
maintain a very firm, tough position? Our Congress returns in
January and if there is a clear-cut reduction in the intensity of
the measures being taken by the Government of Argentina, then
there would in fact be a changing situation where the charge that a
consistent pattern of gross violations exists could be seen as
invalid. Second, it is very important that Argentina find a means
to explain the Argentine position to the world. There is also a
third element and that is that there are many well meaning people in
the United States, though perhaps somewhat naive, who
indiscriminately take the side of those imprisoned in Argentina.
Their attitudes are reinforced by instances where the US
Government has been unable, in the case of arrested U.S. citizens,
to have consular access. The U.S. is not going to defend these
persons if they break your laws but we must have prompt consular
access. In summary there are three issues: the question of timing
of the relaxation of extreme counter-subversion measures;
promoting an understand [sic] of the problems facing Argentina; and
consular access.

. . . .

The Acting Secretary noted that our job is to determine what we can do about this situation. He said we would be remiss if we did not underline again the very serious problem we face with our Congress unless Argentina can properly explain its position and move to a situation in which it is able to soften its counter-subversion measures. This will be necessary in order to avoid the concept of a consistent pattern of gross violations, and the changed situation must be perceived by the American public.

Ambassador Martin remarked that if members of religious groups violate the law it is essential that they not simply "disappear." It should be sufficient to arrest them and bring them to trial. In the United States people simply do not believe that religious men can act in a fashion that warrants summary treatment.

Ambassador Musich then remarked that a negative vote in the Inter-American Development Bank could have a bad effect in Argentina. Assistant Secretary Shlaudeman responded that we also have a problem in that the two loans for $90 million coming together will further concentrate critical attention here. We will not, he said, vote no, but it would be to our mutual advantage if a vote on one of the two pending Argentine loans could be postponed. There is no difficulty with the $60 million loan but we do have a problem with the $30 million loan. We would like to separate the two votes, postponing consideration of the second loan. The situation would then be reexamined at a later date and if there were progress we would not have a problem.

Acting Secretary Robinson said that it would be helpful if the Foreign Minister were to repeat his views to the Secretary in New York. The United States, he said, is anxious to cooperate with Argentina within the limits imposed by our Congress; the United States wishes Argentina success in its endeavors. Foreign Minister

Guzzetti… asked for understanding for the Government of Argentina while it resolves its terrorist problems.

CONFIDENTIAL

**Source:** "Memorandum of Conversation, U.S.-Argentine Relations." (1976, October 6). In C. Osorio (Ed.), *National Security Archive Electronic Briefing Book No. 104: Kissinger to Argentines on Dirty War: "The Quicker You Succeed the Better"* (doc. 5). Washington, DC: George Washington University. Accessed at: http://nsarchive2.gwu.edu/NSAEBB/NSAEBB104/Doc5%20761006.pdf

## DOCUMENT 5

This document includes excerpts of the memorandum regarding the conversation, previously classified "SECRET/NODIS," between Secretary of State Henry Kissinger and Argentine Foreign Minister Cesar Guzzetti, at the Waldorf Astoria Hotel in New York City. Kissinger clearly indicates his support for Argentina's government, as well as an awareness of human rights. His foremost suggestion is to decrease human rights abuses to prevent issues with the us Congress, especially in relation to economic aid.

[Excerpts]

DEPARTMENT OF STATE
*Memorandum of Conversation*

SECRET                                          DATE: October 7, 1976
NODIS

SUBJECT: Secretary's Meeting with Argentine Foreign Minister Guzzetti

DATE, TIME AND PLACE: October 7, 1976; 5:15 P.M., Secretary's Suite, Waldorf Astoria Hotel, New York

PARTICIPANTS:    ARGENTINA
                 Foreign Minister Cesar Augusto Guzzetti

Ambassador to the United States Arnaldo T. Musich
Ambassador to the UN Carlos Ortiz de Rosas

US
The Secretary
Under Secretary Philip Habib
Assistant Secretary Harry W. Shlaudeman
Fernando Rondon (notetaker)
Anthony Hervas (Interpreter)

DISTRIBUTION:   S(Aherne), S, S/S, WH(Rodman)


. . . .


Foreign Minister Guzzetti: ...Mr. Secretary, I'm going to speak in
Spanish. You will recall our meeting in Santiago. I want to talk
about events in Argentina during the last four months. Our
struggle has had very good results in the last four months. The
terrorist organizations have been dismantled. If this direction
continues, by the end of the year the danger will have been set
aside. There will always be isolated attempts, of course.

The Secretary: When will they be overcome? Next Spring?

Foreign Minister Guzzetti: No, by the end of this year.

With respect to economic steps and the results we have achieved,
with your support we have been able to achieve results. The
recovery is continuing. We will begin to go upwards. The facts are
clear enough.

That is not all. Last time we spoke of the refugees. The Chilean
refugee problem continues to be the problem. We are seeking to

provide permanent documentation in the country for refugees or
send them out in agreement with other countries.  With the
cooperation of other countries, we can reduce the pressure.

The Secretary:  You want terrorism in the United States?

Foreign Minister Guzzetti:  No, the refugee problem is not a
terrorist problem.  Many left their countries due to changes of
government.  Many want to live in peace elsewhere.  A small minority
may be terrorist.


. . . .


The Secretary: Look, our basic attitude is that we would like  you
to succeed.  I have an old-fashioned view that friends ought to be
supported.  What is not understood in the United States is that you
have a civil war.  We read about human rights problems but not the
context.  The quicker you succeed the better.

The human rights problem is a growing one.  Your Ambassador can
apprise you.  We want a stable situation.  We won't cause you
unnecessary difficulties.  If you can finish before Congress gets
back, the better.  Whatever freedoms you can restore would help.

On economics, we have Harkin [Amendment].  We will do our utmost
not to apply it to Argentina unless the situation gets out of
control.  There are two loans in the bank.  We have no intention of
voting against them.  We hope you will keep our problems in mind.
Eventually we will be forced into it.

Foreign Minister Guzzetti:  Yesterday, we discussed the problem
with Under Secretary Robinson and Mr. Shlaudeman.  Argentina is
ready to postpone a loan to avoid inconveniences.

The Secretary: You were in Washington?

Foreign Minister Guzzetti: Yes.

There are other credits in Export-Import bank.

The Secretary: No. The Harkin Amendment does not apply to the Export-Import Bank. Proceed with your Export-Import Bank requests. We would like your economic program to succeed and we will do our best to help you. The special problem is only in the IDB.

Foreign Minister Guzzetti: With help received, we can look forward to the effective recuperation of the Argentine economy....

SECRET

NODIS

**Source:** "Secretary's Meeting with Argentine Foreign Minister Guzzetti." (1976, October 7). In C. Osario (Ed.), *National Security Archive Electronic Briefing Book No. 104: Kissinger to Argentines on Dirty War: "The Quicker You Succeed the Better"* (doc. 6). Washington, DC: George Washington University. Accessed at: http://nsarchive2.gwu.edu/NSAEBB/NSAEBB104/Doc6%20761007.pdf

# DOCUMENT 6

In this document, us Ambassador Hill sends a diplomatic cable on October 19, 1976, to document his meeting with Argentine Foreign Minister Guzzetti upon Guzzetti's return from meetings with American government officials in the United States. Guzzetti appeared "euphoric" and "ecstatic" after these meetings, clearly elated from the support and encouragement he perceived to have received from Vice President Rockefeller, as well as the "success" of his meeting with Kissinger. Hill, however, expressed concern that Guzzetti did not understand the "gravity" of the human rights concerns. Hill noted in his final commentary in this cable: "Guzzetti went to [the] U.S. fully expecting to hear some strong, firm, direct warnings on his gov[ernmen]t's human rights practices. Rather, he has returned in a state of jubilation, convinced that there is no real problem with the USG over this issue." Further, Hill was concerned about how this would impact his ability to press for human rights.

[Excerpts]

Department of State

TELEGRAM

PAGE 01    BUENOS 06871    191949Z
71
ACTION SS-25


INFO OCT-01 ISO-00 SSO-00 /026 W
------------------------------ 128730
P 91815Z OCT 76
FM AMEMBASSY BUENOS AIRES
TO SECSTATE WASHDC PRIORITY 7598

 BUENOS AIRES 6871


E.O. 11652: XGDS-2
TAGS: PFOR, SHUM, AR, US
SUBJECT: FOREIGN MINISTER GUZZETTI EUPHORIC OVER VISIT TO
UNITED STATES


1.  FONMIN GUZZETTI RETURNED TO BUENOS AIRES OCT 14-AFTER
HAVING SPENT SOME TWO WEEKS AT THE UN AND IN WASHINGTON. WHEN
I MET HIM AT THE AIRPORT, HE APPEARED TIRED BUT ANXIOUS TO TALK
TO ME AFTER HE HAD REPORTED TO PRESIDENT VIDELA.
SUBSEQUENTLY, HE ASKED ME TO CALL ON HIM AT 6:30 P.M. THE NEXT
DAY (OCT 15).  I DID SO AND AFTER A WAIT OF ONLY A FEW MOMENTS,

HE BOUNDED INTO THE ROOM AND GREETED ME EFFUSIVELY WITH AN
ABRAZO [A HUG], WHICH IS NOT TYPICAL OF HIM. HE TOOK ME TO HIS
PRIVATE OFFICE WHERE FOR 35 MINUTES HE ENTHUSIASTICALLY TOLD
ME OF THE SUCCESS OF HIS VISIT.

2. HE SPOKE FIRST OF HIS LUNCH IN WASHINGTON WITH DEPUTY
SECRETARY ROBINSON, ASST SEC SHLAUDEMAN AND AMBASSADOR MARTIN.
HE EMPHASIZED HOW WELL THEY UNDERSTOOD THE ARGENTINE PEOPLE,
AND SAID THAT "THE CONSENSUS OF THE MEETING WAS TO GET THE
TERRORIST PROBLEM OVER AS SOON AS POSSIBLE." HE SAID HE AGREED
FULLY WITH AMB MARTIN'S WARNING TO "BE CAREFUL WITH THE
CATHOLIC CHURCH AND WITH ANTI-SEMITISM", AND THAT HE HAD
REPORTED THIS TO PRESIDENT VIDELA.

3. GUZZETTI WAS ALMOST ECSTATIC IN DESCRIBING HIS VISIT WITH
VICE PRESIDENT ROCKEFELLER. ONE COULD CLEARLY SENSE THE
PRUSSIAN-TYPE, SIMPLE SUBMARINE COMMANDER RATHER OVERWHELMED
BY HIS MEETING WITH THE POWERFUL AND FAMOUS ROCKEFELLER. HE
COMPLIMENTED THE VICE PRESIDENT ON HIS SPANISH AND HIS
KNOWLEDGE OF ARGENTINA. HE SAID THAT THE VICE PRESIDENT URGED
HIM TO ADVISE PRESIDENT VIDELA TO "FINISH THE TERRORIST PROBLEM
QUICKLY.... THE US WANTED A STRONG ARGENTINA AND WANTED TO
COOPERATE WITH THE GOA."

4. HE CONSIDERED HIS TALK WITH SECRETARY OF STATE KISSINGER A
SUCCESS. THE SECRETARY, HE SAID, HAD REITERATED THE ADVICE
GIVEN TO HIM AT THE SANTIAGO MEETING, HAD URGED ARGENTINA "TO
BE CAREFUL" AND HAD SAID THAT IF THE TERRORIST PROBLEM WAS OVER
BY DECEMBER OR JANUARY, HE (THE SECRETARY) BELIEVED SERIOUS
PROBLEMS COULD BE AVOIDED IN THE US. GUZZETTI SAID THE
SECRETARY HAD ASSURED HIM THAT THE US "WANTS TO HELP
ARGENTINA."

5. GUZZETTI SAID THAT HIS TALKS AT THE UN WITH AMB SCRANTON AND SEC GEN WALDHEIM WERE PROTOCOLARY. HE HAD THOUGHT THAT IN HIS TWO CONVERSATIONS WITH WALDHEIM THE LATTER WOULD RAISE THE ISSUE OF HUMAN RIGHTS, BUT, IN THE EVENT, HE HAD NOT DONE SO. GUZZETTI SAID HE HAD BEEN EMBARRASSED AT THE UN BY THE FAILURE OF THE GOA TO INFORM HIM FULLY AND PROMPTLY CONCERNING THE CAMPO DE MAYO BOMBING ATTEMPT AGAINST PRESIDENT VIDELA. THIS, HE SAID, HAD MADE IT VERY DIFFICULT FOR HIM TO ANSWER QUESTIONS ON THE SUBJECT.

6. GUZZETTI SAID HIS RECEPTION AT THE STATE DEPARTMENT, BY THE SECRETARY AT THE UN, AND THE CEREMONIES DEDICATING THE SAN MARTIN MONUMENT HAD GONE FAR BEYOND HIS EXPECTATIONS. HE EXPRESSED APPRECIATION THAT HIGH OFFICIALS IN THE GOVERNMENT "UNDERSTAND THE ARGENTINE PROBLEM AND STAND WITH US DURING THIS DIFFICULT PERIOD." HE SAID HE WAS "SATISFIED THAT THE STATE DEPT CLEARLY UNDERSTOOD THE PROBLEM THAT THERE WOULD BE NO CONFRONTATION OVER HUMAN RIGHTS."

. . . .

8. IN APPARENT RECOGNITION THAT AT LEAST FOR THE NEXT FEW MONTHS CIRCUMSTANCES WILL BE DIFFICULT, GUZZETTI NOTED THAT HE HOPED FUTURE LOANS FROM THE IDB MIGHT BE POSTPONED "UNTIL STABILITY RETURNS TO ARGENTINA" (READ, TO AVOID THE US VOTING NO). CLEARLY, HE HOPES BY JANUARY THE HUMAN RIGHTS SITUATION WILL BE OVER, AND THAT THE LOAN APPLICATIONS WOULD THEN GO FORWARD, ASSURED OF A FAVORABLE US VOTE.

9. COMMENT: GUZZETTI'S REMARKS BOTH TO ME AND TO THE ARGENTINE PRESS SINCE HIS RETURN ARE NOT THOSE OF A MAN WHO HAS BEEN IMPRESSED WITH THE GRAVITY OF THE HUMAN RIGHTS PROBLEM AS SEEN

FROM THE U.S. BOTH PERSONALLY AND IN PRESS ACCOUNTS OF HIS TRIP,
GUZZETTI'S REACTION INDICATES LITTLE REASON FOR CONCERN OVER
THE HUMAN RIGHTS ISSUE. GUZZETTI WENT TO US FULLY EXPECTING TO
HEAR SOME STRONG, FIRM, DIRECT WARNINGS ON HIS GOVT'S HUMAN
RIGHTS PRACTICES. RATHER THAN THAT, HE HAS RETURNED IN A STATE
OF JUBILATION, CONVINCED THAT THERE IS NO REAL PROBLEM WITH THE
USG OVER THIS ISSUE. BASED ON WHAT GUZZETTI IS DOUBTLESS
REPORTING TO THE GOA, IT MUST NOW BELIEVE THAT IF IT HAS ANY
PROBLEM WITH THE US OVER HUMAN RIGHTS, THEY ARE CONFINED TO
CERTAIN ELEMENTS OF CONGRESS AND WHAT IT REGARDS AS BIASED AND/
OR UNINFORMED MINOR SEGMENTS OF PUBLIC OPINION. WHILE THIS
CONVICTION PERSISTS, IT WILL BE UNREALISTIC AND INEFFECTIVE FOR
THIS EMBASSY TO PRESS REPRESENTATIONS TO THE GOA OVER HUMAN
RIGHTS VIOLATIONS.
HILL.

**Source:** US Embassy (Buenos Aires). (1976, October 19). "Foreign Minister
Guzzetti Euphoric over Visit to United States." In C. Osario (Ed.), *National
Security Archive Electronic Briefing Book No. 104: Kissinger to Argentines on
Dirty War: "The Quicker You Succeed the Better"* (doc. 7). Washington, DC:
George Washington University. Accessed at: http://nsarchive2.gwu.edu/NSAEBB/
NSAEBB104/Doc7%20761019.pdf

## DOCUMENT 7

This document records the March 30, 1977, Memorandum of Conversation
between US Assistant Secretary for Human Rights Patricia Derian and Juan
Carlos Arlia, the Argentine officer leading their Human Rights Working
Group. Assistant Secretary Derian would come to serve a pivotal role
under President Jimmy Carter's administration, forcefully confronting
Argentina's government leaders about their patterns of human rights
abuses. In this meeting, Arlia denies the extent of human rights violations
being mentioned, suggesting the US had been deceived and even that no
pattern of human rights violations existed in Argentina. Derian, however,
affirms the significance of human rights questions to US policy toward

Argentina under Carter: "Nevertheless, although the US government understands the problems faced by the Argentine government, it cannot stand with Argentina due to human rights violations." This is in marked contrast to the tone of previous diplomatic meetings on these matters under prior administrations.

[Excerpts]

MEMORANDUM OF CONVERSATION

March 30, 1977

PARTICIPANTS
From the Argentine
Ministry of Foreign
Relations and Worship:

       Minister Miguel Angel Espeche, Officer in charge of
          North American Affairs (United States and Canada)
       Counselor Juan Carlos Arlia, Officer in charge of
          Human Rights Working Group
       Counselor Edgardo Enrique Flores, Human Rights Working
          Group
       Mr. Atilo N. Molteni, Office of the SubSecretary of Foreign
          Affairs

From the US Government:
       Ms. Patricia Derian, D/HA
       Minister Maxwell Chaplin, Amembassy Buenos Aires
       Mr. Fernando Rondon, ARA/ECA
       Mr. Anthony Freeman, POL, Amembassy Buenos Aires
       Ms. Yvonne Thayer, POL, Amembassy Buenos Aires

PLACE:     Argentine Foreign Ministry, Buenos Aires

DISTRIBUTION: Ambassador Hill

Counselor Arlia graciously welcomed Ms. Derian to Argentina.  He
was pleased that she had made the trip to Argentina and only
wished that the subjects to be discussed at the meeting were
more pleasant ones.  Argentina, he said, has always had a firm and
traditional belief in human rights.  The country's commitment to
human rights is embodied in the Argentine Constitution, which
was modeled on the US Constitution.  However, Argentina is now
facing the most significant aggression in its history--an
aggression not only directed by foreign elements outside
Argentina but an aggression totally foreign and unacceptable to
Argentine nature.  This aggression is manifested in terrorist
subversion.  Argentina has a fervent desire for a return to
democratic ideals and a secure peace.  In order to do that, it is
necessary to combat the terrorist aggression and banish it from
the country.

It has been impossible to maintain Argentina's good image abroad
because of the concentrated and well-financed campaign of the
country's enemies overseas.  Argentina has lacked the time,
resources and ability to counteract the bad image made by the
efforts of leftists abroad.  A period of six months passed from
the time of the military coup in March 1976 to the beginning of the
Argentine government's dialogue with its foreign friends on the
question of human rights.  Much violence during that period
transpired and much of it escaped the immediate control of the
government.  It was the worst period during which the state did
not have a complete monopoly on the forces engaged in repressing
leftist subversion and rightwing terrorists were operating

unchecked. However, since October, the Argentine government has ended organized rightwing terrorism and has had a complete monopoly of force. The human rights working group was consolidated in October directly under the SubSecretary of Foreign Affairs in order to coordinate all human rights questions and concerns brought to it by foreign missions. The working group is staffed entirely by civilian career diplomats--Arlia himself has 25 years diplomatic service--and does not reflect a narrow military point of view.

It should be understood that there is a difference between terrorism from the right and terrorism from the left. Leftist terrorism has the goal of destroying Argentine society and takes the initiative in using violent means to win its objective. Rightwing terrorism is a reaction to the left; its only objective is to fight against leftist subversion. It will be recalled that from the beginning President Videla has consistently condemned all forms of terrorism, be it from the right or the left.

Ms. Derian expressed her pleasure in being able to visit Argentina and meet with members of the Argentine Foreign Ministry. The United States, she said, is extremely sympathetic to the pain that Argentina has and is suffering. She is here to learn as much as she can about the problems of Argentina and to develop information and ideas on what can be done to further the cause of human rights throughout the world. Sometimes one finds that in order to solve one problem, one ends up creating another, which is not her intention nor that of the new US administration. The US government does not want to be the moral arbitor [sic] for the world; it does want to offer its good offices to assist in finding the best solutions. The US public is concerned not to find itself a participant in situations where violations of human

rights are taking place. The US has had some but not much
experience with terrorism. People fear it even though they
might not fully understand the urgency of it. It is hard to judge
a terrorist situation from a distance. Nevertheless, although
the US government understands the problems faced by the
Argentine government, it cannot stand with Argentina due to
human rights violations. Terrorism is too poorly known and
understood to permit ready and easy solutions. Argentina is on
the front line, having to learn to deal with terrorism and find
ways to confront this problem for the rest of the world.

. . . .

Ms. Derian emphasized President Carter's deep commitment to human
rights which she said stems from his very character and
conviction. It was not a device nor a political maneuver. Human
rights is not the only factor in the Administration's foreign
policy but a major consideration, mixed in like egg whites in a
soufflé. After some appreciation of her metaphor, Ms. Derian said
it was even more apt than she originally meant: if the mixture
fails, the soufflé is a failure.

Counselor Arlia responded that he had great respect for President
Carter, but that in his policy toward Argentina, he had only
committed mistakes. One of his errors was accepting false
information from self-interested terrorist elements. For
example, while attending the United Nations Human Rights
Commission meeting in Geneva in February, Arlia on several
occasions saw the US delegate Brady Tyson and his staff talking to
Argentine terrorists, including such persons as leftist lawyers
Gustavo Roca and Garzon Maceda, Roberto Guevara and a Mr.
Matarollo. Gustavo Roca and Garzon Maceda, he said, were the two

who negotiated the Samuelson ransom for the terrorists. Whole
sections of Tyson's speech on Argentina came right from this sort
of person. Another person who testified against Argentina in
Geneva was Uruguayan Senator Enrique Erro, a Communist. Erro had
been arrested during the last Peron government. He was not
charged due to his status as a former senator but he was kept in
prison to control his activities. He was freed in January 1977.
His testimony in Geneva were lies. Contrary to what he said,
there are no shooting galleries in Argentine prisons, no torture
in prisons; food and health standards are high and civilian
doctors who have private clinics provide medical care to
prisoners. The International Red Cross is acting in Argentina and
can confirm Arlia's claims.

In response to Ms. Derian's comment that she had been told by
Argentines that human rights excesses are deplorable but necessary
to root out terrorism, Counselor Arlia said that information was also
not true. It was the American police who had invented third degree
interrogation methods, not the Argentines, he said. Abuses of human
rights may occur in Argentina, but it is not the intent nor the
policy of the Argentine government to violate human rights.
Contrary information comes from wrong-minded sources. . . . . If the
US government uses this information on good faith, it is making a big
mistake. Counselor Arlia mentioned the cases of Paraguayan doctor
Agustin Goriburu and Argentine Professor Mauricio Lopez as examples
of the problem faced by GOA officials of its bad image abroad. No
more than a few days after their disappearances, literally hundreds
of protest letters, some of them on mimeographed forms, and cables
came in to the government. Some arrived in less time than it was
possible for mail to go from the US and Europe to Argentina. GOA is
doing everything it can to find these two men, but no matter what it
does, it will never get over the accusation that it has kidnapped

them. All we are asking of you is that you seek information from us before passing judgment on Argentina.

Counselor Arlia gave Ms. Derian material showing Argentines who have been killed and maimed by terrorist bombs and assassinations during the last several years. Terrorism, he said, has changed. In riots, such as those in Italy recently, students don't throw [leftist philosopher Herbert] Marcuse's book at security officials, they shoot first. It is simply not possible to courteously arrest a terrorist who is shooting at you. Human rights violations, Arlia concluded, exist when a government applies a specific policy. That is not the case in Argentina.....

**Source:** US Embassy (Buenos Aires). (1977, March 30). "Memorandum of Conversation, Patricia Derian, US Assistant Secretary for Human Rights." In US Department of State, *Argentina Declassification Project (1976-1984)*. Freedom of Information Act Virtual Reading Room. Accessed at: https://foia.state.gov/Search/results. aspx?searchText=*&beginDate=19770330&endDate=19770330&publishedBeginDate =&publishedEndDate=&caseNumber=

## DOCUMENT 8

In this document, a diplomatic cable chronicles an August 10, 1977, meeting between Patricia Derian, assistant secretary for human rights, and Admiral Emilio Massera, one of the leaders of the Argentine junta. Here, Derian actively confronts Massera about several human rights matters, including questions about unlawful interrogations, systematic detentions, and torture at the ESMA (Navy Mechanics School), which Massera denied. As noted in the cable, "Mrs. Derian said that on her prior visit she had been told that one of the worst interrogation centers was the Navy Mechanical School in Buenos Aires. The Admiral denied this, saying that the Navy's entire anti-subversive role was carried out by no more than thirty people." After the dictatorship, it would emerge that the ESMA was one of the most notorious torture centers during the dictatorship, as documented in the *Nunca Más* truth commission report (1986), testimonies from survivors, and later human rights trials.

[Excerpts]

Current Class: ███████                                          Page: 1
Current Handling: LIMDIS, STADIS
   Document Number: 1977STATE192822                    Channel: n/a
                         8/15/77 [hand-written]
                   Case Number: 200000044

. . . .


O 151758Z AUG 77
FM SECSTATE WASHDC
TO AMEMBASSY BUENOS AIRES IMMEDIATE


. . . .


SUBJECT: DERIAN VISIT WITH ADMIRAL MASSERA
FOR CHARGÉ CHAPLIN


BEGIN SUMMARY
1. AT HIS REQUEST, U.S. COORDINATOR FOR HUMAN RIGHTS PATT
DERIAN MET WITH JUNTA MEMBER MASSERA ON MORNING OF AUGUST 10.
THE ADMIRAL STRESSED THAT ARGENTINA WAS IN THE PROCESS OF
RETURNING TO NORMAL LEGAL PROCEDURES AND THAT MUCH PROGRESS
HAD BEEN MADE SINCE MS. DERIAN'S LAST VISIT. MRS. [SIC] DERIAN
EXPRESSED HER HOPE THAT NORMALIZATION WOULD BE ACCOMPLISHED
SOON AND IN SUCH A WAY THAT ALL LEVELS OF THE SECURITY APPARATUS
WOULD UNDERSTAND IT.
END SUMMARY.


2. THE ADMIRAL STARTED THE CONVERSATION BY STRESSING THAT....
PROGRESS WAS BEING MADE IN CONTROLLING THE SITUATION, WHILE NOTING
THAT FALSE INFORMATION CIRCULATES, AND SOME INCIDENTS CONTINUE TO
OCCUR ("SOME GROUPS STILL ESCAPE US") HE STRESSED THAT THE END WAS

IN SIGHT.  MRS. DERIAN EXPRESSED HER HOPE THAT THIS WAS THE CASE AND
NOTED TWO THINGS OF PARTICULAR CONCERN TO THE USG: (1) THE LARGE
NUMBER OF DISAPPEARED AND (2) THE CONDITIONS OF BEING HELD
INCOMUNICADO [SIC] WHERE PEOPLE ARE TREATED TOO HARSHLY.  SHE SAID
SHE HOPED NEW PROCEDURES WILL BE INTRODUCED.

3.  ADMIRAL MASSERA SAID HE DID NOT KNOW WHAT NUMBERS PRESIDENT
VIDELA OR ADMIRAL ALLARA HAD PROVIDED REGARDING THE NUMBER OF
PEOPLE CHARGED OR TAKEN ILLEGALLY BUT HE SAID THE LAST FEW
MONTHS SHOWED RAPID PROGRESS....HE ADVISED THAT THERE COULD BE
A DIFFERENCE BETWEEN THE IMPRESSION RECEIVED OF THE CURRENT
SITUATION AND THE ACTUAL REALITY.

4.  MRS. DERIAN EXPRESSED HER CONCERN OVER THE NUMBER OF PEOPLE
WHO DON'T KNOW IF MEMBERS OF THEIR FAMILY ARE DEAD OR ALIVE.  SHE
MENTIONED THAT LABOR LEADERS AND OTHERS HAVE BEEN IN JAIL SINCE
1975.  SHE SAID THAT THE SYSTEM SEEMS TO HAVE GROUND TO A HALT,
E.G., PEOPLE WERE PICKED UP AND NEVER CHARGED, SOME WERE HELD WITH
NO EVIDENCE AGAINST THEM, SOME WERE TRIED AND FOUND INNOCENT BUT
STILL DETAINED.  SHE EXPLAINED THAT AFTER A PERIOD OF TIME THE
GOVERNMENT, HAVING WON THE FIGHT AGAINST TERRORISM, SHOULD SHOW
ITS STRENGTH BY SAYING TO THE PEOPLE THAT IT HAS WON BUT IT NEEDS
HELP IN THIS MOP-UP PHASE.  SHE SAID THE TERRORISTS ACHIEVE THEIR
MAIN OBJECTIVE OF DESTROYING THE LEGAL INSTITUTIONS OF THE STATE
IF THE GOVERNMENT DOESN'T ADMIT IT HAS WON THE WAR AND MUST NOW
RETURN TO THE JUDICIAL SYSTEM BY BRINGING THOSE DETAINED TO
TRIAL.  SHE CITED THE CASE OF JACOBO TIMMERMAN AS AN EXAMPLE,
ADDING HE HAS BEEN MISTREATED WHILE UNDER DETENTION.  ADMIRAL
MASSERA SAID HE DIDN'T BELIEVE TIMMERMAN HAD BEEN MISTREATED
ALTHOUGH HE MAY HAVE SAID HE HAS BEEN.

5.  RETURNING TO THE GENERAL SITUATION, MRS. DERIAN SAID THAT MANY
PEOPLE IN THE ARGENTINE GOVERNMENT HAD TOLD USG REPRESENTATIVES

THAT THE NAVY IS RESPONSIBLE FOR ABUSES WHICH OCCUR WHEN PEOPLE ARE
TAKEN INTO CUSTODY AND INTERROGATED BEFORE THEY ENTER THE SYSTEM.
ADMIRAL MASSERA RESPONDED THAT, WHILE HE DOESN'T WISH TO GIVE THE
APPEARANCE OF "WASHING HIS HANDS OF THE MATTER," INTERNAL SECURITY
IS NOT THE NAVY'S RESPONSIBILITY, THAT THE NAVY HAS NO TERRITORIAL
JURISDICTION AND WHEN IT DOES DO SOMETHING IN THIS AREA IT DOES SO
WITH THE KNOWLEDGE OF THE ARMY. HE SAID THAT THOSE WHO SAY
OTHERWISE ARE TRYING TO DECEIVE. MRS. DERIAN SAID THAT ON HER PRIOR
VISIT SHE HAD BEEN TOLD THAT ONE OF THE WORST INTERROGATION CENTERS
WAS THE NAVY MECHANICAL SCHOOL IN BUENOS AIRES. THE ADMIRAL DENIED
THIS, SAYING THAT THE NAVY'S ENTIRE ANTI-SUBVERSIVE ROLE WAS
CARRIED OUT BY NO MORE THAN THIRTY PEOPLE.

. . . .

7. THE ADMIRAL RESPONDED THAT, WHILE HE COULDN'T TALK OF A TIME
PERIOD, THAT HE HAD NO CRYSTAL BALL WITH WHICH TO PREDICT, ARGENTINA
WAS ON THE ROAD TO NORMALIZATION. HE ADMITTED THAT IN THE ROUGH
BATTLE AGAINST TERRORISM SOME THINGS GOT OUT OF HAND, BUT THAT
THERE HAS BEEN REAL IMPROVEMENT SINCE MARCH. HE REFERRED TO ONE OF
HIS OFFICERS ESPECIALLY DESIGNATED TO RECEIVE PEOPLE LOOKING FOR
THEIR RELATIVES AND SAID HIS CASE LOAD HAS DROPPED MARKEDLY.

. . . .

9. MRS. DERIAN SAID THAT BECAUSE OF THE DISORDER, SO MANY CAN
OPERATE THINKING THEY HAVE THE APPROVAL OF EITHER THE
GOVERNMENT OR THE PEOPLE, THAT THE LEFT WING HAS BEEN LICKED
BUT A MONSTER CREATED. ADMIRAL MASSERA SAID HE DIDN'T SEE IT
THAT WAY. HE SAID THE RIGHT WING IS VERY SMALL IN ARGENTINA
AND THE GOVERNMENT HAS TAKEN STEPS, LIKE THE CLOSING OF THE
MAGAZINE CABILDO. HE SAID THE RIGHT EXISTS ONLY AS A
POLITICAL FORCE. MRS. DERIAN MENTIONED THAT THE INCIDENT

AGAINST THE LAWYERS COULDN'T HAVE OCCURRED WITHOUT SOME
OFFICIAL SUPPORT. ADMIRAL MASSERA ASKED WHAT PRESIDENT
VIDELA HAD TOLD HER ABOUT THIS INCIDENT AND, WHEN SHE
RESPONDED THAT THEY HADN'T DISCUSSED IT, HE SAID THAT
INCIDENTS SUCH AS IT COULD BE COUNTED ON THE FINGERS OF YOUR
HAND.

10. ...HE ASKED MRS. DERIAN TO MAINTAIN AN EQUILIBRIUM REALIZING
THAT WHILE THESE CASES WERE IMPORTANT, THEY WERE OLD AND FEW, AND
THE JUNTA WAS ON THE ROAD TO NORMALIZATION.


. . . .


12. MRS. DERIAN ENDED BY REFERRING TO THE HABEUS CORPUS PETITIONS
SUBMITTED TO THE EXECUTIVE BY THE SUPREME COURT SAYING IT WAS MUCH
ON PEOPLES [SIC] MINDS AND THAT SHE WOULD BE GLAD WHEN ALL THIS WAS
OVER. SHE SAID THAT THE REINSTATEMENT OF LEGAL PROCEDURES WOULD
CERTAINLY HELP RELATIONS BETWEEN OUR TWO COUNTRIES AND STRESSED
THAT WE WERE ANXIOUS TO RETURN TO NORMAL GOOD RELATIONS.

**Source:** Secretary of State. (1977, August 15). "Derian Visit with Admiral
Massera." In US Department of State, *Argentina Declassification Project (1975–
1984)*. Freedom of Information Act Virtual Reading Room. Accessed at: https://
foia.state.gov/Search/results.aspx?searchText=*&beginDate=19770815&endDate
=19770815&publishedBeginDate=&publishedEndDate=&caseNumber=.


# DOCUMENT 9

In this document, a June 27, 1978, diplomatic cable, US Ambassador Raúl
Castro documents Henry Kissinger's visit to Argentina on the occasion of
the World Cup. Although he was invited as a private citizen by President
Videla, Kissinger had meetings with government officials where human
rights matters were discussed and made public statements about political
matters. This document clearly demonstrates Kissinger's ongoing influence in Argentina, even though he was no longer an official in the US

Government. Although acknowledging Kissinger's proclamations that the time for certain tactics had passed in combating terrorism, Castro also remained concerned that Kissinger's "high praise" for how Argentina dealt with terrorism would prompt Argentina to resist human rights reforms.

[Excerpts]

PAGE 01        BUENOS 04937        01 OF 02        272116Z

. . . .

P 272012Z JUN 78
FM AMEMBASSY BUENOS AIRES
TO SECSTATE WASHDC PRIORITY 6283

. . . .

SUBJECT: HENRY KISSINGER VISIT TO ARGENTINA

SUMMARY: FROM ARRIVAL TO DEPARTURE HENRY KISSINGER AND HIS FAMILY
WERE WELL RECEIVED BY ARGENTINE POPULACE. THE GOA LAID OUT RED
CARPET, PULLING OUT STOPS. DR. KISSINGER SPOKE TO DIVERSIFIED
GROUPS--FROM BANKERS TO GAUCHOS. IN MOST INSTANCES, HE
COMPLIMENTED GOA FOR DEFEATING TERRORISTS BUT HE WARNED THAT
TACTICS USED AGAINST THEM THEN ARE NOT JSTIFIABLE [SIC] NOW.
GENERALLY, DR. KISSINGER PUBLICLY AFFIRMED HIS SUPPORT FOR
PRESIDENT CARTER'S FOREIGN POLICY WITH A FEW EXCEPTIONS.

1. DR. KISSINGER, HIS WIFE AND SON ARRIVED IN BA [BUENOS AIRES]
EARLY WEDNESDAY MORNING (JUNE 21). HE WAS MET AT THE AIRPORT BY
A FONOFF [FOREIGN AFFAIRS OFFICE] REP WHO DOGGED HIM THROUGHOUT
HIS VISIT. KISSINGER WAS THE GUEST OF PRESIDENT VIDELA,
SUPPOSEDLY INVITED TO VIEW WORLD CUP. THE FORMER SECRETARY

MADE IT CLEAR DURING HIS FIVE-DAY STAY HE WAS IN ARGENTINA AS
PRIVATE CITIZEN AND NOT A SPOKESMAN FOR USG.

2. KISSINGER'S FIRST ACTIVITY WAS TO LUNCH WITH PRESIDENT VIDELA,
COL. MALLEA GIL (INTERPRETER) AND AMBASSADOR CASTRO AT LOS OLIVOS,
OFFICIAL PRESIDENTIAL RESIDENCE. VIDELA .... PREARRANGED IT SO
KISSINGER AND THE INTERPRETER WOULD MEET WITH HIM PRIVATELY HALF
HOUR BEFORE AMBASSADOR'S ARRIVAL. IMMEDIATELY ON AMBASSADOR'S
ARRIVAL AT 1300 LUNCH WAS SERVED.

3. KISSINGER INFORMED AMBASSADOR THAT DURING PRIVATE SESSION WITH
PRESIDENT HUMAN RIGHTS WERE DISCUSSED. ALLEGEDLY VIDELA WANTED
SUGGESTIONS FROM DR. KISSINGER AS TO HOW TO IMPROVE RELATIONS WITH
USG. THE AMBASSADOR WAS NOT INFORMED WHETHER KISSINGER OFFERED
ANY SOLUTIONS.

. . . .

5. KISSINGER EMPHASIZED LATIN AMERICAN [SIC] MAY BE NEXT ON RUSSIA
AND CUBA'S SCHEDULE. . . .

6. HUMAN RIGHTS WERE DISCUSSED BRIEFLY. KISSINGER SAID IT WAS
UNFORTUNATE MANY AMERICANS STILL THOUGHT ARGENTINA WAS A SOFT DRINK.
HE SAID THIS INDICATED THAT AMERICANS ARE NOT AWARE OF ARGENTINE
HISTORY NOR OF ITS STRUGGLE AGAINST TERRORISM. HE EMPHASIZED THAT
TERRORISM WAS NOT SOLELY OF ARGENTINE ORIGIN BUT INSTEAD IT HAD
BECOME AN INTERNATIONAL CONCEPT. KISSINGER APPLAUDED ARGENTINA'S
EFFORTS IN COMBATTING TERRORISM BUT HE ALSO STRESSED THAT TACTICS
USED IN DEFEATING TERRORISTS HAD NO PLACE IN ARGENTINA TODAY.

7. THROUGHOUT LUNCH VIDELA SEEMED RELAXED AND FRIENDLY. HE TENSED
UP ONLY WHEN ARGENTINA'S PROSPECTS IN THE WORLD CUP WERE DISCUSSED.
HE DISPLAYED NO ANNOYANCE AT USG.

. . . .

12.  ON JUNE 24 KISSINGER PARTICIPATED IN AN OFF THE RECORD PRESS
CONFERENCE AND WAS MADE AN HONORARY MEMBER OF ARGENTINE COUNCIL ON
INTERNATIONAL RELATIONS.  THIS GROUP IS COMPRISED OF FORMER FOREIGN
MINISTERS, WHO HOLD THEMSELVES UP TO THE PUBLIC AS THE "ELITE GROUP"
ON FOREIGN AFFAIRS.  DR. KISSINGER GAVE AN OFF THE CUFF TALK.  HE
STRESSED THAT THERE WAS NO QUESTION BUT THAT AMERICANS LACKED
KNOWLEDGE ABOUT ARGENTINA'S HISTORY.  ESPECIALLY, AMERICANS LACKED
FAMILIARITY WITH ARGENTINA'S EXPERIENCE IN FIGHTING TERRORISM.  HE
EXPLAINED HIS HIS [SIC] OPINION GOA HAD DONE AN OUTSTANDING JOB IN
WIPING OUT TERRORIST FORCES, BUT ALSO CAUTIONED THAT METHODS USED IN
FIGHTING TERRORISM MUST NOT BE PERPETUATED.  HE EXPLAINED A MOVEMENT
TOWARDS NORMALCY MUST TAKE PLACE IF DEMOCRATIC IDEALS ARE TO PREVAIL.

13.  DR. KISSINGER ALSO APPEARED IN A QUESTION AND ANSWER PERIOD
WITH ONE OF ARGENTINA'S POPULAR NEWS COMMENTERS.  DURING THE
INTERVIEW KISSINGER STATED TERRORISTS WERE ONE OF THE GREATEST
VIOLATORS OF HUMAN RIGHTS.  HE SAID IT WAS UNFORTUNATE THAT IN SOME
INSTANCES HUMAN RIGHTS WAS BEING USED AS A WEAPON AGAINST ITS
FRIENDS.

. . . .

COMMENT:  DR. KISSINGER TOLD THE AMBASSADOR HE WOULD NOT CRITICIZE
THE CARTER ADMINISTRATION SO LONG AS HE WAS OVERSEAS.  HE SPOKE
HIGHLY OF PRESIDENT CARTER'S FOREIGN POLICY TO THE AMBASSADOR, BUT
FELT HE WOULD SPEAK OUT AGAINST THE

. . . .

CONCEPT OF ATTEMPTING TO IMPLEMENT HUMAN RIGHTS IN LA [LATIN
AMERICA].  HE SAID HE WOULD WAIT ABOUT TWO WEEKS AFTER HIS RETURN

TO US BEFORE SPEAKING OUT. KISSINGER WORKED CLOSELY WITH EMBASSY PERSONNEL. THEY WERE GOOD GUESTS AND MADE EVERY EFFORT TO GIVE APPEARANCE THEY WERE NOT EMISSARIES OF OPPOSITION TO CURRENT US ADMINISTRATION.

MY ONLY CONCERN IS THAT KISSINGER'S REPEATED HIGH PRAISE FOR ARGENTINA'S ACTION IN WIPING OUT TERRORISM AND HIS STRESS ON THE IMPORTANCE OF ARGENTINA MAY HAVE GONE TO SOME CONSIDERABLE EXTENT TO HIS HOSTS' HEADS. DESPITE HIS DISCLAIMERS THAT THE METHODS USED IN FIGHTING TERRORISM MUST NOT BE PERPETUATED, THERE IS SOME DANGER THAT ARGENTINES MAY USE KISSINGER'S LAUDATORY STATEMENTS AS JUSTIFICATION FOR HARDENING THEIR HUMAN RIGHTS STANCE.
CASTRO

**Source:** US Embassy (Buenos Aires). (1978, June 27). "Henry Kissinger Visit to Argentina." In US Department of State, *Argentina Declassification Project (1975-1984)*. Freedom of Information Act Virtual Reading Room. Accessed at: https://foia.state.gov/Search/results.aspx?searchText=*&beginDate =19780627&endDate=19780627&publishedBeginDate=&publishedEndDate=&caseNumber=

# THE UNITED STATES GOVERNMENT'S RELATIONSHIP WITH GUATEMALA DURING THE GENOCIDE OF THE MAYA (1981–1983)

Samuel Totten

## INTRODUCTION

During the latter half of the twentieth century, the United States government's relationship with Guatemala was nothing short of sordid. Other than the US government's overthrow of the democratically elected government of Guatemalan President Jacobo Árbenz Guzmán in 1954, perhaps the United States' most egregious involvement in Guatemala occurred during the period commonly referred to as "*la violencia*" (1978–84). This was particularly true during the rule of President Romeo Lucas García (July 1, 1978–March 23, 1982) and that of Efraín Ríos Montt (March 23, 1982–August 9, 1983), when massive crimes against humanity and then genocide were perpetrated against the Maya people of the Guatemalan Highlands. During this period the United States provided training for Guatemalan military personnel and the military intelligence unit at its infamous US Army School of the Americas. The Guatemalans were instructed in counterinsurgency tactics, which the Guatemalan military ultimately put to ruthless, brutal, and deadly use. The US government also provided advisers on the ground, an extraordinary amount of funding, and weapons. Those at the highest levels of government in the Reagan administration, including President Reagan, were well informed about the atrocities that were being perpetrated by Guatemala against its own people but, schizophrenically (a) insisted that communists were an existential danger to both Guatemala and the United States, knowing full well that the Government of Guatemala accused the Maya population of being communistic and that it had to be extirpated; (b) called on the Guatemalan government to cease and desist from carrying out atrocities against its citizens; (c) claimed it was difficult to ascertain with any degree of certainty whether it was the Guatemalan military or the rebels who were committing the greatest number of atrocities during the period; (d) argued that Ríos Montt's regime was making significant headway in halting the killings and disappearances of the Maya during the very period when the atrocities were actually increasing in number; (e) conveniently looked the other way as the Guatemalan military did its dirty work; and (f) continued to provide the Guatemalan government and military with weapons, which the latter insisted they needed to successfully combat their foes.

Based on evidence collected by the United Nations-sponsored *Comisión para el Esclarecimiento Histórico* (Commission for Historical Clarification, or CEH), it is now known that some 626 villages were attacked by Government of Guatemala troops and/or their paramilitary units; of these, 440 villages were utterly destroyed (CEH, 1999). During the course of this scorched earth policy/counterinsurgency, not only were homes and other structures burned down, but crops were stolen and/or burned and farm animals were killed. For those leading an agrarian life, the latter constituted the lifeblood of their economic existence.

Furthermore, over 200,000 Guatemalans were killed or "disappeared." At least 83 per cent of those victims were indigenous Maya (CEH, 1999, p. 79). Approximately 93 per cent of the atrocities were carried out by government forces (p. 90). Based on its findings, the commission asserted that the scorched earth campaign that the Government of Guatemala carried out against the Maya constituted "acts of genocide."

The focus of this chapter addresses all of the above and more: (a) when and what the United States government knew vis-à-vis the atrocities being perpetrated by the Government of Guatemala against its Maya population, and (b) how the US government reacted to its knowledge of such atrocities. To this day, many in Guatemala continue to deal with this brutal period in their history. Not only do the survivors continue to struggle with their memories of the horrors (including the torture, murder, and genocide of family members, friends, and community members) but in many cases they continue to face threats from those who supported the former regimes. This is particularly true in regard to those calling for an end to impunity for the genocidaires and for those who have testified in trials against the alleged perpetrators.

## OVERVIEW OF THE GENOCIDE

The insidious impact of colonial rule in Guatemala resulted in hundreds of years of ongoing prejudice, racism, and oppression against the indigenous peoples of Guatemala. The *ladinos* (Spanish conquerors) suppressed, enslaved, and otherwise abused the indigenous peoples. Over the march of time, the descendants of the conquerors continued the abusive treatment of the indigenous peoples, and in particular, the Maya—perceiving the latter as a lesser race and treating them as second-class citizens or worse. Such treatment resulted in the abuse and exploitation of the Maya, ranging from outright discrimination to wholesale disenfranchisement to economic exploitation (including slave labor). Green (1999) cogently argues that "the relationship between political violence and the deeply rooted and historically based structural violence of inequality and impunity suffuses Guatemalan society [today], [and is] expressed through class, ethnicity, and gender divisions and experienced by Mayas as virulent racism" (p. 10). Due to a confluence of factors, in the mid-twentieth century the Maya began demanding just treatment and equal rights, but both government officials and wealthy landowners looked askance at such demands. But it didn't end there; both the government and the landowners essentially set out to crush those making the demands.

While the United Fruit Company, a us corporation, played a huge part in the Guatemalan economy and contributed mightily to keeping the poor in their place throughout the first half of the twentieth century, it was the us government that became a dominant force in relation to the Guatemalan government and its military forces' treatment of the so-called peasants in the latter half of the twentieth century. As previously mentioned, the us government's involvement in Guatemala's affairs reaches back decades, but the 1951 election of Jacobo Árbenz Guzmán, a left-of-center politician, as president of Guatemala seemingly unhinged leaders at the highest level of the us government. While many within the us government looked askance at Árbenz's politics, what particularly incensed them was his administration's passage of a law, Decree 900, whose express purpose was to ensure a more equitable life for all Guatemalans. At the heart of the decree was land reform. Those who were the wealthiest in Guatemala—and who also happened to be large landowners—decried Decree 900, for they saw it as a direct challenge to what they perceived as their entitlement: their power, their wealth, and ultimately their way of life. The United Fruit Company also castigated Árbenz and Decree 900. Many in the us government perceived the reforms as communistic in nature, which was particularly anathema during the so-called Second Red Scare (also referred to as McCarthyism) in the United States.

What many at the highest levels of the us government may have known about—but very few others did—was the close relationship that certain us officials had with the United Fruit Company. For example, President Dwight David Eisenhower's secretary of state, John Foster Dulles, along with the law firm he worked for (Sullivan and Cromwell), had been instrumental years before in negotiating the so-called land giveaways to the United Fruit Company in both Honduras and Guatemala. Furthermore, Dulles' brother, Alan Dulles, the director of the Central Intelligence Agency in Eisenhower's administration not only served as legal counsel for United Fruit but sat on its board of directors. Henry Cabot Lodge, the United

States' ambassador to the UN during the Eisenhower administration, owned a large amount of United Fruit stock. And, to top it off, Ann Whitman, Eisenhower's personal secretary, was married to Ed Whitman, the head of public relations for United Fruit.

Intent on preventing communists from gaining a toehold in Central America, the CIA planned the coup d'état that resulted in the right-wing military regime overthrowing the democratically elected government of Árbenz. The US-backed Guatemalan troops were both trained and armed by the CIA. Purportedly, United Fruit approached both the Truman and Eisenhower administrations, warning them that Árbenz was intent on aligning his regime with the Soviets. While some have questioned whether that was actually Árbenz's intent, what was indisputable was the fact that United Fruit owned the most land in Guatemala and was facing the expropriation of 40 per cent of its landholdings.

Ultimately, the coup d'état set the stage for what was to become a horrific nightmare for the poorest of the poor in Guatemala, and, in particular, the Maya people. In no little part, this resulted from the US government's support of one right-wing Guatemalan government after another, most of which carried out one cycle of violent repression after another. Addressing how the Cold War policies of the United States meshed with the goals and actions of a whole slew of right-wing governments in Guatemala, Manz (2004) writes, "The growing political realities of the Cold War and the United States foreign policy toward Central America gave the Guatemalan military and economic elites complete license to rule in an increasingly authoritarian way. Anti-communism served to justify and conceal the most heinous of crimes, and the United States—except for the [Jimmy] Carter administration—eagerly funneled millions of dollars to military regimes decade after decade, showing no concern for the brutality committed by the armed forces" (p. 21).

It is worth noting that not all those in the Guatemalan military over the years had agreed with its government's ill treatment of Guatemala's indigenous population. In 1960, for example, a small group of rebel officers attempted to carry out a coup d'état but failed. Subsequently, they fled into the mountains in eastern Guatemala. Said to have been inspired by the actions and success of Fidel Castro, Che Guevara, and their fellow rebels in Cuba, the rebel officers in Guatemala immersed themselves in the study of Marxism-Leninism and founded the first organized guerrilla group: *Fuerzas Armadas Rebeldes* (FAR) or Rebel Armed Forces. In the years ahead, FAR would carry out an insurgency against a host of right-wing Guatemalan governments.

Intent on supporting the Guatemalan government in its battle against the rebel forces, the United States sent a contingent of Green Berets to Guatemala in 1966 to assist in the training of Guatemala's soldiers. As previously mentioned, the US government also hosted and trained numerous Guatemalan military leaders at its School of the Americas (SOA). Many of the latter returned to Guatemala and oversaw the government's counterinsurgency efforts, which comprised a wide range of terroristic actions, including but not limited to assassination, summary execution, torture, massacres, "disappearances" (of approximately 40,000 people), *and* genocide.

The training of its military leaders by the SOA paid off, for the Guatemalan army's counterinsurgency campaign (1966–1968) essentially beat FAR into submission. A key aspect of the counterinsurgency campaign was the formation and deployment of death squads. It is estimated that some 8,000 civilians, most of whom were said to be unarmed, were murdered as a result of that particular counterinsurgency campaign.

Stunned by their losses, the rebels initiated a new approach: undertaking political work in the Western Highlands of Guatemala in an attempt to convince those who suffered the most at the hands of the government and its military actions to support them, the rebels. Once the rebels were confident that they had the people's support, they returned to fighting the government.

The government, however, had absolutely no intention of capitulating to the rebels' demands. Perhaps this was most vehemently expressed in 1971 by the newly elected president of Guatemala, General Carlos Arana Osorio: "If it is necessary to turn the country into a cemetery to pacify it, I will not hesitate to do so."

The 20-year period between 1960 and 1980 radically impacted how the indigenous peoples in the highlands perceived the government. In the early 1960s, economic growth in Guatemala positively impacted every class of people. During that period, many were given land as part of the government's "colonization program," which resulted in raising the hopes of people, leading them to begin to think and believe that they just might be on the cusp of controlling their own destinies. However, all that began to radically change by the 1970s. As the economy took a dramatic downturn, it was evident that making a livelihood at subsistence farming was becoming increasingly untenable. Exacerbating matters around this time, powerful military officials also began to virtually steal the very land that had been given to peasants as part of the land redistribution program. Understandably, those who lost their land to rogue military officers were embittered.

During this period, many subsistence farmers began seeking work elsewhere, particularly on large farms of rich landowners. Jonas (2013) asserts that "as producers, [the indigenous] were being semi-proletarianized as a seasonal migrant labor force on the plantations of the Southern Coast, meanwhile often losing even the tiny subsistence plots of land they had traditionally held in the highlands. The combination of their experiences of being evicted from their own lands and their experiences as a migrant semi proletariat radicalized large numbers of highlands Mayas" (p. 377). Making matters even worse, Guatemala was hit with a major earthquake in 1976, resulting in thousands more leaving (actually, in this case, fleeing) their villages in an attempt to eke out an existence elsewhere.

Gradually, as the Highland Maya faced ever-increasing contact with the ladino society, they became more and more protective of their own culture. This was especially so in regard to protecting, and, actually, coveting, their own languages, religious practices, customs, and land. As Jonas (2013) notes, embracing their unique backgrounds and way of life, not to mention "their overall worldview," became "a factor in mobilizing their resistance to the ladino-dominated state" (p. 378).

As the Guatemalan military continued its oppression of the indigenous people (attacking their villages and homes, stealing their land, raping the females, and killing people at will) and the Maya world view began to radically change throughout the 1960s and 1970s, the Maya morphed from passively accepting the repressive and brutal nature of the government into rebelling against it.

There was another highly significant factor at play in the radicalization of the Mayan people, and that was the influence of those Catholic priests who worked alongside—and on the behalf of—the poor. The period as described above (i.e., the downturn of the economy, the indigenous seeking work on the plantations of the rich, and the indigenous being pushed off their own land by brute force at the hands of corrupt military officials) coincided with the rise of the so-called Church of the Poor. The activities of the priests' and, ultimately, the Church itself, which in Guatemala slowly shed its conservative bent, were perceived by the government as working hand-in-hand with the larger "subversive movement" orchestrated by the rebel groups. That did not sit well with the government, and it was something the government was intent on squelching.

A major escalation in the ongoing conflict (whose origins reached back to 1960) between Guatemala's indigenous groups and the Guatemalan government followed the presidential election of General Fernando Romeo Lucas García in 1978. From there, it continued apace when Efraín Ríos Montt became president in the aftermath of a coup d'état that he and junior officers under his command carried out on March 23, 1982, for the express purpose of deposing Lucas García.

In the meantime, the uprising by the rebels and the indigenous peoples they attracted to their cause caught the attention of other repressed people throughout Guatemala, who ended up joining the rebellion. When the rebellion was at its strongest in 1980–81, estimates put the number of supporters and collaborators at around a half million (Adams, 1988, p. 296). In fact, during the early 1980s, one Maya community after another was turning to the insurgents for arms with which "to defend themselves from army incursions and massacres" (Jonas, 2013, p. 358). At the same time, "the new wave of armed struggle was taken very seriously by Guatemala's elites and military leaders as heralding a possible seizure of power by the insurgents" (p. 358).

Fearing a leftist takeover in 1981, the Guatemalan government initiated a scorched earth counterinsurgency effort. Astonishingly, recorded cases of extrajudicial killings rose from 100 in 1978 to over 10,000 in 1981 (CEH, 1999, p. 79).

Displeased, however, with the government's approach to the numerous uprisings across the nation, a coterie in the military, led, as previously mentioned, by General Efraín Ríos Montt, carried out a coup d'état in 1982. Almost immediately, Ríos Montt ratcheted up what had already been a fierce counterinsurgency effort. Throughout 1982 and 1983, the counterinsurgency became increasingly brutal, as government forces destroyed hundreds of villages and killed tens of thousands of innocent people. Jonas (2013) reports that "the army openly acknowledged [that the] goal was literally to 'drain the sea' in which the guerrilla movement operated and to eradicate its civilian support base in the Mayan [sic] highlands" (p. 351).

During this period, "entire sectors of the Maya population became military targets" (Jonas, 2013, p. 359). Indeed, anyone who was Maya was "fair game." Even babies. Even those still in the wombs of those mothers suspected of supporting the rebels. In this regard, Salazar (2014) argues as follows:

In the frontal attack on the Mayas as a group, pueblo, and culture, the perpetrators sought to destroy and severely alter Maya families as well as their capacities for physical reproduction and childbearing, the latter not only through the mass murder of children but also through the forced transfer of surviving Maya children to military and paramilitary families. In sum, one of the genocide's ultimate goals was to obliterate the very existence of Maya families, especially in entire communities identified as long-term "troublemakers."... There was another dimension of this genocidal gender system, that is, the intentional process of destroying Maya children, conceived by agents of genocide as "bad seed" that needed to be eradicated even from the wombs of their mothers, as hundreds of cases testify (ODHAG/REMHI 1998; CEH 1999; Oficina de Derechos Humanso del Arzobispado de Guatemala [ODHAG] 2006). Conceptualizing Maya children as "bad seed" was not casual or invented in a hurry. It was intended to instill not just fear towards the military, but perhaps more importantly, to penetrate the heart of Maya communities, for which seeds are cosmologically and spiritually significant in that they represent the beginning of life of Mother Earth. (pp. 102–3)

Intentionally targeting the Maya with the intent to destroy them "in part or in whole" is exactly why the Ríos Montt regime has been accused of perpetrating genocide.

Between 1981 and 1983, it is estimated that between 100,000 and 150,000 civilians (primarily of Maya descent) were murdered. Based on the actions of the government and the resulting destruction and death, human rights organizations and scholars have concluded that "the army's policies were *systematically directed to destroy some ethnic sub-groups in particular, as well as the Mayan [sic] population in general*" (Jonas, 2013, p. 259; italics in the original).

An estimated 200,000 children lost at least one parent, with many of the children becoming outright orphans. Some 80,000 women lost their husbands to the violence. Approximately 1 million people were forced from their villages, ending up as either internally displaced peoples or refugees.

Ultimately, under the leadership of General Óscar Mejía Victores, Guatemala's military was intent on consolidating control over the entire indigenous population in Guatemala, and military leaders conceived of various, and often brutal, ways to accomplish that goal. First, it formed and mandated that both Maya men and boys join "civilian self-defense patrols." The latter were forced to patrol their own region, frequently against their will, and to "carry out surveillance on their neighbors and at times to commit murder" (Green, 1999, p. 31). Green (1999) convincingly argues that forcing the Maya boys and men to take part in the self-defense patrols "led to severe ruptures in family and community social relations. Not only [did] it undermine the sense of trust and cooperation among family members and neighbors, but the dividing of such loyalties [was] instrumental in perpetuating fear and terror, as family members themselves [were] implicated in acts of violence" (p. 31). Anyone who dared to refuse to serve on a self-defense patrol was generally beaten, if not tortured and/or killed, by government soldiers.

Second, the military also forced Maya civilians into model villages, which were essentially resettlement camps cum concentration camps under the control of the Guatemalan army. The people were promised adequate quarters and food, but the civilians frequently found that they in fact did not receive enough food to keep their families fed.

Third, Inter-Institutional Coordinating Councils were established, "which centralized administration of development projects at every level of government (local, municipal, provincial, national), under military control" (Jonas, 2013, pp. 383–84). In doing so, the military essentially placed the Maya population under constant scrutiny so that their every move was known.

Ultimately, in March 1994, in an effort to end the fighting, both the rebels and the Guatemalan government agreed to a human rights accord. Later, in December 1996, the rebels and government signed a peace treaty, bringing about an end to the brutal and deadly 36-year war.

Like most agreements of this nature, the peace treaty had its strengths and its weaknesses. Addressing the limitations of the peace agreement, Green (1999) argues that "the Guatemalan Peace Accords that resulted from the negotiations defined peace and security in its narrowest terms, equating peace with the absence of war and security with the absence of military threat. These restricted definitions both overlook the multifaceted problems that circumscribe Guatemalan society—economic, ecological, demographic, narcotic, and gender issues—and discount their importance in constructing lasting peace and justice in Guatemala" (p. 51).

In the aftermath of the peace agreement, a Herculean effort got underway to exhume mass graves where many victims of the military had been buried. Indicative of the vast number of graves is the fact that the Catholic Church in Guatemala alone identified 442 massacre sites.

Impunity, however, continued to reign. Adding insult to injury, in 1995 Ríos Montt was elected speaker of Guatemala's congress.

As for the culpability of the US government, in June 1996, a US presidential panel, the Intelligence Oversight Board (1996), found that the CIA "did not keep Congress adequately informed of its activities in Guatemala and was insensitive to human rights abuses there" (n.p.). The phrase "insensitive to human rights abuses there" is a gross understatement, an affront to all of the victims, and constitutes yet another example of adding insult to injury. Continuing, the report found that "several CIA assets [agents] were credibly alleged to have ordered, planned, or participated in serious human rights violations such as assassination, extrajudicial execution, torture or kidnapping while they were assets—and that the CIA was contemporaneously aware of many of the allegations" (n.p.).

In 1998, the *Recuperación de la Memoria Histórica* (Recovery of Historical Memory) project, in a study undertaken by the Human Rights Office of the Archdiocese of Guatemala, published *Guatemala: Nunca Más* (*Guatemala: Never Again*). In addition to delineating the historical context of the period, the report addressed a host of key concerns germane to the violence that tore asunder the fabric of Guatemalan society between 1960 and 1996, including but not limited to the following: those who constituted the perpetrators of the violence; those who constituted the victims; the types of atrocities perpetrated and how they were carried out by Guatemalan military forces and their allies; the fact that literally hundreds of communities were utterly destroyed; the forced cooptation of civilians by the military to carry out its dirty work; and the fact that the government established clandestine prisons and cemeteries during the period.

In February 1999, the UN-sponsored CEH whose express purpose was to "clarify with objectivity, equity and impartiality, the human rights violations and acts of violence" (CEH, 1999, p. 11) during the course of the 36-year war, issued its report on the impact of the latter. In part, the authors state that "the massacres, scorched earth operations, forced disappearances and executions of Mayan [sic] authorities, leaders, and spiritual guides were not only an attempt to destroy the social base of the guerrillas, but above all, to destroy the cultural values that ensured cohesion and collective action in Mayan [sic] communities" (p. 23). The authors of the report concluded, in part, as follows:

110. After studying four selected geographical regions (Maya-Q'anjob'al and Maya-Chuj, in Barillas, Nentón and San Mateo Ixtatán in North Huehuetenango; Maya-Ixil, in Nebaj, Cotzaland Chajul, Quiché; Maya-K'iche' in Joyabaj, Zacualpa and Chiché, Quiché; and Maya-Achi in Rabinal, Baja Verapaz), the CEH is able to confirm that between 1981 and 1983 the [Guatemalan] Army identified groups of the Mayan [sic] population as the internal enemy, considering them to be an actual or potential support base for the guerrillas, with respect to material sustenance, a source of recruits and a place to hide their members. *In this way, the Army, inspired by the National Security Doctrine, defined a concept of internal enemy that went beyond guerrilla sympathisers, combatants or militants to include civilians from specific ethnic groups* [italics added];

111. *"The reiteration of destructive acts, directed against groups of the Mayan [sic] population, within which can be mentioned the elimination of leaders and criminal acts against minors who could not possibly have been military targets, demonstrates that the only common denominator for all the victims was the fact that they belonged to a specific ethnic group and makes it evident that these acts were committed 'with the intent to destroy, in whole or in part' these groups"* (Article II, first paragraph of the Convention [on the Prevention and Punishment of the Crime of Genocide]) [italics added];

115. *The CEH concludes that, among those acts perpetrated with the intent to destroy, in whole or in part, numerous Mayan [sic] groups, are included many actions committed which constituted "serious bodily or mental harm to members of the group"* (Article II.b of the Convention). The resulting destruction of social cohesion of the group, typical of these acts, corresponds to the intent to annihilate the group, physically and spiritually [italics added];

116. The investigation has also proved that the killings, especially those that were indiscriminate massacres, were accompanied by the

razing of villages. This was most significant in the Ixil region, where between 70% and 90% of villages were razed. Also, in the north of Huehuetenango, in Rabinal and in Zacualpa, whole villages were burnt, properties were destroyed and the collectively worked fields and harvests were also burnt, leaving the communities without food;

117. Furthermore, in the four regions which were the object of this special investigation, people were also persecuted during their displacement. The CEH has established that in the Ixil area, displaced persons were bombed. Similarly, those who were captured or gave themselves up voluntarily continued to be the object of violations, in spite of being under the Army's absolute control;

118. *The CEH concludes that some of the acts mentioned in the two previous paragraphs constitute the "deliberate infliction on the group of conditions of life" that could bring about, and in several cases did bring about, "its physical destruction in whole or in part"* (Article II. c. of the Convention) [italics added];

119. The CEH's analysis demonstrates that in the execution of these acts, the national military structures were co-ordinated to allow for the "effective" action of soldiers and members of Civil Patrols in the four regions studied. *Military plan Victory 82, for example, established that "the mission is to annihilate the guerrillas and parallel organizations"; the military plan Firmness 83-1 determined that the Army should support "their operations with a maximum of PAC members, in order to raze all collective works..."* [italics added];

120. The above has convinced the CEH that acts committed with the intent to destroy, in whole or in part, numerous groups of Mayans [sic] were not isolated acts or excesses committed by soldiers who were out of control, nor were they the result of possible improvisation by mid-level Army command. With great consternation, the CEH concludes that many massacres and other human rights violations committed against these groups obeyed a higher, strategically planned policy, manifested in actions which had a logical and coherent sequence;

121. Faced with several options to combat the insurgency, the State chose the one that caused the greatest loss of human life among non-combatant civilians. Rejecting other options, such as a political effort to reach agreements with disaffected non-combatant civilians, moving of people away from the conflict areas, or the arrest of insurgents, the State opted for the annihilation of those they identified as their enemy;

122. In consequence, the CEH concludes that agents of the State of Guatemala, within the framework of counterinsurgency operations carried out between 1981 and 1983, committed acts of genocide against groups of Mayan [sic] people which lived in the four regions analysed. This conclusion is based on the evidence that, in light of Article II of the Convention on the Prevention and Punishment of the Crime of Genocide, the killing of members of Mayan [sic] groups occurred (Article II.a), serious bodily or mental harm was inflicted (Article II.b) and the group was deliberately subjected to living conditions calculated to bring about its physical destruction in whole or in part (Article II.c). The conclusion is also based on the evidence that all these acts were committed "with intent to destroy, in whole or in part" groups identified by their common ethnicity, by reason thereof, whatever the cause, motive or final objective of these acts may have been (Article II, first paragraph);

123. The CEH has information that similar acts occurred and were repeated in other regions inhabited by Mayan [sic] people;

124. Based on the fundamental conclusion that genocide was committed, the CEH, in keeping with its mandate to present an objective judgement on the events of the internal armed confrontation, indicates that, without prejudice to the fact that the active subjects are the intellectual and material authors of the crimes in the acts of genocide committed in Guatemala, the State is also responsible, because the majority of these acts were the product of a policy pre-established by a command superior to the material perpetrators. (CEH, 1999, pp. 39–41)[91]

---

91  For additional discussions as to how the actions of the Government of Guatemala and its paramilitary units against the Maya constituted genocide, see chapter 6, "Guatemalan Army Campaigns of Genocide," in Sanford (2003), and Jonas (2013).

Ultimately, in 2013, Ríos Montt was brought to trial on charges of crimes against humanity and genocide for atrocities perpetrated during the period of his regime. In May 2013, he was found guilty of genocide and sentenced to 80 years for crimes against humanity and genocide. Ten days later, however, the judgment was overturned on technical grounds, which critics claimed was likely politically motivated. In January 2015, a new trial got underway, but Ríos Montt did not appear in court as his lawyers asserted their client was too sick to do so. After the three-judge panel forced Ríos Montt to appear in court, his lawyers argued that one of the judges should recuse herself, since she had written a master's thesis 10 years earlier in which she presented a legal analysis arguing that genocide had been perpetrated by the Ríos Montt regime. The other two judges agreed with Ríos Montt's attorneys and suspended the trial until a different judge could be appointed to the panel. Ultimately, on August 25, 2015, a Guatemalan court announced that while Ríos Montt could stand trial on charges of genocide and crimes against humanity, he could not be sentenced, since the former strongman was suffering from dementia. The trial, the court said, would be held behind closed doors and Ríos Montt could still be found guilty or not guilty, but no matter what he would serve no time. Immediately, his lawyers appealed the ruling, arguing that their client should be excused altogether.

## THE GUATEMALAN GOVERNMENT'S GENOCIDE OF THE MAYA: CULPABILITY OF THE UNITED STATES GOVERNMENT?

The United States government and, to a certain extent, various components of its different military service branches, were not only well informed about the atrocities being perpetrated against the Maya in Guatemala during the 36-year war but had their hands in the fray in a host of different ways. Even a short list of the various officials, US government agencies, and military branches and units that were well informed about the atrocities perpetrated during Guatemala's 36-year war is notable. Among them, for example, were President Ronald Reagan; US Assistant Secretary of State

Elliott Abrams; US Assistant Secretary of State for Inter-American Affairs Thomas Enders; US Ambassador to Guatemala Frederic Chapin; United States Marine Lieutenant Colonel and Deputy Director for Political and Military Affairs with the National Security Agency Oliver North; President Reagan's Deputy National Security Adviser Robert McFarlane; US Special Envoy to Central America Richard B. Stone; and Richard Childress, a national security aide. Many of the latter were not only well informed about the atrocities but integrally involved in one way or other in the United States' dealings with Guatemala, including but not limited to military training, advising Guatemalan governmental and military officials, and overseeing the sale of weapons during the period.

There were a host of other US officials who were, in one way or another, also involved in US dealings with the Government of Guatemala and its military forces in relation to their policies and actions against the Maya of the highlands: unnamed CIA officers, operating out of the CIA station in Guatemala and in Washington, DC; various officers stationed at the US Embassy in Guatemala City; officials in the US Defense Intelligence Agency; and retired US Army General Vernon Walters (who served as Secretary of State Haig's personal emissary to Guatemalan President Fernando Romeo Lucas García). The latter individuals either wrote and sent, received, and/ or were mentioned by name in one or more declassified CIA and US Department of State documents.

Prior to highlighting what various US government officials knew about the atrocities being perpetrated in Guatemala, when they knew it, and what their response was to such knowledge, it is important to note that the United States military was extremely active in Guatemala as early as the 1960s. It is also worth noting that between 1946 and 1995, it is estimated that some 1,500 Guatemalan members of the Guatemalan military attended one or more courses at the SOA. Among such individuals, for example, were Fernando Romeo Lucas García, dictator/president of Guatemala in the late 1970s and early 1980s, against whom 10 Guatemalan communities filed a lawsuit in June 2000, contending he had committed genocide while in office; Efraín Ríos Montt, who was indicted by the Government of Guatemala in the early 2000s as being the one, while president of Guatemala, who oversaw the genocide of the Maya; Colonel Hector Montalban, General Manuel Antonio Callejas y Callejas, and Francisco Ortega Menaldo, all of whom served as directors of the Guatemala's infamous intelligence agency, D-2; and Cesar Quinteros Alvarado, Domingo Velasquez Axpuac, Eduardo Ochoa Barrios, Francisco Edgar Dominguez Lopez, Federico Sobalvarro Meza, Luis Felipe Caballeros Meza, Harry Ponce, and Jose Manuel Rivas Rios, all of whom were top military officials.

Speaking of D-2, the *Nunca Más* report noted that it played "a central role in the conduct of military operations, in massacres, extra-judicial executions, forced disappearances and torture during the period of the genocide and beyond" (vol. 2, p. 65).

In regard to those US officials who were well informed about the atrocities being perpetrated in Guatemala during their period in office in the 1980s, the following questions must be asked: (1) Who knew what, and when did they know it?; and (2) Who was cognizant of the fact that most of the atrocities were being perpetrated by the Guatemalan government (as opposed, for example, to being under the impression that rebels were responsible for a great number of the atrocities)? It is important to pose such questions, because a fair number of officials in the Reagan administration have asserted that, at the time, they were not sure who was responsible for the murders. Today, however, there is conclusive evidence that many of the officials lied about what they knew. In fact, various declassified US government documents provide unassailable evidence that some of those who have claimed ignorance of the facts were indeed lying. How many of the others who lied may never be known.

Another question that merits being asked is this: If the aforementioned US officials did not appreciate the fact that the Guatemalan government was perpetrating the atrocities in the 1980s, how come? It is important to pose this question helps to ascertain whether such individuals were, for example, (a) lying, (b) issuing a half-truth, (c) simply naive, (d) purposely naive, (e) purposely avoiding such knowledge, or (f) half believing and half not believing the facts on the ground, but not inclined to delve further since they were well aware of the Reagan administration's position on anti-communism and its ardent belief that the rebels and indigenous peoples were under the sway of communism, if not outright proponents of it.

Richard Childress, a national security aide during the Reagan administration, for one, was certainly well aware of the atrocities that were being perpetrated under the Ríos Montt regime. For example, on February 2, 1982, he wrote the following secret memo to his colleagues regarding the situation on the ground in Guatemala:

> As we move ahead on our approach to Latin America, we need to consciously address the unique problems posed by Guatemala. Possessed of some of the worst human rights records in the region...it presents a policy dilemma for us. The abysmal human rights record makes it, in its present form, unworthy of USG support....
>
> Beset by a continuous insurgency for at least 15 years, the current leadership is completely committed to a ruthless and unyielding program of suppression. Hardly a soldier could be found that has not killed a "guerrilla." (quoted in Parry, 2013, n.p.)

Both genocide and crimes against humanity were perpetrated against the Maya people in the Western Highlands of Guatemala by the Guatemalan government in the 1980s, which, to a large extent, parallels when Ronald Reagan was in the White House (1981–88). The following comments by New York University historian Greg Grandin (2013) provides damning evidence in regard to just how closely linked President Reagan was with the Government of Guatemala and what Reagan likely knew about the massacres being perpetrated in Guatemala: "Once in office, Reagan continued to supply munitions and training to the Guatemalan army, despite a ban on military aid imposed by the Carter administration (existing contracts were exempt from the ban)....Reagan was consistent in his moral backing for Guatemala's genocidaires. On Dec. 5, 1982, for instance, he met with Rios Montt in Honduras and said he was 'a man of great integrity' and 'totally dedicated to democracy'" (n.p.).

Continuing, Grandin (2013) argues that "other declassified documents reveal that the White House was less concerned with the massacres than with their effectiveness" (n.p.). They were also less concerned with the fact people were being murdered "than they were with countering the bad publicity stemming from reports of the atrocities" (n.p.).

In fact, "the day after Reagan's aforementioned endorsement, Guatemalan soldiers arrived at a village called Dos Erres and started killing. The slaughter went on for three days and by the time it was over at least 162 people, including many children, were dead" (Grandin, 2013, n.p.).

Reagan had a host of right-hand men at his side who were eager to please him, and being keen supporters of the right-wing regimes in Central America, seemingly had no qualms about the ongoing atrocities perpetrated by many of the regimes, including the one in Guatemala. Among the most eager and aggressive in carrying out Reagan's vision was US Assistant Secretary of State Elliott Abrams. In a devastating article, "Guatemala: Will Justice Be Done?" (which appeared in the *New York Review of Books*), noted human rights activist Aryeh Neier (2013) wrote the following: "The State Department's *Country Reports on Human Rights Practices for 1982*, the year in which the CEH found that 48 percent of the killings and disappearances of the thirty-six-year conflict had taken place, asserted that 'there has been a decrease in the level of [government] killing.' The report was published under the direction of Elliott Abrams" (n.p.).

In 1983, Abrams' efforts at spin continued unabated. In a piece titled "The Upside of Genocide," Eric Alterman (2013) had the following to say about Abrams's efforts on the behalf of President Ríos Montt: "*Even after the killings increased in intensity*... Assistant Secretary of State for Human Rights Elliott Abrams credited Ríos Montt with having 'brought considerable progress' on human rights issues and insisted that 'the amount of killing of innocent civilians is being reduced step by step'" (n.p.). As if in an Orwellian novel, Abrams demanded that Congress provide the regime with advanced arms because its alleged "progress need[ed] to be rewarded and encouraged" (n.p.). To this day Abrams is not about to question, let alone condemn, his or the Reagan administration's support of Ríos Montt.

As for us Assistant Secretary of State for Inter-American Affairs Thomas Enders, Alterman (2013) notes that "he wrote to Amnesty International disputing its reporting on the killings in Guatemala and insisted that the government was making 'significant progress' on human rights while the genocide was taking place" (n.p.). This is the same official who had praised Ríos Montt for conducting an "effective insurgency" (Henry, 2003, p. 25). Years later, when he was no longer with the us government, Enders mused, "We didn't think that we could effectively sustain the resistance to the guerrillas in Central America without being willing to give significant public support to their governments.... We were afraid that the approach that had been adopted by the Carter administration, which was highly critical of them and would result in their demoralization, would fail to convince the Soviet Union or the Salvadorans, Hondurans and others that we really meant business" (quoted in Cohn & Thompson, 1995, p. 4). Despite almost overwhelming evidence that the Guatemalan government and its army were engaged in a systematic effort to destroy at least significant parts of the Maya in the Western Highlands, certain Reagan officials continued to praise Ríos Montt for purportedly moderating the army's actions in the highlands. As Parry (2005) notes, in February 1983, a secret CIA cable noted a rise in

"suspect right-wing violence" with kidnappings of students and teachers. Bodies of victims were appearing in ditches and gullies. CIA sources traced these political murders to Rios Montt's order to the "Archivos"[92] in October to "apprehend, hold, interrogate and dispose of suspected guerrillas as they saw fit".... On March 17, 1983, Americas Watch

---

92  Presidential Chiefs of Staff's military intelligence unit, described in the Department of State's report of March 28, 1986, as a "secret group in the President's office that collected information on insurgents and operated against them" (*National Security Archive Electronic Briefing Book No. 32: Guatemala's Disappeared, 1977–1986*, (doc. 30).

representatives condemned the Guatemalan army for human rights atrocities against the Indian population. New York attorney Stephen L. Kass said these findings included proof that the [Guatemalan] government carried out "virtually indiscriminate murder of men, women and children of any farm regarded by the army as possibly supportive of guerrilla insurgents." Rural women suspected of guerrilla sympathies were raped before execution, Kass said. Children were "thrown into burning homes. They are thrown in the air and speared with bayonets. We heard many, many stories of children being picked up by the ankles and swung against poles so their heads are destroyed" [AP, March 17, 1983]. Publicly, however, senior Reagan officials continued to put on a happy face. On June 12, 1983, special envoy Richard B. Stone praised "positive changes" in Rios Montt's government. But Rios Montt's vengeful Christian fundamentalism was hurtling out of control, even by Guatemalan standards. In August 1983, General Oscar Mejía Victores seized power in another coup. (n.p.)

## A SELECT OVERVIEW OF THE MAJOR DOCUMENTS ISSUED BY THE US GOVERNMENT

There is a wealth of declassified US government documents that provide a revealing picture of the US government's interaction with those Guatemalan governments responsible for crimes against humanity and/or genocide of its Maya citizens. Released under the Freedom of Information Act, such documents are variously from the archives of the CIA, the Pentagon, and the US State Department. Such documents are readily accessible to members of the public thanks to the outstanding efforts of the National Security Archive, an independent, non-profit research institute and library based at George Washington University in Washington, DC. Among such documents are, for example, (a) secret memorandums, (b) top secret reports, (c) secret cables, (d) confidential cables, and (e) secret intelligence assessments. Many are invaluable in that they, at least to a certain extent, take some of the guesswork out of the positions/actions of various US presidential administrations—most notably Jimmy Carter's (January 20, 1977–January 20, 1981) and Ronald Reagan's (January 20, 1981–January 20, 1989)—vis-à-vis various Guatemalan regimes' treatment/mistreatment of the Maya people during the late 1970s and 1980s.

Many of the declassified documents provide ample and indisputable evidence that key officials in the Reagan administration (a) were well informed about the massacres that were taking place in Guatemala as well as those who were responsible for them; (b) tended, at times, to look away in an attempt to ignore the real situation on the ground, or, put another way, willingly ignored or purposely blinded themselves to the facts; (c) failed to delve more deeply into the situation to obtain clear and unambiguous evidence in regard to what, exactly, was taking place on the ground in Guatemala; (d) were prone to implementing half measures seemingly to "show" that the administration was ostensibly attempting to rein in the Guatemalan regimes, while knowing full well that such half measures were not going to result in staunching the ongoing killing by the regimes; and, in certain cases, (e) actually supported the tough measures taken by their allies in Guatemala.

At first blush, the actual meaning of some of the information in the documents seems rather opaque. However, when one carefully probes into *who* wrote and disseminated the documents, *when* the documents were written, *why* they were written (i.e., to inform, to warn, to suggest a particular action), *to whom* they were sent, *how* they were classified (i.e., top secret, secret, etc., and/or stamped with warnings as to who the documents should not be shared with, etc.), the *wording* (whether, for example, euphemisms are used), and the *tone* (matter-of-fact, dismissive, blunt, cautious, or tentative), the message inherent in most of the documents become much clearer. The point is this: it is not adequate to simply peruse or quickly read a particular document and leave it at that. Furthermore, to even begin to understand the full import of a document, it is essential for readers to (a) have a solid understanding of an administration's policies/position in the first place and (b) what was transpiring in Guatemala at the time the document was written and disseminated.

Due to space constraints, only seven documents shall be commented on herein. That said, the seven documents selected for discussion are rather revelatory.

A secret memorandum—"Guatemala: What Next?"—which was sent out under the auspices of the US State Department on October 5, 1981, provides an invaluable insight into the fact that the Guatemalan government was intent on exterminating the rebels, their sympathizers and supporters before Ríos Montt even became president in 1982.

Prior to a detailed discussion of the nature of the memo, some background is needed. In 1981, President Reagan sent retired General Vernon Walters on his behalf to meet with President Lucas García in regard to Guatemala's poor human rights record. In no uncertain terms, Lucas García told Walters that while Guatemala certainly desired US military assistance, "the repression will continue...and the guerilla threat will be successfully routed," with or without such assistance.

Initially, the memo—written by Robert L. Jacobs, an official with the US State Department's Bureau of Human Rights and Humanitarian Affairs, and addressed to a Mr. Einaudi (Luigi R. Einaudi, the director of the Office of Policy, Planning, and Coordination in the Bureau of Inter-American Affairs with the US State Department)—appears to suggest that the United States government is extremely concerned that the Government of Guatemala is not only treating its own people in such horrific ways—torturing and killing rebels, their sympathizers, and their supporters—but is also intent on exterminating them all. Upon closer examination, however, it becomes increasingly obvious that the memo is more about appearances than anything else. Indeed, the major concern seems to be about how it would look should the US be accused of supporting such a murderous regime.

Several key issues/concerns are revealed in this memo. First, for example, as early as 1981, the US government obviously knew that the Government of Guatemala was intent on "exterminating the guerrillas." As US officials obviously knew, "extermination" constitutes, at a minimum, a crime against humanity. Second, it is also clear that while the United States purportedly called out the Guatemalan government vis-à-vis its repressive and deadly measures cum human rights violations, the US government was, as mentioned above, more concerned about appearances than the fact that Guatemala was actually intent on exterminating a particular group. Concomitantly, based on the wording of the document, it appears that (and here I am choosing my words carefully) *once the extermination had been completed*, the US was most willing to resume business as usual.

Jacobs opens by stating the following: "I read with keen interest Ambassador Chapin's assessment of General Walters [sic] recent visit to Guatemala. In essence Ambassador Chapin concludes that President Lucas is not going to address our human rights concerns, that we must recognize this fact, and that we must now decide whether national security considerations require that we nevertheless go ahead with security assistance" (Doyle & Osorio, n.d., doc.13). This is a telling statement in light of the fact that Jacobs (and other high-level officials) in the US State Department unequivocally knew that the Government of Guatemala was essentially intent on exterminating "the guerillas, their supporters and their sympathizers." Indeed, he says as much:

Only in time will we and the Guatemalans know whether President Lucas is correct in his conviction that repression will work once again in Guatemala. If he is right and the policy of repression is succeeding and will result in the extermination of the guerillas, their supporters, and their sympathizers there is no need for the U.S. to implicate itself in the repression by supplying the GOG [Government of Guatemala] with security assistance.... Having failed in our efforts to dissuade the GOG from its policy of repression we ought to distance ourselves from the GOG and not involve ourselves in Guatemala's "dirty war." If the repression does work and the guerillas, their supporters and sympathizers are neutralized we can in the aftermath of the repression work to restore normal relations with the successors to President Lucas.

If Lucas is right and the GOG can successfully "go it alone" in its policy of repression, there is no need for the U.S. to provide the GOG with redundant political and military support. The provisioning of such assistance would needlessly render us a complicit party in the repression. (Doyle & Osorio, n.d., doc. 13, p. 2)

It appears that the US government would prefer that the Guatemalan government not use extermination to solve its "problem"; however, if Guatemala proceeds with the extermination, the US is not going to apply any additional pressure in an attempt to force Guatemala to cease and desist. Instead, the US will simply keep the Guatemalan government at arm's length so that Guatemala's actions do not reflect badly on the US and/or have serious repercussions. Then, once Guatemala has settled its "problem" via extermination and everything quiets down again, the US will resume its relationship with Guatemala as if nothing had ever happened. In other words, there is no real concern for the people who are likely to be targeted—including anyone who sympathizes with them—and massacred. None at all. In fact, it is almost as if the "supporters and sympathizers" are simply in the way and that is their tough luck. In that regard, the US government's position is akin to readily accepting that so-called collateral damage is likely to occur, but "Oh, well." The cold-hearted and callous approach of the United States government could not have been stated more clearly. In one respect, it is a clear example of realpolitik at its "best" (or, more aptly put, its worst). In another respect, it speaks volumes about the US government's "adherence" to honoring the protection of basic human rights.

Furthermore, it is interesting, and not a little curious, that Jacobs does not seem to recognize the fact that the Government of Guatemala is seemingly intent on perpetrating genocide (then again, he possibly saw absolutely no value in pointing that possibility out). Equally curious is the fact that the United States government does not seem all that concerned about that fact. Furthermore, it is telling that Jacobs has a propensity to use a euphemism for extermination: repression. It is also rather evident that if the United States government could have been absolutely sure of not being found out—thus avoiding castigation for providing military support to

Guatemala despite the Government of Guatemala's intentions—it would have provided such support without a moment's hesitation.

This document may be the most glaring example of what the United States government knew regarding the mass killings in Guatemala, including when it knew and how it reacted. Guatemala is a classic case of the United States' complicity in genocide, via a combination of purposely ignoring the hard facts, obfuscating the facts, covering up key facts, and, when all is said and done, essentially allowing a genocide to take place.

On February 5, 1982, the Director of Central Intelligence issued a top-secret report (*DCI*[93] *Watch Committee Report*) about Guatemala's military's plans as they related to a location called the Ixil Triangle. Many years later, the report was okayed for release (i.e., declassification) by the CIA; however only one of the 10 paragraphs was not redacted (i.e., totally blacked out). The sole paragraph that remains reads as follows:

5. Guatemala: The Guatemalan military's plans to begin sweeps through the Ixil Triangle area, which has the largest concentration of guerrillas and sympathizers in the country, could lead not only to major clashes, but to serious abuses by the armed forces. Chief of Staff Lucas has cautioned his men not to harm innocent peasants, but he acknowledged that because most Indians in the area support the guerrillas it probably will be necessary to destroy a number of villages. *This sort of activity almost certainly would receive prominent coverage in foreign newspapers.* (Doyle & Osorio, n.d., doc. 14; italics in original)

This top-secret report provides clear and unequivocal evidence that United States was well aware that there was a better-than-even chance that the Guatemalan government would likely commit, at the very least, crimes

---

93 The Office of United States Director of Central Intelligence (DCI) headed up the Central Intelligence Agency (CIA) from 1946 to 2005, serving as the primary intelligence adviser to the US President and the National Security Council. The DCI also served as the coordinator of all US-related intelligence activities between and amongst the various US intelligence agencies from 1981 onward.

against humanity (including murder and extermination), if not genocide, against innocent peasants (i.e., who the government automatically assumed were supporters of the rebels). This is an extrapolation of common knowledge in regard to what the Guatemalan military meant by "destroy a village" and how military personnel actually carried out such destruction. As Schirmer (1998) notes, various officers "who served in the Ixil...have... admitted that unarmed civilians were routinely killed" (p. 52). Continuing, she quotes one of her interviewees, an intelligence officer, as stating the following: "'*Everyone, everyone* was a guerilla; no difference was made in killing them. The big difference in the shift in strategy after the 1982 coup was that we couldn't eliminate them all' (*Todos, todos* no habia diferencia en matarlos. La gran diferencia fue que no podiamos eliminar a todos.) Some were captured and their lives spared so they could serve as informers" (Schirmer, 1998, p. 52; italics in original).

In 1983, Americas Watch reported the following in regard to how Guatemalan military troops carried out the destruction of village after village: "The twin goals of Rios Montt's counterinsurgency strategy have been to eradicate the guerrillas quickly and to reassert the government's control over—i.e., 'pacify,'—the Indian population. The principal tactics of this strategy are bombing, shelling, selective killings and massacres in suspected 'subversive' villages, combined with a scorched earth policy of crop-burning, confiscation of harvests and slaughter of livestock, calculated not only to deny the guerrillas food but also to force peasants to near starvation" (p. 9).

It is important to note that the declassified document under discussion here strongly suggests that the *primary concern* of the DCI was its fear that the international media might report on such atrocities. As for the Guatemalan military's plan itself and the way it was to be carried out—including the possibility of perpetrating genocidal actions—the DCI seems rather blasé. That is, there is no denunciation of such. Of course, it is possible that the DCI did comment on such actions in one or more of the nine paragraphs that were redacted; but then again, that is not likely, for why would such information be redacted?

If those who okayed the release of the above document were willing to allow that single paragraph to remain—which is striking in and of itself, since it addresses the murderous modus operandi of the Guatemalan military—one has to wonder what the other paragraphs consisted of and what they spelled out in regard to what the United States knew about the Guatemalan government's plans and actions and how it (the US) reacted to such. The point is this: words, sentences, and paragraphs are redacted by US government agencies/censors for a reason, and to allow such a paragraph, containing such inflammatory information, to appear in print for anyone and everyone to read raises a host of questions in regard to what was redacted.

In February 1982, the CIA either sent or received a secret cable (reproduced below as Document 2) regarding the Guatemalan army's counterinsurgency operations in El Quiché, Guatemala. (*The information about who sent and received the secret cable was redacted before the cable was declassified/released for access by the public.*)

A large portion of this document has been heavily redacted: at least half of the first page, five lines on the second page, three or four lines on the third page (it's impossible to know for sure since part of the page is blurry), and all of the fourth page.

This document complements Document 1 in that it actually delineates, at least to a certain extent, exactly what took place in the Ixil Triangle during the operation to destroy villages there. Among its most telling contents are the following:

1. In mid-February 1982, the Guatemalan army reinforced its existing force in the central El Quiche Department and launched a sweep operation into the Ixil Triangle. The commanding officers of the units involved have been instructed to destroy all towns and villages which are cooperating with the guerilla army of the poor (EGP) and eliminate all sources of resistance.

2. Since the operation began, several villages have been burned to the ground, and a large number of guerrillas and collaborators have

been killed. [Word redacted] comment: When any army patrol meets resistance and takes fire from a town or village it is assumed that the entire town is hostile and it is subsequently destroyed....

4. [The army's] successes today appear to be limited to the destruction of several "ECP-Controlled Towns" and the killing of Indian collaborators and sympathizers. ([Word redacted] comment: The well documented belief by the army that the entire Ixil Indian population is Pro EGP has created a situation in which the army can be expected to give no quarter to combatants and non-combatants alike.)

The little that is *not redacted* in this document is revelatory. First, it is obvious that virtually anyone and everyone who was a member of the Ixil indigenous population and "ECP-Controlled Towns" were fair game and likely to be killed by Guatemalan troops. Second, another section of the report suggests that those civilians and "Indians" who chose "to collaborate with the army and who seek army protection are to be well treated and cared for in refugee camps," but the fact is the civilians never were well treated or cared for in such camps. In fact, not a few were tortured to force them to provide information; all of them were closely watched and their interactions monitored; they rarely, if ever, received enough food to eat; and they were, in the end, treated like second-class citizens or worse (Krueger & Enge, 1985, pp. vii–viii; 27–52; Sanford, 2003, pp. 78, 112–116, 123, 137, 139–42, 148, 165, 169–74; Streeter, 2013, p. 254).

On October 22, 1982, the American Embassy in Guatemala sent a confidential cable to the US State Department and various American embassies in Central and South America with an analysis of various human rights reports on Guatemala by Amnesty International, the Washington Office on Latin America/Network in Solidarity with the People of Guatemala (WOLA/NISGUA), and the Guatemala Human Rights Commission. In the cable, it is asserted, without proof of any sort, that the aforementioned human rights organizations had been highly influenced by communist groups based in Central America. Furthermore, it states that, since the communists had a vested interest in the outcome of the civil war in Guatemala, their influence of the human rights groups had resulted in blatantly biased human rights reports against the Government of Guatemala.

In part, the cable reads as follows:

> We conclude that a concerted disinformation campaign is being waged in the U.S. against the Guatemalan Government by groups supporting the communist insurgency in Guatemala; this has enlisted the support of conscientious human rights and church organizations which may not fully appreciate that they are being utilized. This is a campaign in which guerrilla mayhem and violations of human rights are ignored; a campaign in which responsibility for atrocities is assigned to the GOG without verifiable evidence; a campaign in which GOG responsibility for atrocities is alleged when evidence shows guerrilla responsibility; a campaign in which atrocities are cited that never occurred. The campaign's object is simple: to deny the Guatemalan army the weapons and equipment needed from the U.S. to defeat the guerrillas. (Doyle & Osorio, n.d., doc. 16, pp. 1–2)

The above excerpt from the larger document (cable) is revealing: first, it seems that US embassy personnel either had little or no idea as to the real cause of the conflict between the rebels and the government or simply did not care. (Based on other declassified US documents from the period, detailed human rights reports, and relatively recent scholarship, it is crystal clear that a lack of concern about the plight of the indigenous population in Guatemala is what drove the perspective of US embassy personnel vis-à-vis this crisis.) As noted at the outset of this chapter, the poor in Guatemala, and particularly the Maya living in the Western Highlands, were historically subjected to extremely shabby treatment by both the Guatemalan government and its military officials. Part and parcel of the latter is that the poor suffered economic and political disenfranchisement, abject poverty, indentured servitude, and theft of their land. In other words, their grievances were real. To be oblivious of such concerns or simply not concerned about them speaks volumes about the lax and/or ideologically driven perspective of US embassy personnel. Second, by assuming and asserting that the crux of the problem in Guatemala was the influence of the communists, US embassy personnel were dismissive of any and all legitimate grievances the poor might have had. Third, the sole concern of US embassy personnel seemed to revolve around the barrier to supplying the Guatemalan government with military assistance. That speaks to the rather cavalier dismissal of the reasons for such a roadblock. Fourth, US embassy personnel seemed to believe that the only solution to the grievances of the poor was to defeat the rebels in any way possible—versus coming up with potential solutions to ameliorate the conditions, and assuage the concerns, of both the poor and those fighting against the government, thus convincing them to put down their weapons.

Finally, the section of the cable that has been highlighted here includes a slew of assertions about the purported actions of the guerrillas, but offers no empirical evidence. Furthermore, the author(s) of the memo makes one disparaging remark and accusation after another against various human rights groups vis-à-vis the accuracy of their reports, but, again, fail to provide any hard evidence that supports such assertions.

Later in the cable, the author(s) write, "If the GOG were indeed engaged in massive extrajudicial executions—a 'mad genocidal' campaign—in the Highlands, one must wonder why Indians are joining civil defense patrols in great numbers, and why thousands of Indians are coming to the army for refuge…" The fact is, the vast number of the Maya who "joined" the civil defense patrols were forced to do so under the threat of duress (meaning sure death at the hands of the Guatemala military or their paramilitary partners). Speaking of the Guatemalan government's "second stage" in its counterinsurgency plan, Patricia K. Hall (1986) noted the following:

> The main aspects of this second stage of the military's counterinsurgency plan, according to army documents, include strengthening and expanding the civil patrols…in the conflict areas. More recently, institutional coordinators were established to give the military control over state and parastatal development agencies.…Extremely sophisticated,

the counterinsurgency plan aims to control the civil population and to destroy the culture and traditions of an ethnic majority in such a way that they continue to exist only in a form that is beneficial to, and manageable by, the status quo....

Membership in the patrols is compulsory in the sense that nonparticipation labels one a subversive, which in Guatemala means almost certain death....As one army colonel explained, "Before, he (the Indian) was Juan Pedro from a certain village (or ethnic group). Now, in the civil patrol, he feels part of Guatemala. Every civil patrol post has its little Guatemalan flag, whether it's of paper, plastic or whatever, and he is beginning to identify with it." An extremely effective control system, the patrols must account for every able-bodied man in the community at all hours of the day and night and for all movement in and out of the community. The army uses civil patrols to do some of its dirty work—at the same time dividing communities—by forcing patrol members to assassinate and torture members of their own villages. Patrol members have little alternative but to comply or be shot for disobeying the local military commander's orders.

It must be understood that while it may appear—as the army claims—that Indians take part willingly in these events, military control is so pervasive in Guatemala that even to show reluctance to participate in these activities would be exceedingly dangerous. (n.p.)

As for puzzlement expressed by the author of the cable—"One must wonder why Indians are joining civil defense patrols in great numbers, and why thousands of Indians are coming to the army for refuge"—the reality was that survivors were forced into such settlements after their own villages had been utterly destroyed. Tellingly, the resettlements were more like a prison than anything else. In this regard, Hall (1986) reported the following:

The most ambitious part of the counterinsurgency plan...is the resettlement program....The four main [settlement areas] are in the [Highland region,] Ixil triangle in Quiche, Chisec in Alta Verapaz, Playa Grande in Quiche, and Chacaj in northern Huehuetenango....

The settlements...share the common purpose of consolidating army control over the indigenous population and creating an infrastructure from which to launch military raids and offensives. So far, all have been constructed in the front line of the military's fight with the guerrilla organization, the EGP (Guerrilla Army of the Poor).

There are various types of settlements. Some, such as Acul and Tzalbal in the Ixil triangle, are model strategic villages that are shown off to visiting journalists, diplomats and aid agency workers. There are many more reconstructed, redesigned "new villages" with fewer services such as Las Pacayas in Alta Verapaz. Often these are villages that were previously destroyed by the army and where massacres took place. Other settlements, where the focus is control, are little more than refugee camps with practically no services.

Finally, [there] is the Acamal "reeducation" center, where the approximately 1,500 exclusively Indian inmates—supposedly former active guerrilla supporters—are being held under strict military control.

At least another 40 new villages are projected for the near future. So far nearly all of the new settlements have been inaugurated with a great deal of publicity....The army is depicted as the benefactor, providing new housing and extensive facilities for the poor Indians who have sought its protection and escaped the clutches of the guerrillas.

While this is the official propaganda, most other observers, such as church people and community leaders, described the slave-like existence in the model villages, the coercion of the inhabitants, the excessive monitoring of their movements and the breaking down of the traditional Indian lifestyle. According to a report published by members of the British Parliamentary Human Rights Group, who visited Guatemala in October 1984, people in the settlements are "subjected to rigorous work schedules, followed by compulsory drill and then patrolling at night; [as well as] compulsory political education and serious food shortages." (n.p.)

In "circa late 1982," during which the genocide against the Maya was in full force, the United States State Department issued a secret report entitled "Guatemala: Reports of Atrocities Mark Army Gains." In part, the report stated the following:

> The government has improved its control over rural areas through a strategic village program in which the rural populace is ordered to move to villages where the army has outposts. A scorched earth policy is then applied in the surrounding area. These tactics have been accompanied by widespread allegations that government troops are regularly guilty of massacres, rape and mayhem. US Embassy investigations have found that some of these reports cannot be verified, that some of the atrocities reported are attributable to the guerrillas, and that still others cannot be attributed with accuracy to either side. The Embassy does not as yet believe that there is sufficient evidence to link government troops to any of the reported massacres. (Doyle & Osorio, n.d., doc. 17, p. 1)

One has to wonder just how thoroughly US embassy personnel in Guatemala looked into the perpetration of the atrocities against the Maya of the Western Highlands. The comments in this secret report suggest that perhaps the US embassy did not really want to know who was doing what to whom in Guatemala. That seems to be the case, for by late 1982 a host of reports about the atrocities in Guatemala had been published by various human rights organizations. Among the reports were, for example, Amnesty International's *Guatemala: A Government Program of Political Murder: The Amnesty Report* (1981); Americas Watch's "Human Rights in Guatemala: No Neutrals Allowed" (1982); Amnesty International's *Guatemala: Massive Extrajudicial Executions in Rural Areas under the Government of General Efrain Rios Montt* (1982); Oxfam's *Witness to Political Violence in Guatemala*; "Impact Audit 2" (Amnesty International, 1982); and Americas Watch's "Guatemala: A Nation of Prisoners" (Simon, 1984). Each of these reports delineate who the perpetrators were and where the atrocities were committed. The problem, of course, is that seemingly no one in the US government wanted to believe that the Guatemalan military and its para-military partners were responsible for most of the atrocities. Furthermore, few, if any, in the US government put any stock into such reports, as the organizations that issued them were perceived by US officials as biased against the Government of Guatemala and/or purportedly, according to various US government sources, heavily influenced by communist sources in Guatemala.

In February 1983, a CIA secret cable [addressee is redacted] asserts that Ríos Montt essentially gave his commanders carte blanche to deal with "the insurgents" as they saw fit. In part, the secret cable reads as follows:

1. [First three lines totally redacted] told Archivo personnel that president (Efrain Rios) Montt promised that no more guerillas will be released as happened in early February when three known guerrillas were set free. [Words redacted] The three were not set free. They were given temporary reprieves from death sentences by a stay of execution issued at the last minute by the supreme court. This is technically a writ of amparo, and the supreme court is still deciding after two weeks of legal maneuvers whether the persons convicted by the special courts will be freed as innocents or whether the sentences of execution by firing squad will be allowed to stand. Archivo personnel were very angry when these guerrillas were not executed. [Word(s) redacted]... that known guerillas will no longer be remanded to the special courts, but rather be dealt with by Archivo.

2. ...Rios Montt said that the increase in threats to his government and other subversive activities was a result of his government's lenient policy toward the application of justice [words redacted]... that Rios Montt implied that [word(s) redacted] was free to do his job as he saw fit.

3. [Words redacted] that after the late October 1982 meeting [Word(s) redacted] informed Archivos officers that they were free to apprehend, hold, interrogate, and dispose of suspected guerrillas as they saw fit. [Word(s) redacted] Although there is no specific informa-

tion available to link the Archivo to any extra-legal activities, there has been a steady increase of suspect, right-wing violence over the past few months. Kidnappings, particularly of students and educators, have increased in number and bodies are again appearing in ditches and in gullies showing the telltale signs of rightist hit squad executions similar to those common under the previous regime. (National Security Archive, n.d., doc. 23, pp. 2, 3)

It is striking that the author of this CIA secret memo actually uses the words "dispose of", which certainly suggests extermination. It is also important to recognize the fact that the author of the document does not say "those found guilty of" but rather that Ríos Montt purportedly asserted that his commanders were free to treat "*suspected* guerillas" (italics added) as they saw fit. In others words, he was giving his troops a green light to kill virtually anyone. Period.

In August 1983, the CIA's Directorate of Intelligence crafted a highly detailed intelligence assessment of Ríos Montt's regime ("Guatemala: Prospects for Political Moderation"). A particularly telling and disturbing section reads as follows:

[W]e believe that the present trend toward more moderate government is likely to continue during the next year or two—provided Rios Montt remains in power. The President has demonstrated a strong personal commitment to civilize Guatemala. He has adopted a counterinsurgency strategy that combines selective repression and civic action. He has taken some steps to reduce human rights abuse and integrate previously excluded social groups—such as Indians, peasant, and urban workers—into the political and economic mainstream;

[Three-quarters of a line redacted] human rights violations have decreased substantially. Although abuses remain, we judge that the climate of fear, the widespread indiscriminate brutality, and—more important—the hostility between peasants and the Army have diminished noticeably. (National Security Archive, n.d., doc 26, p. iv)

It is critical to seriously consider both the wording in this excerpt and what it insinuates in regard to the CIA's perspective vis-à-vis the situation in Guatemala. First, the DOC uses the term "civilize" in the phrase "demonstrated a strong commitment to civilize Guatemala." Essentially, the DOC is implying that the rebels, and by association their supporters, and in fact all Maya, if not all indigenous peoples, are uncivilized, wild, barbarous, brutish, uncultured, etc. And by extension, the DOC is also implying that the latter must be brought under control, and those that are carrying out that task (i.e., Ríos Montt and his soldiers) are (a) contributing to the betterment of society, (b) correct in pursuing such a course, and (c) doing the right—and honorable—thing. In fact, the use of the term "civilize" in this context is extremely ironic; the ones who were truly uncivilized, barbaric, brutish, uncontrolled, and savage were those carrying out the atrocities in their purported effort to civilize others. Indeed, it was Guatemalan government troops and their allied militia who were carrying out genocidal massacres against civilians (including infants, young children, pregnant woman, and the elderly). And they were the ones who were smashing the heads of babies against rocks, cutting fetuses out of the wombs of their mothers, burning children and women alive, mass raping females, torturing their victims, and on and on. (See, for example, Americas Watch, 1983; Burkhalter, 1985; Alexandrov, 2012.)

In this intelligence assessment, it is stated that Ríos Montt "combines selective repression and civic action." There was, as one has surely ascertained by now, absolutely nothing selective about the repression that Ríos Montt and his lackeys carried out. And as for civic action, the entire effort to "pacify" the indigenous groups by providing them with "new housing," "food," and "protection" was largely, if not wholly, a guise for leading them to turn themselves over to authorities so that they could be rounded up and relocated in one central area where they could be watched 24 hours a day and, "if need be," tortured into providing information about the rebels.

Tellingly, the following insights by *Frontline*'s María José Calderón (2011) virtually contradict what the DOC had reported regarding the so-called improved situation in Guatemala in 1983:

During [General Efraín Ríos Montt's] 17-month reign, the worst atrocities against the indigenous population occurred.... Despite the confirmation of massacres in Guatemalan villages across the country by anti-guerilla forces, in early 1983, a newly elected President Ronald Reagan overturned the arms embargo imposed on Guatemala by Carter in 1980. Reagan claimed Guatemala's human rights conditions were improving, and he authorized the sale of military hardware, including weapons and vehicles, to the country's government. *Meanwhile, a then-secret 1983 CIA cable noted a rise in "suspect right-wing violence."* (n.p.; italics added)

Concomitantly, even after Ríos Montt was overthrown in a coup d'état by the Guatemalan military, the mass murder of innocents by Guatemalan government forces continued unabated.

## A MASS OF OTHER DECLASSIFIED DOCUMENTS

Space precludes including even a short discussion of the treasure trove of other declassified documents available that various agencies and individuals within the US government crafted and disseminated in the early to mid-1980s about the massacres of the Maya in the Western Highlands of Guatemala. That said, other documents readers are likely to find informative and thought-provoking are the following, all from the *National Security Archive's Briefing Book No. 32: The Guatemalan Military: What the U.S. Files Reveal* (n.d.): a Department of State secret report, "Guatemala's Disappeared 1977–86" (March 28, 1986); a Department of State secret report, "Article Is Wrong to Report that Nothing Has Changed under Cerezo Presidency" (July 1986); a CIA secret cable, "The D-2 Conducts Human Rights Investigations" (November 1989); and a Department of State secret cable, "Stop Delivery of Military Assistance to Guatemala" (December 16, 1990).[94]

---

94 In 1995, articles in the US press reported that while "overt" US military aid had been stopped in December 1990, millions of dollars from secret CIA funds were funneled to the Guatemalan military in subsequent years. Such funding came to an end only upon becoming publicly known.

## CONCLUSION

The United States government's knowledge of the Guatemalan government's perpetration of atrocities (some as they were perpetrated, others shortly after they were carried out) against the Maya of the Western Highlands was largely common knowledge among many of the most powerful officials in the Reagan administration. A fair number of the now declassified cables and memoranda provide clear and indisputable evidence that many US government officials were more than a little blasé about the mass killing of the Maya and seemingly more concerned with preventing word from getting out that the US government not only knew about the mass killings but more often than not also stood idly by as they were being committed and, in certain cases, actually continued to provide Guatemala with military hardware despite knowing it would be used against the Maya population. When all is said and done, the United States government was not simply a bystander to the genocide perpetrated by the Government of Guatemala against the Maya but was, at least in certain instances and even if inadvertently, a facilitator of the mass killing.

# REFERENCES

Adams, R. (1988). "Conclusions: What Can We Know about the Harvest of Violence?" In R. Carmack (Ed.), *Harvest of Violence* (pp. 274–91). Norman: University of Oklahoma Press.

Alexandrov, N. (2012, March 13). "Guatemala, Ríos Montt and the SOA." *School of the Americas Watch.* Accessed at: www.soaw.org/category-table/3873-guatemala-rios-montt-and-the-soa

Alterman, E. (2013, June 19). "The Upside of Genocide." *Nation.* Accessed at: www.thenation.com/article/174885/upside-genocide

Americas Watch. (1983). "Creating a Desolation and Calling It Peace." New York: Author.

Amnesty International. (1981). *Guatemala: A Government Program of Political Murder: The Amnesty Report.* New York: Author.

Amnesty International. (1982). *Guatemala: Massive Extrajudicial Executions in Rural Areas under the Government of General Efrain Rios Montt.* London: Author.

Burkhalter, H. (1985). *Guatemala Revised. How the Reagan Administration Finds Improvements in Human Rights in Guatemala.* New York: Americas Watch.

Calderón, M.J. (2011). "Timeline: Guatemala's History of Violence." *Frontline.* Accessed at: www.pbs.org/frontlineworld/stories/guatemala704/history/timeline.html

Cohn, G., & Thompson, G. (1995, June 11). "Unearthed: Fatal Secrets When a Wave of Torture and Murder Staggered a Small U.S. Ally, Truth Was a Casualty." *Baltimore Sun*, n.p.

Comisión para el Esclarecimiento Histórico (Commission for Historical Clarification / CEH). (1999). *Guatemala—Memory of Silence: Report of the Commission for Historical Clarification*. Guatemala City: Author.

Doyle, K., & Osorio, C. (Eds.). (n.d.). *National Security Archive Electronic Briefing Book No. 11: U.S. Policy in Guatemala, 1966–1996*. Washington, DC: George Washington University. Accessed at: nsarchive.gwu.edu/NSAEBB/NSAEBB11/docs/

Grandin, G. (2013, May 21). "Guatemalan Slaughter Was Part of Reagan's Hardline." *New York Times*. Accessed at: https://www.nytimes.com/roomfordebate/2013/05/19/what-guilt-does-the-us-bear-in-guatemala/guatemalan-slaughter-was-part-of-reagans-hard-line?mcubz=0

Green, L. (1999). *Fear as a Way of Life: Mayan Widows in Rural Guatemala*. New York: Columbia University Press.

Hall, P.K. (1986). "Military Rule Threatens Guatemala's Highland Maya Indians." *Cultural Survival Quarterly, 10*(2), n.p. https://www.culturalsurvival.org/publications/cultural-survival-quarterly/military-rule-threatens-guatemalas-highland-maya-indians

Henry, J. (2003). *The Blood Bankers: Tales from the Global Underground Economy*. New York: Four Walls Eight Windows.

Human Rights Watch. (1982, November 23). "Human Rights in Guatemala: No Neutrals Allowed." Accessed at: https://www.hrw.org/report/1982/11/23/human-rights-guatemala/no-neutrals-allowed

Intelligence Oversight Board. (1996). *Report on the Guatemala Review: June 28, 1996*. Washington, DC: Author.

Jonas, S. (2013). "Guatemala: Acts of Genocide and Scorched-Earth Counterinsurgency War." In S. Totten & W.S. Parsons (Eds.), *Centuries of Genocide: Critical Essays and Eyewitness Accounts* (pp. 355–93). New York: Routledge.

Krueger, C., & Enge, K. (1985). *Security and Development Conditions in the Guatemalan Highlands*. Washington, DC: Washington Office on Latin America.

Manz, B. (2004). *Paradise in Ashes: A Guatemalan Journey of Courage, Terror, and Hope*. Berkeley: University of California Press.

National Security Archive. (n.d.). *National Security Archive Electronic Briefing Book No. 32: The Guatemala Military: What the U.S. Files Reveal* (vol. 2). Washington, DC: George Washington University. Accessed at: http://nsarchive2.gwu.edu//NSAEBB/NSAEBB32/vol2.html

National Security Archive. (1999). *National Security Archive Electronic Briefing Book No. 15: Guatemalan Death Squad Dossier*. Washington, DC: George Washington University. Accessed at: http://nsarchive2.gwu.edu/NSAEBB/NSAEBB15/

Neier, A. (2013, June 20). "Guatemala: Will Justice Be Done?" *New York Review of Books*. Accessed at: http://www.nybooks.com/articles/2013/06/20/guatemala-will-justice-be-done/

Parry, R. (2005, January 11). "History of Guatemala's Death Squads." Accessed at: https://consortiumnews.com/2005/011005.html

Parry, R. (2013, February 21). "How Reagan Promoted Genocide." Accessed at: https://consortiumnews.com/2013/02/21/how-reagan-promoted-genocide-2/

Recuperación de la Memoria Histórica. (1998). *Guatemala: Nunca Más* (*Guatemala Never Again*) Guatemala City: Oficina de Derechos Humanos del Arzobispado de Guatemala.

Salazar, E.M. (2014). *Global Coloniality of Power in Guatemala: Racism, Genocide, Citizenship*. Lanham, MD: Lexington Books.

Sanford, V. (2003). *Buried Secrets: Truth and Human Rights in Guatemala*. New York: Palgrave/
Macmillan.

Schirmer, J. (1998). *The Guatemalan Military Project: Violence Called Democracy*. Philadelphia:
University of Pennsylvania Press.

Simon, J.-M. (1984, January 1). "Guatemala: A Nation of Prisoners." *Americas Watch Report*.
Accessed at: https://papers.ssrn.com/sol3/papers.cfm?abstract_id=2334200

Streeter, S.M. (2013). "Guatemala." In A. McPherson (Ed.), *Encyclopedia of U.S. Military
Interventions in Latin America* (pp. 251–54). Santa Barbara, CA: ABC-Clio.

# DOCUMENTS

## DOCUMENT 1

This document ("Guatemala: What Next?") provides unique insights into the United States' wishy-washy, wait-and-see position in relation to the Guatemalan government's scorched earth policies against the Maya people of the Guatemalan Highlands. More specifically, this declassified document, which is dated October 5, 1981, is a memo (from Mr. Robert L. Jacobs, an official with the US State Department's Bureau of Human Rights and Humanitarian Affairs to Mr. Luigi L. Einaudi, director of US Policy Planning for Inter-American Affairs) about US Ambassador to Guatemala Frederic L. Chapin's assessment of an attempt by US General Vernon Walters to convince Guatemalan President Lucas that his regime's continued repression of the Maya people would inflame, not cool, the upheaval in the Guatemalan Highlands. Chapin asserts that continued repression of the Maya people by Lucas's regime would not only likely strengthen the rebels' resolve but also help them to attract more individuals to their cause. At the same time, the memo notes that Guatemalan President Lucas is intent on continuing the repression of the rebellion because he perceives it as the Guatemalan government's only means of survival. Furthermore, it is duly noted that Lucas intends to pursue his current policies whether the United States supports his efforts or not.

Tellingly, Jacobs clearly delineates the Guatemalan government's intent in carrying out the repression against the Maya rebels: "the extermination of the guerillas, their supporters, and their sympathizers." Essentially, he is indicating that anyone and everyone who is Maya and even suspected of being friendly with the rebels and/or perceives the rebels' cause as legitimate is not only fair game but will be killed.

Ultimately, Jacobs asserts that while the US government is essentially against supporting the Guatemalan government's ongoing repressive measures, and thus ought to distance itself from the actions of the GOG, what is really needed to make a final decision is an assessment as to whether the rebels represent a real threat to the survival of the current Guatemalan regime or not. Then and only then, he argues, can the United States make a sound judgment as to whether it should "provide the GOG with [more] political and military support" or not. Simply stated, Jacobs is saying that if an assessment suggests that the rebels are as dangerous as Lucas says they are, then the United States should provide weapons and other support for the Guatemalan government, no matter its intent (i.e., war crimes, crimes against humanity, or genocide). Jacobs might well argue that this is putting words into his mouth, but how else can the following be construed?: "If there is no proximate threat—that is the guerillas do not represent a military threat to the survival of the present Guatemala regime over the next 12 months—then it would seem that we can await either the success or failure of the GOG's repressive policies [i.e., "the extermination of the guerillas, their supporters, and their sympathizers"]. The nature of military threat posed by the guerillas can best be assessed by the intelligence community. Before deciding upon any next step in Guatemala we ought, therefore, undertake such an intelligence assessment."

**DEPARTMENT OF STATE**
**Washington, D.C. 20570**

SECRET

MEMORANDUM                                             October 5, 1981

TO:          ARA/PPC - Mr. Einaudi

FROM:        HA/HR - Robert L. Jacobs
SUBJECT:     Guatemala: What Next?
REFERENCE:   Guatemala 6366

I read with keen interest Ambassador Chapin's assessment of
General Walters recent visit to Guatemala (reftel). In essence
Ambassador Chapin concludes that President Lucas is not going to
address our human rights concerns, that we must recognize this
fact, and that we must now decide whether "national security
considerations" require that we nevertheless go ahead with
security assistance.

The following observations and conclusions are predicated
upon the implicit assumption that those around General Lucas --
if not General Lucas himself -- are at least "amorally rational"
-- that is, their fundamental objective is their survival and they
will do nothing which they know will result in their self-
destruction.

In conversation with General Walters, President Lucas made clear
that his government will continue as before -- that the repression
will continue. He reiterated his belief that the repression is working
and that the guerilla threat will be successfully routed. He prefers
U.S. assistance in this effort but believes that he can succeed with
or without U.S. help.

General Walters efforts to persuade President Lucas that the
repression will only spread the guerilla contagion were evidently
unsuccessful.

Historically, of course, we cannot argue that repression always
"fails" nor can Lucas argue that it always "succeeds". Recent
history is replete with examples where repression has been

"successful" in exorcising guerilla threats to a regime's survival.
Argentina and Uruguay are both recent examples which come to mind.
Indeed in Guatemala during the late 1960's and early 1970's a policy
of repression succeeded in routing the guerilla threat to the then
existing regime. However, there are also contemporary examples
where repression "failed" -- Greece under Col. Papadopalous, Iran
under the Shah, Nicaragua under Somoza, and Venezuela under Perez-
Jimenez.

The point is the rather obvious one that only in time will we and
the Guatemalans know whether President Lucas is correct in his
conviction that repression will work once again in Guatemala. If he
is right and the policy of repression is succeeding and will result
in the extermination of the guerillas, their supporters, and their
sympathizers there is no need for the U.S. to implicate itself in
the repression by supplying the GOG with security assistance. We
did not provide such assistance to Argentina in waging its "dirty
war" against the guerillas in that country. Now that that "war" has
been concluded, we are endeavoring to re-establish more normal
relations with Argentina. It would seem that the Argentina
experience is relevant to Guatemala. Having failed in our efforts
to dissuade the GOG from its policy of repression we ought to
distance ourselves from the GOG and not involve ourselves in
Guatemala's "dirty war". If the repression does work and the
guerillas, their supporters and sympathizers are neutralized, we
can in the aftermath of the repression work to restore normal
relations with the successors to President Lucas.

Our conviction that repression will not contain the guerilla
threat but only exacerbate and compound it, will likewise only
become evident over time. At such time as the failure of repression
to contain and eradicate the guerilla threat becomes evident,
demands for a change in policy within the GOG -- and the Army in

particular -- should emerge. At such a juncture the crisis in
relations between Guatemala and ourselves will have politically
"matured" in the sense that it will then be ripe for a successful
U.S. diplomatic initiative. The GOG under internal pressure will
have no choice but to seek political and military assistance from
the U.S. more or less on our terms.

## CONCLUSIONS:

Whether President Lucas is right or wrong in his conviction
that repression will succeed in neutralizing the guerillas,
their supporters and sympathizers, the U.S. posture ought remain
one of distancing itself from the GOG. If Lucas is right and the
GOG can successfully "go it alone" in its policy of repression,
there is no need for the U.S. to provide the GOG with redundant
political and military support.  The provisioning of such
assistance would needlessly render us a complicit party in the
repression. If we are correct in our conviction that the repression
will not succeed and will only exacerbate and compound the guerilla
threat, then we ought to distance ourselves from the GOG until such
time as it arrives at this realization and is prepared to address
our human rights concerns in return for renewed U.S. political and
military support.

The remaining question is whether we indeed have the time to
await either the success or failure of the GOG's present repressive
politics. The answer to that question depends upon an assessment of
whether the guerillas represent a proximate, intermediate, or long-
range threat to the GOG. If there is no proximate threat -- that is
the guerillas do not represent a military threat to the survival of
the present Guatemalan regime over the next 12 months -- then it
would seem that we can await either the success or failure of the
GOG's repressive policies. The nature of military threat posed by
the guerillas can best be assessed by the intelligence community.

Before deciding upon any next step in Guatemala we ought, therefore, undertake such an intelligence assessment.

SECRET

**Source:** US State Department. (1981, October 5). "Memorandum: Guatemala: What Next?" In K. Doyle & C. Osorios (Eds.), *National Security Archive Electronic Briefing Book No. 11: U.S. Policy in Guatemala, 1966-1996* (doc. 13). Washington, DC: George Washington University. Accessed at: http://nsarchive2. gwu.edu/NSAEBB/NSAEBB11/docs/doc13.pdf

## DOCUMENT 2

This document is a secret cable sent by the CIA on February 1982 to an unknown individual (or set of individuals). Its subject is the Guatemalan army's ongoing counterinsurgency operations throughout the Ixil Triangle in El Quiché against the Guerilla Army of the Poor. For whatever reason, when the US government agreed to declassify this document, it redacted the name (or names) of the recipient(s).

Tellingly, a vast portion of the document was blacked out (redacted) by the CIA before it was declassified and released. That, of course, raises a host of questions as to what exactly was redacted and why. Would revealing the information have placed certain individuals in harm's way even some 16 years after the crafting of the memo? Would the information reveal untoward information about the CIA, and thus the US government's, position/ actions? No one, except those who redacted the information, knows; and thus, in the end, such speculation is fruitless.

The information that has not been redacted is basically informational in nature, and in that regard addresses such issues as the following: the fact that the aim of the operation was to destroy all towns and villages and to kill "all Indians" suspected of collaborating, cooperating and/or sympathizing with the Guerilla Army of the Poor; and the army's belief that since the entire indigenous population of Ixil supported the guerrillas, it had "created a situation in which the army [could] be expected to give no quarter to combatants and non-combatants alike."

The author of the memo also asserts that "civilians in the area who agree to collaborate with the army and who seek army protection are to be well treated and cared for in refugee camps for the duration of the operation." What it does not comment on is that those areas to which civilians were taken were essentially concentration or prison camps where the people were closely watched, underfed, and, in fact, generally ill-treated.

Feb 82

1. IN MID-FEBRUARY 1982 THE GUATEMALAN ARMY REINFORCED ITS EXISTING FORCE IN THE CENTRAL EL QUICHE DEPARTMENT AND LAUNCHED A SWEEP OPERATION INTO THE IXIL TRIANGLE. THE COMMANDING OFFICERS OF THE UNITS INVOLVED HAVE BEEN INSTRUCTED TO DESTROY ALL TOWNS AND VILLAGES WHICH ARE COOPERATING WITH THE GUERRILLA ARMY OF THE POOR (EGP) AND ELIMINATE ALL SOURCES OF RESISTANCE. CIVILIANS IN THE AREA WHO AGREE TO COLLABORATE WITH THE ARMY

AND WHO SEEK ARMY PROTECTION ARE TO BE WELL TREATED AND CARED
FOR IN REFUGEE CAMPS FOR THE DURATION OF THE OPERATION. ███████

███████████████████████████████████████████████████████████████

███████████████████████████████████████████████████████████████

███████████████████████████████████████████████████████████████

███████████████████████████████████████████████████████████████

███████████████████████████████████████████████████████████████

███████████████████████████████████████████████████████████████

███████████████████████████████████████████████████████████████

2. THE ARMY INITIALLY PLANNED TO ASSIGN THREE FULL
BATTALIONS (THREE COMPANIES EACH) TO THE IXIL TRIANGLE FOR THE
SWEEP OPERATION, BUT HAS ENCOUNTERED PROBLEMS IN FORMING THREE
NEW BATTALIONS AND HAS HAD TO MOVE COMBAT UNITS FROM OTHER
AREAS INTO EL QUICHE.

███████████████████████████████████████████████████████████████

███████████████████████████████████████████████████████████████

███████████ THERE ARE TWO INFANTRY BATTALIONS AND ONE
ADDITIONAL COMPANY OF AIRBORNE TROOPS PRESENTLY INVOLVED IN
THE SWEEP, AND TWO ADDITIONAL COMPANIES ARE EXPECTED TO ARRIVE
IN THE AREA WITHIN THE NEXT FEW DAYS. THE MAJORITY OF THE UNITS
PRESENTLY OPERATING IN THE IXIL TRIANGLE ARE FROM THE MARISCAL
ZAVALA BRIGADE, HEAD-QUARTERED IN GUATEMALA CITY.

3. SINCE THE OPERATION BEGAN, SEVERAL VILLAGES HAVE BEEN
BURNED TO THE GROUND, AND A LARGE NUMBER OF GUERRILLAS AND
COLLABORATORS HAVE BEEN KILLED. ███ COMMENT: WHEN AN ARMY
PATROL MEETS RESISTANCE AND TAKES FIRE FROM A TOWN OR VILLAGE IT
IS ASSUMED THAT THE ENTIRE TOWN IS HOSTILE AND IT IS
SUBSEQUENTLY DESTROYED. THE ARMY HAS FOUND THAT MOST OF THE
VILLAGES HAVE BEEN ABANDONED BEFORE THE MILITARY FORCES ARRIVE.
AN EMPTY VILLAGE IS ASSUMED TO HAVE BEEN SUPPORTING THE EGP, AND
IT IS DESTROYED. THERE ARE HUNDREDS, POSSIBLY THOUSANDS, OF
REFUGEES IN THE HILLS WITH NO HOMES TO RETURN TO. THE EGP

APPARENTLY CAN NOT PROTECT AND FEED SUCH LARGE NUMBERS AND THE

████████████████████████████████████████████████

████████████████████████████████████████████████

████████████████████████████████████████████████

████████████████████████████████████████████████

REFUGEES, MAINLY IXIL INDIAN PEASANTS, ARE MAKING CONTACT WITH THE ARMY AND OFFERING TO COLLABORATE IN EXCHANGE FOR FOOD AND SHELTER.

   4. THE ARMY HIGH COMMAND IS HIGHLY PLEASED WITH THE INITIAL RESULTS OF THE SWEEP OPERATION, AND BELIEVES THAT IT WILL BE SUCCESSFUL IN DESTROYING THE MAJOR EGP SUPPORT AREA AND WILL BE ABLE TO DRIVE THE EGP OUT OF THE IXIL TRIANGLE. INDIANS WHO HAVE HISTORICALLY BEEN HOSTILE TO THE ARMY ARE NO [SIC] COLLABORATING TO THE EXTENT THAT THE ARMY HAS SUCCESSFULLY FORMED A SELF-DEFENSE FORCE OF IXIL INDIANS IN THE TOWN OF SAN JUAN COTZAL TO PROTECT THE TOWN AGAINST ATTACKS BY THE EGP. THE ARMY HAS YET TO ENCOUNTER ANY MAJOR GUERRILLA FORCE IN THE AREA. ITS SUCCESSES TO DATE APPEAR TO BE LIMITED TO THE DESTRUCTION OF SEVERAL "EGP-CONTROLLED-TOWNS" AND THE KILLING OF INDIAN COLLABORATORS AND SYMPATHIZERS.███ COMMENT: THE WELL DOCUMENTED BELIEF BY THE ARMY THAT THE ENTIRE IXIL INDIAN POPULATION IS PRO-EGP HAS CREATED A SITUATION IN WHICH THE ARMY CAN BE EXPECTED TO GIVE NO QUARTER TO COMBATANTS AND NON-COMBATANTS ALIKE. IT IS CLEAR THAT THE EGP CAN NOT FACE THE ARMY WHEN IT OPERATES IN LARGE UNIT STRENGTH. IT IS ENCOURAGING TO NOTE THAT THE ARMY IS TREATING WELL THOSE INDIANS WHO SEEK ITS PROTECTION AND SUCCOR. IT REMAINS TO BE DETERMINED, HOWEVER, HOW LOYAL THE IXIL INDIANS WILL REMAIN ONCE THE ARMY COMPLETES ITS SWEEP AND MOVES ON TO ANOTHER AREA.

                    SECRET

                    DENIED IN FULL


**[The entire page of print has been blacked out]**

**Source:** CIA. (1982, February). "Cable, Counterinsurgency Operations in El Quiche." In *National Security Archive Electronic Briefing Book No. 11* (doc. 14). Washington, DC: George Washington University.

## DOCUMENT 3

This document, dated October 21, 1982, is a report issued by the American Embassy in Guatemala to the US Secretary of State and the US embassies in the rest of Central America (i.e., Belize, Nicaragua, Mexico, Panama, Costa Rica, El Salvador, and Honduras) in regard to the US embassy's purported attempt in Guatemala to verify alleged massacres in Huehuetenango.

The information presented herein would be laughable were it not so tragic and either so ill-informed or purposely misleading vis-à-vis the general attitude/position and actions of the Guatemalan army. Basically, the report asserts that three officials with the US embassy in Guatemala planned to investigate the areas where alleged large-scale massacres had been carried out by the Guatemalan army against the villages of Finca San Francisco and Petenac. It goes on to state that inclement weather prevented the three officers from reaching the villages and also "notes the helpful and open attitude of the Guatemalan army personnel assisting in the effort," concluding that the "army is completely up front about allowing us to check alleged massacre sites and to speak to whomever we wish."

It is worth noting that, many years later, one of the "alleged" massacres (the San Francisco Massacre of July 18, 1982) served as one of the "illustrative human rights cases" examined by the CEH. Essentially, the commission concluded that the San Francisco massacre constituted a prime example of the sort of atrocities the Guatemalan army was perpetrating against the Maya population in Guatemala at that particular period of time.

**CONFIDENTIAL**

```
CONFIDENTIAL
PAGE 01        GUATEM    07935    01 OF 02   212146Z
ACTION ARA- 16
```

INFO   OCT-00   COPY-01 ADS-00   AID-07   INR-10   SS-10    CIAE-00
       DODE-00  H-01    IO-15    NSCE-00 NSAE-00 SSO-00   SY-06
       HA-08    L-03    PM-09    PA-01    MCT-02   INRE-00  SAL-01
       RP-10    SYE-00  USIE-00 SP-02    SR-04    SPRS-01  /107 W
       _ _ _ _ _ _ _ _ _ _ _ _ _ _ _ _ _ _   007447 212221Z /62


O 212102Z OCT 82
FM AMEMBASSY GUATEMALA
TO SECSTATE WASHDC    IMMEDIATE 1560
INFO AMEMBASSY BELIZE
AMEMBASSY MANAGUA
AMEMBASSY MEXICO
AMEMBASSY PANAMA
AMEMBASSY SAN JOSE
AMEMBASSY SAN SALVADOR
AMEMBASSY TEGUCIGALPA
USCINCSO QUARRY HTS PN


C O N F I D E N T I A L -- SECTION 01 OF 02  GUATEMALA 07935


E.O. 12356:   DECL:    10/21/88
TAGS: PINS, PINR, SHUM, GT
SUBJECT: (C) EMBASSY ATTEMPT TO VERIFY ALLEGED
         MASSACRES IN HUEHUETENANGO


REFS: (A) GUATEMALA 7790
      (B) GUATEMALA 7741


1. (C - ENTIRE TEXT)


2. SUMMARY: THREE MISSION OFFICERS VISITED THE DEPARTMENT OF
HUEHUETENANGO BY AIR ON OCTOBER 20 IN AN ATTEMPT TO CHECK THE
VILLAGES OF FINCA SAN FRANCISCO AND PETANAC, SITES OF ALLEGED

LARGE SCALE MASSACRES PURPORTEDLY CARRIED OUT BY THE
GUATEMALAN ARMY. BAD WEATHER FORCED US TO TURN BACK FROM THE
HIGHEST ELEVATIONS OF NORTHERN HUEHUETENANGO; WE WERE UNABLE
TO REACH EITHER VILLAGE. EMBOFF DID, HOWEVER, REACH THE
CONCLUSION THAT THE ARMY IS COMPLETELY UP FRONT ABOUT ALLOWING
US TO CHECK ALLEGED MASSACRE SITES AND TO SPEAK WITH WHOMEVER
WE WISH.    END SUMMARY.

3. THE PURPOSE OF THIS VISIT WAS TO CHECK FIRST-HAND TWO SITES OF
ALLEGED GOG MASSACRES. REF B, PARA 14, OUTLINED THE BASIC FACTS OF
BOTH CASES: PETANAC, WHERE THE ARMY IS SUPPOSED TO HAVE KILLED 89
PEOPLE ON JULY 14; AND FINCA SAN FRANCISCO (ACTUALLY A SMALL
VILLAGE), WHERE THE ARMY ALLEGEDLY SLAUGHTERED SOME 300 PEOPLE ON
JULY 18. BOTH VILLAGES ARE LOCATED IN THE MUNICIPALITY OF SAN MATEO
IXTATAN. THE ARMY HAS DENIED THAT EITHER INCIDENT TOOK PLACE.

4. WE FLEW TO THE ARMY BASE AT HUEHUETENANGO PROPER ON OCTOBER
20. REF A REPORTED THE BASIC MILITARY, ECONOMIC AND REFUGEE
SITUATION IN HUEHUETENANGO. WE WERE AGAIN INFORMED THAT THE
MILITARY SITUATION IN HUEHUETENANGO IS FAIRLY WELL IN HAND.
NEVERTHELESS, THERE ARE AREAS THAT THE GOG DOES NOT CONTROL,
MOSTLY THE FRINGE AREAS OF THE DEPARTMENT THAT BORDER MEXICO.
GUERRILLAS APPARENTLY CROSS THE BORDER WITH SOME FREQUENCY,
SPREADING MAYHEM, PROPAGANDA AND TERROR. SAN FRANCISCO AND
PETANAC ARE IN SUCH AN AREA, FAR NORTH CENTRAL HUEHUETENANGO.
WE WERE TOLD THAT SAN FRANCISCO AND NEIGHBORING YALAMBOJOCH HAD
BEEN ABANDONED BECAUSE OF GUERRILLA ACTIVITY IN THE AREA.
PETANANC WAS SAID TO HAVE A FEW PEOPLE STILL LIVING
THERE, BUT NO CIVIL DEFENSE PATROL. WE WERE INVITED BY THE
MILITARY AUTHORITIES IN HUEHUETENANGO TO TRAVEL WHEREVER WE
MIGHT WISH, WITH THE CAVEAT THAT WE WERE ON OUR OWN IF WE TOUCHED
DOWN OUTSIDE OF THE AREA SECURED BY THE ARMY. SUITABLY ADVISED, WE
LEFT FOR SAN FRANCISCO. THE WEATHER WAS BAD WHEN WE LEFT AND WORSE

WHEN WE ATTEMPTED TO RISE YET HIGHER IN NORTHERN HUEHUETENANGO. THE PILOT ADVISED US HE COULD NOT REACH THE AREA IN SUCH WEATHER; WE RETURNED TO THE ARMY BASE IN HUEHUETENAGO PROPER.

5. COMMENT: ALTHOUGH WE WERE UNABLE TO REACH SAN FRANCISCO AND PETANAC, THERE ARE SEVERAL POINTS WORTH NOTING ABOUT THE ATTITUDE OF THE ARMY. EMBOFF KNOWS THAT THE RANKING OFFICERS AT THE HUEHUETENANGO BASE WERE PERFECTLY AWARE OF THE PURPOSE OF OUR VISIT. YET. THE COMMANDING, CIVIC ACTION, OPERATIONS AND INTELLIGENCE OFFICERS ALL OFFERED US THE RUN OF THE DEPARTMENT, AND THIS WITHOUT AN ARMY ESCORT. IF THESE OFFICERS HAVE SOMETHING TO HIDE, THEY DO NOT SEEM OVERLY CONCERNED ABOUT US FINDING IT. THEN AGAIN, IF SAN FRANCISCO IS NOW ABANDONED -- AND EMBOFF BELIEVES THAT IT IS -- WE WOULD HAVE FOUND NOTHING TO CONFIRM OR DENY THE MASSACRE REPORTS. PETANAC, HOWEVER, IS APPARENTLY STILL INHABITED. IF THE WEATHER WAS CLEAR, WE COULD HAVE EASILY REACHED EITHER VILLAGE. IN SUM, WE CANNOT AT THIS TIME CONFIRM OR DENY THE REPORTS OF MASSACRES IN THIS AREA; WE CAN, HOWEVER, AFFIRM THAT THE ARMY HAS NO OBJECTION TO OUR CRISSCROSSING THEIR COMBAT ZONES IN SEARCH OF INFORMATION WE DEEM NECESSARY TO POSSESS.

6. THIS TRIP, AT A COST OF APPROXIMATELY $1,600, HAS EXHAUSTED EMBASSY TRAVEL MONEY. WE SHOULD LIKE TO ATTEMPT TO CHECK THESE SITES AGAIN IN BETTER WEATHER. WE WILL NEED, HOWEVER, ADDITIONAL FUNDING FROM ARA.   END COMMENT. CHAPIN

CONFIDENTIAL

Source: US Embassy (Guatemala). (1982, October 21). "Report: Embassy Attempt to Verify Alleged Massacres in Huehuetenango." In K. Doyle & C. Osorios (Eds.), *National Security Archive Electronic Briefing Book No. 11: U.S. Policy in Guatemala, 1966-1996* (doc. 15). Washington, DC: George Washington University. Accessed at: http://nsarchive2.gwu.edu/NSAEBB/NSAEBB11/docs/doc15.pdf

## DOCUMENT 4

This document is entitled "Guatemala: Reports of Atrocity Mark Army Gains" and is dated circa late 1982. It is a secret report issued by the US Department of State. There is no indication on the report to whom it was sent. Essentially, the report provides the descriptions of various scorched earth campaigns carried out by the Government of Guatemala. The scorched earth campaigns were based on what was commonly referred to as the "rifles and beans" policy, which was initiated in July 1982 by President Efraín Ríos Montt. Essentially, the policy was one which alternated between the use of carrots—that is, the offer of food and medicine for those who were fighting with the rebels— and sticks—carrying out a state of siege, meaning a massive military offensive, and forcing "Indians" into Civil Defense Forces. The report also notes that the Guatemalan government had tightened its control over rural areas where the rebels had strongholds via the establishment of strategic hamlets for local communities. It is also reported that there had been widespread allegations of mayhem, massacres, and rape by the Guatemalan troops, but the report goes on to assert that "the Embassy does not as yet believe that there is sufficient evidence to link government troops to any of the reported massacres."

**PAGE ONE REDACTED**

SECRET/NOFORN/NOCONTRACT/ORCON

- 2 -

**2.** GUATEMALA: REPORTS OF ATROCITIES MARK ARMY GAINS

The Guatemalan military is making slow progress against insurgent forces amid widespread allegations of atrocities by the troops. Much of the government's progress can be credited to President Rios Montt's arming of the highland Indians, which could boomerang should they turn against the government in the future. The insurgents, faced with growing opposition from traditionally supportive or at least neutral Indian villages, have begun killing those perceived as not supporting their cause.

*      *      *

The "rifles and beans" policy initiated in July by Rios Montt is characterized by alternating the use of carrots -- such as the offer of amnesty for guerrillas -- and sticks -- the State of Siege, a heavy military offensive, and the organization of the Indians into Civil Defense Forces (CDFs).

Hoping to befriend the Indians, Rios has ordered the Army to distribute food to the "friendly" populace following operations. Similarly, a new code of conduct admonishes the largely illiterate soldiers not to steal "even a pin" from the civilian population. The CDF patrols reportedly have acquitted themselves well against insurgent forces, considering the fact that members are impressed into service and only a minority have firearms. In response, the guerrillas have massacred CDF members, their families, and others in villages believed to support the government.

The government has improved its control over rural areas through a strategic village program in which the rural populace is ordered to move to villages where the army has outposts. A scorched earth policy is then applied in the surrounding area. These tactics have been accompanied by widespread allegations that government troops are regularly guilty of massacres, rape, and mayhem. US Embassy investigations have found that some of these reports cannot be verified, that some of the atrocities reported are attributable to the guerrillas, and that still others cannot be attributed with accuracy to either side. The Embassy does not as yet believe that there is sufficient evidence to link government troops to any of the reported massacres.

Recent government successes have hurt two of the four insurgent groups. Nonetheless, the Cuban-trained Guerrilla Army of the Poor, the largest guerrilla organization, continues to harass the army regularly in much of the highland Departments (provinces) of Huehuetenango and El Quiche. This heavy fighting along the Mexican border in Huehuetenango Department has caused several thousand Guatemalans to seek safety in refugee camps in Mexico. The fighting has generated a number of reports of cross-border fire by Guatemalan troops and at least one report of an incursion into Mexican territory.

SECRET/NOFORN/NOCONTRACT/ORCON

Source: US State Department. (1982). "Report: Guatemala: Reports of Atrocities Mark Army Gains." In K. Doyle & C. Osorios (Eds.), *National Security Archive Electronic Briefing Book No. 11: U.S. Policy In Guatemala, 1966-1996* (doc. 17). Washington, DC: George Washington University. Accessed at: http://nsarchive2. gwu.edu/NSAEBB/NSAEBB11/docs/doc17.pdf

## DOCUMENT 5

This document is a secret cable that was issued by the CIA in February 1983. It deals with the fact that Guatemalan President Efraín Ríos Montt had given carte blanche to the Archivos (the nickname of a notorious intelligence unit within the Guatemalan government whose full name was the Presidential Security Directorate) to deal with the ongoing insurgency by the Maya rebels. (The Archivos formed part of what was known as the Presidential General Staff, which was essentially a large and powerful security organization under the direct command of the presidency. For decades it was known as the command center for political repression in Guatemala.) The name of the recipient of the document has been redacted. In fact, a fairly large amount of information has been redacted from the document, as well as the names of numerous individuals (each of the redactions is duly noted herein).

The cable reports, "There has been a recent steady increase of 'suspect right-wing violence,' with kidnappings—particularly of students and educators—increasing in number, and bodies again appearing in ditches and gullies, a practice that was associated with the previous regime. Since taking power in March 1982, [Guatemalan] President Ríos has experimented with new legal mechanisms for handling captured guerrillas and suspected subversives, but sources report that in October 1982, officers of the Archivos were told that 'known guerrillas will no longer be remanded to the special courts,' and that they [members of the Archivos] were free to 'apprehend, hold, interrogate and dispose of suspected guerrillas as they saw fit.'"

One word and one phrase in the above statement are of particular significance: "suspected" and "dispose of". First, the Archivos could basically pick up, interrogate, and then kill virtually anyone whom it suspected of being a guerrilla. In other words, no evidence of any sort was needed prior to the arrest, interrogation, or execution of an individual; mere suspicion was sufficient. Second, the phrase "dispose of" provides a chilling sense as to how the Guatemalan government perceived both known and suspected guerrillas: no better than garbage.

While the cable itself does not provide *any specific* information linking the Archivos to such actions, in a comment attached to the end of the cable, US Ambassador to Guatemala Frederic Chapin is said to be "firmly convinced" that the recent upsurge in violence had been ordered and directed by "armed services officers close to President Ríos Montt."

SECRET

FEBRUARY 1983

Text: 1. ████████████████████████████████████
████████████████████████████████████████████
████████████████████████████████████████████

TOLD [EL ARCHIVO GENERAL DE CENTRO AMERICA] PERSONNEL THAT
PRESIDENT EFRAIN ((RIOS)) MONTT PROMISED THAT NO MORE GUERRILLAS
WILL BE RELEASED AS HAPPENED IN EARLY FEBRUARY WHEN THREE KNOWN
GUERRILLAS WERE SET FREE. ████████████████████. COMMENT:
THE THREE WERE NOT SET FREE, THEY WERE GIVEN TEMPORARY
REPRIEVES FROM DEATH SENTENCES BY A STAY OF EXECUTION ISSUED AT
THE LAST MINUTE BY THE [GUATEMALAN] SUPREME COURT. THIS IS
TECHNICALLY A WRIT OF AMPARO[95], AND THE SUPREME COURT IS STILL
DECIDING AFTER TWO WEEKS OF LEGAL MANEUVERS WHETHER THE
PERSONS CONVICTED BY THE SPECIAL COURTS WILL BE FREED AS
INNOCENTS OR WHETHER THE SENTENCES OF EXECUTION BY FIRING SQUAD
WILL BE ALLOWED TO STAND). [EL ARCHIVO GENERAL DE CENTRO
AMERICA] PERSONNEL WERE VERY ANGRY WHEN THESE GUERRILLAS WERE
NOT EXECUTED. ████████████████ SAID THAT KNOWN GUERRILLAS
WILL NO LONGER BE REMANDED TO THE SPECIAL COURTS, BUT RATHER
WILL BE DEALT WITH BY [EL ARCHIVO GENERAL DE CENTRO AMERICA].

2. ████████████████████████████████████████
████████████████████████████████████████████

RIOS MONTT DISCUSSED A NUMBER OF INTELLIGENCE AND SECURITY SERVICE
ISSUES INCLUDING THE KIDNAPPING OF RIOS MONTT'S NEPHEW, JOSE MARIO
((RIOS)) MUNDI

---

95  "The writ of *amparo*, like the *habeas corpus*, may be invoked by any person who believes that
any of his/her rights, is being violated. However, one of the great progresses of the *amparo* in
Latin America is that it enables citizens to invoke the action for the violation of any right
protected either explicitly or implicitly by the Constitution or by any applicable international
treaties." From Gloria Orrego Hoyos (2013). "The *Amparo* Context in Latin American
Jurisdiction: An Approach to an Empowering Action." Hauser Global Law School Program.
Accessed at: www.nyulawglobal.org/globalex/Amparo.html

WHICH TOOK PLACE ON 12 OCTOBER 1982. AT THAT TIME, RIOS MONTT WAS VERY ANGRY ABOUT THE RECENT MURDERS OF A POLICE DETECTIVE AND MUNICIPAL INSPECTOR, THE KIDNAPPING OF HIS NEPHEW, AND THE RECENTLY UNCOVERED COUP PLOT LED BY NATIONAL LIBERATION MOVEMENT (MLN) LEADER LEONEL ((SISNIEGA)) [SIC] OTERO. ███████████ ███████████████████ RIOS MONTT SAID THAT THE INCREASE IN THREATS TO HIS GOVERNMENT AND OTHER SUBVERSIVE ACTIVITIES WAS A RESULT OF HIS GOVERNMENT'S LENIENT POLICY TOWARD THE APPLICATION OF JUSTICE ████████████████ THAT RIOS MONTT IMPLIED THAT ██████ █████████ WAS FREE TO DO HIS JOB AS HE SAW FIT.

3. ██████████████████████████████ THAT AFTER THE LATE OCTOBER 1982 MEETING ████████████████ INFORMED [EL ARCHIVO DE GENERAL DE CENTRO AMERICA] OFFICERS THAT THEY WERE FREE TO APPREHEND, HOLD, INTERROGATE, AND DISPOSE OF SUSPECTED GUERRILLAS AS THEY SAW FIT. █████████████ COMMENT: ALTHOUGH THERE IS NO SPECIFIC INFORMATION AVAILABLE TO LINK [EL ARCHIVO GENERAL DE CENTRO AMERICA] TO ANY EXTRA-LEGAL ACTIVITIES, THERE HAS BEEN A STEADY INCREASE OF SUSPECTED RIGHT-WING VIOLENCE OVER THE PAST FEW MONTHS. KIDNAPPINGS, PARTICULARLY OF STUDENTS AND EDUCATORS, HAVE INCREASED IN NUMBER AND IN BODIES ARE AGAIN APPEARING IN DITCHES AND IN GULLIES, SHOWING THE TELLTALE SIGNS OF RIGHTIST HIT SQUAD EXECUTIONS SIMILAR TO THOSE COMMON UNDER THE PREVIOUS REGIME.]

4. ██████████████████████████████████████ THAT [EL ARCHIVO GENERAL DE CENTRO AMERICA] HAS BEEN INVOLVED IN A NUMBER OF RURAL MILITARY OPERATIONS. IN THE MOST RECENT IN LATE JANUARY 1982, 18 [EL ARCHIVO GENERAL DE CENTRO AMERICA] PERSONNEL ACCOMPANIED BY AN ARMY LIEUTENANT PARTICIPATED IN AN OPERATION OUT OF PLAYA GRANDE. EL QUICHE [ILLEGIBLE] GUIDED BY TWO EX-SOLDIERS WHO LIVED IN THE TOWN, THE [EL ARCHIVO GENERAL DE CENTRO AMERICA] PERSONNEL DRESSED IN CIVILIAN CLOTHES,

SURROUNDED A TOWN NEAR CHICAMAN [ILLEGIBLE]. AFTER ASSUMING THEIR POSITIONS AROUND THE TOWN THEY PROCEEDED TO ATTACK WITH REGULAR ARMY TROOPS BACKING THEM UP. THE [EL ARCHIVO GENERAL DE CENTRO AMERICA] PERSONNEL KILLED 37 GUERRILLAS AND CAPTURED TWO OTHERS. ███████████████ COMMENT: ACCORDING TO A MILITARY PRESS RELEASE DATED 31 JANUARY, SOLDIERS FROM PLATA GRANDE DISCOVERED A GUERRILLA HIDEOUT IN THE TOWN OF CHINATZEJA (COORDINATES UNLOCATED). DURING THEIR ATTACK, THE MILITARY KILLED 17 GUERRILLAS AND CAPTURED OLIVE DRAB UNIFORMS, PROPAGANDA AND CLAYMORE MINES. NO FIREARMS WERE SEIZED IN THE ATTACK. IT IS PROBABLE THAT THE NEWS ARTICLE REFERS TO THE SAME ATTACK IN WHICH [EL ARCHIVO GENERAL DE CENTRO AMERICA] PERSONNEL PARTICIPATED.)

5. ███████████████ COMMENT: THE INABILITY OF THE GOG TO DEAL EFFECTIVELY WITH KNOWN TERRORISTS AND GUERRILLA CADRE THROUGH ITS REGULAR JUDICIAL SYTEM PROMPTED THE GOG TO CREATE COURTS OF SPECIAL JURISDICTION UNDER THE MINISTER OF DEFENSE. AS IT BECOMES INCREASINGLY EVIDENT THAT THE SPECIAL COURTS CAN NOT DISPENSE JUSTICE IN A MANNER ACCEPTABLE TO THE ARMY AND THE SECURITY SERVICES, THERE WILL BE INCREASED PRESSURE FROM ALL LEVELS TO BYPASS LEGAL RESTRAINT AND IMPLEMENT SUMMARY PUNISHMENT.)

6. (AMBASSADORS [SIC] COMMENT: I AM FIRMLY CONVINCED THAT THE VIOLENCE DESCRIBED IN PARAGRAPH THREE IS GOVERNMENT OF GUATEMALA ORDERED AND DIRECTED VIOLENCE AND NOT "RIGHT WING VIOLENCE" AND THAT THESE WERE NOT "RIGHTEST HIT SQUAD EXECUTIONS" BUT AGAIN EXECUTIONS ORDERED BY ARMED SERVICE OFFICERS CLOSE TO PRESIDENT RIOS MONTT.)

SECRET

Source: CIA. (1983, February). "Cable, Ríos Montt Gives Carte Blanche to Archivos to Deal with Insurgency." In *National Security Archive Electronic Briefing Book No. 32: The Guatemalan Military: What the U.S. Files Reveal* (vol. II, doc. 23). Washington, DC: George Washington University. Accessed at: http://nsarchive2.gwu.edu//NSAEBB/NSAEBB32/docs/doc23.pdf

## DOCUMENT 6

This document is a declassified confidential cable sent by the American Embassy in Guatemala on February 2, 1984, to the US State Department about recent kidnappings carried out in Guatemala. In the cable, US Ambassador to Guatemala Frederic Chapin provides graphic evidence of two recent kidnappings carried out in broad daylight in Guatemala City, the capital of Guatemala. Chapin essentially asserts that, based on the evidence he's collected, he believes that Guatemalan security forces were behind the disappearances and then goes on to address what he perceives such criminal actions mean in regard to US policy in Guatemala. In doing so, he states the following: "I pointed out the other day in San Salvador the conflict between the desire to incorporate Guatemala into an overall U.S. strategic concept for Central America and the horrible human rights realities in Guatemala. We must come to some resolution in policy terms. Either we can overlook the record and emphasize the strategic concept or we can pursue a higher moral path. We simply cannot flip flop back and forth between the two possible positions." In what sounds like frustration, Chapin calls the US government out on its wishy-washy policies toward Guatemala. While it certainly sounds as if Chapin favors the pursuit of "a higher moral path" in dealing with the ongoing human rights violations by the Guatemalan government, he does not advocate for it per se. The strategic concept that Chapin mentions is one wherein the United States would either ignore the human rights infractions by the Guatemalan government and/or continue to support the Guatemalan government by providing it with funding, weapons, and other material, and possibly training Guatemalan military troops, if not advisers. One is not exactly sure, as Chapin does not spell it out.

CONFIDENTIAL

PAGE 01        GUATEM 01154    01 OF 02   022226Z
ACTION SS-25


INFO   OCT-00 COPY-01    ADS-00       SSO-00        /026 W
                 --------------------------------127070 022251Z /62
O 022216Z FEB 84
FM AMEMBASSY GUATEMALA
TO SECSTATE WASHDC  IMMEDIATE  9568


C O N F I D E N T I A L   SECTION 01 OF 02      GUATEMALA

DEPARTMENT PLEASE PASS TO SECRETARY SHULTZ AND
ASSISTANT SECRETARY ARA MOTLEY FROM AMBASSADOR CHAPIN

E.O. 12356DECL: 2/2/90
TAGS: PGOV, PINS, GT, SHUM
SUBJECT: RECENT KIDNAPPINGS: SIGNS POINT TO
          GOVERNMENT SECURITY FORCES

REF: GUATEMALA 1155

(C) SUMMARY: THE CIRCUMSTANCES OF TWO RECENT GUATEMALA CITY
KIDNAPPINGS CLEARLY SUGGEST THEY WERE PERPETRATED BY
GOVERNMENT SECURITY FORCES. IN ONE CASE THE YOUNG VICTIM WAS

SEIZED BY AN ARMED GROUP IN TWO CARS FROM ONE OF THE CITY'S MAIN
SHOPPING CENTERS, WHILE NATIONAL POLICE STOOD IDLY BY. IN THE
SECOND, MORE FLAGRANT CASE, THE VICTIM WAS CARRIED OUT ON A
STRETCHER FROM A HOSPITAL BY TEN ARMED MEN WITH A BOTTLE OF
INTRAVENOUS FLUID STILL DRIPPING INTO HIS ARM. HE WAS IN THE
EMERGENCY ROOM ABOUT TO UNDERGO SURGERY FOR THE REMOVAL OF
BULLETS RECEIVED EARLIER IN THE DAY FROM AN ASSASSINATION
ATTEMPT. HE WAS THE ONE REMAINING MEMBER OF A FAMILY OF FOUR.
HIS MOTHER AND TWO SIBLINGS HAD PREVIOUSLY BEEN ABDUCTED FROM
THEIR HOME BY ARMED MEN OVER A YEAR AGO IN A CASE UNIVERSALLY
ATTRIBUTED TO GOVERNMENT SECURITY FORCES. HIS MOTHER WAS AN
EMPLOYEE OF THE NATIONAL UNIVERSITY OF SAN CARLOS, A SUSPECTED
HOTBED OF SUBVERSIVE ACTIVITY. THESE NEW SHOCKING ABDUCTIONS
INDICATE THAT THE GOG SECURITY FORCES WILL STRIKE WHENEVER
THERE IS A TARGET OF IMPORTANCE. THE SEPARATE MESSAGE ON
ABDUCTIONS IN HUEHUETENANGO INDICATES THAT THE GOG ARMY WILL DO
LIKEWISE. WE MUST COME TO SOME RESOLUTION IN POLICY TERMS.
EITHER WE CAN OVERLOOK THE RECORD AND EMPHASIZE THE STRATEGIC
CONCEPT OR WE CAN PURSUE A HIGHER MORAL PATH. WE SIMPLY CANNOT
FLIP FLOP BACK AND FORTH BETWEEN THE TWO POSSIBLE POSITIONS.
MUDDLING THROUGH WILL SIMPLY GO NOWHERE. END SUMMARY.

1. (U) TEN MEN ARMED WITH SUBMACHINE GUNS AND AUTOMATIC RIFLES
ENTERED THE ROOSEVELT EMERGENCY HOSPITAL IN GUATEMALA CITY ON
JANUARY 31 AND KIDNAPPED SERGIO VINICIO SAMAYOA MORALES, AGE
29. SAMAYOA WAS SEIZED AS HE WAS ABOUT TO BE TAKEN INTO SURGERY
TWO HOURS AFTER BEING ADMITTED TO THE HOSPITAL SUFFERING FROM
BULLET WOUNDS. HE WAS TAKEN AWAY IN A WHITE PANEL TRUCK BY THE
KIDNAPPERS.

2. (U) SAMAYOA WAS WOUNDED BY TWO ARMED MEN ABOUT 4:30 IN THE
AFTERNOON OF JANUARY 31, ACCORDING TO NEWSPAPER REPORTS, AT HIS
PLACE OF WORK. HE WAS SHOT FIVE TIMES BY HIS ATTACKERS. HOWEVER,

THEY FAILED TO KILL HIM AND AFTER THEY FLED HE WAS TAKEN BY AMBULANCE TO THE EMERGENCY HOSPITAL IN GRAVE CONDITION.

3. (U) TWO HOURS LATER, A GROUP OF ARMED MEN ENTERED THE HOSPITAL'S EMERGENCY WARD, DISARMED THE TWO POLICEMEN ON DUTY AND QUESTIONED THE DUTY PHYSICIAN ABOUT THE WHEREABOUTS OF THE GUNSHOT VICTIM. AFTER HE WAS LOCATED IN THE PREP ROOM FOR SURGERY, HE WAS TAKEN OUT TO THE WAITING VEHICLES, ON A STRETCHER ALONG WITH THE BOTTLE OF INTRAVENOUS FLUID WHICH WAS STILL DRIPPING INTO HIS ARM.

4. (U) THE SAMAYOA MORALES FAMILY HAS SUFFERED FROM SIMILAR VIOLENCE IN THE PAST. ON SEPTEMBER 10, 1982, SAMAYOA'S MOTHER AND TWO BROTHERS WERE KIDNAPPED BY ARMED MEN FROM THE FAMILY RESIDENCE. SERGIO SAMAYOA APPARENTLY ESCAPED ABDUCTION AT THAT TIME ONLY BECAUSE HE WAS NOT PRESENT AT THE TIME OF THE KIDNAPPING. MRS. GRACIELA MORALES DE SAMAYOA WORKED AT SAN CARLOS UNIVERISTY [SIC]. THE KIDNAPPINGS HAVE NEVER BEEN SOLVED, BUT GOVERNMENT SECURITY FORCES ARE BELIEVED TO BE RESPONSIBLE.

5. (C) ON FEBRUARY 1, 1984, HECTOR VILLAGRAN SALAZAR CAME TO THE EMBASSY TO REPORT THE JANUARY 27 ABDUCTION OF SON-IN-LAW JORGE MAURICIO GATICA PAZ. ACCORDING TO MR. VILLAGRAN, HIS DAUGHTER AND SON-IN-LAW WENT TO A LARGE SHOPPING CENTER TO DO SOME GROCERY SHOPPING ON JANUARY 27. MR. GATICA REMAINED IN THE CAR WITH THE DOG WHILE HIS WIFE WENT INTO THE SUPERMARKET. WHEN SHE CAME OUT OF THE STORE, CAR, HUSBAND AND DOG HAD DISAPPEARED. A WITNESS TOLD HER THAT HEAVILY ARMED MEN IN A WHITE PANEL TRUCK PULLED UP BEHIND HER CAR, FORCED HER HUSBAND INTO THE TRUCK, AND DEPARTED RAPIDLY IN BOTH VEHICLES. ALTHOUGH THERE WERE SEVERAL POLICEMEN IN THE PARKING LOT -- THE SHOPPING CENTER IS ONE OF THE LARGEST IN GUATEMALA CITY -- THEY DID NOT INTERVENE AND WOULD

NOT TELL THE WIFE ANYTHING. THE ABDUCTION TOOK PLACE AT AROUND
1730 HOURS.

6. (C) MR. VILLAGRAN -- A PROFESSIONAL ECONOMIST AND A MEMBER OF
THE GUATEMALAN EQUIVALENT OF OUR FEDERAL RESERVE BOARD -- WAS
IN A CONFERENCE WITH FINANCE MINISTER COL. LEONARDO FIGUEROA
VILLATE WHEN HIS WIFE CALLED HIM ABOUT THE KIDNAPPING. HE
IMMEDIATELY ASKED COLONEL FIGUEROA FOR ASSISTANCE. THE LATTER
CALLED DIRECTOR OF POLICE COL. HECTOR RAFAEL BOL DE LA CRUZ, WHO
ADVISED MR. VILLAGRAN TO FILE A COMPLAINT WITH THE POLICE; MR.
VILLAGRAN SUBSEQUENTLY FILED COMPLAINTS WITH THE NATIONAL
POLICE AND THE DIT (DEPARTMENT OF TECHNICAL INVESTIGATIONS). ON
SATURDAY, JAN 28, MR. VILLAGRAN CALLED FOREIGN MINISTER ANDRADE
AND ASKED FOR HIS PERSONAL INTERVENTION; THE FOREIGN MINISTER
PROMISED TO CALL ARMY OFFICIALS ON THE GENERAL STAFF. ON
JANUARY 30, MR. VILLAGRAN ASKED THE MINISTER OF THE ECONOMY TO
TAKE ACTION ON THE CASE. HE ALSO PROMISED TO HELP MR. VILLAGRAN.

7. (C) IN SPITE OF ALL THIS HIGH-LEVEL INTEREST IN THE
WHEREABOUTS OF MR. GATICA, HOWEVER, HIS DISAPPERANCE AND
PRESENT LOCATION REMAIN A MYSTERY. THE BLATANT NATURE OF THE
MODUS OPERANDI OF BOTH ABDUCTIONS POINTS TO GOVERNMENT
SECURITY FORCES AS THE PERPETRATORS. THE KIDNAPPING OF THE
GRAVELY WOUNDED SAMAYOA FROM THE HOSPITAL RECALLS SCENES FROM
"THE GODFATHER" BUT IN THE MOVIE, THE VICTIM SURVIVED.

8. AMBASSADOR'S COMMENTS: DESPITE THE FACT THAT THE ILL-
REPUTED ARCHIVOS HAVE BEEN STOOD DOWN AT LEAST TEMPORARILY,
THESE NEW SHOCKING ABDUCTIONS INDICATE THAT THE GOG SECURITY
FORCES WILL STRIKE WHENEVER THERE IS A TARGET OF IMPORTANCE. THE
SEPARATE MESSAGE ON ABDUCTIONS IN HUEHUETENANGO INDICATES THAT
THE GOG ARMY WILL DO LIKEWISE. I POINTED OUT THE OTHER DAY IN SAN
SALVADOR THE CONFLICT BETWEEN THE DESIRE TO INCORPORATE

GUATEMALA INTO AN OVERALL U.S. STRATEGIC CONCEPT FOR CENTRAL AMERICA AND THE HORRIBLE HUMAN RIGHTS REALITIES IN GUATEMELA. WE MUST COME TO SOME RESOLUTION IN POLICY TERMS. EITHER WE CAN OVERLOOK THE RECORD AND EMPHASIZE THE STRATEGIC CONCEPT OR WE CAN PURSUE A HIGHER MORAL PATH. WE SIMPLY CANNOT FLIP FLOP BACK AND FORTH BETWEEN THE TWO POSSIBLE POSITIONS. MUDDLING THROUGH WILL SIMPLY GO NOWHERE.

-

CHAPIN

NOTE BY OC/T: NOT PASSED ABOVE ADDRESSES.

CONFIDENTIAL

**SOURCE**: US Embassy (Guatemala). (1984, February 2). "Cable, Recent Kidnappings: Signs Point to Government Security Forces." In National Security Archive Electronic Briefing Book No. 15: Guatemalan Death Squad Dossier: Internal Military Log Reveals Fate of 183 "Disappeared" (doc. 4). Washington, DC: George Washington University. Accessed at: http://nsarchive2.gwu.edu/NSAEBB/NSAEBB15/docs/doc04.pdf

# CALCULATED AVOIDANCE: THE CLINTON ADMINISTRATION AND THE 100-DAY GENOCIDE IN RWANDA (1994)

Samuel Totten and Gerald Caplan

It is arguable that the fate of Rwanda's Tutsi in 1994 was sealed exactly six months earlier elsewhere in Africa. Though vastly outnumbered by Somali militia loyal to warlord Mohamed Farrah Aidid, on October 3 and 4 us troops launched a raid that went bad in Mogadishu, Somalia. Subsequently, 18 us soldiers were killed and 74 wounded (and some 800 to 1,000 Somalians were killed) as they and their fellow troops attempted to rescue the survivors and "secure and recover" the dead crew members of two Black Hawk helicopters that had been shot down during the mission to capture two of Aidid's top men. They were in the country as part of a UN mission, but this was an exclusively American operation.

The body of a dead American soldier, wearing only his undershorts, was dragged around Mogadishu behind a jeep. The incident was caught on video which was played relentlessly by CNN until a vast number of Americans had seen it. The humiliation of a us soldier within the larger humiliation of the failed mission and the 18 dead was intolerable to Americans.

Fear of a repeat of the events similar to those in Somalia shaped us policy for several years hence, with many commentators identifying the

Battle of Mogadishu as the key reason behind the US' failure to intervene in later conflicts such as the Rwandan Genocide in 1994. According to former United States Deputy Chief to the Mission in Somalia Walter Clarke, "The ghosts of Somalia continue to haunt US policy.... Our lack of response in Rwanda was a fear of getting involved in something like a Somalia all over again" (PBS 2001, n.p.).

Republican members of the US Congress had long been hostile to the United Nations and had repeatedly attempted to withhold US dues and peacekeeping fees owed to the UN. If they even knew, these Republicans never cared that the costly Black Hawk attack was solely a US, not a UN, initiative (Millwood, 1996, p. 36).

The following April, both the Republicans and Democrats in Congress were almost entirely indifferent to the actual situation in Rwanda. Indeed, both were ignorant about and uninterested in the country. In straightforward terms of national interest, America had nothing at stake in Rwanda. There were no conventional interests to be protected. Rwanda had no attractive natural resources. There were no powerful lobbyists knocking on politicians' doors on behalf of Rwanda's Tutsi. As a result, precious few American politicians gave two minutes' thought to Rwanda's plight, even at the peak of the genocide.

This situation was hardly unfamiliar. In an administration report on Rwanda in 1992 under US President Bill Clinton's predecessor, President George H.W. Bush, described US–Rwandan relations as "excellent," and stated that "there is no evidence of any systematic human rights abuses by the military or any other element of the government in Rwanda" (Human Rights Watch, 1994, p. 21). However, a series of anti-Tutsi pogroms had already led to escalating tensions in Kigali (the capital of Rwanda). In fact, Hutu extremists "directed massacres of hundreds of Tutsi in mid-October 1990 and in five other episodes before the 1994 genocide" (Des Forges, 1999, p. 4).

Soon after Clinton was inaugurated, James Woods, long-time deputy assistant secretary for African Affairs, was instructed by Clinton aides that neither Rwanda nor Burundi was of interest to the new administration.

"Look, if something happens in Rwanda-Burundi, we don't care.... US national interest is not involved.... Just make it go away." A few months later, after the Black Hawk fiasco, Woods realized that if Rwanda blew up, "we probably wouldn't react" (PBS, 1999b, n.p.).

In the end, American policy under Clinton remained essentially indifferent to Rwanda, much as it had been before. Tellingly, the United States demonstrated its new post–"Black Hawk Down" anti-interventionist inclination almost immediately after the tragedy in Somalia. The Somali debacle happened on October 3, 1993. By coincidence, the UN Security Council voted on a United Nations Assistance Mission in Rwanda (UNAMIR) only two days later. The US voted in favor of the mission, but half-heartedly, making sure the mandate was weak (a chapter VI or peacekeeping mandate versus a chapter VII or peace enforcement mandate) and that the US would not be asked to contribute any troops to the mission.

Soon after, work began within the administration on the development of a formal US peacekeeping doctrine, embodied in a presidential policy directive known as PDD-25, "Presidential Decision Directive: Clinton Administration Policy on Reforming Multilateral Peace Operations." This directive was not finalized for almost a year, but its thrust influenced US policy immediately. It included 16 factors that policymakers had to take into account before deciding whether to support peacekeeping initiatives. In effect, as US officials fully understood, the checklist ensured that only in the most remarkable circumstances would the US support and get involved in peacekeeping activities. The genocide in Rwanda was not considered remarkable enough, as the world soon learned.

The warnings issued by General Romeo Dallaire (the commander of UNAMIR) had no impact either. At the end of March 1994, with many in Kigali warning of dire if not catastrophic possibilities, UNAMIR's mandate was extended. But it was not strengthened. Nor were more reinforcements added, mostly due to the US' influence within the Security Council (Gourevitch, 1998, p. 50; Kuperman, 1998, n.p.). An immutable pattern had been set.

Once Rwandan President Juvénal Habyrimana's plane was shot down on April 6, 1994, and the killing began the following day, the American embassy in Kigali, like all other foreign missions, worried first about its own citizens in Rwanda. It began an evacuation of American officials over-land by car south to Burundi, but Washington also dispatched 300 Marines to Burundi. The Marines, however, were not to intervene to protect the victims of the genocide in Rwanda, but were on alert in case they were needed to assist in the evacuation of American expatriates. No Tutsi, nor even long-term local employees of the US embassy, were evacuated; a good number were soon murdered (Nkurinziza, 2015, n.p.).

Even once the genocide began, the US essentially indicated it had no national interest in Rwanda. This was a bipartisan position. The Republicans backed the Clinton administration's stance. "I don't think we have any national interest there," Robert Dole, a senior Republican politician, asserted on April 10. "The Americans are out of it, and as far as I'm con-cerned, that ought to be the end of it" (quoted in Elaine Sciolino, 1994, n.p.). By the time all the Americans and other foreigners had been evacuated, barely three days after the shooting down of Habyrimana's plane, some 20,000 Rwandans, all Tutsi or moderate Hutu, had already been killed.

Despite what President Clinton and other officials in his administration later claimed, it took little time for the Clinton administration to get a good sense of what was actually transpiring in Rwanda. In fact, one US govern-ment document after another produced by the Clinton administration during and about the 1994 genocide in Rwanda attests to that fact.

Early on the morning after the plane crash, 10 Belgian soldiers with UNAMIR were brutally murdered by Rwandan government troops. In response, Belgium abruptly withdrew its contingent from UNAMIR, a mor-tal blow to General Dallaire's capacity. Almost immediately, the Belgian government began lobbying for the complete removal of UNAMIR from Rwanda. However, Belgium did not want to withdraw alone, ignomini-ously; it wanted others to share the blame. US Secretary of State Warren Christopher agreed to back Belgian pleas for a full UN withdrawal.

US policy in the first weeks after the genocide may seem extraordinary today, but it was crystal clear and unambiguous then: no US military intervention, insistent demands for a withdrawal of all of Dallaire's forces, and no support for a new, more robust UN mission that would challenge the killers. Each of these positions is clearly delineated in declassified US documents.

Thanks to the US, Belgium now had the cover it needed. Led by Madeleine Albright, US ambassador to the UN, a compromise was negotiated, calling for UNAMIR's already derisory numbers to be dramatically reduced. General Dallaire was to be left with 270 men, although he maneuvered to keep 400. Albright later claimed that she privately fought her own administration on this matter, but there is little evidence of her doing so at the time. Be that as it may, exactly two weeks after the genocide began, with perhaps 100,000 already dead, the United States led the UN Security Council in seriously undermining UNAMIR's already minimal capacity to intervene (United Nations Independent Inquiry, 1999, p. 21).

For the next month, as the genocide was being systematically executed, the Security Council failed to bolster its mission to Rwanda, leaving countless more Tutsi to die than otherwise might have. The US, led by Ambassador Albright, played the key role in blocking more expeditious action by the Council (Des Forges, 1999, p. 618). Finally, on May 17, embarrassed by their own dereliction of duty, the Security Council authorized an expanded UNAMIR II to consist of 5,500 personnel (UN Security Council, 1994, pp. 1–2).

Even then, the US contrived to undermine the resolution. The Pentagon mysteriously required an additional seven weeks just to negotiate a contract for delivering armed personnel carriers to the field; ostensibly, it proved difficult to arrange appropriate financial terms for "maintenance and spare parts" (PBS, 1999a, n.p.). When the genocide ended in mid-July with the final Rwandan Patriotic Force victory, not a single new UN "blue helmet" had landed in Kigali.

This deadly and pathetic farce reflected the United States' determined non-engagement in the genocide. In fact, the US chose not to label events in Rwanda a genocide at all, though administration officials knew perfectly well that it was. The low point of this charade came at a press conference on June 10, 1994, when a spokesperson for the State Department, Christine Shelley, had the following exchange with reporters:

REPORTER: How would you describe the events taking place in Rwanda?

SHELLEY: Based on the evidence we have seen from observations on the ground, we have every reason to believe that acts of genocide have occurred in Rwanda.

REPORTER: How many "acts of genocide" does it take to make "genocide"?

SHELLEY: As you know, there is a legal definition of this. There has been a lot of discussion about how the definition applies under the definition of "genocide" contained in the 1948 Convention. If you're looking at that for your determination about genocide, clearly, not all of the killings that have taken place in Rwanda are killings to which you might apply that label. Some of the difficulties over actually arriving at a definition of "genocide" and formulations on genocide are the reasons why—particularly, in late May, the U.N. Human Rights Commission, with the very strong support by the United States, appointed a Special Rapporteur for Rwanda, specifically to compile the information on possible violations of human rights and on acts which constitute breaches of international humanitarian law and crimes against humanity, including acts of genocide. His preliminary report, which is due later this month, will provide the additional information about the human rights violations—the types, and presumably how they might be characterized—and that is something that we have to wait for. As to the distinctions between the words, we're trying to call. What we have seen so far, as best as we can, and based, again, on the evidence, we have every reason to believe that acts of genocide have occurred.

REPORTER: How many acts of genocide does it take to make genocide?

SHELLEY: Alan, that's just not a question that I'm in a position to answer.

REPORTER: Well, is it true that you have specific guidance not to use the word "genocide" in isolation but always to preface it with these words "acts of"?

SHELLEY: I have guidance which I try to use as best as I can. There are formulations that we are using that we are trying to be consistent of our use of. I don't have an absolute categorical prescription against something, but I have the definitions. I have phraseology which has been carefully examined and arrived at as best as we can apply to exactly the situation and the actions which have taken place.

REPORTER: Christine, I've noticed the wording from yesterday to today has changed somewhat. Yesterday it was "acts of genocide may have occurred," and now you're saying, "we believe they're likely to occur." Has there been a change from yesterday to today on our view of that situation?

SHELLEY: I don't know if there has been a change in our view. This is after careful examination by a lot of those who are involved in very careful tracking of this, including also the lawyers, because there are obligations which arise in connection with the use of the term...

REPORTER: You say genocide happens when certain acts happen, and you say that these acts have happened in Rwanda, so why can't you say that genocide has happened?

SHELLY: We had said consistently prior to that that we believed that acts of genocide may have occurred in Rwanda, and we strongly supported full investigation and documentation of those crimes against humanity with a view to being able to make not only the evaluation of itself but to be able to describe it as accurately as we can...

REPORTER: Christine, as a signatory to the convention, is the United States required to do anything once it has established that acts of genocide have occurred?

SHELLEY: The issue as to what obligations it might entail for the US Government, as you know, the US has strongly supported the introduction of a peacekeeping force in Rwanda as soon as possible to try to protect the individuals at risk and to assist in this supply of humanitarian assistance. The UN has commitments on the part of 10 nations to provide troops for this operation. The US is going to assist with that in financial, logistical and material support. We believe that this international force is the proper response to protect the individuals at risk. In addition to that, as we said, because of the facts of the situation, certainly the most recent ones that have come out, it's the reason why we are also pursuing this via the United Nations Rights Commission and the decision specifically to send the human rights officers to there to be able to do the investigations and the necessary documentation to evaluate the breaches of international law and crimes against humanity which includes the acts of genocide. (US State Department, 1994a)

Poor Shelley was merely following her instructions. This exchange has featured in various films about the genocide, both documentaries and otherwise, and leaves Shelley something close to a laughingstock. The enmity it engendered seemed misplaced.

According to Tony Marley, who was a political military adviser for the US State Department (1992–95), during a period when literally tens, and then hundreds of thousands of Tutsi and moderate Hutu were being savagely killed in Rwanda, the Clinton administration debated, via teleconferences, whether the massive amount of killing being perpetrated in Rwanda constituted genocide or not. In part, he stated the following after the fact:

> There were those, and I was among them, that took a much more pragmatic view: "Let's look at the dictionary definition of genocide and it either is or isn't genocide." And to separate the definition from the political decision of whether or not something was to be done. Those that wanted nothing done didn't want to even acknowledge the fact that it could be genocide because that would weaken their argument that nothing should be done. They didn't want to say it was genocide. When they knew it was, they first moved through this charade of referring to it as acts of genocide. People were aware it was genocide and then approached the issue more either in institutional interest, institutional bureaucratic interest terms or in U.S. national interest. But at least we did advance the argument, the crucial credible question of whether or not to do something. (PBS, 1999c)

During one of the aforementioned teleconferences, a Clinton administration official broached the issue as to whether there might be an averse impact for the Democrats in the congressional elections scheduled for later that year were the US government to acknowledge that genocide was taking place in Rwanda and then did nothing to staunch it. The official was proposing that such a concern should be factored into the consideration as to whether or not "genocide" should be used by the administration to describe the events unfolding in Rwanda (PBS, 1999c). During the entire three months of the genocide, President Bill Clinton never assembled his top policy advisers to discuss the killings. Similarly, National Security Adviser Anthony Lake never gathered the "principals" who were the cabinet-level members of the foreign policy team. Rwanda was never deemed an urgent priority. Ignoring it paid no political price; on the contrary, the editorial boards of major American newspapers actually discouraged US intervention during the genocide. Of course, like the administration, the papers lamented the killings, but they believed, as *The Washington Post* editorial of April 17, 1994, put it, "The United States has no recognizable national interest in taking a role, certainly not a leading role" (n.p.). Washington was, to say the least, not caught up in Rwanda.

But a few US officials were engaged. Seeing that no troops were forthcoming from the US or elsewhere, some considered other measures to minimize the suffering. General Dallaire pleaded with New York, and some Clinton officials agreed, that something had to be done to "neutralize" Radio-Télévision Libre des Mille Collines (RTLMC), the extremely popular and influential génocidaire-controlled hate radio station that was actively pushing the genocide forward.

How could the US prevent RTLM from broadcasting murderous instructions directly to the population? This question actually received high-level attention at the end of April when National Security Adviser Anthony Lake raised the matter with Secretary of Defense William Perry. Three possibilities seemed feasible. The United States could destroy the station's antenna. It could transmit "counter-broadcasts" urging perpetrators to stop the genocide. Or it could jam RTLM's incendiary broadcasts. Pentagon officials, however, found reasons to reject all the proposals. On May 5, Frank Wisner (1994), the undersecretary of defense for policy, prepared a memo (stamped "Confidential," but now declassified) for Sandy Berger, the deputy assistant to the president with the National Security Council, demonstrating the unwillingness of the US government to make even trivial financial sacrifices to diminish the killing:

We have looked at options to stop the broadcasts within the Pentagon, discussed them interagency and concluded jamming is an ineffective and expensive mechanism that will not accomplish the objective the N[ational] S[ecurity] C[ouncil] Advisor seeks.... (p. 1)

Pentagon planners understood perfectly well that stopping the genocide required a military solution. But of course neither they nor the White House wanted any part in such a solution. So the US opted for the worst of all possibilities: neither a military solution nor any other forms of intervention that would surely save some, and perhaps many, lives.

In fact, the US government did just about everything it could to avoid taking any action to attempt to halt the genocide and save people. And it came up with one justification after another for its inaction. The words and insights of Prudence Bushnell, who was US deputy assistant secretary of state for African Affairs during the genocide, speaks to those justifications:

I chaired these God-awful interagency videoconferences. We'd sit in this tiny airless room looking at four TV monitors—NSC [National Security Council], CIA, and two for DOD [Department of Defense]—and talk with clenched jaws about what could be done. I at least wanted the hate radio that was encouraging people to continue the genocide to be jammed....

The first thing I was told is that jamming is against international law. Then I was told it would be too expensive, then that DOD didn't have the planes, and finally, that all of the jamming equipment was being used in Haiti, one excuse after another. At one point, a JCS [Joint Chiefs of Staff] colleague leaned forward to admonish me: "Pru, radios don't kill people, people kill people...."

We had no interest in that country: "Look at what they did to Belgian peacekeepers." "It takes too long to put a peacekeeping operation together." "What would our exit strategy be?" "These things happen in

Africa." "We couldn't have stopped it." I could go on....(Association for Diplomatic Studies and Training, 2008, pp. 63–64, 68)

Nevertheless, the US was not finished with its betrayal of Rwanda. The Clinton administration had promised to provide armored support if African nations provided soldiers. But the Pentagon continued to stall. On May 19, the UN formally requested 50 US armored personnel carriers (APCs). On May 31, the United States agreed to send the APCs from Germany to Entebbe, Uganda, directly adjacent to Rwanda. But endless squabbles between the Pentagon and UN planners arose. Who would pay for the vehicles? Should they be tracked or wheeled? Would the UN buy them or simply lease them? And who would pay the shipping costs? The tragedy was that a single phone call demanding swift action by President Clinton would have instantly cleared up all these logistical questions.

Compounding the disputes was the fact that DOD regulations prevented the US army from preparing the vehicles for transport until contracts had been signed. The DOD demanded that it be reimbursed $15 million for shipping spare parts and equipment to and from Rwanda. In June the White House finally intervened. On June 19, a month after the UN request, the United States began transporting the APCs, but they were missing the radios and heavy machine guns that would be needed if UN troops came under fire (Gordon, 1994, p. 10). By the time the APCs arrived, the genocide was over, halted by Rwandan Patriotic Front forces under the command of Tutsi leader Paul Kagame.

## AN EXAMINATION OF DECLASSIFIED GOVERNMENT DOCUMENTS

Today, it is common knowledge that from the very beginning to the very end of the 1994 genocide in Rwanda (April 7 to July 4), the administration of President Bill Clinton did just about everything in its power to avoid (a) increasing the number of troops in the UN peacekeeping force already in Rwanda (UNAMIR), (b) supporting a change in the mandate of UNAMIR from a chapter VI (or peacekeeping force) to a chapter VII (or peace enforcement force), and (c) placing US troops on the ground in Rwanda. Ample proof of all the aforementioned situations is not only found in scores of declassified US government documents but in declassified documents originating at the UN issued by the governments of various nations across the globe (e.g., New Zealand, England, and France), and in statements to the press by Clinton administration spokespersons.

To date, hundreds of pages of US documents have been released, most due to Freedom of Information requests by the National Security Archive project based at George Washington University in Washington, DC. In 2014 alone, the National Security Archive and the United States Holocaust Memorial Museum worked together to gain the release of 300 previously secret US government cables dealing with the 1994 genocide in Rwanda. Remarkably, to date, well over 20,000 declassified US, UN, French, and Belgian cables about the Rwandan genocide are now available for examination and use by researchers (students and professionals alike).

Speaking about the newly released documents (all 300 of which are available online), Tom Blanton of the National Security Archive asserted that "it's clear, in hindsight, that the pullout of peacekeeping was the green light for genocide" (quoted in Landler, 2014, p. A11). As Landler (2014) duly notes in his *New York Times* article "Declassified U.N. Cables Reveal Turning Point in Rwanda Crisis of 1994," "On April 12, 1994, six days after a plane carrying Rwanda's president was shot down, setting off a wave of killings, Madeleine K. Albright, the American ambassador to the United Nations at the time, sent a cable to the State Department proposing that the United States take the lead in pushing to withdraw most of the United Nations peacekeeping force operating there" (p. A11). While the aforementioned 300 secret cables provide invaluable insights and evidence into how the Clinton administration dealt with the genocide, they do not provide the entire story. In fact, "one of the missing pieces in the newly declassified trove of documents, researchers said, are roughly 100 internal White House emails on Rwanda, which would shed light on the marching orders Ms. Albright was getting from the White House" (Landler, 2014, p. A11).

What follows is an analysis of several declassified documents that provide unique insights into how the Clinton administration reacted to the ever-increasing violence in Rwanda in 1994. The documents are discussed in the chronological order in which they were written or transmitted.

On September 30, 1993, seven months before the outset of the 1994 genocide in Rwanda on April 6, someone within the US government crafted and disseminated a document titled "Assessment: Peacekeeping Operations in Rwanda." The document, which is marked "SECRET NOFORN WNINTEL ORCON," does not note who wrote it; which agency or department disseminated it; or which individuals, departments, or agencies received it. What is astonishing about this "intelligence assessment" is just how wrong those in the Clinton administration were about the crisis brewing in Rwanda. In fact, the information is so overwhelmingly incorrect it is hard to imagine that someone, for some reason, was not purposely planting such information. The document reports, with only certain caveats but with absolute confidence and mind-boggling inaccuracy, that:

- The military, political, social, economic, and operational conditions in Rwanda favor an economical and easily executed peacekeeping operation. (p. 1)
- The actual conduct of peacekeeping operations should be easier than elsewhere in Africa. (p. 3)
- The proposed UNAMIR structure and operational plan is technically sound and is likely to succeed.
- The UNAMIR plan has an excellent probability of success. Competent execution of the plan will greatly enhance Rwandan stability over the next 3–4 years. This will further enhance political and social stability in the region, and facilitate international efforts to restore stability and effective government in Uganda and Zaire, and nurture the fledgling democracy in Burundi. (United States Government, 1993, p. 6)

The Clinton administration came to these conclusions despite the fact that such organizations as Human Rights Watch and Amnesty International had been issuing one report after another throughout 1992 and 1993 vis-à-vis the upheaval in Rwanda, including Hutus targeting Tutsi politicians, Hutu police officers brutalizing Tutsi citizens, and violent Hutu gangs terrorizing and attacking their Tutsi neighbors. On February 8, 1993, for example, Amnesty International issued a report titled "Rwanda: Death Threats/Possible Extrajudicial Execution." In part, it read,

> AI has received reports that people who assisted an international inquiry into human rights violations in Rwanda have received death threats from government and security officials. One man, Muhikira, a member of the Tutsi minority, was apparently forced to commit suicide on the night of 13 January 1993 after armed Hutu gangs surrounded his house. The gangs were reportedly accompanied by local police, who did not intervene. Muhikira was apparently targeted because his son had acted as an interpreter to the commission of inquiry. His son has reportedly fled his home. No action has apparently been taken against the gangs responsible for his father's death. (n.p.)

In June 1993, just 10 months before the outbreak of the genocide in Rwanda, Human Rights Watch issued a report in which it stated the following: "More than 300 Tutsi and members of political parties opposed to Rwandan President Juvenal Habyarimana were massacred in northwestern Rwanda in late January 1993 by private militia at the direction of local and central government authorities. The Rwandan government has acknowledged previous human rights violations and made extensive commitments to improvements, but it has done little to follow up such statements" (n.p.).

And so it went through March, April, May, June, July, and into August of 1993. On August 11, 1993, the UN Commission on Human Rights issued a report on human rights violations across the globe. A section titled "Extrajudicial, Summary or Arbitrary Executions Addendum" included a report by Special Rapporteur B.W. Ndiaye about his mission to Rwanda from April 8 through April 17, 1993. In part, the report read,

This report would not be complete without a reference to one of the most tragic consequences of the present situation in Rwanda—the displacement of populations within the country. Before the violation of the cease-fire Agreement by the FPR [Rwandan Patriotic Front] on 8 February 1993, 350,000 persons had already fled in terror from the combat zones and the areas of intercommunal violence, leaving behind them all their possessions and their lands, situated mainly in the north, the most fertile region of the country. Since then, the number of displaced persons has risen to 900,000 and possibly 1 million. This means that almost one in seven Rwandese has been displaced by war. An unknown number of displaced persons are also living in the area held by the FPR on the border with Uganda in the north of the country. Some of them have reportedly been deported to that country. To these must be added an indeterminate number of persons who, as a result of local acts of violence whose presumed perpetrators are still at large, live in a permanent state of terror and dare not move back into their homes, cultivating their fields in the daytime and spending the night in the open or with members of their families. (UN Commission on Human Rights, 1993, n.p.)

Why the disconnect? It is difficult to know the exact reasons. Undoubtedly, certain individuals who were in the Clinton administration could answer the question, but to date no one has. At least not directly.

In recent years, some former members of the Clinton administration have issued comments that seem to hint at possible answers. For example, according to Colum Lynch (2015), Prudence Bushnell (deputy assistant secretary of state for African Affairs) essentially claimed "that top policymakers in the Clinton administration paid little attention to events in Rwanda leading up to the genocide" (n.p.). Seemingly emphasizing her point, Bushnell said, "I was way down the totem pole and I had responsibility for the Rwanda portfolio. That shows you how important it was in the U.S. government" (quoted in Lynch, 2015, n.p.).

Bushnell also claimed that Clinton was seemingly uninterested in Africa. "Early in the Clinton term, I was not able to get a new, democratically elected president in Africa, a former human rights activist, to see the president because, I was told, 'President Clinton would find him boring'" (Bushnell quoted in Lynch, 2015, n.p.). Undoubtedly, the Clinton administration's "hands-off" approach to hotspots was, at least in part (if not in large part), impacted by the aforementioned debacle in Somalia in October 1993. But that still does not explain how and why the US came up with such incorrect information about the situation in Rwanda.

Tellingly, though, the Clinton administration had been arguing against any involvement in Rwanda *before* the US debacle in Somalia. For example, in a US State Department cable ("Evening Notes 9/28—The NSC Is Downbeat on a Rwanda Operation") to the United States Mission at the United Nations (USUN) dated September 29, 1993, Richard Clarke, the chairman of the National Security Council's Counter-Terrorism Security Group, is said to have "intimated that Rwanda may be the case the NSC is looking for [*sic*] to prove the U.S. can say 'no' to a new peacekeeping operation" (p. 5). Part and parcel of what led Clarke to suggest this was the Clinton administration's general lack of faith in UN peacekeeping operations. To a great extent, the administration was duly influenced by reports of various US politicians in regard to the amount of money the US contributed to such missions, and their discomfort over the possibility of US troops falling under the command of UN "blue helmet" operations. The document continues to read: "Given the lack of enthusiasm in the rest of the government for the Rwandan operation, AF [Bureau of African Affairs] is going to have to come up with a much more plausible set of objectives for the operation if it is to come to fruition. A major problem plaguing Rwanda is the constantly shifting objectives and size of the force. On the other hand, if as the USUN reports, a Rwanda resolution has 10 votes in the UNSC, we may have to say no with a veto" (US State Department, p. 1).

The Clinton administration continued its lackadaisical approach to the crisis brewing in Rwanda right up to the outbreak of the genocide in the early morning hours of April 7, 1994, following the shooting down of Rwandan President Habyarimana's plane as he was returning to Kigali from a meeting in Arusha, Tanzania, whose focus was on finding a way to end the ethnic conflict in Rwanda and Burundi. On April 8, the US National Photographic Interpretation Center issued a document stamped "Secret," entitled "Runway Blocked, Kigali, Rwanda." The documented stated, "this is the principal airfield in Rwanda, supporting international and domestic civilian air traffic and the Rwandan Air Force" (p. 1). On the right side of the document is a large rectangle titled "White House Situation Room. Rwanda," which comprises three columns of surnames, including Lake, McLarty, Halperin, Clarke, Rice, and Tenet. The significance of this document is that it clearly proves that the United States government was conducting reconnaissance surveillance at the very outbreak of the violence that would degenerate into the 1994 genocide, and that key officials in the White House not only had ready access to such information but were provided with it almost immediately (meaning, within hours of its collection). Undoubtedly, such information continued to be supplied to those at the highest levels of the US government, which essentially contradicts President Bill Clinton's assertion in Rwanda on March 25, 1998:

> I am directing my administration to improve, with the international community, our system for identifying and spotlighting nations in danger of genocidal violence, so that we can assure worldwide awareness of impending threats. It may seem strange to you here, especially the many of you who lost members of your family, but all over the world there were people like me sitting in offices, day after day after day, who did not fully appreciate the depth and the speed with which you were being engulfed by this unimaginable terror. (p. 2)

On April 9, 1994, Richard Clarke (chairman of the US National Security Council) sent a memo ("Rwanda: Next Steps, for Sunday and Beyond") marked "Secret" to a host of high-level officials in the Clinton administration in which he called for the termination of the UNAMIR: "We make a lot of noise about terminating UN forces that aren't working. Well, few could be as clearly not working. We should work with the French to gain a consensus to terminate the UN mission" (n.p.).

By that time, thousands of Tutsi had already been slaughtered, but Clarke was obviously not concerned about that fact. Indeed, he could hardly have cared less about the humanitarian crisis. Rather, he concerned himself with shutting down UNAMIR, which did not include a single member of the United States military. The significance of this memo is that from early on—indeed, just two days into the paroxysm of violence that engulfed Rwanda—at least some high-level officials in the US government were intent on and pushing for the total dismantling of UNAMIR, no matter how much carnage ensued.

On April 11, 1994, Lieutenant Colonel Harvin, with the office of the US deputy assistant secretary of defense for Middle East Africa, prepared a memorandum (marked "Confidential") that constituted talking points for the Under Secretary of Defense for Policy Frank Wisner in his upcoming meeting with Henry Kissinger, the former secretary of state in the Nixon administration. These talking points reveal that US officials sensed that Rwanda was about to turn into a bloodbath, and, despite that, the US was not willing to do anything but engage in diplomatic efforts. In other words, the US was not about to attempt to halt the mass killing of hundreds of thousands that the US government was fairly sure was on the horizon. The memorandum reads as follows:

- *What is State doing now?*
  Expect little beyond diplomatic statements.

- *Is the USG willing to get involved?*
  Not inside Rwanda or Burundi until peace is restored. We played an important role in brokering the Arusha Accords. As the only "honest broker" left on the field (given the intense hatred of Belgium by the Rwandan Hutus and of France by the Tutsis) we could (and should) play a critical diplomatic role in urging the parties to adhere to the Arusha peace agreement. We would want to start our security assistance program once the peace process is back on track.

- *What are the humanitarian issues, and what can DoD do?*
  …Unless both sides can be convinced to [commit to] the peace process,
  a massive (hundreds of thousands of deaths) bloodbath will ensue that
  will likely spill over into Burundi. (Ferroggiaro, 2001, n.p.)

In his introduction to the above document from the National Security
Archive website, William Ferroggiaro commented as follows:

This document—apparently produced as a briefer for a dinner between
Under Secretary Frank Wisner, the third ranking official at the
Pentagon, and former Secretary of State Henry Kissinger—shows the
Pentagon's candid assessment about events in Rwanda only five days
after the shooting down of the Rwandan president's plane. Pentagon
Africa analysts conclude: if the peace process fails, "a massive bloodbath (hundreds of thousands of deaths) will ensue"; the "UN will likely
withdraw all forces"; and the US will not get involved "until peace is
restored." That these shocking details are offered as dinner conversation reveals the extent to which Pentagon analysts accepted it as
inevitable. (Ferroggiaro, 2001, n.p.)

On April 12, 1994, the USUN sent the following cable (labeled
"Confidential) with the imprimatur of US Ambassador to the UN Madeline
Albright, to the US secretary of state (and other actors within the US government), regarding the United States government's perspective on the
future roles of UNAMIR and France in Rwanda. (A great amount of this
document has been redacted in its now declassified form):

AT PRESENT THE AIRPORT IS STILL OPEN AND UNDER FRENCH-
BELGIAN CONTROL. HOWEVER, THERE IS NO SIGNAL THAT THE
UN IS NEARING A DECISION BECAUSE RELATIVE CALM HAS
DESCENDED ON KIGALI AND UNAMIR TROOPS ARE NOT
PRESENTLY THE TARGET OF HOSTILITIES. YET THIS MIGHT BE A

WINDOW OF RELATIVE OPPORTUNITY TO EVACUATE UNAMIR FORCES; THERE IS A REAL POSSIBILITY THAT IT MIGHT BECOME MORE DIFFICULT TO EVACUATE UNAMIR ONCE THE FRENCH AND BELGIANS LEAVE. IN THIS RESPECT, IT IS WORTH CONSIDERING TAKING THE LEAD IN THE SECURITY COUNCIL TO AUTHORIZE THE EVACUATION OF THE BULK OF UNAMIR, WHILE LEAVING BEHIND A SKELETAL STAFF THAT MIGHT BE ABLE TO FACILITATE A CEASE-FIRE AND ANY FUTURE POLITICAL NEGOTIATIONS [original in all capitals]. (Ferroggiaro, 2017, n.p.)

By the date of this memo (April 12th), the mass killing of Tutsi and moderate Hutu had been underway for six days.

On April 13, 1994, Donatella Lorch reported the following in *The New York Times*:

The streets of this capital city [Kigali], empty of residents, was a terrifying obstacle course today of drunken soldiers and marauding gangs of looters dressed in a patchwork of uniforms, armed with machetes, spears, bows and arrows and automatic weapons.

Children carried hand grenades, and open-back trucks, loaded with angry men waving weapons at passing cars, sped through the city. As night fell, screams could be heard coming from a church compound where more than 2,000 Rwandans had taken refuge. A short time later, after the sound of machine-gun fire, the screaming stopped.

As tribal and political violence that began last week continued unabated, with tens of thousands of deaths reported, the evacuation of foreigners began... Thousands of rotting bodies that have littered the streets were cleared up with bulldozers and trucks on Tuesday....

Eighteen Belgian nuns and lay brothers abandoned a hilltop hospital for the insane, leaving behind 200 patients, The Associated Press reported. As the Belgians were picked up by an armored Belgian convoy, the hospital administrator, Gerard Van Selst, said he had no illusions about the fate of the patients or of the 500 Tutsi refugees camped out there. "They're finished," he said. "A huge number will be killed." (Lorch, 1994, p. 1)

On April 15, in a meeting at the UN concerning the fate of UNAMIR, the United States "dropped the bombshell" that it no longer supported UNAMIR's continued presence in Rwanda. The actual words to that effect, though, have been redacted from the US government document (archived under the title "US Drops Bombshell on Security Council – 4/15"), which had been sent from the USUN to the US secretary of state and the White House on April 15, 1994. However, the exact words of the US representative were relayed by other nations' representatives to their respective governments, and thus a record of the complete statement does exist. For example, in a document simply titled "Rwanda," the UK's representative David Hannay (1994) fired off a cable to the leaders of his government about the US government's position. In part, Hannay stated the following:

> Belgian hyperactivity irritates Council members. Ghana and Bangladesh indicate readiness to maintain their contingents. NAM [Non-Aligned Movement caucus] wants UNAMIR to remain in place at its current strength. Americans refuse to countenance any Council decision other than withdrawal, but acknowledge for the moment the NAM's preferred outcome does not require such a decision as UNAMIR is already authorized.... I suggest suspension of UNAMIR's deployment and retention of the Secretary-General's Special Representative in the field, with appropriate support, to continue efforts to secure a cease-fire. Key players (US, France, Nigeria) agree to my suggestions.... Walker (US) said that the US believed the Rwandan armed parties bore full responsibility for the continued violence and instability. The US did not believe there was a role now in Rwanda for a United Nations peacekeeping force. They supported the decision of the Belgian Government to withdraw immediately.... The US did not believe the war parties in Rwanda were likely to respect UNAMIR's mandate, or capable of guaranteeing the safety of UN peace-

keeping personnel in Rwanda.... The US would support a political initiative by the Secretary-General to promote reconciliation among the parties.... Walker underlined that US opposition to retaining a UNAMIR presence in Rwanda under current conditions was firm. It was based on a conviction that the Security Council had an obligation to ensure that peacekeeping operations were viable and capable of fulfilling their mandates, and that peacekeeping personnel were not knowingly put in an untenable situation. When the parties documented that they were willing and able to work towards a peaceful settlement the US would be willing to reconsider whether renewed UN peacekeeping could facilitate lasting peace. (pp. 3–4)

What Hannay did not comment on was the United States government's disingenuous position. That is, he failed to point out that if the US had been willing to call for and attempt to convince the UN Security Council to implement a robust (meaning well staffed and well resourced) chapter VII peace enforcement mission in Rwanda, then the UN troops would have, literally, had a fighting chance to save the targeted populations *and* to fend for themselves as they attempted to counter the Hutu extremists' actions. Instead, the United States was making all of its decisions predicated on the assumption that the only UN force available was the tiny UNAMIR force with its vague chapter VI mandate (peacekeeping). The primary distinctions between a chapter VI mandate (peacekeeping) and a chapter VII mandate (peace enforcement) are incredibly significant:

Chapter 6, "Pacific Settlement of Disputes," stipulates that parties to a dispute should use peaceful methods of resolving disputes, such as negotiation and mediation. It authorizes the Security Council to issue recommendations, but they are generally considered advisory and not binding. Chapter 7, "Action with Respect to Threats to the Peace, Breaches of the Peace, and Acts of Aggression," authorizes more forceful methods such as economic coercion and severance of diplomatic relations. Should those measures prove inadequate, the Security

Council may then "take such action by air, sea, or land forces as may be necessary to maintain or restore international peace and security." (United States Institute of Peace, n.d., n.p.)

On April 19, 1994, Eric P. Schwartz, an official with the National Security Council, sent a memorandum ("Pull-out of UNAMIR") marked "Confidential" to Susan E. Rice and Donald K. Steinberg. In the memo, Schwartz mentions the word "genocide," a term which would shortly become verboten within the Clinton administration, at least as it applied to the events unfolding in Rwanda in April, May, and June of 1994. This memo is one of the few issued by US government personnel that expresses real alarm for the safety of the potential victims:

> I just heard from Human Rights Watch, pleading that we oppose a quick UNAMIR pullout from Rwanda. Human Rights Watch seemed to indicate that UNAMIR is protecting thousands (25,000?) Rwandans and if they pull out, the Rwandans will quickly become victims of genocide.
>
> Is this true? If so, shouldn't it be a major factor informing high-level decision-making on this issue? Has it been?
>
> I am expecting to receive a fax on this shortly and will see that you get it. (Schwartz, 1994, p. 1)

Whether Schwartz received a reply to his memorandum is, as far as can be ascertained, unknown. That said, it wouldn't be surprising if all this email set in motion was the Clinton administration's strenuous effort to avoid using "the G-word" at all costs.

As previously noted, one of the most infamous examples of the duplicity by Clinton administration officials in its efforts not to call the genocide in Rwanda "genocide" took place on April 28, some three weeks into the tragedy unfolding all across Rwanda. On that day, State Department Spokeswoman Christine Shelley was asked the following by a reporter: "Does the State Department have a view as to whether or not what is happening is genocide?" Shelley stammered: "Well, as I think you know, the use of the term 'genocide' has a very precise legal meaning, although it's not strictly a legal determination. There are other factors in there, as well. When...looking at a situation to make a determination about that, before we begin to use that term, we have to know as much as possible about the facts of the situation" (US State Department, 1994, n.p.).

On May 1, 1994, four weeks into the genocide, the US government showed its true colors in the document "Discussion Paper: Rwanda," which was marked "Secret." The first item under a section entitled "Issues for Discussion," which was prepared by various US governmental agencies (including the Joints Chief of Staff), reads as follows: "Genocide Investigation: Language that calls for an international investigation of human rights abuses and possible violations of the genocide convention." This was immediately followed with the warning "Be careful. Legal at State was worried about this yesterday—Genocide finding could commit USG to actually 'do something'" (Ferroggiaro, 2017, p. 1).

That warning encapsulates and epitomizes the Clinton administration's position in regard to the slaughter that was pulling hundreds of thousands into its deadly maw in Rwanda. That which demanded decisive, quick, and resolute action was met with just about every type of equivocation the administration could come up with.

The warning provides unambiguous evidence that bureaucrats in the legal department were more concerned with making sure other US governmental bureaucrats avoided calling the genocide "genocide" than the victims being caught up in its murderous maw. The legal department feared that the use of the term "genocide" might result in the US being pressured to honor its promise to act in the face of genocide since it had ratified the United Nations Genocide Convention. Being the good bureaucrats they were, most followed the warning precisely and did their level best to adhere to the US State Department's admonition, while what was to become one of the swiftest genocides perpetrated in centuries played its murderous self out.

By that time, the world had been well informed that mass murder—no matter what it might technically be deemed (crimes against humanity, massacres, or genocide)—had been (and continued to be) perpetrated in Rwanda. The titles of various newspaper and magazine articles about what was transpiring in Rwanda at the time provides ample evidence of that: "Thousands Massacred in Rwanda" (Hilsum, 1994); "Deaths in Rwanda Fighting Said to Be 20,000 or More" (Schmidt, 1994); "U.N. Forces Shelter Thousands in Rwanda" (Lewis, 1994); "U.N. in Rwanda Says It Is Powerless to Halt the Violence" (Lorch, 1994a); "Tribes Battle for Rwandan Capital; New Massacres Reported" (Associated Press, 1994); "Corpses Everywhere: Once More, Tens of Thousands Massacred" (Masland, Hammer, Breslau, & Tanaka, 1994); "Rwandan Refugees Describe Horrors after a Bloody Trek" (Lorch, 1994b); "Streets of Slaughter: Tribal Bloodlust and Political Rivalry Turn the Country into an Unimaginable Hell of Killing, Looting and Anarchy" (Mutsio, 1994); and "Deeper into the Abyss: An Orgy of Tribal Slaughter Kills Thousands as Foreigners Flee for Their Lives" (Hammer, Stanger, & Sparkman, 1994).

The stammering by those in the Clinton administration was far from over. On May 4, 1994, in response to a reporter's question as to whether the UNCG should be invoked, US Ambassador to the UN Madeline Albright uttered: "I think, as you know, this became a legal definitional thing. Unfortunately, in terms of, as horrendous as all these things are, there becomes a definitional question" (PBS, 2004, p. 1). As one wag commented, she was "a perfect Clinton staffer."

As previously mentioned, on May 5, 1994, US Under Secretary of Defense Frank G. Wisner sent out a confidential memorandum ("Memorandum for Deputy Assistant to the President for National Security Affairs, National Security Council") on the subject of jamming civilian radio broadcasts in Rwanda, which essentially argued that any effort to jam the broadcasts issued by the Hutus against the Tutsi would be too expensive. At the same time, Wisner argued in favor of using funds to provide relief supplies to those survivors who had made it out of Rwanda. More specifically, he stated the following:

Commando Solo, an Air National Guard Asset, is the only suitable DoD jamming platform. It costs $8500 per flight hour and requires a semi-secure area of operations due to its vulnerability and limited self-protection.

I believe it would be wiser to use air to assist in Rwanda in the relief effort, particularly in neighboring countries, like Tanzania. This weekend we will be assisting with air lifts to Tanzania (blankets and plastic sheeting) and an American NGO, AmeriCares (blankets and plastic sheeting). (n.p.)

Undoubtedly, the cost per flight hour was exorbitant. At the same time, though, it is key to recognize the fact that RTLMC personnel were, in fact, calling on, prodding, and cajoling Hutu to go into their streets and neighborhoods to undertake "work," which was a code word for killing Tutsi. Essentially, Wisner's (and the US government's) concern about the cost of jamming the radio station outweighed the value of saving individual human lives—tens of thousands of them.

In regard to the issue of jamming the Hutu-controlled radio station, others in the US government broached the issue of First Amendment rights, and, in particular, freedom of speech. Some argued that by jamming Radio Rwanda signals the US government would essentially be guilty of contravening the First Amendment rights of the Hutu personnel calling on their brethren to wantonly kill their Tutsi neighbors. Such contorted thinking is nothing short of Kafkaesque.

On June 14, 1994, Donald K. Steinberg, an official with the National Security Council, sent a memorandum to the White House in which he delineated talking points for President Clinton vis-à-vis the United States' reaction to the tragedy that was still unfolding in Rwanda. It is a classic example of a government bureaucrat's concern with "appearance" versus reality; that is, the talking points focus on making the United States and Clinton look good, while assiduously avoiding anything in regard to what the US could do to stanch the killing.

Rwanda

I've been deeply concerned over the continuing tragedy in Rwanda. We are providing $68 million in humanitarian assistance for Rwandan refugees, including food, medicine, blankets and other supplies. Our military is flying in three planeloads a day of food into Burundi.

-- This is by far the lion's share of the humanitarian relief effort. Our efforts have helped to save lives throughout the neighboring countries.

-- We've also sent disaster relief teams into Rwanda to assist the distribution of humanitarian relief there.

-- We share the frustration over the slowness in drawing together an international peacekeeping force. That is why we've been so involved in the process of getting peacekeepers into Rwanda. The Vice President's meeting with UN Secretary General Boutros Ghali, OAU Secretary General Salim Salim and Tanzanian President Mwinyi in South Africa on May 10 helped drive this process, leading to a UNSC Resolution less than a week later to authorize 5500 troops.

-- We've helped the UN planning process and mobilized to provide equipment, airlift, training and financial support for the operation.

-- We've contacted numerous African countries to get their support for the mission. We're helping the UN peacekeeping secretariat coordinate the dozen or so country forces that have to be merged into this mission.

-- We previously sent military equipment in Europe to assist its quick delivery. For example, we have 50 armored personnel carriers for this mission in Germany about to be shipped to Kampala, where they will be used for the training of Ghanaian troops and driven to Kigali.

-- We have every reason to believe that [acts of genocide have] [genocide has] occurred in Rwanda, as defined under the 1948 convention. That's why we've supported so strongly the introduction of 5500 UN peacekeepers into Rwanda and why we have urged the U.N. Human Rights Commission to send a special rapporteur to Rwanda to investigate these acts of genocide and ensure that those responsible for acts of genocide be held accountable for their deeds.

-- (If asked) The Genocide Convention does not impose a responsibility on the part of any government to take any specific action. We believe that creation of the peacekeeping force, the appointment of a special rapporteur and our massive humanitarian assistance effort is an appropriate response. (Steinberg, 1994)

Anyone aware of the United States government's position(s), reactions, and inactions between April 7 (when the mass killing began) and the date of Steinberg's memorandum (June 14) knows full well that this government (the Clinton administration) was hardly the voice of action and, in fact, was the voice of hesitation, self-interest, dissembling, half-truths, obfuscation, and lies, rather than any true concern for the hundreds of thousands of innocents who were being slaughtered.

Ultimately, on June 27, 1994, during remarks he made to the White House Conference on Africa, President Bill Clinton, for the first time publicly, used the word "genocide" to describe what had been (and at the time still was) taking place in Rwanda. Tellingly, this was over two and a half months after the mass killing had been triggered back in early April. On June 27, Clinton said: "We've insisted that those who are committing genocide be brought to justice." Despite the fact that he had never used the term "genocide" to describe the events in Rwanda up until that very moment, Clinton used the past tense.

Equally interesting and telling is that Clinton did not use any variation of the term "genocide" again to describe the events unfolding in Rwanda until July 15, 1994, by which time the genocide had been halted. "The United States cannot allow representatives of a regime that supports genocidal massacre to remain on our soil," Clinton announced as he shut down the Rwandan Embassy to the United States.

## CONCLUSION

At every stage of the crisis in Rwanda, the United States had a variety of options to at least slow down the genocide and save Tutsi lives. Instead of leaving it to mid-level officials to communicate with the Rwandan leadership behind the scenes, senior officials in the Clinton administration could have taken control of the process. President Clinton could have intervened personally and directly. The US could have publicly and frequently denounced the slaughter. The Clinton administration could have branded the crimes "genocide" at a far earlier stage. It could have called for the expulsion of the Rwandan delegation from its seat on the UN Security Council. It could have threatened to prosecute those complicit in the genocide. It could have deployed Pentagon instruments to jam the deadly radio broadcasts.

Instead of acting as it did—demanding a UN withdrawal, quibbling over costs, and coming forward with a plan better suited to caring for refugees than to stopping massacres (and even that was belated)—US officials could have worked to make UNAMIR a force to contend with. They could have urged their Belgian allies to stay and protect Rwandan civilians. The White House could have done everything in its considerable power to make sure that UNAMIR was immediately reinforced. Senior officials could have rallied troops from other nations and could have supplied strategic airlift and logistic support to a coalition that it had helped create. In short, the United States could have led the world. None of these things, not a single one, happened.

This was no accident. Much of the world has regarded the United States' failure to intervene in the 1994 Rwanda genocide to have been a profound failure of statesmanship. From the point of view of the victims, it was of course that and much more. The Clinton administration, supported completely by its Republican opponents, wanted no part of Rwanda and succeeded in making sure the US played no part in ending the genocide. That between 500,000 and 1 million Tutsi and moderate Hutu lost their lives to this decision is a separate matter. That the US succeeded in achieving its political objective explains virtually all US actions throughout the

100 days of killing. The United States was not "missing in action" during the genocide. On the contrary, it was actively protecting what it considered its self-interest.

As a symbol of the US position, perhaps the fate of Madeleine Albright stands out most clearly. As President Clinton's ambassador to the UN, Albright was directly responsible for the failure of the Security Council to burnish UNAMIR's mandate and capacity. Little more than two years after the end of the genocide, the president nominated her as his secretary of state—a major promotion to the highest cabinet position in the land. Other major players in the Clinton administration who actively carried out their instructions, like Susan Rice and Anthony Lake, ended up holding senior positions either in the Obama administration or at the United Nations. Rice was appointed national security adviser. Lake, Clinton's own national security adviser, became executive director of UNICEF. No bad deed goes unawarded, it seems.

# REFERENCES

Albright, Madeline. (1994, April 12). "TFRWOL: Future of UNAMIR and French Roles in Rwanda." In W. Ferroggiaro (Ed.), National Security Archive Briefing Book No. 511: 1994 Rwanda Pullout Driven by Clinton White House, U.N. Equivocation (doc. 14). Washington, DC: George Washington University. Accessed at: http://nsarchive2.gwu.edu/NSAEBB/NSAEBB511/docs/DOCUMENT%2014.pdf

Amnesty International. (1993). "UA 30/93 - Rwanda: Death Threats/Possible Extrajudicial Execution: Human Rights Activists and Others Who Assisted with a Commission of Inquiry into Human Rights Violations in Rwanda, Including: Muhikira and His Son Eustache Mupenzi." London: Author.

Associated Press. (1994, April 16). "Tribes Battle for Rwandan Capital, New Massacres Reported." The New York Times, n.p. Accessed at: http://www.nytimes.com/1994/04/16/world/tribes-battle-for-rwandan-capital-new-massacres-reported.html?mcubz=0

Association for Diplomatic Studies and Training. (2008). "Ambassador Prudence Bushnell." In Frontline Diplomacy: Foreign Affairs Oral History Project. Arlington, VA: National Foreign Affairs Training Center.

Clarke, R. (1994, April 9). "Rwanda: Next Steps, for Sunday and Beyond." In MDR Case no. 2014–0278. Little Rock, AR: William J. Clinton Presidential Library.

Clinton, W. (1998, March 25). "Remarks to the People of Rwanda." American President Speech Archive. Miller Center, University of Virginia. Accessed at: https://millercenter.org/the-presidency/presidential-speeches/march-25-1998-remarks-people-rwanda

Des Forges, A. (1999). *Leave None to Tell the Story: Genocide in Rwanda*. New York: Human Rights Watch.

Ferroggiaro, W. (2001, August 20). "Introduction to Document 3. In W. Ferroggiaro (Ed.), *National Security Archive Electronic Briefing Book: The US and the Genocide in Rwanda 1994: Evidence of Inaction*. Accessed at: http://nsarchive2.gwu.edu//NSAEBB/NSAEBB53/index.html

Gordon, M.R. (1994, June 9). "UN's Rwanda Deployment Slowed by Lack of Vehicles." *The New York Times*, p. A10.

Gourevitch, P. (1998). *We Wish to Inform You That Tomorrow We Will Be Killed with Our Families: Stories from Rwanda*. New York: Farrar Straus & Giroux.

Hannay, D. (1994, April 16). "Rwanda." In W. Ferroggiaro (Ed.), *National Security Archive Electronic Briefing Book No. 511: 1994 Rwanda Pullout Driven by Clinton White House, U.N. Equivocation* (doc. 17). Washington, DC: George Washington University. Accessed at: http://nsarchive2.gwu.edu/NSAEBB/NSAEBB511/docs/DOCUMENT%2017.pdf

Human Rights Watch. (1993, June 10). *Beyond the Rhetoric: Continuing Human Rights Abuses in Rwanda*. New York: Author. Accessed at: https://www.hrw.org/report/1993/06/01/beyond-rhetoric/continuing-human-rights-abuses-rwanda

Human Rights Watch. (1994, January). "Arming Rwanda: The Arms Trade and Human Rights – Abuses in the Rwandan War." *Human Rights Watch Arms Project*, 6(1), 1–39.

Human Rights Watch. (2004, March 29). *Rwanda: Lessons Learned*. New York: Author. Accessed at: Author. Accessed at: https://www.hrw.org/report/2004/03/29/rwanda-lessons-learned/ten-years-after-genocide

Huband, M. (1994, April 12). "UN Troops Stand by and Watch Carnage." *The Guardian*. Accessed at: https://www.theguardian.com/world/1994/apr/12/rwanda.fromthearchive

Kuperman, A. (1998, December 29). "The Rwanda Failure." *The Washington Post*. Accessed at: https://www.washingtonpost.com/archive/opinions/1998/12/29/the-rwanda-failure/df77dcd5-111e-4f32-835e-6569b3a88d58/?utm_term=.c41c1772937b

Landler, M. (2014, June 3). "Declassified U.N. Cables Reveal Turning Point in Rwanda Crisis of 1994." *The New York Times*, p. A11.

Lorch, D. (1994a, April 14). "Anarchy Rules Rwanda's Capital and Drunken Soldiers Roam the City." *The New York Times*. Accessed at: http://www.nytimes.com/1994/04/14/world/anarchy-rules-rwanda-s-capital-and-drunken-soldiers-roam-city.html?pagewanted=all

Lorch, D. (1994b, April 15). "UN in Rwanda Says It Is Powerless to Halt Violence." *The New York Times*, n.p.

Lynch, C. (2015, April 5). "Exclusive: 'Rwanda Revisited.'" *Foreign Policy*. Accessed at: https://foreignpolicy.com/2015/04/05/rwanda-revisited-genocide-united-states-state-department/

Millwood, D. (Ed.). (1996). *The International Response to Conflict and Genocide: Lessons from the Rwanda Experience*. Copenhagen: Steering Committee of the Joint Evaluation of Emergency Assistance to Rwanda.

National Photographic Interpretation Center. (1994, April 8). "Runway Blocked, Kigali, Rwanda." Clinton Library, MDR Case no. 2014-0278. Little Rock, AR: William J. Clinton Presidential Library.

Nkurinziza, M. (2015, April 18). "Rwanda: US Embassy Honours 26 Staff Killed in Genocide." *The New Times*. Accessed at: allafrica.com/stories/201504201160.html

PBS. (1999a, January 26). "Ambush in Mogadishu: Interview with Walter Clarke." *Frontline*. Accessed at: http://www.pbs.org/wgbh/pages/frontline/shows/ambush/interviews/clarke.html

PBS. (1999b, January 26). "Triumph of Evil (Interview with James Woods)." *Frontline*. Accessed at: http://www.pbs.org/wgbh/pages/frontline/shows/evil/interviews/woods.html

PBS. (1999c, January 26). "Triumph of Evil (Interview with Tony Marley)." *Frontline*. Accessed at: http://www.pbs.org/wgbh/pages/frontline/shows/evil/interviews/marley.html

PBS. (2004, April 9). "Ghosts of Rwanda." *Frontline*. Accessed at: www.pbs.org/wgbh/pages/frontline/shows/ghosts/etc/script.html

Schwartz, E.P. (1994, April 19). "Pull-Out of UNAMIR." In W. Ferroggiaro (Ed.), *National Security Archive Electronic Briefing Book No. 511: 1994 Rwanda Pullout Driven by Clinton White House, U.N. Equivocation* (doc. 18). Washington, DC: George Washington University. Accessed at: http://nsarchive2.gwu.edu/NSAEBB/NSAEBB511/docs/DOCUMENT%2018.pdf

Sciolino, E. (1994, April 15). "For West, Rwanda Is Not Worth the Political Candle." *The New York Times*. Accessed at: http://www.nytimes.com/1994/04/15/world/for-west-rwanda-is-not-worth-the-political-candle.html

Steinberg, Donald. (1994, June 14). "Points for POTUS with Members." In W. Ferroggiaro (Ed.), *National Security Archive Electronic Briefing Book No. 511: 1994 Rwanda Pullout Driven by Clinton White House, U.N. Equivocation* (doc. 20). Washington, DC: George Washington University. Accessed at: http://nsarchive2.gwu.edu/NSAEBB/NSAEBB511/docs/DOCUMENT%2020.pdf

UN Commission on Human Rights. (1993, August 11). "Question of the Violation of Human Rights and Fundamental Freedoms in Any Part of the World, with Particular Reference to Colonial and Other Dependent Countries and Territories." Extrajudicial, Summary or Arbitrary Executions Addendum. Report by B.W. Ndiaye, Special Rapporteur on His Mission to Rwanda from 8 to 17 April 1993. New York: United Nations.

UN Security Council. (1994). *Resolution 918 (1994): Adopted by the Security Council at Its 3377th Meeting, on 17 May 1994*. S/RES/918. New York: United Nations.

United Nations Independent Inquiry. (1999). *Report of the Independent Inquiry into the Actions of the United Nations during the 1994 Genocide in Rwanda*. S/1999/1257. New York: United Nations.

United States Government. (1993, September 20). "Assessment: Peacekeeping Operations in Rwanda." MDR Case no. 2014-0278. Little Rock, AR: William J. Clinton Presidential Library.

United States Institute of Peace. (n.d.). "Chapters 6 and 7." In USIP (Ed.), *Glossary of Terms for Conflict Management and Peacebuilding*. Washington, DC: Author.

United States Mission to the United Nations (USUN). (1994). "TFRWOL: US Drops Bombshell on Security Council—4/15." MDR Case no. 2014-0278. Little Rock, AR: William J. Clinton Presidential Library.

US Department of State. (1994a, April 15). "Cable Number 099440, to US Mission to the United Nations, New York, 'Talking Points for UNAMIR Withdrawal.'" In W. Ferroggiaro (Ed.), *National Security Archive Electronic Briefing Book : The U.S. and the Genocide in Rwanda 1994: Evidence of Inaction* (doc. 4). Washington, DC: George Washington University. Accessed at: http://nsarchive2.gwu.edu//NSAEBB/NSAEBB53/index.html

US Department of State. (1994b, April 28). *Daily Press Briefing*. Washington, DC: Author.

US Department of State. (1994c, June 10). *Daily Press Briefing*. Washington, DC: Author.

US Secretary of State. (1993, September 28). "Evening Notes 9/28." In W. Ferroggario, *National Security Archive Electronic Briefing Book No. 511: 1994 Rwanda Pullout Driven by Clinton White House, U.N. Equivocation* (doc. 2). Washington, DC: George Washington University. Accessed at: http://nsarchive2.gwu.edu/NSAEBB/NSAEBB511/docs/DOCUMENT%202.pdf

*The Washington Post* (1994, April 17). "One, Two, Many Rwandas?" Accessed at: https://www.washingtonpost.com/archive/opinions/1994/04/17/one-two-many-rwandas/aeee86e7-2b87-45e9-aeod-7a3b4c118ce9/?utm_term=.5ffef90aaf6c

Wisner, F. G. (1994, May 5). "Rwanda: Jamming Civilian Radio Broadcasts." In W. Ferroggario (Ed.), *National Security Archive Electronic Briefing Book: The US and the Genocide in Rwanda 1994: Evidence of Inaction* (doc. 10). Washington, DC: George Washington University. Accessed at: http://nsarchive2.gwu.edu//NSAEBB/NSAEBB53/rw050594.pdf

# DOCUMENTS

The following documents are declassified US documents that were written and disseminated by various members of the Clinton administration during the 100 days of the 1994 genocide in Rwanda. Each document provides unique insights into how and why Clinton administration officials reacted to what was taking place in Rwanda.

The National Security Archive based at George Washington University in Washington, DC, graciously provided permission to reprint each of the documents that appear herein.

## DOCUMENT 1

This document is a memorandum from US Lieutenant Colonel Harvin to Frank Wisner, the US under-secretary of defense for policy (the third ranking official at the Pentagon), and essentially constitutes a series of "talking points" on the political situations in Rwanda and Burundi in preparation for Wisner's upcoming dinner meeting with former Secretary of State Henry Kissinger. Dated April 11, 1994, just four days after the outbreak of the genocide in Rwanda, the document presents a clear and unequivocal picture of what the Pentagon knew about the events unfolding in Rwanda, during a time when many in the Clinton administration acted as if they were operating in the dark. The Pentagon's Africa analysts conclude that if the peace process fails (a) "a massive bloodbath" (resulting in hundreds of thousands of deaths) will ensue; (b) the "UN will likely withdraw all forces"; and (c) the US will not get involved in the situation "until peace is restored."

Certainly the most astounding aspect of this document is the very matter of fact assertion that in the face of hundreds of thousands possibly facing their death there was absolutely no plan or consideration by the US government to, at the least, step up and urge the United Nations to immediately act to attempt to curtail the killing, and stanch what surely would constitute a case of crimes against humanity, if not genocide.

**April 11, 1994**

**|-94|16533**

**EXECUTIVE SUMMARY/COVER BRIEF**

MEMORANDUM FOR UNDER SECRETARY OF DEFENSE FOR POLICY

THROUGH:      Assistant Secretary of Defense for International Security Affairs

FROM:      Deputy Assistant Secretary of Defense for Middle East Africa

Prepared by: LtCol Harvin:MEA:x78824

SUBJECT:      Talking Points On Rwanda/Burundi (U)

PURPOSE:      INFORMATION -- Talking points for your dinner tonight with Mr. Kissinger.

DISCUSSION:      (U) Action Officers in H&RA, PK/PE, and MEA collaborated on the attached talking points.

COORDINATION

ASD/SOLIC _____

ASD/SR &R _____

Atch: a/s

## RWANDA/BURUNDI

■ **What is State doing now?**

Just beginning to look at next steps (DCM Leader will brief
at State tomorrow).

Expect little beyond diplomatic statements.


■ **What next in Rwanda?**

Rwanda Patriotic Front (RPF) will maintain 48-hour cease-
fire to allow ex-pats to depart.

UN will likely withdraw all UN forces.

Following the 48-hour cease-fire period, RPF forces will
attempt to take Kigali and will come into open warfare with
any remaining French, Belgian, or UN forces.

Civilians will increasingly be drawn into the conflict and
fighting will likely spread to Burundi.

AmEmbassy Bujumbura is under "Ordered Departure" and is
drawing down from its 46 official/31 dependents to essential
personnel only (planning on 22, could drop lower).

Unofficial U.S. personnel normally number between 100-150,
but many may have already departed.


■ **Will Burundi's new democratic, Hutu-led Government fall?**

Probably. Given the close tribal ties to the parties in
Rwanda, it is highly likely that inter-tribal killings will
spread. A NEO should not be necessary given the prior
warning foreign citizens are getting.


■ **Is the USG willing to get involved?**

Not inside Rwanda or Burundi until peace is restored.

We played an important role in brokering the Arusha Accords.

As the only "honest broker" left on the field (given the
intense hatred of Belgium by the Rwandan Hutus and of France

by the Tutsis) we could (and should) play a critical diplomatic role in urging the parties to adhere to the Arusha peace agreement. We would want to restart our security assistance program once the peace process is back on track.

■ **What is happening at the U.N.?**

Security Council is meeting today to discuss future of UNAMIR, probably will take no action -- everyone waiting for UNAMIR Commander's recommendations. USUN has not been given guidance. There is some support in the USG for leaving the Commander and a small support staff in Kigali. He seems to be the only person who can talk to both sides.

■ **What are the humanitarian issues, and what can DoD do?**

Since last Wednesday, 5,000 refugees have fled Rwanda to Zaire, 5,000 Burundi [sic] have fled to Tanzania in anticipation of more violence, and UNHCR in Tanzania is expecting 100-250,000 more. UNHCR has refugee support food in Zaire for 10 days. DoD may be asked to airlift relief supplies. If State requests, H&RA can provide MREs, Humanitarian Daily Rations, consumable medical and other supplies for disaster relief.

C O N F I D E N T I A L

**Rwanda**

**DoD Policy Options**

■ Because of the fluidity of the situation and the obvious requirement to focus on the NEO, State has not yet begun to look at its next steps re: U.S. Policy towards Rwanda and will not do so for a few days. DCM Joyce Leader will brief at State tomorrow. AMB [Ambassador] Rawson will remain in Burundi for a few day [sic]. The Burundi Government wants the additional US Marines in Bujumbura to

depart as soon as all AmCits [American citizens] are out of Rwanda
-- we support that request. (State Rwanda TF)

■ State will likely shut down its Rwanda Task Force NLT Wednesday
morning. (State Rwanda TF)

■ We believe State will initially limit itself to diplomatic
statements in support of the UN, the French, the Belgians, and the
necessity for both sides to resume the peace process. Of note:
this crisis will likely raise questions at the UN about the wisdom
of including lightly armed troops in a Chapter VI PKO instead of
only unarmed observers (who would probably have been well-treated
like most other un-armed ex-pats).

■ Unless both sides can be convinced to return to the peace
process, a massive (hundreds of thousands of deaths) bloodbath
will ensue that would likely spill over into Burundi. In addition,
millions of refugees will flee into neighboring Uganda, Tanzania,
and Zaire, far exceeding the absorptive capacity of those nations.
Since neither the French nor the Belgians have the trust of both
sides in the conflict, they are unlikely to be able to convince the
parties to return to the peace process -- thus there will be role
to play for the U.S. as the "honest broker."

■ One of the primary U.S. representatives at the last round of
peace negotiations was an ISA alum, LTC Tony Marley, who is assigned
to the Africa Regional Affairs office at State. He is known and
trusted by both sides and will likely be called upon to play a
significant role once more if the peace process can be put in motion.

■ When the peace process is back on track, we should resume our
security assistance program:

Recent Security Assistance Summary ($ in Millions):

|  | FY91 | FY92 | FY93 | FY94 | FY95 |
|---|---|---|---|---|---|
|  |  |  |  |  | (PROPOSED) |
| FMF | 0.0 | 0.0 | 0.0 | 0.0 | 0.0 |
| CIVIC ACTION | .135 | .150 | 0.0 | 0.0 | 0.0 |
| BIODIVERSITY | .525 | N/A | .525 | N/A | N/A |
| IMET/DIRECT TRNG. | .060 | .070 | .127 | .075 | .150 |
| IMET STUDENTS | 3 | 3 | 5 | 4 | 8 |

Prepared by LtCol Harvin, 11 April 94, x788824

**Source:** "Memorandum from Deputy Assistant Secretary of Defense for Middle East/Africa, through Assistant Secretary of Defense for International Security Affairs, to Under Secretary of Defense for Policy, 'Talking Points On Rwanda/ Burundi.'" (1994, April 11). In W. Ferroggario (Ed.), *National Security Archive Briefing Book: The US and the Genocide in Rwanda 1994: Evidence of Inaction* (doc. 3). Washington, DC: George Washington University. Accessed at: http://nsarchive2.gwu.edu//NSAEBB/NSAEBB53/rw041194.pdf

# DOCUMENT 2

This document, which was crafted and sent on April 12, 1994, just five days after the outbreak of genocide in Rwanda, is a confidential memorandum from US Ambassador to the United Nations Madeleine Albright to US Secretary of State Warren Christopher. Essentially, Albright urges the US to seriously consider taking the lead at the UN Security Council in calling for the evacuation of the bulk of the UN peacekeeping mission in Rwanda. By April 12th, the world knew that tens of thousands of people had already been killed, and that there seemingly was no end in sight to the killing. Certainly a more humanitarian approach would have been for Albright to call for upgrading the current UN peacekeeping mission (UNAMIR) from a Chapter VI mission (peacekeeping) to a Chapter VII mission (peace enforcement, which would have provided the mission with more personnel, heavier weapons, and a green light to actually go out and attempt to save the potential victims).

Concluding her report, Albright stated: "Relative calm has descended on Kigali and UNAMIR troops are not presently the target of hostilities." Calm? Journalist Mark Huband (1994) reported something quite different. More specifically, in his article "UN Troops Stand by and Watch Carnage," published in *The Guardian* on April 12, 1994, Huband reported the following:

> "[A]rmy trucks filled with foreign evacuees were blocked ... [by] a massacre where machete- and knife-wielding Rwandans lined the roads smiling as their victims lay dying. As the convoy [passed by again] less than an houre later, up the hill lay a pile of corpses. [W]omen, old and young, were led to the pile and beat... until they no longer moved, within view of where the evacuees packed their children, pet dogs, teddy bears into trucks."

CONFIDENTIAL

```
PAGE 01   USUN N   01503   121743Z
ACTION IO-16


INFO   LOG-00   AF-01   AID-01   ARA-01   CCO-00   CIAE-00   C-01
       OASY-00  DOEE-00  EAP-01   EB-01    EUR-01   HA-09    H-01
       TEDE-00  INR-00   L-01    ADS-00    NEA-01   NSAE-00  OIC-02
       OIG-04   OMB-01   PA-01   PM-00     PRS-01   P-01     SNP-00
       SP-00    SR-00    SS-00    STR-01   TRSE-00  T-00     USIE-00
       SA-01    RPE-01   SNIS-00  NISC-02  PMB-00   /050W
                        -------------------- 3AF2CA 121744Z /38
O 121738Z APR 94 ZFF4
FM USMISSION USUN NEW YORK
TO SECSTATE WASHDC NIACT IMMEDIATE 5612
WHITEHOUSE WASHDC IMMEDIATE
AMEMBASSY PARIS IMMEDIATE
AMEMBASSY BRUSSELS IMMEDIATE
AMEMBASSY NAIROBI PRIORITY
```

AMEMBASSY BUJUMBURA PRIORITY
JOINT STAFF WASHDC
SECDEF WASHDC
USCINCEUR VAIHINGEN GE
AMEMBASSY OTTAWA
UN SECURITY COUNCIL COLLECTIVE
AMEMBASSY KAMPALA
AMEMBASSY DAR ES SALAAM
AMEMBASSY ADDIS ABABA


C O N F I D E N T I A L  USUN NEW YORK 001503


DEPT FOR TASK FORCE, P/TARNOFF, IO/WARD, AF/MOOSE
WHITEHOUSE PASS TO NSC FOR SRICE, DMOZENA
JOINT STAFF FOR CHAIRMAN, DIR JS, J3;
SECDEF FOR OSD/ISA

E.O.12356:    DECL:OADR
TAGS: MOPS, PREL, MARR, PGOV, KDEM, RW, UNSC, CG

SUBJECT: TFRWOL: FUTURE UNAMIR AND FRENCH ROLES IN RWANDA

REFTEL: PARIS 9724

1. CONFIDENTIAL - ENTIRE TEXT.

2. USUN FORESEES TWO ISSUES THAT DEMAND WASHINGTON'S IMMEDIATE
CONSIDERATION.

3. THE OTHER IMMEDIATE ISSUE IS UNAMIR'S FUTURE. AT PRESENT THE AIRPORT IS STILL OPEN AND UNDER FRENCH-BELGIAN CONTROL. HOWEVER, THERE IS NO SIGNAL THAT THE UN IS NEARING A DECISION BECAUSE RELATIVE CALM HAS DESCENDED ON KIGALI AND UNAMIR TROOPS ARE NOT PRESENTLY THE TARGET OF HOSTILITIES. YET THIS MIGHT BE A WINDOW OF RELATIVE OPPORTUNITY TO EVACUATE UNAMIR FORCES; THERE IS A REAL POSSIBILITY THAT IT MIGHT BECOME MORE DIFFICULT TO EVACUATE UNAMIR ONCE THE FRENCH AND BELGIANS LEAVE. IN THIS RESPECT, IT IS WORTH CONSIDERING TAKING THE LEAD IN THE SECURITY COUNCIL TO AUTHORIZE THE EVACUATION OF THE BULK OF UNAMIR, WHILE LEAVING BEHIND A SKELETAL STAFF THAT MIGHT BE ABLE TO FACILITATE A CEASE-FIRE AND ANY FUTURE POLITICAL NEGOTIATIONS.

4. BUJUMBURA MINIMIZE CONSIDERED.

ALBRIGHT

**CONFIDENTIAL**

**Source:** Albright, Madeline. (1994, April 12). "TFRWOL: Future of UNAMIR and French Roles in Rwanda." In W. Ferroggiaro (Ed.), *National Security Archive Briefing Book No. 511: 1994 Rwanda Pullout Driven by Clinton White House, U.N. Equivocation* (doc. 14). Washington, DC: George Washington University. Accessed at: http://nsarchive2.gwu.edu/NSAEBB/NSAEBB511/docs/DOCUMENT%2014.pdf

## DOCUMENT 3

This now declassified cable was sent by US Secretary of State Warren Christopher to the USUN (and in particular, to US Ambassador to the UN Madeline Albright) on April 15, 1994. Essentially, the cable contains "talking points" for the USUN to use in calling for the withdrawal of the UNAMIR. In part, the cable reads as follows: "The [US State] Department has considered the prospect of additional widescale conflict and violence in Rwanda, and the threat that the relative immunity afforded to remaining foreign and civilian personnel will end on April 15. Taking these factors into account Department believes that there is insufficient justification to retain a UN peacekeeping presence in Rwanda and that the international community must give highest priority to full, orderly withdrawal of all UNAMIR personnel as soon as possible." Knowing full well that the genocide was now underway in all its force, that tens and of thousands of people had already been murdered and that the mass murder was not likely to end anytime soon without a major military effort to halt the killing, the US Department of State solely speaks of pulling out the peacekeeping force, failing to utter a word urging the UN to immediately send a large and well-equipped Chapter VII peacekeeping force to Rwanda to attempt to stanch the killing.

Continuing, the memo reads: "We are willing to support and encourage a political initiative by the secretary general to promote reconciliation among the parties. Experience suggests that any serious negotiations among the parties will take place outside Rwanda; therefore, UN security forces will not be required. Our opposition to retaining a UNAMIR presence in Rwanda is firm." Basically, Christopher is saying that as far as the United States is concerned, all of the innocent people facing potential murder are on their own, and that at another time, outside of Rwanda, the US would be happy to engage in diplomatic negotiations with the parties engaged in the conflict (meaning the Rwandan government and the extremist Hutu doing the killing, and the rebel force—the Rwandan Patriotic Force—fighting the Hutu). Again, nothing is said about the other party: those civilians (all Tutsi and moderate Hutu) who are not armed and facing potential death at the hands of the génocidares.

```
Current Class: CONFIDENTIAL
Current Handling: n/a
```

```
PAGE 01      STATE     099440  150430Z
ORIGIN IO-16


INFO  LOG-00  AF-01  AMAD-01  ARA-01  CIAE-00  C-01  OASY-00
ANHR-01  EAP-01  EUR-01  HA-09  H-01  TEDE-00  INR-00
L-01  ADS-00  NEA-01  NSAE-00  NSCE-00  OIC-02  OIG-04
OMB-01  PA-01  PM-00  PRS-01  P-01  SNP-00  SP-00
SSO-00  SS-00  TRSE-00  T-00  USIE-00  SA-01  PMB-00
   046R


DRAFTED BY:  IO/UNP: CPATTERSON: CNP
APPROVED BY:    IO: GFWARD
IO/UNP: JSNYDER  USUN/W: DSCHEFFER  AF: PBUSHNELL  TFRWO1: ARENDER
L/UNA: EBLOOM                       AF/ KAISTON
PM: AMARGULIES                      P: EBRIMMER
OSD: PDAHLQUIST  JCS: BATTAGLINI    NSC: KKENYS/S:  HKT S/S-O: MROBINSOO
                ------- 3C2560 150432Z /38
O   150428Z   APR 94
FM SECSTATE WASHDC
TO USMISSION USUN NEW YORK IMMEDIATE
INFO UN SECURITY COUNCIL COLLECTIVE IMMEDIATE
AMEMBASSY BRUSSELS IMMEDIATE
JOINT STAFF WASHDC 0000
AMEMBASSY ADDIS ABABA
AMEBASSY BUJUMBURA
AMEMBASSY NAIROBI
AMEMBASSY DAR ES SALAAM
SECDEF WASHDC 0000
AMEMBASSY DHAKA
AMEMBASSY ACCRA


                    CONFIDENTIAL
```

PAGE 02     STATE      099440 150430Z
C O N F I D E N T I A L STATE 099440


E.O.     12356 DECL: OADR
TAGS: PREL, MARR, MOPS, UN
SUBJECT: TALKING POINTS ON UNAMIR WITHDRAWAL


A) USUN 1553,   B) USUN 1533,   C TELCON   IO/UNP-USUN   4/14
1. CONFIDENTIAL  -  ENTIRE TEXT.


2. THIS IS AN ACTION CABLE  -  SEE BELOW.


3. DEPARTMENT HAS GIVEN CAREFUL CONSIDERATION TO THE DRAFT
RESOLUTION (REF A) AND TO THE VIEWS OF OTHER SECURITY COUNCIL
(UNSC) MEMBERS REGARDING THE STATUS AND FUTURE OF THE CURRENT
PEACEKEEPING FORCE IN RWANDA. THE POLITICAL AND HUMANITARIAN
REASONS PUT FORTH FOR RETENTION OF UNAMIR ELEMENTS IN RWANDA
HAVE BEEN TAKEN INTO ACCCOUNT FULLY IN OUR DETERMINATION OF THE
APPROPRIATE INTERNATIONAL RESPONSE TO DEVELOPMENTS IN RWANDA
SINCE PASSAGE OF UNSC RESOLUTION 909 ON AFRIL [SIC] 5.


4. DEPARTMENT HAS CONSIDERED THE PROSPECT OF ADDITIONAL
WIDESCALE CONFLICT AND VIOLENCE IN RWANDA, AND THE THREAT THAT
THE RELATIVE IMMUNITY AFFORDED TO REMAINING FOREIGN CIVILIAN
AND MILITARY PERSONNEL WILL END ON APRIL 15.


TAKING THESE FACTORS INTO ACCOUNT DEPARTMENT BELIEVES THAT
THERE IS INSUFFICIENT JUSTIFICATION TO RETAIN A UN PEACEKEEPING
PRESENCE IN RWANDA AND THAT THE INTERNATIONAL COMMUNITY MUST
GIVE HIGHEST PRIORITY TO FULL, ORDERLY WITHDRAWAL OF ALL UNAMIR
PERSONNEL AS SOON AS POSSIBLE.


5. COGNIZANT THAT FULL WITHDRAWAL MAY NOT BE ABLE TO BE
IMPLEMENTED PRIOR TO THE END OF THE CURRENT DEADLINE SET Y [sic]

THE RPF, WE BELIEVE THAT UN NEGOTIATORS SHOULD FOCUS THEIR EFFORTS ON ENSURING THAT THE WITHDRAWAL OF UNAMIR PERSONNEL IS NOT IMPEDED AND THAT THE WARRING RWANDAN PARTIES REFRAIN FROM ATTACKING OR THREATENING THESE PERSONNEL. WE ALSO BELIEVE THAT UNAMIR SHOULD TAKE STEPS TO ENSURE THE SAFETY OF RWANDAN CIVILIANS UNDER ITS PROTECTION, CONSISTENT WITH ITS MANDATE AND PROVIDED THAT THE SAFETY OF UNAMIR PERSONNEL IS NOT JEOPARDIZED.

## ACTION REQUESTED

6. DRAWING ON THE FOREGOING, USUN IS INSTRUCTED TO INFORM NSC COLLEAGUES THAT THE UNITED STATES BELIEVES THAT THE FIRST PRIORITY OF THE SECURITY COUNCIL IS TO INSTRUCT THE SECRETARY GENERAL TO IMPLEMENT AN ORDERLY WITHDRAWAL OF ALL/ALL UNAMIR FORCES FROM RWANDA, TAKING THE NECESSARY STEPS TO ENSURE THAT THE WARRING PARTIES IN RWANDA RESFECT [SIC] THE SAFETY OF UNAMIR AND OTHER FOREIGN CIVILIAN AND MILITARY PERSONNEL UNTIL SUCH TIME AS THEIR EVACUATION HAS EEN [sic] COMPLETED. MISSION IS ALSO INSTRUCTED TO MAKE CLEAR TO OTHER UNSC MEMBERS THAT THE UNITED STATES DOES NOT BELIEVE THAT A SECURITY COUNCIL RESOLUTION IS NECESSARY TO IMPLEMENT THIS WITHDRAWAL. (THE SYG HAS AUTHORITY TO ORDER THIS WITHDRAWAL UNDER THESE CIRCUMSTANCES) AND THAT WE WILL OPPOSE ANY EFFORT AT THIS TIME TO PERSERVE A UNAMIR PRESENCE IN RWANDA.

7. MISSION MAY DRAW ON THE FOLLOWING POINTS IN PRESENTING THE U.S. POSITION:

-- THE UNITED STATES SHARES THE SHOCK AND OUTRAGE OF THE INTERNATIONAL COMMUNITY OVER THE EVENTS IN RWANDA IN RECENT DAYS.

-- WE CONDEMN UNEQUIVOCALLY THE RENEWED FIGHTING AND WIDESPREAD VIOLENCE, AND THE ATTACKS ON INTERNATIONAL PEACEKEEPERS, FOREIGN CIVILIANS, AND INNOCENT RWANDAN CITIZENS.

-- THE RWANDAN ARMED PARTIES MUST BEAR FULL RESPONSIBILITY FOR THE TRAGIC SITUATION, AND CONTINUED VIOLENCE AND INSTABILITY, IN THEIR COUNTRY.

-- IN THE CURRENT ENVIRONMENT IN RWANDA, THERE IS NO ROLE FOR A UNITED NATIONS PEACEKEEPING FORCE.

-- THOSE NATIONS THAT CONTRIBUTED TROOPS TO UNAMIR HAVE ACTED RESPONSIBLY AND TO THEIR UTMOST ABILITY, AND HAVE EXERTED COMMENDABLE EFFORTS TO PROVIDE HUMANITARIAN PROTECTION TO FOREIGN, AS WELL AS RWANDAN, CIVILIANS.

-- THOSE FORCES THAT PARTICIPTED IN UNAMIR ARE TO BE COMMENDED FOR THEIR EFFORTS IN A HOSTILE AND THREATENING ENVIRONMENT.

-- WE ENDORSE THE DECISION OF UNAMIR CONTRIBUTORS TO WITHDRAW THEIR FORCES FROM RWANDA FOR THEIR SAFETY, HOFING [SIC] THAT SUCH WITHDRAWAL WILL BE CARRIED OUT IN AN ORDERLY MANNER AND THAT MEASURES WILL BE TAKEN TO OBTAIN COMMITMENTS FROM THE RWANDAN PARTIES TO RESPECT THE SAFETY OF RWANDAN AND FOREIGN CIVILIANS AFTER THE UN PERSONNEL HAVE WITHDRAWN.

-- WE DO NOT BELIEVE THAT THE WARRING PARTIES IN RWANDA ARE LIKELY TO RESPECT UNAMIR'S MANDATE NOR, IN THE PRESENT ENVIRONMENT, ARE THEY CAPABLE OF ADEQUATELY ENSURING THE SAFETY OF UN PEACEKEEPING PERSONNEL IN RWANDA.

-- THERE MAY BE A ROLE FOR THE UN TO PLAY IN FACILITATING EGOTIATIONS [SIC] AMONG THE WARRING PARTIES BUT THAT IS A ROLE FOR A REPRESENTATIVE OF THE SECRETARY GENERAL, NOT FOR UNAMIR. WE ARE WILLING TO SUPPORT AND ENCOURAGE A POLITICAL INITATIVE BY THE SECRETARY GENERAL TO PROMOTE RECONCILIATION AMONG THE PARTIES.

--- EXPERIENCE SUGGESTS THAT ANY SERIOUS NEGOTIATIONS AMONG THE PARTIES WILL TAKE PLACE OUTSIDE RWANDA; THEREFORE, UN SECURITY FORCES WILL NOT BE REQUIRED.

-- OUR OPPOSITION TO RETAINING A UNAMIR PRESENCE IN RWANDA IS FIRM. IT IS BASED ON OUR CONVICTION THAT THE SECURITY COUNCIL HAS AN OBLIGATION TO ENSURE THAT PEACEKEEPING OPERATIONS ARE VIABLE, THAT THEY ARE CAPABLE OF FULFILLING THEIR MANDATES, AND THAT UN PEACEKEEPING PERSONNEL ARE NOT PLACED OR RETAINED, KNOWINGLY, IN AN NTENABLE [SIC] SITUATION.

-- THE UNITED STATES HOPES THAT THE PARTIES IN RWANDA, WITH THE ASSISTANCE OF MEDIATORS FROM THE INTERNATIONAL COMMUNITY AS APPROPRIATE, WILL BE ABLE TO END THE VIOLENCE IN THEIR COUNTRY, MOVE TOWARD RECONCILATION, AND BEGIN A PROCESS THAT WILL LEAD TO A DURABLE PEACE.

-- WHEN THE PARTIES DEMONSTRATE THAT THEY ARE WILLING AND ABLE TO WORK IN THE INTERESTS OF THE RWANDAN PEOPLE TOWARD A LASTING RESOLUTION OF THEIR CONFLICT, WE WILL BE WILLING TO RECONSIDER WHETHER A RENEWED ROLE FOR UN PEACEKEEPING CAN FACILITATE AND BUILD A LASTING FEACE [SIC] IN THEIR COUNTRY.

-- UNTIL THAT TIME, HOWEVER, PRIORITY MUST BE GIVEN TO ENSURING THE SAFE WITHDRAWAL OF UN PEACEKEEPERS AND OTHER INTERNATIONAL PERSONNEL AND CIVILIANS IN DANGER IN RWANDA. TO ATTEMFT [SIC] TO SUSTAIN A PEACEKEPPING OPERATION IN THE PRESENT ENVIRONMENT WOULD ONLY UNDERMINE THE SECURITY COUNCIL'S RESPONSIBILITIES FOR INTERNATIONAL PEACEKEEPING. CHRISTOPHER

CONFIDENTIAL

Source: US Department of State. (1994, April 15). "Cable Number 099440, to US Mission to the United Nations, New York, 'Talking Points for UNAMIR Withdrawal.'" In W. Ferroggiaro (Ed.), *National Security Archive Electronic Briefing Book : The U.S. and the Genocide in Rwanda 1994: Evidence of Inaction* (doc. 4). Washington, DC: George Washington University. Accessed at: http:// nsarchive2.gwu.edu//NSAEBB/NSAEBB53/index.html

## DOCUMENT 4

This now declassified confidential memorandum concerning the pullout of UNAMIR was sent by US National Security staffer Eric Schwartz to Susan Rice and Donald Steinberg on April 19, 1994. In this very brief but telling memorandum, Schwartz notes that Human Rights Watch, a major international human rights organization, had contacted him and pleaded that the United States oppose pulling UNAMIR out of Rwanda. He explains that Human Rights Watch indicated to him that "UNAMIR is protecting thousands (25,000?) of Rwandans and if they pull out, the Rwandans will quickly become victims of genocide." Schwartz goes on to ask Rice and Steinberg, "is this true? If so, shouldn't it be a major factor informing high-level decision-making on this issue? Has it been?"

Interestingly, it is one of the few declassified US documents dealing with the Rwandan genocide in which an individual broaches a question about the plight and fate of the targeted victims. He then virtually suggests that the US government should seriously consider such concerns in its decision-making processes.

To put the matter in perspective, just four days before, on April 15, a *New York Times* article entitled "UN in Rwanda Says It is Powerless to Halt Violence," by Lorch reported the following:

Marauding groups of looters and soldiers remained in control of the... deserted streets, as reports of mass killings filtered out to the thousands of Rwandans...stranded in churches, schools and [homes] with no armed protection...[D]runken men with machetes, spears, truncheons and automatic weapons manned checkpoints throughout the city. The International Committee of the Red Cross temporarily suspended relief operations today when [G]unmen stopped one of its truck carrying six wounded Rwandans, pulled the Rwandans out and killed them. "It is machete massacres," said Philippe Gaillard, the chief Red Cross representative here.

On June 15, in an editorial entitled "Shameful Dawdling in Rwanda," *The New York Times* commented as follows on the Clinton administration's position on the unfolding genocide:

[A] paralyzed Pentagon quibbles over nickels and dimes instead of rushing U.S. armored vehicles to...U.N. peacekeepers....Instead, [Clinton Administration] spokesmen have been instructed to say that 'acts of genocide may have occurred.'

A day later, on April 16, 1994, an article entitled "Tribes Battle for Rwandan Capital, New Massacres Reported," reported the following:

Gangs [armed] with machetes roamed the streets...adding new bodies to the piles of decaying corpses....[Nearly] 1,200 Tutsis...were massacred Wednesday at a church in Musha...hacked to death by gangs...In a separate massacre, Polish missionaries said they could hear the slashing of machetes and moans and calls for help when marauders slaughtered about 80 Tutsis at a Roman Catholic Church in Kigali last Saturday (Associated Press, 1994, n.p.).

### NATIONAL SECURITY COUNCIL

19-Apr-1994 13:27 EDT

CONFIDENTIAL

MEMORANDUM FOR:
    Susan E. Rice     (RICE)
    Donald K. Steinberg    (STEINBERG)

FROM:     Eric P. Schwartz
          (SCHWARTZ)

SUBJECT:     PULL-OUT OF UNAMIR

I just heard from Human Rights Watch, pleading that we oppose a quick
UNAMIR pull-out from Rwanda. Human Rights Watch seemed to indicate
that UNAMIR is protecting thousands (25,000?) [of] Rwandans and if
they pull out, the Rwandans will quickly become victims of genocide.

Is this true? If so, shouldn't it be a major factor informing high-
level decision-making on this issue? Has it been?

I am expecting to receive a fax on this shortly and will see that
you get it.

Eric
CC: Records                 (RECORDS)
_____
Additional Header Information Follows
_____
Date Created: 19-April-1994 13:24
Deletable Flag: Y
DOCNUM: 036828
VMS Filename: OA$SHARE27:ZVEKJ7Y73.WPL
AI Folder: APR94
Message Format:
Message Status: READ
Date Modified: 19Apr-1994-13:24
Forward Flag: YES
Read-Receipt Requested: NO
Delivery-Receipt Requested: NO
Message Priority: FIRST_CLASS

**Source:** Schwartz, Eric. (1994, April 19). "Pull-out of UNAMIR." In W. Ferroggario (Ed.), *National Security Archive Electronic Briefing Book No. 511: 1994 Rwanda Pullout Driven by Clinton White House, U.N. Equivocation* (doc. 18). Washington, DC: George Washington University. Accessed at: http://nsarchive2.gwu.edu/NSAEBB/NSAEBB511/docs/DOCUMENT%2018.pdf

## DOCUMENT 5

On May 13, 1994, US Senators Paul Simon (D-IL) and Jim Jeffords (R-VT) sent the following letter to President Bill Clinton in which they "criticized his Administration's lack of 'leadership'" in responding to the genocide in Rwanda. In doing so, they asserted that "swift and sound decision-making is needed." Moreover, the senators urged Clinton to push Congress to enact sanctions and an arms embargo against Rwanda. They also urged him to push the United Nations to change the current UN mission in Rwanda (UNAMIR) from a Chapter VI or peacekeeping mission to a Chapter VI or peace enforcement mission, stating, "an end to the slaughter is not possible without this action." They also urged Clinton to push for a much larger force than what was currently in Rwanda.

What is notable about this letter, other than the noble effort by the two senators, is that neither the US Senate nor the US House of Representatives, let alone Congress as a whole, approached Clinton about their concern for the victims of the genocide, let alone in regard what the United States could and/or should do to help stanch the genocide.

**United States Senate**

**COMMITTEE ON FOREIGN RELATIONS**

**Washington, D.C. 20510-6225**

13 May 1994

President William J. Clinton

White House

1600 Pennsylvania Ave.

Washington, DC


Dear Mr. President:

We are concerned about the continuing disaster in Rwanda, and the failure of the international community to halt or even diminish the slaughter taking place there.

We have been consulting with those who work with the refugee community including a Rwandan who barely escaped from the disaster; General Romeo Dallaire, the Canadian military leader in charge of the remnant of United Nations troops in the capital city of Kigali; and others.

We suggest the following action be considered immediately and acted upon swiftly:

1. The United States should send a signal to the present government, such as it is, and to those who rebel, that a government which does not strive to halt the civil war, eliminate the massacres, and assist in getting food to hungry people, regardless of ethnic background, will not receive assistance from the United States, and we will encourage the community of nations to follow a similar policy.

2. The United States should take steps to discourage the importation of arms into Rwanda.

3. The United States should press the United Nations Security Council to immediately approve an increase in authorized UN force levels of the United Nations Assistance Mission to Rwanda (UNAMIR). General Dallaire, the UN forces commander in Rwanda, has indicated that a minimum of 5,000 troops would be necessary to ensure a credible UN presence. He believes a force of 8,000 would effectively achieve the desired results. The force should have the mandate to (a) stop the massacres; (b) protect civilians throughout the country; and (c) facilitate the delivery of

humanitarian assistance. General Dallaire believes a force of that size could effectively achieve the desired result. Obviously there are risks, but an end to the slaughter is not possible without this action. These can be primarily African-nation troops, though some non-African troops should participate. The United States should assist the United Nations with finances and provide some basic equipment to some of the less well-equipped forces.

Delays, or simply doing nothing, are not acceptable substitutes for a foreign policy of leadership. Human life is at stake, and swift and sound decision-making is needed.

We request that you ask your top military and diplomatic personnel to immediately analyze the soundness of our proposals, and to report back to you quickly so that timely action can be taken.

Sincerely,

Paul Simon                                    Jim Jeffords
U.S. Senator                                  U.S. Senator

**CLASSIFED BY:   DIR AFR REGION**
C O N F I D E N T IAL

Source: Simon, P., & Jefford, J. (1994, May 13). "Letter to the President." In W. Ferroggario (Ed.), *National Security Archive Electronic Briefing Book: The U.S. and the Genocide in Rwanda 1994: Information, Intelligence, and the U.S. Response* (doc. 48). Washington, DC: George Washington University. Accessed at: http://nsarchive2.gwu.edu/NSAEBB/NSAEBB117/RW48.pdf

# DOCUMENT 6

In this previously classified confidential memorandum dated June 14, 1994, Donald Steinberg, senior director for African Affairs on the National Security Council, outlines a set of "talking points" for President Clinton in preparation for a meeting of Clinton and members of Congress about the ongoing genocide in Rwanda. In this memo that was sent to the White House, Steinberg states, "I think it would do the President well to stand up himself and say that genocide has occurred in Rwanda. Period. He is in the unique position to break through the globbledy-gook that the rest of us are required to say. If he does it, it will make it seem like he himself is frustrated over the bureaucracy's inability to call a spade a spade—that would be a good thing." The irony, of course, is that it wasn't some amorphous "bureaucracy" that was not calling a spade a spade, but the order that no one in the administration use the word "genocide" when speaking about the events in Rwanda came from those on high within the administration.

Steinberg further suggests that Clinton consider saying the following: "We have every reason to believe that [acts of genocide have] [genocide has] occurred in Rwanda, as defined under the 1948 Convention." He further suggests that if Clinton is asked what obligations a nation has that has ratified the UNCG, he should simply say, "The Genocide Convention does not impose a responsibility on the part of any government to take any specific action." Be that as it may, this suggestion simply constitutes one more attempt to extricate the US government from its commitment, as a result of its signing the UNCG, to prevent genocide. It perfectly mirrors, however, the Clinton administration's torturous contortions to do nothing of real substance to prevent the horrific murder of innocent people (women, children, babies, and the elderly, among others).

NATIONAL SECURITY COUNCIL

14-JUN-1994 11:50 EDT

CONFIDENTIAL

MEMORANDUM FOR: SEE BELOW

FROM:    Donald K. Steinberg
         (STEINBERG)

SUBJECT:    Points for POTUS with Members [of Congress]

Jeremy:

     Attached is a page of talking points on Rwanda. We need to
get a decision from Tony on the bracketted [sic] language -- not
only for the meeting with the Members, but for public as well. I
think it would do the President well to stand up himself and say
that genocide has occurred in Rwanda. Period. He is in the
unique position to break through the globbledy-gook that the
rest of us are required to say. If he does it, it will make it
seem like he himself is frustrated over the bureaucracy's
inability to call a spade a spade -- that would be a good
thing...We have addressed below the question of what obligation
that entails, or if he thinks we are responding adequately.

                                                     Don


### Rwanda

-- I've been deeply concerned over the continuing tragedy in
Rwanda. We have are [sic] providing $68 million in humanitarian
assistance for Rwandan refugees, including food, medicine,
blankets and other supplies. Our military is flying three
planeloads a day of food into Burundi.

- This is by far the lion's share of the humanitarian relief
  effort. Our efforts have helped to save lives throughout the
  neighboring countries.

- We've also sent disaster relief teams into Rwanda to assist
  the distribution of humanitarian relief there.

-- We share the frustration over the slowness in drawing together
   an international peacekeeping force. That is why we've been so
   involved in the process of getting peacekeepers into Rwanda.
   The Vice President's meeting with UN Secretary General Boutros
   Ghali, OAU Secretary General Salim Salim and Tanzanian President
   Mwinyi in South Africa on May 10 helped drive this process,
   leading to a UNSC Resolution less than a week later to authorize
   5500 troops.

   ■ We've helped the UN planning process and mobilized to
     provide equipment, airlift, training and financial support
     for the operation.

   ■ We've contacted numerous African countries to get their
     support for the mission. We're helping the UN peacekeeping
     secretariat coordinate the dozen or so country forces that
     have to be merged into this mission.

   ■ We previously sent military equipment in Europe to assist
     its quick delivery. For example, we have 50 armored personnel
     carriers for this mission in Germany about to be shipped to
     Kampala, where they will be used for the training of Ghanaian
     troops and driven to Kigali.

-- We have every reason to believe that [acts of genocide have]
   [genocide has] occurred in Rwanda, as defined under the 1948
   convention. That's why we've supported so strongly the
   introduction of 5500 UN peacekeepers into Rwanda and why we
   have urged the U.N. Human Rights Commission to send a special
   rapporteur to Rwanda to investigate these acts of genocide and
   ensure that those responsible for acts of genocide be held
   accountable for their deeds.

- (if asked) The Genocide Convention does not impose a
  responsibility on the part of any government to take any
  specific action. We believe that the creation of the
  peacekeeping force, the appointment of a special rapporteur
  and our massive humanitarian assistance effort is an
  appropriate response.

Distribution:

FOR: George M. Andricos          (ANDRICOS)

FOR: Christina L. Funches        (FUNCHES)

FOR: Jeremy D. Rosner            (ROSNER)

FOR: Eric Liu            (LIU)

FOR: William C. Danvers          (DANVERS)

CC: Records            (RECORDS)

------------------------------

Additional Header Information Follows

------------------------------

Date Created: 14-June-1994 11:49

Deletable Flag: Y

DOCNUM: 043650

VMS Filename: OA$SHARA9: ZVGOGWQ26.WPL

AI Folder: JUN94

Message Format:

Message Status: READ

Date Modified: 14 Jun-1994 11:49

Forward Flag: YES

Read-Receipt Requested: NO

Delivery-Receipt Requested: NO

Message Priority: FIRST_CLASS

**Source:** Steinberg, Donald. (1994, June 14). "Points for POTUS with Members."
In W. Ferroggiaro (Ed.), *National Security Archive Electronic Briefing Book
No. 511: 1994 Rwanda Pullout Driven by Clinton White House, U.N. Equivocation*
(doc. 20). Washington, DC: George Washington University. Accessed at: http://
nsarchive2.gwu.edu/NSAEBB/NSAEBB511/docs/DOCUMENT%2020.pdf

# AFTERWORD

Samuel Totten

As one reads the various chapters in *Dirty Hands and Vicious Deeds: The US Government's Complicity in Crimes Against Humanity and Genocide*, certain motifs and patterns begin to appear. Among some of the more important ones are the following: a tendency, at times, by US presidents and their top advisers to lie to Congress, the media, and the public about actions the president and/or his cabinet members, advisers, or minions carried out; the involvement of the CIA in criminal actions, including the planning and carrying out of coup d'états against democratically elected leaders of other nations; political malfeasance by various US presidents, vice presidents, and presidential advisers; the breaking of US embargos on arms sales to certain nations by various US presidential administrations; secret actions by US officials that infringe on various international conventions to which the US was a signatory; a tendency by US presidents and his minions to ignore atrocities (some of which amounted to genocide) being perpetrated by another government which the US had a close relationship with; the misuse of the classification ("Confidential," "Secret," or "Top Secret") of certain documents to hide questionable and/or criminal decisions by US government officials; the fact that few citizens outside the government have the slightest idea what the US government is doing in their name; and the brazen positions or actions of certain US presidents with nary a concern as to what he promised when he was sworn in as the President of the United States.

These and other issues raise a whole host of concerns about the operation of the US government, including but not limited to: the moral compasses of those who are elected to represent the people of the United States; issues of moral and political responsibility by those elected and appointed to high positions in the government; how prone certain high officials in the US government have been to classify something as "Secret" when it was not a matter of national security, but rather political malfeasance and/or criminal and/or immoral actions; whether the so-called checks and balances system the US prides itself on is really operating the way it was originally intended; how those culprits who are found to have committed criminal and/or immoral acts while in office should be dealt with (both those who are currently in their positions, as well as those who committed them 10, 20, or 30 years ago); whether there should be a statute of limitations for such individuals in various presidential administrations who committed criminal acts; what individual citizens can, or should, do to not only make their displeasure known about such criminal and/or immoral actions, but what they can do to attempt to ensure that they will not be committed in the future.

All of these issues and concerns are ripe for discussion, debate, and action by US citizens (including students in classes studying crimes against humanity and/or genocide). Not only would the discussion and debate of such issues likely result in high level thinking and engaging verbal exchanges, but in their own inimitable way, they would contribute to the ongoing discussion that scholars and practitioners concerned with preventing crimes against humanity and genocide have wrestled with for decades—including how to prevent crimes against humanity and genocide from being perpetrated.

There is nothing, of course, that limits a reader's reactions solely to discussion or debate. Readers (including students) could write up their concerns, responses, or suggestions in various ways, many of which could be aimed at various audiences, including US officials, the media, or the general public (the voters). They could, for example, take the form of any of the following: submitting angry letters to US senators and members of

Congress; submitting letters or guest editorials/commentaries for publication to local or state newspapers; send letters of concern to well-known columnists with major newspapers, such as *The New York Times*, *The Washington Post*, *The Wall Street Journal*, or *The Christian Science Monitor*, who are known to address major issues in their columns (and could possibly lead to the columnist taking up the issue, placing the letter in a blog, or quoting the author in another piece); contribute an article to an online newspaper (i.e., *The Conversation*); draft petitions that could be signed by family members, friends, neighbors, and colleagues, and then submit them to the White House, the us Congress (or individual members of Congress), newspapers (such as *The Huffington Post*), or post them online. Teachers could grade the efforts and/or offer extra credit to those students who wish to take on such tasks.

University or college graduate students could do all of the above as well as write (individually, in pairs, or as a class) short research notes that could be submitted to an array of refereed journals (i.e., *Journal of Genocide Research*, *Genocide Studies International*, *Genocide Studies and Prevention: An International Journal*, *Human Rights Review*).

It is one thing to have knowledge about crucial matters of importance, but quite another to use it. Readers of *Dirty Hands and Vicious Deeds: The us Government's Complicity in Crimes Against Humanity and Genocide* will have gleaned information about a host of cases about how the United States government has repeatedly been complicit in the perpetration of crimes against humanity and/or genocide by other nations. This is information of which many, if not most, citizens of the United States (not to mention citizens of other nations) know little, if anything, about. Indeed, most readers will likely discover that their loved ones, friends, and colleagues have absolutely no clue that such events actually occurred. In light of that, it is worth seriously considering what one can do with his/her newfound knowledge in an effort to inform others about such facts and, if one has the drive and will to do so, to try to prevent similar actions from being committed in the future.

This book should be of equal concern to citizens outside of the United States. One would be naive to think that other nations' governments have not been complicit in one way or another in another nation's perpetration of crimes against humanity or genocide.

To read and learn about the disturbing facts and cases discussed in *Dirty Hands and Vicious Deeds: The US Government's Complicity in Crimes Against Humanity and Genocide* is, in and of itself, important. Not only are readers better informed, but perhaps they will examine their leaders' and governments' actions from this point forward with a more careful, if not skeptical, eye. That, it seems apparent, is direly needed.

But to leave it at that is not enough, is it? To have such knowledge and do nothing in the face of similar cases that rear their ugly heads in the near or far future is, in a very real sense, to become a bystander of sorts to crimes against humanity and/or genocide. And surely, that is not a legacy anyone wants.

# APPENDIX I

## CRIMES AGAINST HUMANITY

murder;

extermination;

enslavement;

deportation or forcible transfer of population;

imprisonment;

torture;

rape, sexual slavery, enforced prostitution, forced pregnancy, enforced sterilization, or any other form of sexual violence of comparable gravity;

persecution against an identifiable group on political, racial, national, ethnic, cultural, religious, or gender grounds;

enforced disappearance of persons;

the crime of apartheid; and

other inhumane acts of a similar character intentionally causing great suffering or serious bodily or mental injury.

SOURCE: United Nations General Assembly. (1998, July 17). Rome Statute of the International Criminal Court. Accessed at: http://www.refworld.org/docid/3ae6b3a84.html

# APPENDIX II

## CONVENTION ON THE PREVENTION AND PUNISHMENT OF THE CRIME OF GENOCIDE

*Adopted by Resolution 260 (III) A, of the United Nations General Assembly, December 9, 1948.*

### ARTICLE 1

The Contracting Parties confirm that genocide, whether committed in time of peace or in time of war, is a crime under international law which they undertake to prevent and to punish.

### ARTICLE 2

In the present Convention, genocide means any of the following acts committed with intent to destroy, in whole or in part, a national, ethnical, racial or religious group, as such:

- (a) Killing members of the group;
- (b) Causing serious bodily or mental harm to members of the group;
- (c) Deliberately inflicting on the group conditions of life calculated to bring about its physical destruction in whole or in part;
- (d) Imposing measures intended to prevent births within the group;
- (e) Forcibly transferring children of the group to another group.

## ARTICLE 3

The following acts shall be punishable:

- (a) Genocide;
- (b) Conspiracy to commit genocide;
- (c) Direct and public incitement to commit genocide;
- (d) Attempt to commit genocide;
- (e) Complicity in genocide.

## ARTICLE 4

Persons committing genocide or any of the other acts enumerated in Article 3 shall be punished, whether they are constitutionally responsible rulers, public officials or private individuals.

## ARTICLE 5

The Contracting Parties undertake to enact, in accordance with their respective Constitutions, the necessary legislation to give effect to the provisions of the present Convention and, in particular, to provide effective penalties for persons guilty of genocide or any of the other acts enumerated in Article 3.

## ARTICLE 6

Persons charged with genocide or any of the other acts enumerated in Article 3 shall be tried by a competent tribunal of the State in the territory of which the act was committed, or by such international penal tribunal as may have jurisdiction with respect to those Contracting Parties which shall have accepted its jurisdiction.

## ARTICLE 7

Genocide and the other acts enumerated in Article 3 shall not be considered as political crimes for the purpose of extradition.

The Contracting Parties pledge themselves in such cases to grant extradition in accordance with their laws and treaties in force.

## ARTICLE 8

Any Contracting Party may call upon the competent organs of the United Nations to take such action under the Charter of the United Nations as they consider appropriate for the prevention and suppression of acts of genocide or any of the other acts enumerated in Article 3.

## ARTICLE 9

Disputes between the Contracting Parties relating to the interpretation, application or fulfilment of the present Convention, including those relating to the responsibility of a State for genocide or any of the other acts enumerated in Article 3, shall be submitted to the International Court of Justice at the request of any of the parties to the dispute.

## ARTICLE 10

The present Convention, of which the Chinese, English, French, Russian and Spanish texts are equally authentic, shall bear the date of 9 December 1948.

## ARTICLE 11

The present Convention shall be open until 31 December 1949 for signature on behalf of any Member of the United Nations and of any non-member State to which an invitation to sign has been addressed by the General Assembly.

The present Convention shall be ratified, and the instruments of ratification shall be deposited with the Secretary-General of the United Nations.

After 1 January 1950, the present Convention may be acceded to on behalf of any Member of the United Nations and of any non-member State which has received an invitation as aforesaid.

Instruments of accession shall be deposited with the Secretary-General of the United Nations.

## ARTICLE 12

Any Contracting Party may at any time, by notification addressed to the Secretary-General of the United Nations, extend the application of the present Convention to all or any of the territories for the conduct of whose foreign relations that Contracting Party is responsible.

## ARTICLE 13

On the day when the first 20 instruments of ratification or accession have been deposited, the Secretary-General shall draw up a proces-verbal and transmit a copy of it to each Member of the United Nations and to each of the non-member States contemplated in Article 11.

The present Convention shall come into force on the ninetieth day following the date of deposit of the twentieth instrument of ratification or accession.

Any ratification or accession effected subsequent to the latter date shall become effective on the ninetieth day following the deposit of the instrument of ratification or accession.

## ARTICLE 14

The present Convention shall remain in effect for a period of 10 years as from the date of its coming into force.

It shall thereafter remain in force for successive periods of five years for such Contracting Parties as have not denounced it at least six months before the expiration of the current period.

Denunciation shall be effected by a written notification addressed to the Secretary-General of the United Nations.

## ARTICLE 15

If, as a result of denunciations, the number of Parties to the present Convention should become less than 16, the Convention shall cease to be in force as from the date on which the last of these denunciations shall become effective.

## ARTICLE 16

A request for the revision of the present Convention may be made at any time by any Contracting Party by means of a notification in writing addressed to the Secretary-General.

The General Assembly shall decide upon the steps, if any, to be taken in respect of such request.

## ARTICLE 17

The Secretary-General of the United Nations shall notify all Members of the United Nations and the non-member States contemplated in Article 11 of the following:

- (a) Signatures, ratifications and accessions received in accordance with Article 11;
- (b) Notifications received in accordance with Article 12;
- (c) The date upon which the present Convention comes into force in accordance with Article 13;
- (d) Denunciations received in accordance with Article 14;
- (e) The abrogation of the Convention in accordance with Article 15;
- (f) Notifications received in accordance with Article 16.

## ARTICLE 18

The original of the present Convention shall be deposited in the archives of the United Nations.

A certified copy of the Convention shall be transmitted to all Members of the United Nations and to the non-member States contemplated in Article 11.

## ARTICLE 19

The present Convention shall be registered by the Secretary-General of the United Nations on the date of its coming into force.

SOURCE: Convention on the Prevention and Punishment of the Crime of Genocide, United Nations. Created on August 16, 1994. Last edited on January 27, 1997.

# ACKNOWLEDGEMENTS

I wish to sincerely thank Ms. Natalie Fingerhut, History Editor at the University of Toronto Press, for her initial interest in the proposal for this book, her kind and helpful support and assistance throughout the project, and her genuine enthusiasm throughout.

Without the declassified documents accessed at George Washington University's National Security Archive, this book would not have been possible. A hearty thank you to the Archive for its incredible dedication to seeing to it that key U.S. government documents are declassified, and for making them available to researchers for projects of this sort.

I wish to sincerely thank Ms. Sarah Adams, Editorial Coordinator for the Higher Education Division at the University of Toronto Press, for her incredible patience, attention to detail, hard work, and overall kindness throughout this project. After having written and published four books, co-authored two, edited fourteen, and co-edited five, I can honestly say I have never worked with a more dedicated or delightful individual in publishing than Sarah.

Finally, a huge thanks you to all of the contributors to this book. It was a real pleasure working with all of you, and I'd do it again.

# ABOUT THE AUTHORS

**Gerry Caplan** is an independent scholar based in Canada. He has a master's in Canadian history from the University of Toronto and a doctorate in African history from the School of Oriental and African Studies, University of London. Caplan is an internationally recognized expert on the Rwanda genocide.

In 2000, Caplan authored *Rwanda: The Preventable Genocide* for the Organization of African Unity's International Panel of Eminent Personalities to Investigate the 1994 Genocide in Rwanda.

**Christopher R.W. Dietrich** earned his PhD in history at the University of Texas at Austin in 2012. Since then, he has been an Assistant Professor in History and American Studies at Fordham University in New York City. He studies the history of US foreign relations in the twentieth century, with an emphasis on transnational networks, political economy, anti-colonialism, and international law. He has received fellowships from Yale University, the American Historical Association, and the National History Center, and his work has been published in *Diplomacy & Statecraft*, the *International History Review*, and *Diplomatic History*. His first monograph, *Oil Revolution: Sovereign Rights and the Economic Culture of Decolonization, 1945 to 1979* is forthcoming with Cambridge University Press.

**Salim Mansur**, PhD (University of Toronto), is an Associate Professor in Political Science at Western University in London (Ontario), Canada. Mansur's research interests and publications focus on international relations, comparative politics with reference to South Asia and the Middle East, and political theory. Mansur has published widely in such journals as the *Journal of South Asian and Middle Eastern Studies, Arab Studies Quarterly, Middle East Quarterly, The American Journal of Islamic Social Sciences, Jerusalem Quarterly,* and *Middle East Affairs Journal.*

Mansur is also a recipient of the prestigious Stephen S. Wise Humanitarian Award "Profiles in Courage," presented by the American Jewish Congress in 2006.

**Joseph Nevins** received his PhD in geography from the University of California, Los Angeles. He is currently an Associate Professor in the Department of Earth Science and Geography at Vassar College in Poughkeepsie, New York. His research interests include socio-territorial boundaries and mobility, violence and inequality, human rights atrocities and accountability, and political ecology. Among his books is *A Not-So-Distant Horror: Mass Violence in East Timor* (Ithaca, NY: Cornell University Press, 2005).

**Kai M. Thaler** is a PhD candidate in the Department of Government at Harvard University. He works on revolutions, civil wars, political violence, regime change, genocide, and the political economy of development. He holds a BA in political science from Yale University and an MSocSc in sociology from the University of Cape Town. His publications include "Foreshadowing Future Slaughter: From the Indonesian Killings of 1965–66 to Genocide in East Timor," *Genocide Studies and Prevention* , 7(2/3), 204–22; "Ideology and Violence in Civil Wars: Theory and Evidence from Mozambique and Angola," *Civil Wars,* 14(4) (2012), 546–47; and *Armed Violence and Disability: The Untold Story* (with R. Thapa; Brussels: Handicap International, 2012). He was previously an Affiliated Researcher of the Portuguese Institute of International Relations and Security (IPRIS), for whom he wrote about topics including post-genocide relations between East Timor and Indonesia.

**Samuel Totten** is Professor Emeritus, University of Arkansas, Fayetteville. He was a Fulbright Scholar at National University of Rwanda in 2008. For the past decade he has conducted fieldwork in refugee camps along the Chad-Darfur-Sudan border, and over the past four years in the war-torn Nuba Mountains in Sudan.

During the summer of 2004, Totten served as one of the 24 investigators with the US State Department's Atrocities Documentation Project, which involved interviewing refugees from the war raging in Darfur who were residing in refugee camps along the Chad-Darfur-Sudan border. The data collected in the aforementioned interviews was used by then US Secretary of State Colin Powell to ascertain that the Government of Sudan had committed genocide against the black Africans of Darfur, and was possibly still doing so, which he duly reported to the US Foreign Relations Committee on September 9, 2004.

Among some of the books he has written, edited, or co-edited on genocide are *Last Lectures: The Prevention and Intervention of Genocide* (London, UK: Routledge, 2018); Sudan's Nuba Mountains People Under Siege: Accounts by Humanitarians in the Battle Zone (Jefferson, NC: McFarland Publishers, 2017); *Genocide by Attrition: Nuba Mountains, Sudan,* 2nd ed. (New Brunswick, NJ: Transaction Publishers, 2015); *An Oral and Documentary History of the Darfur Genocide* (Santa Barbara, CA: Praeger Security International, 2012); *We Cannot Forget: Interviews with Survivors of the 1994 Genocide in Rwanda* (co-edited with R. Ubaldo; New Brunswick, NJ: Rutgers University Press, 2011); and *Centuries of Genocide: Critical Essays and Eyewitness Accounts,* 5th ed. (co-edited with W.S. Parsons; New York: Routledge, forthcoming).

**Natasha Zaretsky** is a cultural anthropologist focusing on human rights, genocide, migration, and the politics of memory and truth in the Americas. A former Fulbright Scholar, she holds her PhD in cultural anthropology from Princeton University (2008). Currently, she is a Visiting Scholar at the Center for the Study of Genocide and Human Rights (CGHR) at Rutgers University (Newark, New Jersey), and a Senior Lecturer at New York University (New York City). At the CGHR, she chairs the Latin America Working Group and co-leads the Argentina Trial Monitor, a project that chronicles the landmark human rights trials related to state violence committed at the Higher School of Mechanics of the Navy (in Spanish, *Escuela Superior de Mecánica de la Armada*, or ESMA) during Argentina's military dictatorship. She has also been awarded post-doctoral fellowships at Princeton University and Rutgers University, where she was recently an Aresty Visiting Scholar (2014) in the Jewish Studies Department. She has taught courses in anthropology, Latin American studies, human rights, and comparative genocide at Princeton University, Rutgers University, and New York University.

Her recent book, *Landscapes of Memory and Impunity: The Aftermath of the AMIA Bombing in Jewish Argentina* (co-edited with A.H. Levine; New York: Brill, 2015), examines the significance of memorial practices as spaces for citizenship and survival in the wake of violence. Her writing about human rights in Latin America and the aftermath of genocide has appeared in *The Tablet*, *Latin America Goes Global*, and *Foreign Affairs*. Broader research interests include the role of memory and truth in rebuilding communities and nations in the Americas, and the impact of genocide and human rights on diaspora communities. Currently, she is finishing a manuscript about memory and transitional justice in Argentina, *Justice in the Land of Memory*.

# INDEX